THE GAP-YEAR GUIDEBOOK 2003/4

Maybe this will inspire you but don't stay away from Daddy too long xx

Editor:
Susannah Hecht

Assistant Editor:
Catherine Travers

John Catt Educational Limited

Published in 2003 by John Catt Educational Ltd,
Great Glemham, Saxmundham, Suffolk IP17 2DH, UK
Tel: 01728 663666   Fax: 01728 663415
E–mail: info@gap-year.com   Website: **www.gap-year.com**

First published by Peridot Press in 1992
Eleventh edition 2003
© 2003 John Catt Educational Ltd.

Managing Director: Jonathan Evans
Editor in Chief & Publisher: Derek Bingham

All rights reserved. No part of this publication may be reproduced, stored in a retrieval system, transmitted in any form or by any means, electronic, mechanical, photocopying, recording, or otherwise, without the prior permission of the publishers.

Opinions expressed in this publication are those of the contributors, and are not necessarily those of the publishers or the sponsors. We cannot accept responsibility for any errors or omissions.

The Sex Discrimination Act 1975.
The publishers have taken all reasonable steps to avoid a contravention of Section 38 of the Sex Discrimination Act 1975. However, it should be noted that (save where there is an express provision to the contrary) where words have been used which denote the masculine gender only, they shall, pursuant and subject to the said Act, for the purpose of this publication, be deemed to include the feminine gender and vice versa.

British Library Cataloguing in Publication Data.
ISBN: 0 901577 81 2

Designed and typeset by John Catt Educational Limited, Great Glemham, Saxmundham, Suffolk IP17 2DH.

Printed and bound in Great Britain by Bell & Bain Ltd, 303 Burnfield Road, Thornliebank, Glasgow G46 7UQ

CONTENTS

Introduction 7

Your gap year abroad

1 Working abroad 15
  Planning ahead 15
      (Choosing where to work, Visas *etc*)
  Au pairing 17
      (Europe, North America)
  Internships 26
  Sport Instructors 30
  Teaching English as a Foreign Language (TEFL) ...37
  Seasonal work 45
      (Europe, North America, Australia & NZ)

2 Volunteering abroad 65
  Voluntary organisations 70

3 Learning abroad 121
  Languages..121
      Language courses
          (Multi-languages, Arabic, Chinese, Dutch
          French, German, Greek, Indonesian,
          Italian, Japanese, Portuguese,
          Russian, Spanish)
      Learn while you earn
  Sport 168
  Arts & Culture 185
      Art, culture, design & fashion, drama
  Spending an academic year abroad 198

CONTENTS
The Gap-Year Guidebook 2003/4

4 Tips for travellers **203**
    Being Prepared 204
        Getting organised
        Planning the route
        Insurance
    What to take 215
    Health & safety 221
    Getting about: Trains, buses and planes 233
        (Inter-Railing, Eurostar, Trans-Siberian Express,
        Greyhound, bargain flights, rtw tickets)
        Travelling by car
        Cruise Ships
    Accommodation 242
    Keeping in touch 242
        Phone, E-mail, Snail-mail

5 Travel companies **247**

Your gap year in the UK

6 Business skills **261**
    Skills for work 261
    Colleges offering business skills courses 267

7 Extra skills **285**
    Archaeology, Art, Cookery, Drama,
    Driving, Languages, Music,
    Photography, Sports)

8 Working in the UK **315**
    Finding a job 316
    Gap year employers 322
        Arts festivals
        Seasonal Work
        General companies

9 Volunteering in the UK **339**

Appendices

Appendix 1 357

Retakes 359
    Choosing a tutorial college
    Colleges accredited by BAC and CIFE
Applying to university 365
    Application process
    A level results
    Deferred entry, rescheduled entry, or late application?
    Special subjects
    Financing your studies
Universities in the UK..371

Appendix 2 379

Country reports 379

Gap-Year Shop - in association with Homeway 409

With thanks to Grizelda for the illustration on the cover and for her cartoons throughout the book.

Not convinced a gap year is for you?

Here's what some returning gappers have to say...

"... it completely changes your outlook on life."

Caroline taught in a traditional village high in the Himalayas 70 miles from Kathmandu.

"The experience increased my confidence and diplomatic skills. I would recommend it to anyone as a chance to prepare mentally and emotionally for what lies ahead."

Jeannie worked with endangered Huemule deer in Chile, taught in the small village of Lago Verde and trekked in the Andes.

"You will come away with a different outlook on life. This experience has certainly boosted my confidence and I can't wait to back again next year."

Kerry was a volunteer at the Rugby 2001 PEAK holiday at Bilton Grange and had such a good time that she is returning next year.

"I had the opportunity to do things that most people my age can only dream of. I feel now that I am better equipped for the life ahead of me."

Oliver taught computing and commerce in South Africa.

"I urge anyone who is thinking about taking a year out to go for it!"

Sally took part in a variety of conservation projects in Costa Rica including working on a protected beach for leatherback turtle nesting.

"A visit to my local Volunteer Bureau led to the start of a new life for me. My experience as a volunteer in the Philippines has given me a new direction in life. It has changed me as a person."

Sheryl taught pre-school children at Dumaguete, tutoring basic English and maths.

Introduction

Gap years are becoming more and more popular; every year tens of thousands of gappers are calling time out and going out into the world. Companies and organisations are responding by providing an ever-increasing variety of opportunities, from digging wells in remote African villages to drama courses in New York.

And increasingly parents, universities and employers see gap years as an important step in personal development. A 'good' gap year will give you a chance to prove yourself and to stretch your personal boundaries. By discovering new people, places and circumstances it is an opportunity to learn self-reliance, to stand on your own two feet, to make your own decisions and to learn to deal with adults as an adult yourself.

So who goes on a gap year? Anybody and everybody, from all walks of life. A gap year doesn't have to cost a fortune, and there are ways to make your year out pay for itself. According UKSA (May 2002), 'gap years are no longer the preserve of just students. Of the 200,000 people that took a gap year in 2000, one in five were adult professionals.'

Traditionally gap years are taken after A levels, and provide a welcome and deserved rest from the slog of study and the anxiety of exams, exam results and applying for university places. Most universities (not necessarily all) think gap years are great because gappers come to them fresher, wiser, more mature, and able to cope with looking after themselves, not to mention being less jaded about more studying.

Some universities, especially if you're applying to a very popular course, don't welcome gap years. So some students opt to take their gap year after graduating and before getting a 'proper' job. These gappers can take a year out secure in the knowledge that their studies are over, their degree is in the bag, and they now have a chance to cut free before responsibilities take over.

Whenever you take your year out, no one should think that taking a gap year is an easy option. Sitting around watching day-time TV and going to the pub for 12 months doesn't count as a gap year and would quickly become boring. If you're going to make the most of the opportunity then you need to make sure you do something that you find exciting, fun and challenging. This may mean travelling to Thailand, helping with conservation work in Scotland or learning to snowboard. With a whole year ahead of you you could even manage all three if you wanted. The point is to do what you think is right, to do something that gives you a sense of achievement.

The trick to a good gap year is to get the organisation sorted. That doesn't mean you can't be spontaneous, but it would be a real drag if you got to the border of Nepal and found you hadn't got the right visa! Or, while you're in Australia, you get the chance of a great job working with a local TV company but they can't take you on because you couldn't be bothered to get a work permit sorted before you left the UK. Organising your gap year doesn't have to be dull – it can be an opportunity to look forward to the exciting 12 months to come – and as you're making your plans you might find out about new things.

So where do you start? Right here – this newly updated edition of *The Gap-Year Guidebook* is packed with ideas, advice, projects and hundreds of contacts.

You may never get this chance again – at least not for several years – so make the most of it, learn from it and above all, enjoy it.

After 9/11 and Bali is a gap year safe?

After recent events the world is a less safe place for travellers. Terrorists are targetting places known to be frequented by British tourists and you should always check with the Foreign Office whether a country is safe to travel to, and if there are any areas that you should avoid.

This shouldn't stop you from taking a gap year, but it may influence where to go. Don't dismiss Europe – you could end up teaching in Poland, studying art in Florence or Inter-Railing across the whole continent.

Personal safety should always be your number one priority. A real adult won't put themselves in danger rather than risk someone thinking that they're stupid or scared. If in doubt – don't. We strongly recommend that you take a gap safety course before you go. It's not as dull as it sounds - the two companies that we know about (see page 230) have staff who are ex-SAS! They'll teach you how to recognise danger (from people as well as natural disasters), and how to look after yourself in a bad situation – it could be the thing that saves your life.

A year off: the figures

Contrary to expectations, the number of students who took up university and college places in Autumn 2002 was the highest ever. According to provisional UCAS figures (at 9 October 2002), the number of applicants increased by 1.8% from 451,467 in 2001 to 459,395 in 2002, and the number of accepted applicants increased by 2.8% from 355,765 to 365,897.

For some, the decision to take a year off is made well in advance. Many students have already chosen to defer university entrance because there are things they would like to use the time to do. For 2002 entry, 39,706 applicants made at least one application for deferred entry. Some students choose not to apply at all until after they get their A level grades.

Other students find themselves taking a gap year on shorter notice. For example, you may take a year off because your A level grades are not what you had expected – either too low to win the university place you accepted, or high enough to win a place at a better university. Whatever the reason, the result is a gap year.

How to use this book

We've divided it into two: Your Gap Year Abroad and Your Gap Year in the UK. Even if you have a fairly good idea of where you want to go, read the other sections to give you ideas. If you want to go somewhere sunny, but can't afford just to travel, you could spend some time in the UK working to save money first. Or why not get a qualification that will help you get a job abroad – how about working as a scuba diving instructor in Sydney?

The information under the travel section includes important advice, even if you're going abroad with a company or charity – ultimately you are responsible for your own well being and safety.

Gap Year Fun – Worldwide

Getting behind the wheel of your own car and embarking on a gap year between school and university must be two of the most exciting rites of passage from schooldays to university and beyond. Both quite literally widen your horizons but the benefits of a gap year are likely to be much more far-reaching and enduring.

The wealth of options for would-be gappers can be bewildering. Possibilities include: helping others in the UK or abroad; expeditions; travel; experiencing another lifestyle or culture; learning new skills or developing existing interests; taking time off from academic study; earning money to finance the rest of the year or university. Whatever you choose, a gap year provides the opportunity to break away from the inevitably tighter restraints of school and family.

Clearly, a gap year will not be the right choice for everyone and it's essential to consider the possible downsides before making up your mind. Will you lose academic motivation if you take so long away from study? How will you finance such a long period that is bound to involve considerable expense? Is it right to delay your working (and paid!) life for another year? Can you cope with the risk and discomfort associated with life in a completely new environment, possibly thousands of miles from home?

The crucial thing is to make a well-considered decision. Think carefully about what you want to get out of or put into your gap year and begin your research and planning as soon as possible. An ideal gap year will probably consist of a well-structured combination of two, three or more of the range of options available. It's always a good idea to check the attitude of your chosen universities before committing yourself - particularly if you are embarking on longer courses such as medicine. You may end up deciding to take a gap year after university although it must be said that the decision is more difficult at that stage, and will become harder with every passing year.

An encouraging factor as you lay your plans is that universities and employers increasingly look favourably on a gap year, provided that it is well-constructed and planned. You do not have to fill every moment with worthwhile and self-denying activity, but simply wandering around the world courtesy of your father's credit card cuts little ice.

With this proviso, the vast majority of universities look on a gap year as a valuable maturing experience, which inevitably improves communication skills and develops a wider understanding of the world away from the protected environment of school. Moreover, many gap year activities can have a direct relevance to your chosen course – travel for languages, volunteering for medicine, expeditions for geography, and relevant work experience for law all spring readily to mind. And the evidence suggests that those who have undertaken a worthwhile gap year are less likely to drop out of university.

An added bonus is that evidence of preparation for a well-structured year out will make a very favourable impression in section 10 of your UCAS application – another reason for planning as soon as possible, however difficult that may seem given that you will be making university and course choices simultaneously. You don't have to have everything signed and sealed but you do need to show evidence that you have a good idea of what you want to do and have begun your planning.

Employers are likely to take a similar view. They like the initiative that a well-planned year out shows and recognise that such time helps to develop non-academic skills that are vital in the workplace – not least the ability to work with others in new circumstances. An applicant with a gap year under his or her belt is simply more experienced than one without and this is seen as every bit as valuable as an additional A level.

It's worth bearing in mind that parents may well have mixed feelings about waving goodbye to you for a year. The more considered your choice of activities and the better your planning the more likely they are to give the green light – and often end up wishing that they could go themselves!

Of all the options available, volunteering in this country or abroad can be one of the most personally rewarding as well as attracting all the advantages outlined above. For those who are contemplating a spell of volunteering a good place to start is to contact WorldWide Volunteering for Young People, a charity specialising in helping potential volunteers to identify placements that suit their background, circumstances and aspirations. WorldWide Volunteering has developed the UK's most comprehensive database of full-time volunteering opportunities around the world with over 250,000 placements each year in more than 200 countries.

WorldWide Volunteering's search and match CD-ROM software enables volunteers to match in considerable detail their own wishes against the requirements of over 900 volunteer organisations. There is, literally, something for everyone and access will soon be available online for a small fee.

Placements range from those that cost nothing, and even provide 'pocket money', to those that cost many hundreds, even thousands of pounds. They last anything from a week to a year and are located in the next-door county and on the other side of the world. Many schools and colleges subscribe to the programme so that their students will be able to track down the database with little difficulty. For those without easy access, a growing number of public careers centres, libraries and other organisations have the database – details of these are posted on **www.worldwidevolunteering.org.uk** (WorldWide Volunteering's website). If all else fails, details of the WorldWide Volunteering postal enquiry service are also available on the website.

So if you like the idea of helping children with disabilities in the South of England or trying your hand at iguana farming at a conservation site in Nicaragua, WorldWide Volunteering is an excellent place to start. Whether or not volunteering takes up all or part of your gap year you could be about to embark on the adventure of a lifetime. Why not give your rite of passage the extra zest that will come from knowing that you have given something of yourself to others as well as having a great experience?

Roger Potter, Director of WorldWide Volunteering for Young People

WorldWide Volunteering for Young People

Higher Orchard
Sandford Orcas
Dorset DT9 4RP
UK

Tel: +44 (0) 1963 220036
Fax: +44 (0) 1963 220525

E-mail: worldvol@worldvol.co.uk
Website: www.worldwidevolunteering.org.uk

Your Gap Year Abroad

Are you:

> forward thinking?

> independent?

> intent on **engineering** as a career?

> ready for a really worthwhile **gap year**?

Would you like to combine Study, Language, Travel and Work in Europe?

The pinnacle of gap years for engineering students, providing a unique experience if you:

> **want** engineering experience before university and you would like to go abroad for a few months.

> **want** to meet new people and enjoy the social scene

> **want** to learn about management techniques, interpersonal skills and teambuilding in preparation for your future career.

> **recognise** that language skills are an asset in the workplace and want to develop a foreign language, as well as find out more about European work methods and culture

> **would like** the chance to be independent and enjoy personal development

> **are** keen to get ahead of your peers at university

COURSE DESCRIPTION

> 1-week teambuilding at an expedition centre, followed by the academic session which includes familiarisation in all engineering disciplines, supervisory management techniques, IT, computer-aided design with City & Guilds accreditation. CATS points are available for this part of the course.

> Tuition at a European language school, learning or developing to technical level a modern foreign language.

> Work placement in European industry which will involve a variety of departments within a company, such as planning, design, production, marketing and finance

LENGTH OF PROGRAMME

> 11-weeks academic study in engineering, management, IT
> 4-weeks language study
> 13-weeks work placement in Europe

QUALIFICATIONS REQUIRED

Deferred engineering-related degree place at University

COST INVOLVED

All tuition, accommodation and return travel, etc is arranged by The Smallpeice Trust. The cost for the entire programme is £4,950 per student, payable in two instalments.

COUNTRIES COVERED

UK; Eire; Germany; France; Belgium; Spain; Austria; Norway; Finland

AGE RANGE

18+

WHEN?

The programme starts in September and finishes the following May

The Smallpeice Trust
Holly House, 74 Upper Holly Walk
Leamington Spa, Warks CV32 4JL

Tel: 01926 333200 Fax: 01926 333202
gen@smallpeicetrust.org.uk
www.smallpeicetrust.org.uk

1 Working Abroad

So you desperately want to go abroad but you really can't afford it and the bit you have managed to save won't cover much more than an airfare?

A great way to experience a different culture is to live and *work* in it. You might think this could get a bit dull, but most jobs give you enough spare time in the evenings and at weekends to enjoy yourself and make friends. You'll be meeting locals and experiencing what the country is really like. You don't have to be tied to one place for your whole gap year – you can work for a bit and save up for your travels. That way you can learn more about the place and get the inside information from the locals about the best places to see before you set off.

There are loads of different jobs you can get abroad even if you don't speak any languages. From au pair and ski chalet jobs, waitressing and bar work to summer camp staff and teaching English. If you're lucky, you might even find an internship with pay – which would look good on your CV.

Planning ahead

Choosing your destination

Now you just need to choose where to go. Since the terrorist attacks on New York and Bali, international tourism has really dropped off. But even in a globally disrupted economy there are still pockets of job stability: seasonal farm work still needs to be done and being an English-speaker is always an advantage when looking for jobs in tourism at ski resorts, beach bars and hotel receptions – because English is the internationally used language.

With the political situation in mind, you might want to consider staying in Europe. If you are a UK citizen or hold an EU (European Union) passport, you can work in any other EU member country without a visa or work permit and there are countless jobs available to students who can speak the right languages. Not all European countries are EU members – go to the European Union website (**http://europa.eu.in**) to check.

If you do want to be more adventurous then check the Foreign Office website for the list of countries they consider too dangerous to go to.

Before you go, make sure you have all the paperwork you need, including visas and work permits, and that you understand all the regulations and restrictions. You can get into serious trouble if you work without the necessary documents – you probably don't want to be deported during your gap year! Some countries will only grant you a visa or work permit if you can prove you already have a job lined up for when you arrive. The best place to get information is the embassy in London for the country you're going to – there's a link on **www.gap-year.com** to the embassy websites, or look in the country info section at the back of this book for embassy phone numbers. It's worth taking a couple of copies of all your paperwork and leaving one copy at home with someone reliable and packing another copy separate from the papers themselves just in case they get stolen or lost.

It's also a good idea to take a some spare copies of your CV and photocopies of your relevant qualifications with you. Even if you already have a job set up before you go over there, you might not like it and want to apply for another job. If you can get your CV translated into the local language to take with you, that's even better.

When you're getting your insurance, remember to check that you'll be covered if you're working. We've heard of at least one person who wasn't covered because his stuff was damaged while he was working – an expensive mistake. Read through the travel section in *Chapter 4: Tips for Travellers* for ideas and travel advice.

Finding a job

You'll need to be proactive: only the luckiest people (usually in a totally unrealistic Hollywood movie) walk down the street and get offered a job – and if it does happen to you, be careful, it may be a con! Finding a job may take time and effort. The more places you can get your CV the more likely you are to get a job. Register with all the international employment agencies that are free and make sure you know what the agency fee will be if you get employed. If you use an agency, always insist on talking to someone who has used them before – that way you'll really find out what the deal is.

If you want to go to a particular place, do a search to see if there's a website for that area and then send or e-mail your CV with a short covering note to any interesting local companies. Don't expect to be flooded with replies. Some companies are simply too busy to respond to every enquiry – but you may get lucky and have exactly the skills or qualifications they're looking for.

Some companies will also advertise vacant posts on specialist employment websites which often have an international section. You can register with the sites too, usually for free.

Tell everyone you know, including relatives and your parents' friends, that you are looking for a job abroad – someone may know someone who has a company abroad who can help you or let you stay with them.

Of course it's always easier to find employment when you're living locally. Lots of jobs are advertised in the local papers, or even just by 'staff wanted' notices put up in windows. So if you get there and hate the job you've got, don't put up with it, or come running home – see if you can find something better.

Over the next few pages we have listed ideas on types of employment and any companies we know about that will find you work. Always ask a company to put you in contact with someone they have placed before – if they say no then don't use them: they may have something to hide.

Au pairing

Being an au pair is a good way to immerse yourself in a different culture, learn a new language and hopefully save some extra cash. You should be given enough time out of work to take some language courses as well as have fun.

Au pairing used to be considered similar to babysitting, but since the Louise Woodward case in 1998 (the conviction of an English nanny in the USA for the murder, later reduced to manslaughter, of a baby in her charge) people have become more cautious about taking on work abroad as a nanny, and nanny/au pair agencies found themselves having to give legal advice. But if you want to get to grips with a foreign language and don't fancy forking out for food and a dismal flat, being an au pair can be a brilliant solution. It involves living with a foreign family, often in Europe, for several months.

The internet is now an excellent source of information on au pair work worldwide. You can usually register for free and your name will be matched to the families around the world that have registered on the site that meet your specifications (but make sure you make human contact at home and abroad before you make your final decision).

The safest bet, however, may be to look for a placement through a UK-based au pair agency. It's also better for the prospective family abroad, since they will be dealing with a UK agency (possibly working together with an agency in the family's own country) that has met you, interviewed you and taken up references. Remember they're going to be taking you into their family home and trusting you with their children.

Qualifications are not needed to be an au pair, although obviously some experience with children is a bonus. Many au pair agencies now require written references, police checks and other proof of suitability. One starting point for finding au pair agencies in the UK is to see if they are members of the Recruitment and Employment Confederation (REC), which has a website listing all its members and covering au pair employment in many countries, or of the International Au Pair Association. There are of course (as in other areas of business) also good agencies which do not belong to trade associations, either because they are too small to afford the membership fees, or because they are well-established and have a good independent reputation.

International
Au Pair Association

Bredgade 25 H
DK-1260 Copenhagen K
Denmark
Tel: +45 3333 9600
Fax: +45 3393 9676
www.iapa.org

Agencies should ask for an interview and references, and maybe a medical certificate. It may soon be illegal for agencies to charge you a fee to find you an au pairing placement: the DTI (Department of Trade and Industry) is currently revising the Conduct of Employment Agencies and Employment Business Regulations 1976. The proposal recommends that the fees be abolished, and may come into effect later this year. Currently however the maximum registration fee is £40. If you have a complaint against a UK agency it's best to take it up with the Employment Agency Standards Helpline, Tel: +44 (0) 845 955 5105.

Make sure the agency has connections where you'll be working, get a list of other local au pairs so you have support when you're out there, and take time finding a suitable family. The fewer children the better, and you should expect your own room. It's also worth checking what there is to do in your free time – you don't want to spend every weekend in your bedroom because you're stuck in the middle of nowhere.

Before you go, check you have written confirmation of the hours, duties and pay agreed as well as copies of important documents such as passport, birth certificate, and translations of any academic certificates to prove your student status. Extra passport photos are a good idea (even if they're not needed, the chronic pose usually gets a good laugh from the children), as is the number and address of the local British Consulate just in case.

Au pairing in Europe

European law stipulates that au pairs should not be younger than 17 and should provide a current medical certificate for an au pair job (participating in normal family duties); that an employment agreement should be made in writing between the au pair and host family, with conditions of employment clearly defined; that the au pair should receive pocket money (exempt from tax) and have enough free time to study; and that the au pair should not be expected to work more than five hours a day and have at least one full free day a week. The agreement also set up a 'model contract' for young people placed as au pairs. This is now the accepted definition for au pair jobs in the EU, but not necessarily in other countries. Some countries have different local rules. Take a look at **http://conventions.coe.int/treaty/en/Treaties/Html/068.htm** for this and the details of the European Agreement.

In return for board, lodgings and pocket money of around £60 a week (€100) in Europe (less in Greece, Italy or Spain), you will look after the children and do light domestic chores like ironing, cooking, tidying their bedrooms and doing their washing, for up to five hours a day (six hours in France or Germany), five days a week, as well as spending two or three evenings a week baby-sitting. If you are asked to work more than this then technically you are not doing the work of an au pair, but of a mother's help (which pays more). Or slave. Remember that an au pair is classified as 'non-experienced', and you should not be left in sole charge of a young baby (never shake a baby). If the family gives you more responsibility than you can handle say so; if they don't stop – quit.

If you fancy sipping strong black coffee on a Parisian boulevard you can try working in France as an au pair. In exchange for 30 hours work a week (leaving most evenings and weekends free to enjoy the nightlife) you receive full board and accommodation, as well as pocket money. Fluent French isn't necessary. GCSE standard will do, as many parents want you to speak English with the kids.

Living with a French-speaking family will improve your French out of all recognition, particularly your accent. If you hear it from dawn to dusk, you'll pick it up more effectively than from any textbook. If you live in Paris, you'll probably get a chance to see another part of France when you accompany the family on their summer holiday.

Demand for British au pairs in Paris is higher than ever, and at its highest at the start of summer. Every parent wants their children to learn English, but with the rising popularity of Franco-German government-sponsored youth employment programmes, the number of Europeans willing to take au pair jobs has fallen.

It's important to complete all the necessary paperwork for living and working in another country. Most agencies will organise the paperwork side for you, and make sure the legal documents are in order before you leave. Most French agencies require a set of passport photos, a photocopy of your passport, two references (preferably translated into French), and your most recent academic qualifications, as well as a hand-written letter in French to your prospective family which tells them something about you, your reasons for becoming an au pair and any future aspirations. The agency may also ask for a medical certificate (showing you are free of deadly contagious diseases *etc*) dated less than three months before you leave, and translated into French. Au pairs also have to have a medical examination on arrival in France.

The French Consulate advises you to check that the family you stay with obtains a 'mother's help' work contract (*accord de placement au pair d'un stagiaire aide-familiale*). If you are a non-EU citizen you are expected to do this before you leave for France, but British au pairs do not need to.

Consulat Britannique

9 Avenue Hoch
75008 Paris, France
Tel: +33 1 44 513100

French Consulate

21 Cromwell Road
London SW7 2EN, England
Tel: +44 (0) 20 7838 2000
see: www.gap-year.com

You can expect to earn pocket money of around €270 a month and get a free orange travel card in Paris – valid for the metro and buses. You also get state medical insurance. According to the Accueil Familial, a family that demands more than 30 hours a week work from an au pair is in breach of the law.

Accueil Familial des Jeunes Etrangers

23 Rue du Cherche Midi
75006 Paris, France   Tel: +33 1 4222 5034

This agency places young people with families in the suburbs of Paris as well as in the city itself and in other towns throughout France where recognised language schools are situated.

Accueil International

2a rue Ducastel, 7
8100 Saint-Germain-en-Laye
France   Tel: +33 1 3973 0498

Based outside the centre of Paris and run by Edith Drilhon, this agency places au pairs all over France but specialises in western Paris. Arranges 30-hour week au pair placements.

ACI (Alliance Culturelle Internationale)
4 Avenue Felix Fauré
06000 Nice, France   Tel: +33 4 9313 4413

ACI places au pairs between 18 and 28 years old. Telephone interviews are possible. It can also accept a few au pairs for a month or two in the summer as paying guests in families (no charge if the stay is in July or August). ACI operates within a large catchment area in the South of France, from Menton to Marseille, Aix-en-Provence, Arles, Var, St Tropez and Corsica. In touristy areas of the Côte d'Azur au pair placements can last for two months in summer (July-August) or six months; and at other times of the year from six months to a year.

Childcare International
Trafalgar House, Grenville Place
London NW7 3SA   Tel: +44 (0)20 8906 3116

Childcare International is the UK agent for APIA, and sends au pairs to Europe, the USA, Canada, Australia and South Africa.

England & Overseas Nanny/Au Pair Bureau
Suite 21-23, Kent House
87, Regent Street, Piccadilly
London W1R 7HF, England   Tel: +44 (0) 20 7494 2929

Thirty-one years old, this bureau has 32 overseas representatives and places au pairs aged 17 to 27 around the world including North America and the Middle East. Mostly in Europe.

Pebbles Unlimited
UK Office, 58 Northcourt Road
Worthing, Sussex BN14 7DT, England   Tel: +44 (0) 1903 529 637

Pebbles Unlimited is a friendly and professional agency run by sisters Antonia and Zoe. Both have worked as Au Pairs, so have first-hand knowledge of the job. Fluent French speaker Zoe is based on the Côte D'Azur, which means she is able to offer total support at all times. The company interviews all their families and you are given the chance to speak with the family before making your final decision. Registration is free and you get £40-£55 pocket money per week – but you do pay your own travel costs. You need to be of British/EU nationality, aged between 18-27, and have GCSE French. Pebbles has vacancies in the South of France from May onwards.

visit: www.gap-year.com

Solihull Au Pair & Nanny Agency
5 Parklands
Blossomfield Road
Solihull
West Midlands B91 91NG   Tel: +44 (0) 7973 886 979
England   Fax: +44 (0) 121 705 1512

This agency offers au pair and nanny positions in major European Cities, mainly France, Italy and Spain.

Au pairing in North America

The term 'au pair' has a very different connotation in America – much closer to what we would consider to be a nanny. You must be 18 or over and it is considered to be a full-time position – the au pair is often in sole charge of the children.

All au pair programmes are legislated and regulated by US law, which means (at the time of going to press), that all au pairs receive $139.05 (about £96) pocket money in return for 45 hours work a week, regardless of the agency. You can expect a good standard of living, full-board, a room and use of a car.

There are support networks for au pairs once you arrive in the US: agencies should provide assigned co-ordinators who will act as mediators between the au pair and the family if there are problems – and it is possible to be reassigned to a different family.

Looking after children aged under two is more demanding and therefore most agencies ask that you have at least 200 hours of experience with that age group and are at least 19 years old.

The USA has a confusing bureaucratic system, and if you're not careful you risk earning money illegally and even being deported. That's why it is important to go to an agency that runs an honest scheme.

British and English-speaking Europeans can go to the USA on a 'cultural exchange' with a J1 visa which is valid for a year. Candidates must be between 18 and 26 years of age, have a secondary education, experience or training in childcare, hold a clean drivers' licence and be in good health.

According to Au Pair in America (APIA), US government regulations stipulate that au pairs must attend education courses (because au pair work is seen primarily as a cultural exchange) 'putting in a minimum of three hours a week during term-time. This is financed by the host family up to a limit of $500.'

AU PAIRING IN N AMERICA

Because of strict government regulations, most agencies that organise au pairs in the USA offer very similar services. However it's worth registering with a number of agencies if only to have a range of 'perfect match' host families to choose from.

The US embassy is very long-winded if you're trying to find out about au pair work (there's a link from **www.gap-year.com** to the embassy's website). It really is better to contact an agency direct, but you do need to know about visas, and for that they are the best people.

US Embassy (Visas) 5 Upper Grosvenor Street
London W1A 2JB
Tel: 090 6820 0290

The following are just some of the agencies that can find you au pairing work in North America.

Au Pair in America (APIA)

37 Queen's Gate
London SW7 5HR, England

Tel: +44 (0) 20 7581 7311
see: www.gap-year.com

APIA offers you the choice of three programmes to America: Au Pair in America, Au Pair Extraordinaire and EduCare in America. The APIA package includes free return flights to New York from London, medical insurance (candidates must contribute $100 toward medical insurance), a month travel period and a four-day orientation course near New York covering first aid, culture shock and what is expected in general childcare. Au Pairs receive a weekly payment of $139.05 and a $500 study allowance in exchange for up to 45 hours of childcare plus room and board.

If you have a childcare qualification and are at least 20 years old with two years of recent childcare experience under your belt, you could earn $200 per week as an Au Pair Extraordinaire. EduCare has fewer childcare hours and is available for those of you interested in a taste of US college life.

All three programmes require a $400 'good faith deposit' (about £277) that is payable when you are matched with a host family, and candidates will be reimbursed their deposit (including the educational component) after completing the 12 months. To participate you must be aged 18 to 26 and have a driving licence. You will be invited to meet a local interviewer to complete the application process. APIA's US office will match you with a family based on your experience, interests and skills.

The chance to have **the best year of your life**

- Spend a year with an American Family
- Make new friends & learn about the USA
- Benefit from exciting study programmes
- Enjoy a month of independent travel

www.aupairamerica.co.uk
Tel: 020 7581 7311
Email: info@aupairamerica.co.uk

Au Pair in America   Au Pair Extraordinaire   EduCare in America

www.gap-year.com

links to thousands of gap year opportunities

- Work in the UK and abroad
- Sports Courses
- Business skills
- Volunteering
- Travelling
- Languages

A JOHN CATT EDUCATIONAL LIMITED PRODUCT

Childcare International

Trafalgar House
Grenville Place
London NW7 3SA   Tel: 020 8906 3116

Childcare International is the UK agent for APIA, and sends au pairs to Europe, the USA, Canada, Australia and South Africa.

EF Au Pair

EF Centre Boston
One Education Street
Cambridge MA 02141
USA   Tel: +1 800 333 6056

Although EF Au Pair (an affiliate of EF International Language Schools) deals mostly with non-English speaking Europeans, people from Britain have a huge language advantage and are always well-received. EF Au Pair says it can place au pairs in every state of the USA except Hawaii.

Solihull Au Pair & Nanny Agency

5 Parklands
Blossomfield Road
Solihull
West Midlands B91 91NG   Tel: +44 (0) 7973 886 979
England   Fax: +44 (0) 121 705 1512

If you want to spend a year in the USA, the Solihull Au Pair & Nanny Agency will put you in touch with families who have been vetted by AuPairCare San Francisco in the States.

Au Pairs need to be able to stay for a full 12 months, (there's also an opportunity to travel for the 13th month) and must be aged between 18 and 26. Childcare experience is essential, although formal qualifications are not necessary. A driving licence is obligatory.

Au Pairs have their own bedrooms and live as family members, receiving $138.00 per week, plus two week's paid holiday and possibly some holidays with the host family. Au Pairs are sent on a legal J1 visa and they are required to study a subject of their own choosing in the USA on a part-time basis.

Fares are paid to and from New York and onwards to the host family. There is a 24-hour helpline telephone number and a four-day orientation in central New York Hotel.

visit: www.gap-year.com

Internships

If you would like to use your gap year to gain some relevant work experience, then why not sign up for an internship? It will give your CV a competitive edge and it will give you an insight into what that job is really like and whether you like it or not.

Many international organisations and companies (especially in the USA) offer 'internships'. Traditionally these are one-year paid employment postings for undergraduate or graduate students, arranged from a university. Many internships are not open to pre-university students.

Before you sign up as an intern make sure you're clear just what your placement will involve. An 'internship' should mean you are able to do interesting paid work related to your degree studies, current or future, for at least six months. Sitting behind a reception desk in an august institution for very little money is not an internship, but a badly-paid job. Be warned, internships in the USA can be difficult to get without paying for the privilege unless you have personal contacts with the organisation you hope to work for. This is because the USA has a strict job-related work permit system and won't hand out these permits for jobs that American nationals can do themselves. The USA authorities also need to be convinced that the work experience offered provides an opportunity to the UK student that he or she cannot get back home. If the companies that we've got listed below can't help you, take a look at these websites:

www.internjobs.com
www.internships-usa.com
www.itu.int/aboutitu/staffing.html

www.summerjobs.com
www.internabroad.com

Alliances Abroad

2423 Pennsylvania Avenue NW
Washington DC 20037
USA

Tel: +1 (202) 467 9467
Fax: +1 (202) 467 9460

Alliances Abroad is one of only a few educational travel companies in the world that offers international students paid internships and summer work programmes in the United States. With dozens of locations and numerous employers around the country for you to choose from, they'll help you find work that turns into the experience of a lifetime. All you do is choose the location, length of time you're willing to stay, and give them an idea of the type of position you will consider. Their experienced staff in America will do the rest. Positions are available in many categories including import-export, communication, tourism, social work, information technology, secretarial work, economics, law, marketing, banking finance, public relations and many more.

CCUSA

Unit 4CC, Green Dragon House
64-70 High Street
Croydon CR0 9XN, England

Tel: +44 (0) 20 8688 9051
Fax: +44 (0) 20 8680 4539
see: www.gap-year.com

If you're looking for something a bit different to do whilst making money, getting a tan, meeting and working with new people from different cultures, seeing new places, and enhancing your CV, CCUSA will find a programme to achieve this. Over the last 16 years, CCUSA have organised safe and secure working holidays for over 100,000 students from all over the world.

CCUSA's Work Experience USA programme enables you to live and work in America for a summer on a J1 five-month work and travel visa (available to students only). You can choose a secure guaranteed job from their extensive job directory, for example: working on a ranch in Colorado, in the Grand Canyon National Park in California, at a resort on New York or even in a casino in Nevada! Or you can find your own placement if you prefer.

Or, if you want to try somewhere a bit more unusual, you can spend either three or six months in the Brazilian sunshine. You'll live with a host family and work in a job of your choice.

All CCUSA programmes offer guaranteed placement before departure, return flights, visas, insurance, airport pickup, local orientation, and full-time support before, during and after the programme.

CCUSA offers many other programmes, please see their other listings in this chapter in the sections on *Seasonal Work in North America*, *Seasonal Work in Australia and New Zealand* and *Seasonal Work in Europe* for full details.

CIEE (Council on International Educational Exchange)

52 Poland Street
London W1F 7AB, England

Tel: +44 (0) 20 7478 2020
Fax: +44 (0) 20 7734 7322

CIEE's Internship USA programme offers more serious jobs aimed at providing valuable work experience. You have to be a current student (at HND or above) or a recent graduate and the internship you apply for (you have to do the legwork on this) should be related to your degree subject. The fees start from £270 for the first two months and £30 for each additional month, up to 18 in total – this includes your legal sponsorship (necessary for the visa) as well as insurance and all CIEE's support services and e-mail advisory service on finding your ideal internship.

INTERNSHIPS

Working Abroad

Don Quijote

PO Box 218, Stoneleigh
Epsom
Surrey KT19 0YF
England

Tel: +44 (0) 20 8786 8081
Fax: +44 (0) 20 8786 8086
see: www.gap-year.com

The Don Quijote internship programme has three phases: about six weeks intensive Spanish course (depending on your language ability), professional orientation and finally a three-month placement (which can sometimes be extended). Placements are in private sector companies, governmental organisations, NGOs, schools, colleges and universities – depending on your language ability, skills and work experience.

Entrance requirements are high and each step is competitive with an expectation of high levels of performance.

Euro Academy

24 Clarendon Place
London SE13 5EY
England

Tel: +44 (0) 20 8297 0505
Fax: +44 (0) 20 8297 0984

Though mainly a language school, Euro Academy also offers work placements in Europe and the USA and voluntary programmes combined with language in Costa Rica.

i-to-i

9 Blenheim Terrace
Leeds LS2 9HZ
England

Tel: +44 (0) 870 333 2332
Fax: +44 (0) 113 242 2171
see: www.gap-year.com

i-to-i provides internships in journalism, media, business and medicine. You can also combine this with another of i-to-i's projects. For details see i-to-i's listings under *Work Abroad: TEFL* and *Volunteering Abroad*.

InterExchange

161 Sixth Avenue
New York, NY 10013, USA

Tel: +1 (212) 924 0446
Fax: +1 (212) 924 0575

InterExchange run a four-month summer internship programme and an international practical training programme. The international practical training programme lasts six, 12 or 18 months and is aimed at students who have already spent at least two years in higher education. Placements are very career-orientated, and can be in the following fields: information media and communication; management, business, commerce and finance; the sciences, engineering, architecture, mathematics and industrial occupations; and public administration and law.

Mountbatten Internship Programme

5th Floor
Abbey House
74-76 St John Street
London EC1M 4DZ
England

Tel: +44 (0) 20 7253 7759
Fax: +44 (0) 20 7831 7018
see: www.gap-year.com

This organisation aims to promote educational and business links between the USA and the UK. It arranges 12-month internship programmes in New York with a variety of American companies which sponsor the programme. By the end of the course you should have gained the 'Certificate in International Business Practice', accredited by UCLES. To take part in this programme you need to be at least 21 and to have studied to higher education level. A type speed of 50 wpm is also recommended.

Smallpeice Trust

74 Upper Holly Walk
Leamington Spa
Warwickshire CV32 4JL
England

Tel: +44 (0) 1926 333200
Fax: +44 (0) 1926 333202
see: www.gap-year.com

The Smallpeice Trust runs the **Smallpeice Engineering Gap Year**, a gap year programme for students who defer their entry to university on an engineering-related degree course.

This pinnacle of engineering gap years uniquely combines study, language, travel and work in Europe:

- three months academic study at a UK university
- one month language tuition at a language school in France, Germany or Spain
- three months work placement in one of nine European countries.

The entire programme is arranged and subsidised through The Trust, and starts in September, finishing the following May. The cost per student is £4950, payable in two instalments, which includes all tuition, accommodation, placements, return travel *etc*. No other opportunity offers such a firm grounding in engineering, together with personal development, to put students 'head and shoulders' above their peers at university.

Sport instructors

Working as a sports instructor is a great way to use your skills to earn money during your gap year. It's also a good way to finance living in a foreign country and maybe some travel after the job ends.

Ski resorts are probably the biggest sports instructor employers, but for every sport that exists – from kayaking to cricket, from sailing to snowboarding – there will be people who want to learn more, and you might be the person to teach them. Snowboarding and all watersports are really popular at the moment. The great thing is that there are jobs for sport instructors all around the world – from Bermuda to Belgium; from Boston to Bavaria.

If you don't already have your instructor qualifications then you could spend the first part of your gap year getting qualified (take a look at *Chapter 3 Learning abroad: Sport*) – lots of the sports schools will help you get a job, although it's always worth asking before you sign up for the course. Also check that the qualification they are offering is what the resorts want.

You can contact resorts/sports schools direct (find them on the internet) or go through an agency, though some agencies have age restrictions and may want specific qualifications. As always, the internet is a good place to search for jobs. Take a look at: **www.skijobs.net**, **www.skiingthenet.com** or **www.jobmonkey.com**. These are just a few we found after doing a quick search – there are bound to be loads more. If you find a really helpful site you could share your luck by telling other gappers on the www.gap-year.com message board.

If you can't find what you're looking for in the list of companies below, try searching the internet for national and international associations – explain to them that you're looking for work using your sports skills and ask for their help – they may be able to put you in touch with companies or local groups. Make sure you have an up-to-date relevant CV ready to go which lists all your sporting achievements and qualifications and which highlights your leadership skills.

Gail sails through

After finishing University, I got a job in a marketing department, but soon got bored, and felt the need to do something different and exciting.

After my 12 weeks training, I decided to apply to work at UKSA after being inspired on my training.

For me, the best experience has been teaching disadvantaged, special needs or disabled students. However, different people will gain different experiences, and develop new skills. Everyone on my course changed, whether it was in confidence, maturity, presentation skills or communications skills.

It was a great way to spend a gap year. These days employers are looking to see that gap year students have used their time to best develop their skills, not just travelled around. I am now working in the marketing department at UKSA, using my university training in the Watersports field.

Gail

SPORT INSTRUCTORS

Acorn Adventure

22 Worcester Road, Stourbridge
West Midlands DY8 1AN, England   Tel: +44 (0)1384 446057

Acorn Adventure runs adventure holiday camps based in nine centres in France, Italy, Spain and the UK – their main customers are school groups. They operate from April until September and have a good range of rewarding positions available, employing approximately 300 staff annually.

Pay starts from National Minimum Wage in the UK with additional qualification bonuses and returning staff bonuses. As an example of pay in European centres, a BCU Level 3 Canoe Coach would be expected to earn an average of £140 per week with food and accommodation included.

Acorn offers comprehensive training packages, including National Governing Body qualifications as well as free uniform and free travel.

Base Camp Group

Howick, Balls Cross, Petworth   Tel: +44 (0) 1403 820899
West Sussex GU28 9JY, England   Fax: +44 (0) 1403 820 899

The Gap Snowsports Programme (GSP) at Base Camp Group is specifically designed for people taking a year out, predominantly before or after university, who would like to learn to become ski or snowboard instructors in one season. The 11-week programme based in the resort of Meribel (the largest in the world) offers students the opportunity to achieve BASI (British Association of Snowsport Instructors) qualifications that are widely accepted in Europe as well as all around the world.

Gappers can choose from a combination of BASI certification courses and various modules taught by instructors from Snow-Systems Ski School. The GSP prepares students for their BASI 3 as well as teaching students how to ski off-piste, bumps and race, and boarders how to freeride and perform tricks. Students are able to explore and specialise in the various disciplines of skiing and snowboarding while experiencing life in the mountains and learning to become an instructor.

The Programme costs around £5795 and includes: snow systems instruction (six hours per day, five days per week); modular snowsports programme; preparation for all instructor examination courses; registration as a BASI associate member; trainee instructors course for skiers or the Foundation Course for snowboarders (worth £290); 'Les 3 Vallees' season ski pass (seven days per week); First Aid course; accommodation; continental breakfast and evening meal; return flights and airport transfer; French classes. But you will have to pay for your own insurance, snowsports equipment and Base Camp Group ski or snowboard-

Working Abroad

SPORT INSTRUCTORS

ing outfit. The Ski Instructor Training Course or Snowboard Instructor Training Course (on completion of the Trainee Instructors Course or Foundation Course) is an extra £390. Base Camp Group also offers a post programme service that finds work as an instructor for anyone who has completed the programme, especially during uni holidays.

BASI (British Association of Snowsport Instructors)

Glenmore, Aviemore Tel: +44 (0) 1479 861 717
Invernesshire PH22 1QU, Scotland Fax: +44 (0) 1479 861 718

BASI runs a full-time ten-week course for potential instructors (you need to be an experienced skier) from January to April for £4000+. These courses are held in Switzerland, Italy, Andorra and (at a slightly higher price) America. At the end there is an assessment and, if successful, you gain an instructor's licence. BASI advises you to book well ahead.

Flying Fish

25 Union Road, Cowes Tel: +44 (0) 1983 280 641
Isle of Wight PO31 7TW, England see: www.gap-year.com

Flying Fish offers training courses that lead to watersports jobs in the Mediterranean and Australia. Why not start with one of their courses in Sydney or Greece? Tel (Australia): +61 (0) 2 99 76 6714.

Goal-Line Soccer Clinics

PO Box 1642, Corvallis Tel: +1 (541) 753 5833
OR 97339-1642, USA Fax: +1 (541) 753 0811

Goal-Line offers paid soccer coaching vacations for qualified applicants. Their programme operates in a number of communities in the Pacific Northwest (Washington, Oregon) of the USA.

Summer camp sessions begin in early July and end mid-August. Remuneration for 1st year coaches is $300/week.

Marine Divers
(British Sub-Aqua Club School 388) Hong Kong

3E, Block 18, Dynasty View, 11 Ma Wo Road
Tai Po, New Territories, Hong Kong, China Tel: +852 2656 9399

Become a BSAC Open Water Instructor. In six to eight weeks train from beginner to instructor. Training and fun in Hong Kong (The City of Life), with optional five-day trip to the Philippines. Various packages. Dive the World once qualified – and get paid! Possible employment opportunities.

A full time job?

'Anyone out there looking for the best way of spending a year out? At Mark Warner, the most rewarding of times await you at our exclusive Alpine Chalethotels and Mediterranean Beach Clubs.

For winter and summer we want energetically focused staff such as **chefs**, **nannies**, **waiting & bar staff**, **handymen**, **nightwatchmen** and **kitchen porters**. We also want to hear from **watersport and activity instructors** looking for a season in the sun, plus **ski hosts** for our resorts in France, Italy and Austria.

Your destination will be an exciting challenge that includes tremendous fun, valuable experience and an attractive package.

Make yourself a hot prospect and call Mark Warner Resorts Recruitment on 020 7761 7300, or check out the website.

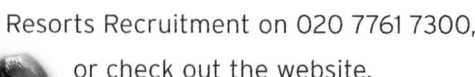

markwarner
beach & ski

markwarner.co.uk

Working Abroad   **SPORT INSTRUCTORS**

Mark Warner
George House
61-65 Kensington Church Street
London W8 4BA, England

Tel: +44 (0) 20 7761 7300
see: www.gap-year.com

Mark Warner offers a variety of jobs, depending on your age. In the summer you could be a pool attendant, aerobics instructor, tennis coach or watersports instructor – in Corsica, Sardinia, Greece, Turkey or Italy.

Nonstopski
1A Bickersteth Road
London SW17 9SE
England

Tel: +44 (0) 20 8772 7852
Fax: +44 (0) 20 8772 7852
see: www.gap-year.com

Nonstopski offers four and 11-week ski and snowboard instructor courses in Fernie, Canada's 'Powder Capital.' Students receive expert tuition from professional coaches in preparation for their internationally recognised ski (CSIA) and/or snowboard (CASI) instructor qualifications. The course also includes tuition in mountain safety and avalanche awareness, survival skills (a night spent in an igloo up the mountain!) winter first aid, foreign languages, photography, TEFL and cookery.

Weekend trips are arranged to Canadian cities, National Parks, hot springs, cat skiing, other ski resorts and the USA. All abilities are welcome and numbers are limited so early booking is advisable. Situated in the heart of the Rockies, Fernie is the fourth largest ski resort in Canada, rated third in the Best Ski Destinations (CNN.com) and has one of the highest average snowfalls (875cm) in North America providing phenomenal ski conditions.

PGL
PGL Recruitment Team, Alton Court
Penyard Lane, Ross-on-Wye
Herefordshire HR9 5GL, England

Tel: +44 (0) 1989 767 833
Fax: +44 (0) 1989 767 760

PGL runs activity holidays and courses for children. Each year the company employs over 2000 young people to work as instructors, group leaders and support staff at its centres in the UK, France and Spain. Positions are available between February and October each year. Ideally you should be able to start before May and be able to commit for a minimum of eight weeks. You must also be over 18 years of age. You'll receive full board and accommodation in addition to £60-£90 per week, depending on your role.

To work as an instructor or group leader you should have relevant experience. You don't need to be qualified as PGL provides training programmes to help staff gain the necessary skills and qualifications.

Teaching & Projects Abroad

Gerrard House, Rustington
West Sussex BN16 1AW
England

Tel: +44 (0) 1903 859 911
Fax: +44 (0) 1903 785 779
see: www.gap-year.com

Teaching & Projects Abroad is as an agency which organises voluntary work placements abroad. As its name suggests, many of the work opportunities it offers are in teaching – in such far flung places as China, Ghana, India, Sri Lanka, Mexico, Bolivia, Chile, Russia, Ukraine, Mongolia, Nepal, Peru, Romania, South Africa, Thailand and Togo. Placements in India, South Africa and Thailand can include teaching sports.

The organisation also offers a variety of other work opportunities – in medicine, veterinary medicine, social work, archaeology, conservation, business and architecture. You could find yourself working with Zing Pong, designer of the Shanghai Opera House. Or you could work in journalism with radio stations in Ghana and Mexico or newspapers in India, Mongolia, Romania and Russia. There is a range of business opportunities in Shanghai, including advertising, human resources, electronics, engineering, IT, accountancy and finance.

The medical placements (in China, India, Ghana, Mexico, Mongolia, Romania and Russia) include anything from dentistry to physiotherapy, and you may even find yourself attending, but definitely not performing, an operation – something to impress medical school with. There's also a conservation placement in Mexico where you can help protect the endangered Olive Ridley Sea Turtle.

Placements start any time and last from as little as one month to as long as a year. Charges range from £995 for three months in Romania to around £1800, and include food, lodging, travel, insurance and local back-up. The organisation holds several open days which give you the opportunity to meet staff and people who have already participated in programmes arranged by Teaching & Projects Abroad.

Travellers Worldwide

7 Mulberry Close, Ferring
West Sussex BN12 5HY
England

Tel: +44 (0) 1903 700478
Fax: +44 (0) 1903 502595
see: www.gap-year.com

Travellers Worldwide organises teaching placements in northern and southern India, Nepal, Sri Lanka and South Africa, and has two new projects in China (near Beijing) and Ghana. You could also teach in Russia in Moscow, St Petersburg, Siberia or in Kiev (where beer is a few pence a litre) in the Ukraine. You usually live with a local family and you don't need formal qualifications – you can teach conversational English or your favourite subject: maths, music, **sport** or whatever it might be. There is a new cultural exchange programme in

Cuba, including a Spanish language course. There are also various conservation and work placements in most of these countries. There's no pay, but your food and lodging are free. Prices range from £895 (three months in Moscow) to £1295 (three months in Ghana), both excluding airfares and insurance. Apply any time.

Teaching English as a Foreign Language

TEFL (Teaching English as a Foreign Language) is the ideal combination of doing something useful (if you're any good) and earning some money whilst enjoying life in another culture. You don't actually need to be able to speak another language, though it probably helps. It's also a good idea if you're interested in teaching – you'll soon find out whether you have a talent for it or not.

There are a lot of organisations happy to persuade you that a TEFL qualification is a very useful thing to have. Probably too many, in fact, because it's quite difficult for under-21s to get TEFL work abroad. Ask course organisers if they can help to find you TEFL jobs abroad as well as train you.

Formal TEFL courses are available at colleges throughout the UK, but there is only one TEFL qualification recognised by the British Council and open to 18-year-olds, and that is the Trinity College Certificate in TESOL (Teaching English to Speakers of Other Languages). Another certificate worth taking is CELTA, which is also widely recognised and open to those aged 18+.

Courses that do not lead to these qualifications are probably only worth doing if linked to a voluntary work placement, and for voluntary work a short course will usually be recommended by the organisation concerned. But you don't have to have any certificates to teach English informally (or as an au pair) abroad, and a short course will give you some idea of how to teach, increase your confidence and give you some lesson plans. Weekend courses tend to focus on theory and longer courses usually involve some sort of teaching practice.

How to find TEFL work

There are always fluctuations in the availability of work for people who can teach English, particularly outside the EU. As mentioned above, if you take a TEFL course, the training company should be able to help you find a TEFL job.

In most countries it is possible to give private lessons. The best way to find out more about individual countries is to contact the relevant embassy in the UK, which will give you up-to-date details of visas, salaries, qualifications needed and a view about the availability of work. You can also find embassy websites on www.gap-year.com. TEFL jobs are advertised in *The Times Educational Supplement* (on Fridays), the *Guardian* (on Tuesdays), in the education section of *The Independent* and in the *EFL Gazette*.

Teaching English in private lessons

Giving private tuition, either formally or in conversation classes, is a good way to earn extra cash. Advertisements can be placed in local schools, universities, newspapers and shops when you've been in a country long enough to know the local language and be streetwise. Be careful about wording your advertisement, particularly if you are young and female. Do not give any indication of your gender, and never write: 'Young English girl gives English lessons' – you could get some heavy-breathing phone calls. Try to meet prospective students in a public place before inviting them to your home or going to theirs.

Academy of Prague

Prague Schools, Na Sekyrce 1392/2	Tel: +420 (2) 333 22 742
Prague 6 160 00, Czech Republic	Fax: +420 (2) 333 23 779

You can get certified to teach English as a foreign language worldwide with Prague TEFL. No previous teaching experience is required. Their four-week intensive Trinity Certificate TESOL course is a practical and theoretical training course designed to produce teachers with the proper skills and techniques needed in order to teach English abroad. The course costs $1244/£829. Half board and all-inclusive prices are also available.

The course consists of a series of lectures, lessons, seminars, classes, workshops and demonstrations which aim not only to teach the theory of TEFL, but also how to put it into practice in the classroom. The staff at Prague TEFL work closely with trainees on finding teaching opportunities worldwide. Job guidance is available to all graduates and some may even be hired at their in-house language school, Prague Schools.

Alliances Abroad

2423 Pennsylvania Avenue NW	Tel: +1 (202) 467 9467
Washington DC 20037, USA	Fax: +1 (202) 467 9460

Alliances Abroad has an extensive range of teaching opportunities across the world. For example, in China you are placed in a school for three months to a year. All positions include free accommodation, and some include partial board, plus you will be paid a competitive salary. Positions tend to be with universities and trade schools.

In Spain you teach the family you're living with in exchange for accommodation and meals and getting to live the Spanish way of life. Whichever country you choose to teach in, the experienced Alliances Abroad staff will help you with all of your travel needs, including travel arrangements, recommendations on what to do while abroad, visa/work permit procurement, airport transfers and all that other organisational stuff.

EF International Languages

74 Roupell Street
London SE1 8SS, England

Tel: +44 (0) 8707 200735
see: www.gap-year.com

Learn a language, teach English and travel to two fantastic destinations. Choose from Europe (Nice, and Barcelona), South America (Quito, Chile, Mexico, Columbia), China (various locations), Russia (St Petersburg, Moscow) and North Africa (Casablanca). This ten-month programme starts with a TEFL training course in the UK, is followed by a three-month language course at one of EF's International Languages Schools, and finishes with a six-month placement as an English Teacher in a second destination. Prices start at £5400 and include TEFL course, language programme, accommodation, flights and living allowance on the teaching placement.

The Espero Language Centre

Szkola Jezykow Obcych 'Espero'
al. Jana Pawla II 17/1
47-220 Kedzierzyn-Kozle
Poland

Tel: +48 77 4838325
Fax: +48 77 4838325

If you fancy a more unusual teaching experience, what about Poland? The Espero Language Centre, 50km from the Czech border in the small town of Kedzierzyn-Kozle, are keen for 'responsible and cheerful' gap year students to teach English. You would be teaching 15-20 classes a week, mainly conversational English, to Polish locals from 3.30pm to 7.30pm.

Here's the crunch – you wouldn't be paid! The main cost to you will be your travel to Poland and a bus pass ($18/month). Accommodation and food are free – you stay with a local Polish 'host' family, so this would be a great way to experience the culture and learn about Polish traditions and customs as well as day-to-day life. Write to Barbara Piechocka, Director of Study, if you are interested. She is happy to put you in touch with one of the gappers teaching there last year.

Inlingua International

Belpstrasse 11
3007 Bern, Switzerland

Tel: +41 31 388 7777
Fax: +41 31 388 7766

Inlingua International runs TESOL (Teaching English to Speakers of Other Languages) in its colleges throughout Europe. For example, for a cost of £995 you could take the five-week full-time TESOL course leading to a Trinity TESOL certificate at its college in Cheltenham. Once you are qualified, you can make use of the Inlingua recruitment service and the many jobs listed on its website to start earning yourself some money. Inlingua does point out that it can't absolutely guarantee to find you a job.

i-to-i

9 Blenheim Terrace
Leeds LS2 9HZ
England

Tel: +44 (0) 870 333 2332
Fax: +44 (0) 113 242 2171
see: www.gap-year.com

i-to-i, a highly respected gap year organisation, pioneered the 20-hour, intensive TEFL course. The i-to-i TEFL course fully prepares participants to teach English abroad with maximum convenience – both of time and money. Fully qualified TEFL tutors conduct courses all over the UK and Ireland, and, whether you want to travel and teach or simply try something different, the i-to-i TEFL course is open to everyone. Also, with their innovative online course (see link from www.gap-year.com) i-to-i's TEFL training is available anywhere in the world, so you can even earn a certificate whilst travelling. The i-to-i TEFL course is both creative and dynamic, and enables you to plan, prepare and teach your own lessons with confidence. Employment information is also provided. The cost for the live or online course is £195, and will award you a TEFL certificate.

JET – Japan Exchange and Teaching Programme

JET Desk, Embassy of Japan
101-104 Piccadilly
London W1J 7JT, England

Tel: +44 (0) 20 7465 6668/6670
see: www.gap-year.com

If you have a bachelors degree in any subject then you can apply to take part in the JET programme. JET recruits from 39 countries, and in 2002 the programme had 6250 participants, over 600 of them from the UK. You spend a year working roughly 35 hours per week as an Assistant Language Teacher (ALT) in local schools and discovering Japanese culture. You don't need a TEFL qualification, although it's helpful, and you'll need to demonstrate excellent spoken and written English along with a genuine interest in all things Japanese. If you already have a good level of Japanese, you can join JET as a Coordinator for International Relations (CIR), where you'll work in local government to promote international activities in your area.

You get paid generously – ¥3,600,000 (roughly £18,300) per annum for ALTs after Japanese taxes are deducted. Rented accommodation will be found for you by the organisation you work for. Placements are in cities, towns and villages throughout Japan. JET recruits via embassies and consulates in participating countries – their main website, **www.mofa.go.jp/j_info/visit/jet/**, has links to these. Entry is quite competitive, and interviews usually take place from November February. There's an orientation programme in both London and Tokyo, and JET will also provide you with Japanese language books and CDs, a work visa, return flights and an in-country support service.

Muyal Liang Trust

53 Blenheim Crescent　　　　　　Tel: +44 (0) 20 7229 4774
London W11 2EG, England　　　　see: www.gap-year.com

The Muyal Liang Trust places teachers in the Denjong Pedma Cheoling Academy, a school for disadvantaged children and orphans. Placements run from March to December and you'll be expected to teach all subjects as well as English.

The school is located in Sikkim, north of Darjeeling. The Indian government restricts foreign visitors to a two-month stay in Sikkim, a sensitive area due to its proximity to the Chinese border. However, permits can be extended for those interested in a longer-term commitment. Teachers will be provided with room and board at Pemayangtse, a 17th century Buddhist monastery in the Himalayan foothills, with magnificent views of Kangchendzonga, the world's third highest mountain. The contact in India is Capt Yapo S Yongda, Muyal Liang Trust, Yongda Hill, Drakchung Dzong, West Sikkim 737113, India. Tel: +91 3595 50656.

Oxford House College

28 Market Place
London W1W 8AW
England　　　　　　　　　　　　Tel: +44 (0) 20 7580 9785

Oxford House College provides a CELTA (UCLES examining body) certificate and runs a wide range of courses. The main full-time course running four weeks costs £680 including exam fee. There's also a part-time course covering the same ground at £750 including the exam fee, which runs for 13 weeks, three evenings a week plus three Saturdays. If you call in at Oxford House they'll show you their 'giant jobs board' where they post notices of TEFL job vacancies worldwide.

Saxoncourt & English Worldwide

124 New Bond Street
London W1S 1DX
England

Tel: +44 (0) 20 7491 1911
Fax: +44 (0) 207 493 3657

Saxoncourt is an EFL recruitment consultancy placing over 600 English instructors with private language schools in up to 20 different countries worldwide each year.

If you don't yet have your TEFL qualification, Saxoncourt also runs full-time four-week courses in London and Oxford, leading to either the Trinity TESOL diploma or the Cambridge CELTA qualification.

Shane English School

59 South Molton Street
London W1K 5SN, England

Tel: +44 (0) 20 7499 8533

This central London school runs ten one-week Gap Teaching Skills courses a year, preparing about 1000 gap year students for teaching posts abroad – not just teaching English, but other subjects too. You

don't come away with a recognised qualification, and many of the places on this course are for GAP (GAP Activity Projects) participants who already have a teaching placement set up for them. It costs £125 for one week and you practise teaching on your peers.

Syndicat Mixte Montaigu-Rocheservière

Rocheservière
Hotel de l'Intercommunalite
35 Avenue Villebois Mareuil   Tel: +33 (0) 2 51 46 45 45
85607 Montaigu, Cedex, France   Fax: +33 (0) 2 51 46 45 40

This French organisation receives local government funding to teach English in primary schools, offering four posts annually – and it also employs a fifth person to work as a language assistant in a local college and lycée.

TTI (Teacher Training International School of English)

148-150 Camden High Street   Tel: +44 (0) 800 174 031
London NW1 ONE, England   Fax: +44 (0) 800 174 031

TTI runs a TEFL course (three times a week for six weeks: £630) at the end of which you gain its TEFL certificate. The course includes grammar awareness, teaching practice and written assessments. You can make up your mind about the course at a 'taster day', costing £35, once every six weeks.

Teaching & Projects Abroad

Gerrard House
Rustington   Tel: +44 (0) 1903 859 911
West Sussex BN16 1AW   Fax: +44 (0) 1903 785 779
England   see: www.gap-year.com

Teaching & Projects Abroad organises teaching placements in such far-flung places as China, Ghana, India, Sri Lanka, Mexico, Bolivia, Chile, Russia, Ukraine, Mongolia, Nepal, Peru, Romania, South Africa, Thailand and Togo. You pay them a deposit, tell them where you want to go and for how long, and if they can't find what you're looking for, your deposit is returned in full. Fees range from £995 for three months in Romania up to £1800 – this includes food, lodging, travel, insurance and local back-up. Though strictly speaking not a work placement as you don't get paid, this is ideal if you want some teaching experience in an unusual setting. The organisation holds several open days which give you the opportunity to meet staff and people who have already participated in programmes arranged by Teaching & Projects Abroad.

TEFL Training

Friend's Close, Stonefield, Witney
Oxfordshire OX8 8PX, England

Tel: +44 (0) 1993 891 686
Fax: +44 (0) 1993 891 686

TEFL Training runs about 17 intensive study weekends a year (£170 or £145 with student card) and a follow-through course (£65) of 80 hours of home study. Together they result in a certificate for 100 hours, accredited by the professional teaching body, the College of Teachers. It also produces a self-study pack for £170 which includes a video, and will help you find a job through its contacts with schools abroad.

Xuzhou Normal College

20 Kuihe Xiyan, Xuzhou Normal College
Xuzhou, China

Tel: +86 5163 822 022
Fax: +86 5163 822 022

Xuzhou Normal College in China has two positions for teachers from English-speaking countries to teach oral English for one year, starting in September. No previous experience is required, and your salary would be the same as that of the local college teachers. On average you would be teaching 10-12 English lessons, five working days per week. Accommodation is free and you are entitled to three months' holiday – summer holiday starts in June, and other holidays include winter holiday and public holidays. In addition, the college also offers two or three touring holidays free of charge. The college says these posts are ideal if you would like the opportunity to explore China while teaching English there.

The College: Xuzhou Normal College is maintained by local government and has roughly 1000 students and 130 staff. Its students are highly praised and many are now working as English teachers, music teachers and art teachers in kindergartens, primary schools and middle schools. This year, the college intends to enrol 100 new students majoring in English Education who will work as English teachers in primary schools and middle schools once they have graduated.

The City: Xuzhou, with a population of over 6 million, is in the north of Jiangsu, which is one of the most prosperous provinces in China. As an old city, Xuzhou is famous for its long history and historical relics, and won the name of 'Historical City of China'. Xuzhou owns one of the busiest railway lines and has convenient train and air links. The school lies in the south of the city within easy reach of supermarkets, department stores, theatre, park, restaurants, university, library and museums.

The Head Teacher, Mrs Xianghua Zhang, says "we are looking forward to hearing from you. If you want to know more, don't hesitate to contact us. Welcome to our school! Welcome to China!" Please send your CV first to the UK contact, Dr Xiang Zhang (Tel: +44 (0) 1235 203758 evening only, email: Xiang.Zhang@ntlworld.com) or send your application direct to Mrs Xianghua Zhang at the college.

Working Abroad

Seasonal work

'Seasonal work' covers a wide variety of jobs including working with kids on summer camps in the States and grape picking in the South of France. Although seasonal work doesn't tend to give you 'career experience' it can pay quite well and it doesn't last all year so you get time to travel. We've grouped the following companies and organisations according to where they're offering work in the world.

Seasonal work in Europe

The following companies should be able to help you get casual work in Europe, or try doing a search on the internet or using gap year message boards to find out if any other gappers know what's available.

Acorn Adventure

22 Worcester Road
Stourbridge
West Midlands DY8 1AN, England   Tel: +44 (0)1384 446057

Acorn Adventure runs adventure holiday camps based in nine centres in France, Italy, Spain and the UK – their main customers are school groups. They operate from April until September and have a good range of rewarding positions available, employing approximately 300 staff annually.

Pay starts from National Minimum Wage in the UK with additional qualification bonuses and returning staff bonuses. As an example of pay in European centres, a BCU Level 3 Canoe Coach would be expected to earn an average of £140 per week with food and accommodation included.

Acorn offers comprehensive training packages, including National Governing Body qualifications as well as free uniform and free travel.

Camp Beaumont

The Old Rectory
Beeston Regis   Tel: +44 (0) 1263 823000
Norfolk NR27 9NG, England   Fax: +44 (0) 1263 823002

It is useful to have a TEFL qualification if you want to work at Camp Beaumont's summer camp in France. Jobs last for five to eight weeks during the summer holidays: recruiting continues until late June. Basic pay starts at £144 a week but varies depending on experience and qualifications. The contact numbers for Camp Beaumont's Beaumont House office are: Tel: +44 (0) 1603 284280, Fax: +44 (0) 1603 284250.

visit: www.gap-year.com

SEASONAL WORK: EUROPE

Working Abroad

CCUSA

Unit 4CC
Green Dragon House
64-70 High Street
Croydon CR0 9XN
England

Tel: +44 (0) 20 8688 9051
Fax: +44 (0) 20 8680 4539
see: www.gap-year.com

If you are looking for something a bit different to do whilst making money, getting a tan, meeting and working with new people from different cultures, seeing new places, and enhancing you CV, CCUSA will find a programme to achieve this. Over the last 16 years, CCUSA have organised safe and secure working holidays for over 100,000 students from all over the world. CCUSA Camp Counselors Russia gives you the chance to work with children for four or eight weeks at a Russian summer camp.

All CCUSA programmes offer guaranteed placement before departure, return flights, visas, insurance, airport pickup, local orientation, and full-time support before, during and after the programme.

CCUSA offers many other programmes, please see their other listings in this chapter in the sections on *Seasonal Work in North America*, *Seasonal Work in Australia and New Zealand* and *Internships* for full details.

Euro Academy

24 Clarendon Place
London SE13 5EY
England

Tel: +44 (0) 20 8297 0505
Fax: +44 (0) 20 8297 0984

Though mainly a language school, Euro Academy also offers work placements in Europe.

Eurocamp

Overseas Recruitment Department
Hartford Manor,
Greenbank Lane
Northwich
Cheshire CW8 1HW, England

Tel: +44 (0) 1606 787 522

Eurocamp organises camping holidays throughout Europe and employs people of 18 and over to work from April to September. You can be a courier, help clean the accommodation, put up and take down tents or supervise. Wages start at £100 per week. Applications begin October.

Working Abroad   **SEASONAL WORK: EUROPE**

Flying Fish

25 Union Road, Cowes
Isle of Wight PO31 7TW   Tel: +44 (0) 1983 280 641
England   see: www.gap-year.com

Flying Fish runs sailing, surfing, windsurfing and diving gap programmes which lead to professional qualifications and jobs in the sun. For example you can join professional dive training in Australia; go on a work placement in the Mediterranean sailing industry; and do international yacht training in the UK and Australia. Qualifications include PADI dive awards and RYA Windsurfing Yachting and Dinghy Sailing certificates. A comprehensive training guide is available. Tel (Australia): +61 (0) 2 99 76 6714.

French Encounters

63 Fordhouse Road
Bromsgrove   Tel: +44 (0) 1527 873645
Worcestershire B60 2LU   Fax: +44 (0) 1527 832794
England   see: www.gap-year.com

Every year French Encounters employs eight gap year students to act as *animateurs/animatrices* in their two châteaux centres in Seine Maritime for the season (mid-February to mid-June). The work includes tour guiding, functioning as couriers, entertainers, supervisors and role models to 10- to 13-year-old British children in school groups (all domestic chores such as cooking, meal service and general cleaning are done by other staff).

You're paid about £60 a week, with a £15 weekend allowance. Full board and lodging, travel costs to and from Normandy and reasonable incidental and miscellaneous expenses during the season are covered. All insurance requirements are included – you don't even need an E111, as the French Encounters policy is fully comprehensive. Because French Encounters is a small family company, its employees become part of the family and are well looked after!

It is the ideal opportunity to speak and practice French in a real, working context and to perfect those linguistic skills required for a successful start to a degree programme. Every encouragement is given by the owners – there's even a library of books and videos available for the team.

The two-week initial training programme for *animateurs* is extremely thorough and incorporates a French Red Cross first aid course and professional presentation skills coaching. It should prove a huge learning curve in terms of teaching and supervision techniques. You

Looking for a meaningful year out?

Why not work as an 'animateur'
with
French Encounters
the specialists in high level educational
and language field trips for schools

Do you want to:
earn while you learn?
develop a variety of essential transferrable skills?
(business, management, human relations)
improve your communication and presentation skills?
enhance your CV and increase your employment potential?
learn to be a guide, courier and entertainer?
perfect your French language skills?
use your initiative?
live and work in a château in Normandy?
acquire some practical first aid skills?
work as part of a dynamic team?
and, of course, have fun in the process?

What previous animateurs have said about their experience:

"It marked me for life!" 1986
"I still remember my time at FE with fondness" 1996
"A great time - I learned so much and had a such fun." 1998
"It was really hard work, but worth every minute.
It was better than anything I've done since." 1999
"The first time I took a group out I was terrified.
By the end I could cope with anything. 2000
"It's a fast way to grow up and get paid too" 2002

Interested?
contact French Encounters
63 Fordhouse Road Bromsgrove Worcs B60 2LU
Tel: 01527 873645 Tel/Fax: 01527 832794
email: admin@frenchencounters.com
www.frenchencounters.com

will get training to develop your courier skills, tour guide techniques and all that these entail. How to manage groups, organise itineraries, use your personal initiative, take responsibility for groups and even how to use a microphone are just some of the things you will learn.

During the season, a week is made available for the preparation and assessment of an English Speaking Board Professional Presentation Skills Certificate: very useful to add to your CV.

Although you might not consider this an exotic gap year project, most previous *animateurs* say they learned a great deal, had enormous fun and were sad when the season came to an end – in fact many have stayed friends with the owners for years.

Holidaybreak

Overseas Recruitment Dept
Hartford Manor
Greenbank Lane
Northwich
Cheshire CW8 1HW   Tel: +44 (0) 1606 787522
England   Fax: +44 (0) 870 366 7640

Holiday Break (Eurocamp and Key Camp) organises camping holidays throughout Europe (excluding the UK) and employs people of 18 and over to help from April/May to July or September/October. Jobs last for at least two months. You can be a courier, (helping customers plus cleaning accommodation), provide activities for children, put up or take down tents or supervise. Minimum wage is £100 per week. Travel costs, uniform, accommodation and subsidised insurance are also provided.

Jobs in the Alps

17 High Street, Gretton
Northamptonshire NN17 3DE   Tel: +44 (0) 7050 121648
England   Fax: +44 (0) 1536 771914

Jobs in the Alps offers seasonal jobs in mountain resorts for gap year students who have good French or German, usually A-level or equivalent, and want to use or improve their language skills whilst enjoying winter skiing or summer sports.

All jobs pay a good wage and usually include free board and accommodation. The winter ski season is from mid-December to April, and applications are best in by early September. The summer season varies but is about mid-June to mid-September – applications should be made by April.

SEASONAL WORK: EUROPE

Mark Warner

George House
61-65 Kensington Church Street
London W8 4BA   Tel: +44 (0) 20 7761 7300
England   see: www.gap-year.com

Mark Warner offers a variety of jobs, depending on your age. In winter you could be a chef, handyman, nanny, bar or chalet person or ski host. In the summer you could also be a pool attendant, aerobics instructor, a member of the waiting staff, tennis coach (qualifications needed) or watersports instructor – in Corsica, Sardinia, Greece, Turkey or Italy.

PGL

PGL Recruitment Team
Alton Court
Penyard Lane
Ross-on-Wye
Herefordshire HR9 5GL   Tel: +44 (0) 1989 767 833
England   Fax: +44 (0) 1989 767 760

Each year PGL employs over 2000 people to work at its children's activity centres in the UK, France and Spain. You'll receive full board and accommodation in addition to £60-£90 per week (depending on your role). You don't need specific experience unless you want to teach sailing, windsurfing, canoeing or pony-trekking. PGL provides instructor training if you do not have the necessary qualifications. There are also vacancies for support staff and for people who work with children.

Positions are available between February and October; it's best to apply as early as possible. You must be 18 years of age and ideally able to start before the end of May.

Solaire Holidays

1158 Stratford Road
Hall Green
Birmingham B28 8AF
England   Tel: +44 (0) 121 7785061

Solaire Holidays organises camping holidays in France and Spain and needs help during the summer – especially general couriers, children's couriers, bar staff and maintenance staff. Pay ranges from £84 to £140 a week plus bonuses with free accommodation and travel.

Seasonal work in North America

Working for a summer in the USA shouldn't be a problem, although after the terrorist attacks in New York the US government was said to be planning a new 'monitoring system' for US visa holders that would result in higher visa application fees. There are different categories of J1 visa and you need the right one: a student visa, for example, counts anyone on a gap year with an unconditional offer of a university or college place as a 'student'.

Many of the organisations listed below can help you find both work visas and employment offers, particularly at some of the 10,000 summer camps in the USA, but check out the small print about pay, accommodation and other expenses. The blanket minimum wage in the USA is $5.15, which doesn't buy you much. It is possible, however, to support yourself and save enough for travel after you finish working – and there's a lot to see in the USA.

If camp life doesn't appeal, there's a broad range of travel and work programmes. Each programme carries its own opportunities and eligibility restrictions, so it's worth doing plenty of research in advance. Some organisers have directories of job opportunities, often within companies that have a history of taking on people from such programmes.

Alliances Abroad

2423 Pennsylvania Avenue NW
Washington DC 20037, USA

Tel: +1 (202) 467 9467
Fax: +1 (202) 467 9460

Alliances Abroad is one of only a few educational travel companies in the world offering international students paid internships and summer work programmes in the United States.

With dozens of locations and numerous employers around the country for you to choose from, they'll help you find work that turns into the experience of a lifetime. All you do is choose the location, length of time you're willing to stay, and give them an idea of the type of position you will consider. Their experienced staff in America will do the rest.

Positions are available in many categories including import-export, communication, tourism, social work, information technology, secretarial work, economics, law, marketing, banking, finance, public relations and many more.

BUNAC (British Universities North America Club)

16 Bowling Green Lane
London EC1R 0QH, England

Tel: +44 (0) 20 7251 3472
see: www.gap-year.com

Spend a summer working as a counsellor on a children's summer camp in the USA. BUNAC arranges your placement, visa, flights, insur-

working adventures
WORLDWIDE

Make the most of your long summer holidays or 'year out' with BUNAC's wide range of exciting work and travel programmes.

- Work on a children's summer camp on *Summer Camp USA* and *KAMP*
- Twelve months to work and travel on *Work Canada, Gap Canada, Work Australia* or *Work New Zealand*
- Summer vacation work in the USA and Canada
- Three to eighteen month internship with *OPT USA*
- Work on a voluntary project on *Volunteer Costa Rica*

Tel: 020 7251 3472

Contact: Gary Yardley, BUNAC, 16 Bowling Green Lane
London, EC1R 0QH. E-mail: enquiries@bunac.org.uk

WWW.BUNAC.ORG

Looking to add skills to your **CV** and see more of the **world**?

ance, accommodation and food. About 3500 young people experience this unique and rewarding type of working holiday each year through BUNAC. Applicants need to be over 19 on June 1st 2003 and must be able to travel to the USA no later than mid June. Experience of working with groups of children in a leadership role is required. Sporty students with experience of instructing activities such as soccer, tennis, swimming, horse-riding, golf and sailing are in demand as are applicants with experience of teaching arts and crafts, drama and music.

Summer Camp USA offers a low up-front cost chance to go on a working holiday. You have to pay £59 registration fee, about £120 for insurance and approximately £45 visa fee to the US Embassy. BUNAC deducts the cost of your airfare from your earnings. You get a minimum of $670 in hand spending money for working six to nine weeks if you are under 21; this rises to $730 if you are over 21.

BUNAC also has a number of other working holiday programmes to the USA: Work America (casual summer work in the USA); KAMP (the Kitchen and Maintenance Programme which provides behind-the-scenes support work on children's summer camps); and OPT USA (career-related training internships).

Canada

BUNAC's Work Canada and Gap Canada programmes give gap year students the chance to spend two to 12 months working in this beautiful and friendly country. Applicants must be British or Irish passport holders aged 18-29 and have an unconditional place to start university. BUNAC will arrange your flexible casual work visa and provide comprehensive pre-departure and arrival orientations. Most participants arrange work on arrival in Canada and are advised by SWAP, BUNAC's partner in Canada. Many gap year students choose to spend the winter working in ski resorts such as Whistler, Lake Louise and Banff whilst others prefer the city life in Vancouver or Toronto.

Camp America
37A Queen's Gate
London SW7 5HR, England

Tel: +44 (0) 20 7581 7333
see: www.gap-year.com

An American adventure: do you want to spend a summer in America full of fun, excitement and new challenges? Would you like the opportunity to make friends from all over the world and travel around another continent? If your answer is "Yes", then Camp America may well be for you.

Each year Camp America sends thousands of young people to work on summer camps and resorts in the States between June and August. You could be working with children teaching sports, arts and life

Summer Work and Travel in the USA!

Do you brim with enthusiasm? Are you friendly and easy going? Do you have a sense of humour and a talent for teamwork?

Camp America are looking for enthusiastic young people to work with kids this summer, teaching them sports, arts and life skills at summer camps in the USA. If you are over 18 on June 1st and are available from then until August, Camp America offer you the summer of a lifetime!

You'll get:

- Fantastic experience for your CV!
- Free return flights
- Free meals and accommodation
- Pocket money
- 24 hour support and assistance
- 10 weeks to travel the USA!

For a brochure:
web: www.campamerica.co.uk e-mail: brochure@campamerica.co.uk
tel: 020 7581 7333 or send this page to:
Camp America, Dept GYG03, 37a Queen's Gate, London SW7 5HR.

www.campamerica.co.uk

Name: _____ Postcode: _____

Address: _____ Telephone: _____

_____ Email: _____

_____ Date of Birth: _____

_____ Uni/College: _____

GYG03

skills. Alternatively you could be cooking or cleaning for them, helping with the camp's administration or working in catering at a resort. Whichever job you choose, you'll get to see what the USA is really like.

Apply to Camp America and you will receive: a free return flight from London to New York; free accommodation and meals for nine weeks (12-16 if working on a resort); pocket money; time for independent travel. Sound exciting? Then what are you waiting for?

CCUSA

Unit 4CC, Green Dragon House
64-70 High Street
Croydon CR0 9XN
England

Tel: +44 (0) 20 8688 9051
Fax: +44 (0) 20 8680 4539
see: www.gap-year.com

If you are looking for something a bit different to do whilst making money, getting a tan, meeting and working with new people from different cultures, seeing new places, and enhancing you CV, CCUSA will find a programme to achieve this. Over the last 16 years, CCUSA have organised safe and secure working holidays for over 100,000 students from all over the world.

If you like working with kids and you have nine weeks to spare this summer then the CCUSA Camp Counselors USA programme is perfect for you. CCUSA works with over 900 summer camps in beautiful locations in America. You don't need any experience or qualifications but you do need to be at least 18 years old.

All CCUSA programmes offer guaranteed placement before departure, return flights, visas, insurance, airport pickup, local orientation, and full-time support before, during and after the programme.

CCUSA offers many other programmes, please see their other listings in this chapter in the sections on *Seasonal Work in Europe*, *Seasonal Work in Australia and New Zealand* and *Internships* for full details.

Changing Worlds

11 Doctors Lane, Chaldon
Surrey CR3 5AE
England

Tel: +44 (0) 1883 340 960
Fax: +44 (0) 1883 330783
see: www.gap-year.com

Changing Worlds offers paid work placements in the Canadian Rockies. Demanding hotel work is rewarded by reasonable pay, an excellent social life, accommodation and time to ski on days off. Workers must be capable of working a full 40-hour week and remaining positive.

Prices start at £1795 and include return flight, finding a suitable job, assistance with work permits, a one-day UK briefing and assistance from the Changing Worlds representative in-country who will meet you and take you to your work placement. Some work experience is expected. Fundraising advice is available although most workers take paid UK jobs prior to their placement. To be eligible for the placement in Canada you need to be going on to university.

CIEE (Council on International Educational Exchange)

52 Poland Street
London W1F 7AB, England
Tel: +44 (0) 20 7478 2020
Fax: +44 (0) 20 7734 7322

CIEE's Work and Travel USA programme is for up to four months of seasonal work (June to October) in the USA and the deposit is £70. Although most students take seasonal summer jobs, past participants have enhanced their CVs with everything from office temping to career-related summer placements.

Check on the CIEE website to read about those who have been and done it or chat to others who are thinking about it on the bulletin boards. The work and travel programme gives you far more freedom than the internship programme, although it does entail a certain amount of confidence in your job-seeking abilities. You could do almost any job from bar work in New York to film work in California.

Euro Academy

24 Clarendon Place
London SE13 5EY
England
Tel: +44 (0) 20 8297 0505
Fax: +44 (0) 20 8297 0984

Though mainly a language school, Euro Academy also offers work placements in the USA.

Gap Challenge

at World Challenge Expeditions
Black Arrow House
2 Chandos Road
London NW10 6NF
England
Tel: +44 (0) 20 8728 7272
and +44 (0) 20 8728 7200
see: www.gap-year.com

Gap Challenge provides individuals aged between 18 and 24 with exciting opportunities to take a well-structured gap year, living and working in one of 12 countries and doing something really constructive in their gap year. It is a highly flexible programme that offers the choice of a variety of rewarding and worthwhile voluntary placements

ranging from teaching in Tanzania or conservation work in the rainforests of Belize to care work in Malaysia.

Placements last for between two and nine months and with a 12-month return flight there is plenty of opportunity for independent travel afterwards. Whilst away, Gap Challengers are offered advice and support from in-country agents and benefit from World Challenge Expedition's comprehensive 24-hour emergency back-up systems.

Seasonal work in Australia and New Zealand

Australasia is the most popular destination for gappers, so there will be a lot of other backpackers after jobs too – but there are usually plenty of jobs to go round, and many backpackers travel from one casual job to another as a way of paying for their travel. It's a good way to meet people too.

Just surfing the internet from the UK (using keywords like 'Australia jobs' or 'vacation work Australia') gives you an idea of what's on offer. Australian job websites worth a look include:

www.monster.com.au   www.ozsearch.com.au
www.youthjobs.com.au

You may notice that job adverts often carry a note that 'only people with the right to work in Australia may apply for this position'. You can apply or register online, but your chances of getting it before you have a ticket and a visa lined up are not be high.

Australian High Commission   Australia House, Strand
London WC2 4LA
Visa enquiries: 090 6550 8900 (£1/min)
www.australia.org.uk

Department of Immigration   Australia
www.immi.gov.au

So getting the right type of visa is a priority. The key point is that to do casual work in Australia you will need a Working Holiday Maker (WHM) visa, which costs £65. It allows you to travel and take occasional work for up to a year. The year begins the day you enter Australia, so if you never arrive you don't lose anything – but once you've used up your WHM visa you'll never be allowed another one.

To qualify for a WHM you need to be aged between 18-30 with no dependants, and be a citizen of a country with reciprocal work agreements with Australia (– these countries include the UK, Republic of Ireland, Canada and various European and Far Eastern countries). You'll need to prove that you have at least £2000 in the bank and enough money for your return fare. Application must be by post (you can download the application form from the website), which takes four to five weeks, and since you have to send your passport, you'll be confined to the UK for that period. You can find information on all types of visas, including the Student Visa, on the Australian High Commission website, **www.australia.org.uk**.

Many organisations arrange paid work placements in Australia and New Zealand, and some also organise voluntary work assignments in those and other countries. Some of these will also sort out your paperwork such as visas and work permits for you – although you may have to pay extra for this service. Below are listed some useful organisations to check out when you're looking for work in Australasia.

Alliances Abroad

2423 Pennsylvania Avenue NW
Washington DC 20037, USA

Tel: +1 (202) 467 9467
Fax: +1 (202) 467 9460

The Alliances Abroad Rural Australia work programme will place you in a paid position on a ranch, station, farm or roadhouse in rural Australia. Work positions include farm work, domestic or childcare work on the farm, or rural hospitality.

To start you off there's a five-day orientation programme on a working farm near Brisbane and then you journey into the Outback for your adventure!

Accommodation and meals are provided as well as a salary. The work programme allows you to experience all that Australia has to offer – making lifelong friends halfway around the world, backpacking, diving, climbing and journeying throughout the Outback – while earning money! Their experienced staff will help you with all of your travel needs, including travel arrangements, recommendations on what to do while abroad, visa/work permit procurement, airport transfers and all that other organisational stuff.

BUNAC (British Universities North America Club)

16 Bowling Green Lane
London EC1R 0QH, England

Tel: +44 (0) 20 7251 3472
see: www.gap-year.com

BUNAC, best known for its programmes in the USA and Canada, also offers Work Australia and Work New Zealand programmes. BUNAC arranges visas, group departures, an organised stop over, arrival accommodation, orientation and access to a resource office throughout your stay.

BUNAC's subsidiary IEP hosts all participants whilst in Australia and New Zealand. Departures are from London and Los Angeles and the extended validity tickets allow trips of up to 18 months' duration.

CCUSA

Unit 4CC, Green Dragon House
64-70 High Street
Croydon CR0 9XN, England

Tel: +44 (0) 20 8688 9051
Fax: +44 (0) 20 8680 4539
see: www.gap-year.com

If you are looking for something a bit different to do whilst making money, getting a tan, meeting and working with new people from different cultures, seeing new places, and enhancing you CV, CCUSA will find a programme to achieve this. Over the last 16 years, CCUSA have organised safe and secure working holidays for over 100,000 students from all over the world.

CCUSA's Work Experience Down Under programme offers a 12-month work and travel visa for both Australia and New Zealand helps you find a job. All CCUSA programmes offer guaranteed placement before departure, return flights, visas, insurance, airport pickup, local orientation, and full-time support before, during and after the programme.

CCUSA offers many other programmes, please see their other listings in this chapter in the sections on *Seasonal Work in Europe, Seasonal Work in North America* and *Internships* for full details.

Changing Worlds

11 Doctors Lane, Chaldon
Surrey CR3 5AE
England

Tel: +44 (0) 1883 340 960
Fax: +44 (0) 1883 330783
see: www.gap-year.com

Changing Worlds offers paid work placements in New Zealand and Queensland, Australia. In the Bay of Islands region of North Island, Changing Worlds organises a range of jobs including hotel work and farm work. Those working in hotels will enjoy local rates of pay. Those working on farms will be paid pocket money and will be well looked after by a local family. Changing worlds also offers a voluntary placement on a tall ship for those with ocean-going experience.

In Australia workers do farm work in Queensland in return for a real taste of Aussie life, pocket money and a blend of hard work and fun. Placements are available working in a zoo and on a fauna park.

In all cases workers must be capable of working a full 40-hour week and remaining positive. Prices start at £2295 and include return flights, finding a suitable job, assistance with work permits, a one-day UK briefing and assistance from the Changing Worlds representative who will meet you and take you to your placement. Some work experience is useful. Fundraising advice is available although most workers take UK paid jobs prior to their placement. To be eligible you need to be between 18 and 25 for New Zealand and up to 30 for Australia.

 *changing worlds*

A year out with changing worlds, change your life forever.

For details of our paid placements,
telephone: 01883 340960 or
visit: www.changingworlds.co.uk

Changing Worlds: 11 Doctors Lane Chaldon Surrey CR3 5AE UK

Australia

Canada

New Zealand

Flying Fish
25 Union Road, Cowes
Isle of Wight PO31 7TW, England

Tel: +44 (0) 1983 280 641
see: www.gap-year.com

Flying Fish runs sailing, surfing, windsurfing and diving gap programmes which lead to professional qualifications and jobs in the sun. For example you can join professional dive training in Australia; go on a work placement in the Mediterranean sailing industry; and do international yacht training in the UK and Australia. Qualifications include PADI dive awards and RYA Windsurfing Yachting and Dinghy Sailing certificates. A comprehensive training guide is available. Tel (Australia): +61 (0) 2 99 76 6714.

newzealandvisas.com

Tel: +44 (0) 1270 626626

Cheshire-based newzealandvisas.com specialises in services for travellers to New Zealand/Australia. In particular they organise working holiday visas for these countries. For a charge of £50 (including Embassy fee) they will post out the application form pack, submit it to New Zealand House then post back (recorded delivery) the passport with visa label. They also offer their own travel insurance which covers young people working in New Zealand/Australia – £211 for fully comprehensive worldwide cover for 12 months. This is helpful as many insurance policies do not cover actually working.

The company also offers a Meet & Greet service upon arrival into New Zealand and, last but not least, tax back.

Visitoz
4c Queen's Gate Place
London SW7 5NT, England

Tel: +44 (0) 20 7581 8627

Visitoz programmes allow gap year students or graduates with a working holiday visa to get short-term jobs in Australia to earn money so that they can continue their travels. On arrival in Australia, students are taken to the Burnet family's house or associate farm and given basic training. Jobs range from working on a cattle ranch as a jackeroo or jilleroo to work in tourist stations and trail-riding centres or being a mother's help. They even have places on a crocodile farm. Visitoz says it has over 1000 varied employers on its books, so it can guarantee work in a wide variety of jobs, each job lasting for up to three months. Arrangements are made for bank accounts, Medicare cards (Australian Health Service) and tax file numbers. Reassuring for worried parents, if irritating for independent-minded students, is that the Burnets encourage people to phone home regularly. Pay rates vary but are usually good (typically about AU$300 a week in hand), and free board and lodging are usually included. Contact William Taunton-Burnet at the address above. Application fee to Visitoz is £10, and the Visitoz programme charge is £385.

Work Oz
First Floor, 68 Plasturton Avenue
Cardiff CF11 9HJ, Wales   Tel: +44 (0) 29 2022 2211

Work Oz, run by ex-High Commission employees, specialises in helping British gappers work, live and play in Oz. They have a special Gap-Year Australia package costing £265 per person. Amongst a long, long list of things, the package includes: Working Holiday Visa application fee and application assistance; transport to hostel from airport and first four nights' share accommodation; four meals during your first four days; membership to the Worldwide Workers network; guaranteed employment – WWW guarantee employment in Sydney within 14 days of registration; free internet access; free phonecard – with AU$5 credit and great rates to the UK and Ireland; social discounts; travel discounts; hop-on hop-off City Harbour Cruise; and a full day exploring the Blue Mountains.

Even if you don't want to take the full Gap-Year Package they will give free work visa advice and can process your visa application for £99 (you also get a useful free Employment Handbook and information about how to register with a doctor in Australia, get a Medicare card and an Australian tax file number). They'll assess your application before it goes off to make sure it's been done correctly (saving you having it sent back if you've made a mistake, which could cost you another five weeks). For an extra £49 you get a World Wide Workers package which gives you an AU$5 phonecard, employment advice and free internet access from the WWW offices in Byron Bay, Cairns, Melbourne and Sydney, travel discounts, discounted jugs of beer with fellow travellers on Fridays and Saturdays and – in Sydney only – a guarantee of work within 14 days of registration.

 Volunteering Abroad

Voluntary work abroad can be one of the most rewarding ways to spend all or part of your gap year. Most gappers who do it come back with memories they never lose and a new perspective on the world.

Taking part in an organised voluntary work project can give you the opportunity to learn about a different culture, meet new people and learn to communicate with people who may not understand your way of life let alone your language. You will come away with an amazing sense of achievement and hopefully pride in what you have done.

You could find yourself working with people living in unbelievable poverty, disease, hunger – something which may give you a different perspective on life.

More and more organisations are arranging voluntary placements abroad for gappers, so there's a huge choice of companies and types of voluntary placement. There's also a huge number of people wanting to go on these trips so companies can afford to be picky – you may find you have to prove to them that you should be selected to go before they will accept your money! It can be as much about them choosing you as you choosing them.

The companies have a point: they put a lot of effort into getting you out there and if you can't stick it, everyone loses out, including the person who could have been chosen instead of you. Voluntary work can be tough. You may be out in the middle of nowhere, with no western influence to be seen; food, language – the entire culture might be totally different to what you're used to and there may not be many English-speakers around: *you* will have to cope with culture shock and feeling lonely, isolated and homesick.

Idealist or hedonist?

Because voluntary work is so popular with gappers, commercial companies are starting to get in on the act and the idealism associated with voluntary work is coming under severe commercial pressure. A few organisations offer packages that are little more than tourism dressed up as voluntary work – at a price. Make sure you are clear about what you will be doing before you sign up and part with your money.

Also, be honest with yourself about what you want – there's nothing wrong with wanting to travel and have 'a good time'. If you get there, hate it and have to come home early you'll feel so disappointed and have such a sense of failure. If you want to do something 'useful' but you're not sure you want to commit your whole gap year, then why not arrange to join a project for a few months and then go travelling?

When to start applying

Application can close early, particularly for expeditions and conservation projects needing complex funding or tied in with international government programmes. If you'd like to go on one of these projects, planning should usually start about a year ahead, in the autumn term. Others can be taken up at very short notice – Gap Challenge, for example, can take in applications during the August period when you are getting A level results or going through clearing and book you on a project that starts in September. If you don't have much time before your gap year starts (maybe you didn't get the grades you expected, or you've made a last-minute decision to defer uni for a year) it is always worth contacting a voluntary organisation about a project you're interested in in case they've had a last-minute cancellation.

True riches

When I arrived on the tarmac at Trivandrum airport, I not only stepped into another country – but another world. Each one of my five senses was tested to the full. The vibrant, beautiful colours, the noise, the smells and taste in the air – a combination of traffic fumes and spices – literally bombard you. The ramshackled homes, the traffic chaos – with cars, bicycles, lorries, carts drawn by oxen, goats, pigs and pedestrians all vying for space on the road and all seemingly travelling in different directions – the auto-rickshaws (clearly made for two but crammed full with uniformed kiddies on their way to school, people eating on the roadside, whole families on the backs of motorbikes. Here you feel you are truly alive!

Visiting the various children's schools you realize how lucky we are in the UK. Four out-of-date computers shared between 2000 or so high school students, slates and chalk instead of exercise books, classrooms separated by wooden dividers, planks of wood for benches... Yet despite this apparent lack of resources, the children appear contented, appreciative and dedicated to learning – their discipline towards their studies and their respect for their teachers fills me with admiration. Despite the relative poverty, the children at the Kings World Trust for Children seem richer somehow. Their loving nature, the way they look out for one another, respect each other, and above all, their adorable smiling faces simply melt my heart.

The whole two-week experience in southern India has had a great impact on me – I urge anyone to become a volunteer.

Lynsey, King's World Trust for Children, 2002

What to expect

Ranging from placements lasting a couple of weeks to teaching for a whole academic year, most placements provide only free accommodation and food – very few provide pocket money.

Gappers who are expecting cuddly tiger cubs or cute children and a nice apartment with MTV on tap and one long party will soon be on the next flight home. You'll need to be resourceful, be able to teach, build, inspire confidence, communicate and share what you know. Physical and mental fitness, staying power, and the ability to get on with people are essential.

Peter from Africa and Asia Venture explains: "We are looking for self-motivated and reliable positive thinkers. You need to be self-reliant and able to cope when you turn up at a Nepali school and find a basic room, no curtains and that the loo is a 'long-drop' down the garden. Perhaps surprisingly we get very few drop outs: in eight years only 16 people have come back early – that's out of 2500!"

Some other points are worth emphasising. You might feel safer going with a big voluntary organisation because they should be able to offer help in a nasty situation. Experience is certainly important where organisations are concerned. But often a small, specialist organisation is more knowledgeable about a country, a school or other destination. Size and status have little bearing on competence. A charity can be more efficient than a commercial company, and a commercial company can show more sensitivity than a charity. There are few general rules – talk to someone who's been.

Organisations vary as to how much back-up they offer volunteers, from virtually holding your hand throughout your stay and even after you come back to the 'sink or swim' method. If you're going to get the most out of your volunteering gap year, then be honest with yourself about what you need: if you feel patronised at the slightest hint of advice then you might get annoyed with too much interference from the organisation. Though do bear in mind that they probably know more than you do about the placement, what sort of vaccinations you're going to need, what will be useful to take with you, and how to get the visas and permits you will need. Equally if you're shy or nervous it might be as well to go with an organisation that sends volunteers in pairs or groups.

Talk to a few organisations before you decide which one to go with and, probably more useful, talk to some previous volunteers. They will be able to tell you what it's really like; don't just ask them if they enjoyed it, get them to describe what they did, what they liked and why, what they didn't like and what they'd do differently – of course companies are never likely to put you in touch with someone who'll say it was rubbish.

The truth is that over in Tanzania, or wherever you're sent, you can't count on much. Regardless of the reputation of the voluntary work organisation you choose, or the competence of voluntary work co-ordinators in a particular country, it's the luck of the draw whether the school you are put in, for example, really values you – or if a family you stay with treats you well. We've had countless stories of students being given information by organisations about postings which have turned out to be inaccurate. It's worth checking what training is given and what support there is in-country, but be aware that you may not get what you expect – you need to be adaptable and make the most of your situation.

What's the cost?

It varies hugely – some companies just expect you to pay for the airfare – others expect you to raise thousands of pounds for funding. It can be hard to combine raising money with studying for A levels, but there are a lot of ways to do it. As usual, the earlier you start, the easier it will be.

One way is to work and save, but you may find it more fun to do something different. The organisation that you go with should be able to give advice, but options include organising sponsored events (abseiling down a tall local building), writing to companies or trusts asking for sponsorship, car-boot sales or just plain scrounging. The last resort is to go cap-in-hand to your parents, either for a loan or a gift, but this can be unsatisfying and they may simply not be able to afford it. If you can manage to earn enough money, or at least a sizeable portion of it, then you're more likely to get a sense of achievement from the whole thing. If your parents or relatives do want to help, you could ask for useful items for Christmas or birthday presents – like a rucksack for example.

Finding your own project

If you've searched through www.gap-year.com and have decided that you would prefer to do your own thing, there are thousands more volunteer projects abroad that you can find on the internet. International bodies like the UN (United Nations) provide lists of voluntary work organisations by country, as do some universities. Alternatively just type 'voluntary work Morocco', for example, into a search engine and follow the leads. You could find just the project you had in mind, or something completely different. If you find the 'perfect project' on the internet without going through a UK organisation, however, you are taking extra risks and you should make sure you get contact phone numbers for references (preferably from recently-returned British volunteers). Payment in advance from the UK is not a good idea unless the organisation has been thoroughly checked out with real human beings. Read all the small print in contracts.

Safety first

If you're going with a good organisation they shouldn't send you anywhere too dangerous – but it's always worth finding out about where you're going for yourself. To find out if you may be visiting a politically volatile and dangerous area of the world, it's a very good idea to check out the Foreign Office's Travel Advice page on **www.fco.gov.uk** or via **www.gap-year.com**. The Foreign Office site also has lots of advice on visas, insurance and other things that need to be sorted out before you go, and advice on what to do in an emergency abroad. It's also worth reading Chapter 4 of this book for travel tips.

VOLUNTARY ORGANISATIONS *Volunteering Abroad*

Voluntary Organisations

Listed over the next pages are organisations offering overseas projects ranging from short-term teaching posts to one-year placements and challenging expeditions.

Between them the organisations listed offer well over 5000 volunteer placements on projects abroad each year, covering more than a hundred countries.

The real experience

I worked on a farm in Ghana – it was all arranged by Save the Earth Network. However, organisations such as this, entirely naturally, don't quite appreciate the 'western' way of organising such projects, and so when I arrived at the airport (STEN isn't that widely publicised – so I still had my doubts) to be met by Ebenezer in his flowery shirt (no ID presented) and then wander round the deserted streets of Accra for an hour or two looking for a taxi (with Eben singing 'Stand By Me' at the top of his voice) and then to be taken to a deserted settlement in the middle of the night to be greeted by two very burly young men, one of whom purported to be a reverend, I really did think I was about to meet my death!

As it was, everything was absolutely fine, and I really did experience the full force of Ghanaian hospitality. So don't worry, but be ready for a bit of a rough ride at the beginning. I was certainly very well looked after during my stay; Ebenezer is obviously very concerned about the welfare of his charges. I had to go to hospital at one point because I was ill, and I've never had so many visitors before!

To get the most out of a farming placement like this I think a fair amount of personal motivation is very necessary too. The good thing is that you are very much thrown fully into the Ghanaian life. I had already spent six months in India with GAP, which I absolutely loved, but because I was at a placement with a partner and had a network of Western contacts, I probably missed out on talking much to the local people. In Ghana it was totally the opposite and I learnt an unbelievable amount about every possible aspect of Ghanaian life. A very valuable and vivid experience. Harvesting mushrooms at 5.30am, planting cassava, fetching water from the lake, making charcoal the way they did it in the 1700s, picking sweet peppers, and teaching the kids in the evening and loads of other stuff.

Judith

visit: www.gap-year.com

Africa & Asia Venture

10 Market Place, Devizes
Wiltshire SN10 1HT
England

Tel: +44 (0) 1380 729009
Fax: +44 (0) 1380 720 060
see: www.gap-year.com

Africa and Asia Venture (AV) is a voluntary work organisation started in 1994 by ex-Army officers Peter Bell and Nigel Warren, who were living in Kenya. AV now takes 500 students per year on teaching placements, which consist of three months in a primary or secondary school, with a month's travel afterwards, including a safari.

There are placements in Africa (Botswana, Kenya, Tanzania, Malawi and Uganda), the Indian Himalayas and Nepal. There are also teaching placements for graduates in Malawi and Tanzania, and a Community and Conservation programme for school-leavers and graduates in Kenya. AV provides a training course first, including advice on teaching, health and safety, language and lifestyle, and full back-up in each country.

Cost is about £2440 including course, accommodation, living allowances, safari, insurance and a contribution towards educating an African or Asian student. Departures are in September, January and April. References provided.

African Conservation Experience

Applications Department
PO Box 9706, Solihull
West Midlands B91 3FF
England

Tel: 0870 241 5816 (UK only)
see: www.gap-year.com

ACE is run by Rob Harris, who lived in South Africa for 35 years and knows its game reserves well. He has links with some 20 game and nature reserves in the southern African bush where he places volunteers, and is sending out 200+ a year to Botswana, Namibia, South Africa and Zimbabwe.

Work can involve game capture and tagging, game counts, habit observation, checking game fences, anti-poaching patrols, controlled burning and everyday reserve maintenance. You could be living in a thatched rondavel or sharing a house with other staff. Fees range from an average £2500 for four-week placements (lowest £1795 for four weeks in the Kaggakamma reserve) to an average £3500 for 12-week placements, and cover flights, transfers, accommodation and food. No pocket money. If you want to phone or fax from abroad, use this number: +44 1404 811404

Volunteering Abroad

VOLUNTARY ORGANISATIONS

African Conservation Trust

PO Box 310, Link Hills
3652 South Africa

Tel: +27 31 2016180
Fax: +27 31 2016180

The mission of the African Conservation Trust is to provide a means for conservation projects to become self-funding through active participation by the public. This gives ordinary people a chance to make a positive and real contribution to environmental conservation by funding and participating in the research effort as volunteers.

The trust has initiated the Lake Malawi Hippo Project with the University of Malawi and the University of Natal to quantify and map the entire Hippopotamus (*Hippopotamus amphibius*) population of the western shore of Lake Malawi. This project is entirely volunteer-funded and staffed. Other projects in Malawi are a reforestation project, an environmental education project and a research base construction project. A three-month period on any of these projects will cost £950.

AFS Community Projects Overseas

Leeming House, Vicar Lane
Leeds LS2 7JF, England

Tel: +44 (0) 113 242 6136
see: www.gap-year.com

AFS is part of an international network with 54 partner countries that offers a range of intercultural learning opportunities. Every year AFS places young people, generally from the age of 18-29, on its International Volunteer Programme to a variety of countries in South America and South Africa. AFS projects are mainly in social welfare, community development, healthcare, education and environmental areas. The programmes usually last for six months (starting in January/February or July/August). AFS provides pre-departure orientation and language tuition on arrival in the host country. Participants generally live with AFS host families and are well supported by AFS volunteers and staff throughout their stay. Participants are supported to fundraise £2950 to cover the cost, which includes airfares, insurance, in-country support, food and accommodation.

AgriVenture

YFC Centre, NAC
Stoneleigh Park, Kenilworth
Warwickshire CV8 2LG, England

Tel: +44 (0) 800 7832186

Travel, work, excitement! AgriVenture offers young people aged 18–30 the opportunity to travel and work in Australia, New Zealand, Canada, America and Japan. They take care of all the practical aspects of your trip, from tickets, work permits and insurance to finding you a

visit: www.gap-year.com

job in the country of your choice. AgriVenture will provide accommodation (you live and work with host families who have been carefully selected and approved), help with training, give you a standard allowance and time off for holiday.

They offer jobs in the following areas:
   Agriculture – on a livestock or cropping enterprise
   Horticulture – in an orchard, market garden or nursery
   Agri-mix – working on the farm and in the home
   Horti-mix – splitting your time between home and horticulture
   Home Management – working in and around the farm home.

AgriVenture is an excellent introduction to a new culture and a different working world. The challenge of thinking for yourself, travelling and working abroad will make you much more confident and prepared for life ahead.

AIM (Africa Inland Mission)

2 Vorley Road
London N19 5HE, England   Tel: +44 (0) 20 7281 1184

AIM looks for volunteers with a specifically Christian outlook to teach in rural schools in Kenya and Uganda. Usually this is for a full year, starting in late August/September, but volunteers can take time off in the holidays to travel. There are also some two-term placements running from January to August. AIM says the small number of school postings it arranges are thoroughly researched and students are usually placed in pairs. Volunteers need to raise about £3000 for the two-term assignment and £4000 for the full-year one. Apply at least six months in advance.

Alliances Abroad

2423 Pennsylvania Avenue NW
Washington DC 20037   Tel: +1 (202) 467 9467
USA   Fax: +1 (202) 467 9460

Alliances Abroad gears its volunteer programme towards individuals looking for the opportunity to work and be of service in a developing country and makes sure the programme matches your interests, prior experience, abilities and language ability. You can choose from Costa Rica, South Africa, Venezuela and Hawaii.

There's a great variety of placements. In Costa Rica volunteer positions include working in environment and national parks and there's at least a month of language training (if you're not already fluent in Spanish). While in South Africa you can help out the zoologists and vets in the wildlife centre of the world. The Hawaii programme offers volunteer

Volunteering Abroad   **VOLUNTARY ORGANISATIONS**

placements from one week to one year on an organic farm. The Venezuela programme offers adventure travel combined with a volunteer placement. Most of the Alliances Abroad programmes include guaranteed placement before departure, airport pickup, local orientation, and full-time support before, during and after the programme.

Archaeology Abroad

Institute of Archaeology, University College
31-34 Gordon Square
London WC1H 0PY, England   Fax: +44 (0) 207 383 2572

Archaeology Abroad produces a bulletin with details of dig opportunities abroad.

ATD Fourth World

48 Addington Square   Tel: +44 (0) 20 7703 3231
London SE5 7LB, England   Fax: +44 (0)207 252 4276

Unlike other organisations in this section, ATD does not normally place gap year students on projects abroad (its long term placements are likely to last from one to three years). However, what you can do if you'd like to be useful while mixing with other nationalities is join one of its summer workcamps, where you could be doing manual labour in Europe to help fund families in poverty in the third world. Summer work camps last for one or two weeks from July to early September and you pay £50 for two weeks. For example, you could lug stones or other tools in Champeaux or Mery-sur-Oise in France or Neudorf, 80km north of Berlin in Germany.

There are also a couple of placements on the 'Social Year' which brings together 20 or so gap year students from across Europe. You are placed in an ATD Fourth World team in a European country for nine months.

Brathay Exploration Group

Brathay Hall, Ambleside   Tel: +44 (0) 15394 33942
Cumbria LA22 0HP, England   Fax: +44 (0) 15394 33942

Brathay provides 'challenging experiences for young people' aged 15-25. It runs a range of expeditions from one to five weeks long which vary each year. Shorter programmes offer, for example, an introduction to mountains in the Lake District.

Students can remain in the UK or travel as far as Tanzania, North America, Mongolia, South Africa, New Zealand, Norway, Malaysia, Morocco (maybe trekking in the sub-Sahara followed by conservation

visit: www.gap-year.com   *75*

work in an oasis), or the European Alps. No fieldwork experience or specific skills are required, and Brathay takes a wide variety of people. Programmes run between July and early September and there's no application deadline.

Bright Light

3 Fentiman Road
London SW8 1LD, England

Tel: +44 (0) 20 7582 1582
Fax: +44 (0) 20 7582 2379

Bright Light is a not-for-profit organisation that runs gap year drama and education projects in Kenya, Uganda, Tanzania and Ethiopia. You get to learn about East African drama, dance and music as well as teaching African children about Western drama and British culture.

The programme lasts three months and is split into three phases. First you spend time working with African theatre professionals, learning about traditional African narrative dance and oral literature, as well as helping with performances.

The second phase consists of volunteer teaching in schools. You introduce small groups of children to Western concepts of drama and help them to produce their first play.

Finally, you get the chance to produce your own play and then spend time at Lake Naivasha where you can reflect on your experiences. When you return home you may even get the opportunity to workshop your performances at the Old Vic in London.

Tours depart in January and May and cost £2440 including all food, travel, accommodation and insurance.

BSES Expeditions

at The Royal Geographical Society
1 Kensington Gore
London SW7 2AR, England

Tel: +44 (0) 20 7591 3141
see: www.gap-year.com

This charitable organisation runs six-week expeditions in the summer and three- or four-month gap year expeditions to wilderness areas abroad to conduct scientific fieldwork on behalf of universities, research institutes or host nation. It also runs conservation and environments projects. BSES sends people aged 16½ to 20 abroad (and unpaid leaders aged 21 and over). The application deadline for summer expeditions is Christmas the year before. In summer 2003 BSES will be visiting Greenland, Kyrgyzstan and Lesotho. Their special gap year project for 2003, 'The Footsteps of Shackleton', is a three-month expedition to the Falkland Islands, South Georgia and Chile. In 2004 the proposed summer destinations are Tanzania, Alaska and Iceland

Find yourself here
with over 200 projects in 14 countries

Media
Health
Building
Teaching
Conservation
Community Work

i-to-i

Volunteer travel & TEFL courses
Visit www.i-to-i.com
or ring 0870 333 2332

and the 'gap year expedition' will be to Oman. The financial contribution varies depending on the expedition.

BTCV

36 St Mary's Street, Wallingford
Oxfordshire OX10 0EU
England

Tel: +44 (0) 1491 821 600
Fax: +44 (0) 1491 839 646
see: www.gap-year.com

BTCV not only runs working conservation holidays in Britain, but also, by working in partnership with other organisations, runs conservation work holidays abroad in more than 25 countries. These are short, ranging from one-week trips in Europe (about £300) to six weeks turtle research in Thailand (£925 excluding flights). You end up in a mixed group of all ages, but not all of them will be doing conservation work alongside you.

Camphill Communities in the UK

William Morris House
Stonehouse
Gloucestershire GL10 3SH, England

Tel: +44 (0) 7941 360039
Fax: +44 (0) 1453 825807

Camphill is a worldwide network of communities (schools, colleges or adult centres) dedicated to work and life with children, adolescents or adults with developmental and other disabilities. The first such community – Camphill Rudolf Steiner School in Scotland – was founded in 1940 by the child psychiatrist Karl Koenig. The insights of the Austrian philosopher and innovator Rudolf Steiner provide a basis for pedagogical and therapeutic approaches, socio/economic forms and the cultural and spiritual creativity of the communities.

Life and work as a volunteer/co-worker in Camphill communities is demanding, diverse and rich. As a co-worker you need to be physically and emotionally healthy. Flexibility, openness and a serious willingness to work with developmentally disabled children or adults and other co-workers are essential. Co-workers are role models for those in their care, and a high level of maturity and judgement will be expected from you at all times. The safety and wellbeing, both physical and mental, of your companions is of primary importance, therefore the consumption of alcohol, as well as excessive smoking is strongly discouraged. Room, board, and pocket money for personal needs are all provided.

As a member of a household, you will be taking part in all domestic tasks. You will be responsible for direct care activities for the companions in your household as needed. Depending on the nature of your community – school, college or adult centre – you will participate in classroom and therapy support, vocational and/or workshop activities. You will also support the companions in their life skills and recreational activities.

Most communities ask that co-workers commit themselves for at least one full year. Induction and orientation courses are offered to first-timers, providing a basic introduction to the guidance of people with special needs, to Camphill life and anthroposophy.

Most Camphill communities are keen to have committed gap year students join them for a year, although some centres specify a minimum age of 19 or 20 years. If you are interested in spending your gap year with them, please visit their website for more information and contact details for specific communities. Their site also carries a list of current vacancies in the various UK communities.

Changing Worlds

11 Doctors Lane, Chaldon
Surrey CR3 5AE
England

Tel: +44 (0) 1883 340 960
Fax: +44 (0) 1883 330783
see: www.gap-year.com

Changing Worlds offers challenging voluntary work placements in Tanzania, Chile, Southern India, Nepal and Romania. To succeed you must have drive and a desire to make a real contribution. "The hardest thing I have ever done but the best thing I have done" is how returned volunteer Beth summarised her time at an orphanage in Southern India. Most volunteers teach although there is a growing number of care work placements in orphanages. Volunteers with sport, music and drama are always popular. After a two-day briefing in the UK volunteers travel out as a group to their destinations where they are taken to the orientation course run by the representative. After a few days volunteers go in small groups to live and work in local schools and projects. Changing worlds prides itself on being a small organisation that knows each volunteer; assistance is always available in-country and in the UK. Volunteers must be aged between 18 and 35 (most are 18-23) and preferably educated to A level. Prices are around £2000 and include return flight and transfer to the placement, courses, accommodation, and all UK and overseas support. Additionally volunteers must budget for visas, insurance, pocket money and food in some cases. Fundraising advice is given at interview.

CMS (Church Mission Society)

Partnership House, 157 Waterloo Road
London SE1 8UU, England

Tel: +44 (0) 20 7928 8681

Offering more of a learning experience than a giving one, the CMS runs three- to five-week Encounter programmes in Africa, Asia, the

Middle East and Eastern Europe for Christians aged 18-30. The projects are 'an opportunity for Christians to discover what it means to be a Christian in another culture', and involve meeting and occasionally working alongside local people. Costs vary from £750 to £950 depending on the country. Application details are available from the Encounter Teams Coordinator.

Concordia

Heversham House
20-22 Boundary Road, Hove
East Sussex BN3 4ET, England

Tel: +44 (0) 1273 422 218
Fax: +44 (0) 1273 421182

Concordia organises international volunteer placements for 16-30 year olds. Standard projects are available in Europe, North Africa, North America, the Middle East and Japan and a limited number of places on projects in Latin America, Asia and Sub Saharan Africa. Volunteers join teams of international volunteers working on conservation, renovation, arts/cultural based or social projects (including children's playschemes and work with adults or children with mental or physical disabilities). There is a registration fee of between £75-£115 depending on the country and volunteers pay their own travel expenses. Board and accommodation is free of charge. Projects last two to four weeks and run from June to September with some winter/spring opportunities.

Concordia also arranges farm or tourism placements with families in Norway (two to six months) and Switzerland (three to eight weeks). Accommodation and small wage provided by the host family.

Coral Cay Conservation

The Tower, 13th Floor
125 High Street,
Colliers Wood
London SW19 2JG, England

Tel: +44 (0) 870 750 0668

Fax: +44 (0) 870 750 0667
see: www.gap-year.com

Coral Cay Conservation (CCC) is a not-for-profit organisation that sends teams of volunteers to survey some of the world's most endangered coral reefs and tropical forests. Working at the invitation of and in partnership with government bodies, NGOs, local communities and education groups, CCC volunteers have been responsible for the establishment of World Heritage Sites, marine reserves and wildlife sanctuaries.

CCC currently has expeditions in Fiji, the Philippines, Malaysia and Honduras. For the ultimate experience, volunteers can split their time between a marine expedition and a forest expedition: in the Philippines volunteers can dive the fabled Coral Triangle, one of the world's most biodiverse areas of coral reef, and then trek the amazing

visit: www.gap-year.com

The English-Speaking Union
A Registered Charity

Would you like to spend your year out between school and university at an American or Canadian High School?

Scholarships are worth around $30,000 each and cover the cost of tuition, board and lodging.

For further information contact:

The Education Officer, The English-Speaking Union,
37 Charles Street, London W1J 5ED
Tel: 020-7529 1550   Fax: 020-7495 6108
Email: mary_dawson@esu.org

---

registered charity 1005452

ANYTHING CAN HAPPEN

that's the whole point

well-led, tough, rainforest conservation
projects and cultural placements
Borneo, Belize and Amazon Guyana

trekforce.org.uk
020 7828 2275

Negros Rainforest – home to hundreds of endemic mammals, birds and insects!

Although volunteers require no scientific background, applicants must be 16 or over, fit, enthusiastic and hardworking. Combining marine and terrestrial scientific research with international travel and cultural exploration, CCC offers its volunteers a unique career-building opportunity and a once in a lifetime experience.

Marine expeditions start at £700 and rainforest expeditions start at £350. Scuba training up to PADI Rescue Diver is provided on location. Costs include Skills Development Training, accommodation and food. Flights not included.

Cross-Cultural Solutions

47 Potter Avenue, New Rochelle Tel: +1 914 632 0022
NY 10801, USA   see: www.gap-year.com

Experience a country from a whole new perspective through a Cross-Cultural Solutions volunteer programme in Brazil, China, Costa Rica, Ghana, India, Peru, Russia, Thailand or Tanzania. By participating in a Cross-Cultural Solutions programme, you will have the opportunity to work side-by-side *with* local people on *locally designed and driven* projects, allowing you to see a country through the eyes of its people.

Cross-Cultural Solutions is a recognised leader in the international volunteer field, sending hundreds of volunteers overseas every year.

Programmes have a unique three-part design. Part one is an individualised volunteer placement on a sustainable community development project with infants and children, teenagers, adults, the elderly, and people with special needs like HIV/AIDS patients, or the mentally or physically disabled. Part two is Perspectives Programming, including an in-depth orientation, insight into cultural norms, language assistance, guest speakers and special events. Guest speakers are chosen for their leadership in a variety of fields relevant to community development and provide meaningful insight to the overall experience. Special events may include attending a holiday festival with sitar and tabla performances in India or learning about traditional healing in Ghana.

Part three is your free time to explore your surroundings. Through each of these elements, you will be able to fully immerse yourself into the culture.

Programmes range from two to 12 weeks and fees start at $1985 (approx. £1280). The Cross Cultural Solutions programme allows you to participate in meaningful community development while getting to see a country from a whole new perspective.

Cross-Cultural Solutions is setting up a UK information office – see their website for up-to-date details and UK contact information.

Crusaders

2 Romeland Hill
St Albans Tel: +44 (0) 1727 855 422
Hertfordshire AL3 4ET, England Fax: +44 (0) 1727 848 518

This is a Christian organisation which offers young people aged 14-20 the chance to 'work for God'. Crusaders runs a variety of programmes, one of which is CRUSOE (Crusaders Overseas Expeditions). Volunteers, who must be committed Christians, stay for two to four weeks between July and August in Central or South America, Africa or Asia.

There are also programmes for 14-16 year-olds in Europe. Projects involve practical work (such as building) and working with street children, orphans and other evangelistic projects. Successful candidates need to raise £550 to go to Europe or £1700 (depending on your destination) to cover costs, if going to other continents. This includes a contribution to the project you'll be working on.

Discover Nepal

GPO Box: 20209 Tel: +977 1 413690
Kathmandu Fax: +977 1 255487
Nepal see: www.gap-year.com

Discover Nepal organises an impressive range of Nepal-related projects – from a festival to celebrate migratory birds to a Jubilee celebration of the climbing of Mount Everest. For gap year students, it runs programmes for volunteers lasting two months.

You will start with a comprehensive orientation period giving an interesting introduction to Nepali life as well as the opportunity to do some sightseeing. In between going on a five-day trek in the Kathmandu Valley and a three-day jungle safari, you'll learn about Nepali history, culture and wildlife, get an introduction to the Nepali language, be shown some basic teaching techniques and be treated to a cultural show with Nepali Cuisine.

You will then be put into mixed-nationality groups and placed in secondary schools to begin your work of helping with English teaching and extra-curricular activities. Programmes start in January, April, June and October. The basic cost of participation is US$1200, plus the cost of any resources and materials you choose to bring (the company suggests picture books, story books, notebooks, stationery, toys, puzzles, board games, outdoor games, videos about your home country, magazines, brochures and cassettes).

| VOLUNTARY ORGANISATIONS | *Volunteering Abroad* |

Dorset Expeditionary Society

Budmouth Technology College
Weymouth, Dorset DT4 9SY
England

Tel: +44 (0) 1305 775 599
see: www.gap-year.com

Not, as you might expect, a society for people who want to explore bluebell-and-daisied Dorset (though it does organise expeditions in Scotland), but a charity which organises 'safe adventurous opportunities' for people usually aged 15-21.

The Dorset Expeditionary Society approves up to six overseas expeditions each year. All-inclusive costs range from £500 to £2000 and all the expeditions take place in July and August. You may be able to try Mount Kenya, as part of a three-week project which includes working in a health centre and a primary school, white-water rafting and a safari in Masai Mara, all in Kenya. Or you could be trekking through the Ladakh 'moonlands' high up in Himalayan India, and across the Zanskar Mountains.

Earthwatch

267 Banbury Road, Oxford
Oxfordshire OX2 7HT
England

Tel: +44 (0) 1865 318 831
Fax: +44 (0) 01865 311383
see: www.gap-year.com

Fancy doing something a bit different this year – saving hippos in Ghana, monitoring Amazon turtles, or looking for hominids in Southern India? International environmental charity Earthwatch currently offers 130 projects in 45 countries: from endangered ecosystems and biodiversity to archaeology, world health and global change.

Paying volunteers are given the opportunity to explore remote, rugged and often little-known parts of the world safely whilst helping scientists to carry out vital conservation and cultural research. Prices range from £495 to £2199. Food, accommodation and training are included but flights are extra. Projects usually last for two weeks and most expeditions are open to anyone over 16.

ESU (English-Speaking Union)

Dartmouth House
37 Charles Street
London W1J 5ED
England

Tel: +44 (0) 20 7529 1550
Fax: +44 (0) 20 7495 6108
see: www.gap-year.com

Not strictly voluntary work: the ESU is a charity which organises educational exchange places in high schools (mostly boarding) in the US and Canada, awarding up to 40 scholarships a year to gap year students. You could end up in a school in the middle of New York or in the middle of an Indiana field, and your assignment will be from two to three terms. Tuition and board are free, but you need to allow around £2500 for fares and pocket money.

It works rather like a dating agency: the schools decide what sort of student they want, and see if you match up. (Unfortunately it works one way only: you can't choose the school). But if, say, your gigs with a tenor sax are already famous in Nuneaton and a school in New Orleans wants a young jazz-playing Brit, you could just get lucky.

The Espero Language Centre

Szkola Jezykow Obcych 'Espero'
al. Jana Pawla II 17/1
47-220 Kedzierzyn-Kozle   Tel: +48 77 4838325
Poland   Fax: +48 77 4838325

If you fancy a more unusual teaching experience, what about Poland? The Espero Language Centre, 50km from the Czech border in the small town of Kedzierzyn-Kozle, are keen for 'responsible and cheerful' gap year students to teach English. You would be teaching 15-20 classes a week, mainly conversational English, to Polish locals from 3.30pm to 7.30pm.

Here's the crunch – you wouldn't be paid! The main cost to you will be your travel to Poland and a bus pass ($18/month). Accommodation and food are free – you stay with a local Polish 'host' family, so this would be a great way to experience the culture and learn about Polish traditions and customs as well as day-to-day life. Write to Barbara Piechocka, Director of Study, if you are interested. She is happy to put you in touch with one of the gappers teaching there last year.

Euro Academy

24 Clarendon Place   Tel: +44 (0) 20 8297 0505
London SE13 5EY, England   Fax: +44 (0) 20 8297 0984

Though mainly a language school, Euro Academy also organises voluntary programmes combined with language in Costa Rica.

Frontier

50-52 Rivington Street   Tel: +44 (0) 20 7613 2422
London EC2A 3QP   Fax: +44 (0) 20 7613 2992
England   see: www.gap-year.com

Frontier sends 'flexible and committed' volunteers (minimum age 17) on 28-day, 10-week or 20-week conservation expeditions to

 changing worlds

A year out with changing worlds, change your life forever.

For details of our voluntary placements,
telephone: 01883 340960 or
visit: www.changingworlds.co.uk

Chile
India
Nepal
Romania
Tanzania

Changing Worlds: 11 Doctors Lane Chaldon Surrey CR3 5AE UK

Madagascar, Tanzania and Vietnam. Volunteers participate in marine or land-based environmental research to protect threatened tropical ecosystems (rainforest, savanna, coral reef and mangrove areas).

Work includes biodiversity surveys, disturbance and resource-use assessments, socio-economic work, expedition and research skills training and practical projects. No prior experience or skills necessary as full training is provided leading to an internationally recognised BTEC qualification in Tropical Habitat Conservation or Expedition Management (Biodiversity Research). Applications accepted all year round. Cost: £1850 (28-day expedition), from £2200 (10-week expedition) and from £3600 (20-week expedition).

GAP Activity Projects

GAP House
44 Queen's Road
Reading, Berkshire RG1 4BB
England   Tel: +44 (0) 1189 594914

GAP (30 years old in 2002) says it arranges more gap year attachments than any other voluntary organisation, and that its short-term teaching, social work, caring/medical work and conservation assignments and outward bound projects are heavily oversubscribed. It now places about 1500 applicants in 34 countries in a year. Placements vary from four to 12 months.

GAP's volunteer project managers stress that they consider the needs of the overseas host as well as the student looking for a placement. Those leaving school in the summer can send for a full brochure and application form at any time, and placements can sometimes be filled at the last minute. Interviews begin in October all over the country and run until all the places are filled in the summer. The earlier you apply, the better your chances of getting the assignment you want, although GAP accepts applications throughout the year. The cost of going on a GAP assignment varies from under £850 to £1350 (plus airfares) depending on the destination. It breaks down like this: non-refundable registration fee £40 (which gets you an interview); GAP fee £725 (including non-refundable deposit £75); insurance from £60 to £160 (you can arrange your own). A teaching course is necessary for schools projects and will cost from £120 for a one-week course.

GAP also runs a Business Partnership Scheme to help GAP volunteers think about their future career when they return from placements. GAP Business Partners such as Barclays, the Metropolitan Police, PricewaterhouseCoopers, Rolls-Royce and Unilever have access to a database containing volunteers' details with a view to offering them recruitment opportunities.

visit: www.gap-year.com

VOLUNTARY ORGANISATIONS — Volunteering Abroad

Gap Challenge

at World Challenge Expeditions
Black Arrow House, 2 Chandos Road
London NW10 6NF, England

Tel: +44 (0) 20 8728 7272
and +44 (0) 20 8728 7200
see: www.gap-year.com

Gap Challenge provides individuals aged between 18 and 24 with exciting opportunities to take a well-structured gap year, living and working in one of 12 countries around and doing something really constructive in their gap year. It is a highly flexible programme that offers the choice of a variety of rewarding and worthwhile paid or voluntary placements ranging from teaching in Tanzania or conservation work in the rainforests of Belize to paid hotel work in the Canadian Rockies. Placements last for between two and nine months and with a 12-month return flight there is plenty of opportunity for independent travel afterwards. Whilst away, Gap Challengers are offered advice and support from in-country agents and benefit from World Challenge Expedition's comprehensive 24-hour emergency back-up systems.

Glencree Centre for Reconciliation

Glencree, Enniskerry
Co Wicklow, Republic of Ireland

Tel: +353 1282 9711

This centre holds workshops on conflict resolution and is an autonomous non-governmental organisation working 'with everybody who tries to bring peace in whatever area of society'. Contact Naoise Kelly for information about short-term volunteer posts (two months in summer, if you like gardening and cooking) or one-year 'Learn and Serve' posts, all at Glencree.

Global Action Nepal

Baldwins, Eastlands Lane, Cowfold
West Sussex RH13 8AY, England

Tel: +44 (0) 1403 864704
Fax: +44 (0) 1403 864088

Global Action Nepal was founded in 1996 to improve the education of children in Nepal. GAN's projects and work are always closely in harness with grass roots level needs, focusing on community-led, participatory development.

As a charity where the sharing of ideas and direct contact with local communities is so important, GAN is very dependent on hard-working, dedicated and open-minded volunteers. The success of many of their projects in Nepal is a direct result of their commitment and skills. GAN's main activities in Nepal involve working in government schools for sustainable, long-term improvement that will last well beyond the length of the six months that each volunteer spends there.

Volunteers will spend the majority of their time working on our CITE (Clinic for the Improvement of Teachers of English) programme – a programme which enables Nepali English Teachers to work better within their classrooms and gives them the skills and training which they lack.

GAN offers full training and support to volunteers, and aims to keep costs as low as possible while maximising the use of their time spent in Nepal.

Global Vision International
Amwell Farm House, St Albans
Hertfordshire AL4 8EJ, England   Tel: +44 (0) 1582 831 300

Global Vision International runs conservation expeditions, research projects and independent voluntary work opportunities around the world.

GVI expeditions offers the adventurous individual the chance to work as part of a structured team or as an independent alongside host country organisations. With projects all over the world you can join expeditions as diverse as: turtle protection programmes in Panama, working with street children in Ecuador and China, rainforest expeditions in South America and pioneering wildlife research expeditions in Africa. GVI also offers individuals the chance to apply for positions with their award-winning and high-profile projects including their exciting new initiative with the South African National Parks Board.

Further opportunities run all over the world, no experience is necessary and expeditions depart all year round and run from two weeks to 12 months. Their motto is: 'Global Vision International, Expeditions that don't Cost the Earth'.

Greenforce
11-15 Betterton Street
Covent Garden   Tel: 0870 770 2646 / +44 (0) 20 7470 8888
London WC2H 9BP   Fax: 0870 7702547 / +44 (0) 207 470 8889
England   see: www.gap-year.com

If you're concerned about the environment and want to do your bit to help preserve what's left of biodiversity on planet Earth then why not become a volunteer researcher on a Greenforce expedition? Greenforce runs a series of 10-week marine and terrestrial expeditions around the world, all of which are based on wildlife conservation. No previous experience is necessary as they train all volunteers from scratch, and marine volunteers get free diver training.

Choose from tracking large mammals in Zambia, investigating the tree canopy of the Amazon rainforest, or diving the coral reefs of the Bahamas, Fiji or Borneo. Whichever project you join you will find a

varied and fascinating programme which has a direct impact on conservation in that country.

For the scientists amongst you there are opportunities to collect data towards a dissertation (provided you agree the topic prior to the expedition). You will learn a wide range of fieldwork techniques, and can get involved in taxonomic classification and data analysis. If you're thinking of developing a career in conservation, ask about their traineeship scheme – it could be the first step for you.

Expedition life can be a challenge – be prepared to live a spartan existence, and to pull your weight in a small, well-organised team. Check out the website for their latest projects.

Habitat for Humanity (Great Britain)

11 Parsons Street, Banbury
Oxfordshire OX16 5LW
England

Tel: +44 (0) 1295 264240 ext.208
Fax: +44 (0) 1295 264230
see: www.gap-year.com

The Habitat for Humanity's Global Village programme is a chance for gappers with practical skills to shine. They are sending over 25 teams all over the world, including Romania, Zambia, Sri Lanka, Poland and South Africa, to build housing for and with the local population. This is a real way to get to talk to local people from a completely different culture. The aim is not only to provide homes, but also to raise awareness of the need for low cost housing. They are particularly looking for team leaders – training is given. Programmes last for between three and four weeks. The Habitat for Humanity programmes (such as the Jimmy Carter Work Project, where Jimmy Carter and his wife pitch in with building homes in Africa) are known for their upbeat atmosphere. You can either go along on your own, or make up a team with friends. You do have to pay for your own trip, and costs obviously vary according to location. Global Village programme co-ordinator Rod Watson will be happy to fill you in with more details.

Himalayan Light Foundation

GPO Box 1219
Kathmandu, Nepal

Tel: +977 (1) 420 842

The Himalayan Light Foundation (HLF) is a Kathmandu-based non-profit NGO (non-governmental organisation) working to make renewable energy technologies more accessible to rural Nepal. HLF organises programmes that link energy with education, and income-generating activities such as sewing and weaving. These include a 'hands on' development project called Solar Sisters. Less than 3% of Nepal's rural population has electricity, so volunteers provide Nepali women in handicraft production centres and educational programmes with affordable solar lighting systems. Volunteers donate funds to cover a solar electricity system and their in-country costs, then travel to Nepal to install the solar panels themselves after a training course (no prior knowledge of solar power is necessary). Twenty extra systems were installed in a Bongadovan village in one month. Each project is two weeks long and costs about £830.

In addition, HLF itself welcomes volunteers who can commit to full-time work for at least five months. Work involves project coordination and development; computer literacy is essential and you have to bring a laptop computer. Volunteers are based in Kathmandu, with occasional field trips into rural Nepal, and cover their own food and accommodation costs, though HLF can help organise a stay with a Nepali family. HLF asks volunteers to contribute £105 to the organisation. There's a possibility of combining HLF and Solar Sisters projects.

HiPACT

PO Box 770, York House
Empire Way, Wembley
Middlesex HA9 0PA, England

Tel: +44 (0) 208 900 1221
Fax: +44 (0) 208 900 0330
see: www.gap-year.com

HiPACT is an association of British universities which aims to widen participation in higher education. It offers opportunities to volunteer both in the UK and abroad. HiPACT has a long-term project in Nigeria, where you could find yourself supporting teachers, development officers or admin staff in local primary and secondary schools. The programme usually lasts between four and 12 weeks between July and September. You pay no fees to HiPACT – you'll have find the money for your flights, insurance, vaccinations and any spending money, but food and accommodation (with local host families, in anything from a jungle hut to a local government official's residence) will be provided for free. HiPACT is keen to emphasise that there is no commitment for you to fundraise – although if you choose to, they're unlikely to stand in your way!

ICYE (Inter Cultural Youth Exchange)

Latin America House
Kingsgate Place
London NW6 4TA, England

Tel: +44 (0) 20 7681 0983
Fax: +44 (0) 20 7681 0983
see: www.gap-year.com

Do you fancy spending a year abroad getting to know another country and its culture? Each year ICYE sends young people aged between 18 and 30 to work in voluntary projects overseas in Africa, Asia, Europe and South America. Volunteers work in a range of projects including counselling centres, human rights NGOs, farms, orphanages and schools for the disabled... No specific qualifications, experience or language skills are required. Instead they are looking for people who are willing to learn new skills, open to new experiences and committed to inter-cultural understanding.

Interserve

325 Kennington Road
London SE11 4QH Tel: +44 (0) 20 7735 8227
England Fax: +44 (0) 20 7587 5362

Interserve is a self-financing international missionary society, working mainly in Asia (Bangladesh, India, Mongolia, Nepal) and in the Arab world. Their gap year programme 'On Track' places volunteers with local churches and organisations in a variety of roles such as children's work, teaching English, administration and other projects.

Placements are for one to 12 months; volunteers must be 18 or over and active members of their local home church. Applications should be made as early as possible. The cost depends on the location and duration of the placement. There is an orientation/training weekend before departure, further orientation in-country and debriefing on return.

i-to-i

9 Blenheim Terrace Tel: +44 (0) 870 333 2332
Leeds LS2 9HZ Fax: +44 (0) 113 242 2171
England see: www.gap-year.com

i-to-i caters for individuals of 17 to 70 seeking an inspirational world experience. i-to-i's volunteer work placements, known as i-Ventures, are all about cultural immersion. There are over 300 projects in 15 countries where volunteers are sent year-round to work in a variety of schools, orphanages, hospitals, colleges and conservation centres, for anywhere from two weeks to six months. You could be teaching Buddhist Monks in Nepal, reading the news on Radio Ghana, caring for young sea turtles on the Caribbean shores of Costa Rica, or replanting saplings in the Ecuadorian rainforests. English teaching i-Ventures are available in Bolivia, China, Costa Rica, Ecuador, Ghana, Honduras, India, Mongolia, Nepal, Sri Lanka, South Korea (a paid placement) and Thailand; and there are conservation i-Ventures in Australia, Bolivia, Costa Rica, Ecuador, Ghana, Honduras, India, Ireland, South Africa, Sri Lanka and Thailand.

i-to-i also provides internships in journalism, media, business and medicine. For added variety, you can also combine two projects in the same or different countries, in which case you get a £100 discount on the second placement. Fees for placements range from £750 to £1695

visit: www.gap-year.com

12 month volunteering placements

Selection, training, in-country support, flights, insurance and debriefing arranged.

35 Years experience

www.projecttrust.org.uk

Looking for something different For your holiday or gap year?

BSES EXPEDITIONS

Combine adventure travel with conservation and science projects in overseas wilderness environments. Founded by Murray Levick of Scott's first epic South Pole expedition, BSES have over 70 years experience of youth development and expeditions.

SUMMER 2003/4		GAP YEAR
GREENLAND	ALASKA	**FOOTSTEPS OF SHACKLETON**
KYRGYZSTAN	ICELAND	(The Falkland Islands, South Georgia, Chile,)
LESOTHO	TANZANIA	OMAN

Registered Charity 802196

CALL FOR DETAILS AND OUR BROCHURE

BSES Expeditions, at the Royal Geographical Society,
1 Kensington Gore, London. SW7 2AR Tel: 020 7591 3141
Email: bses@rgs.org Internet: www.bses.org.uk

and include comprehensive insurance, global staff support network, predeparture preparation, TEFL training, airport pick-up, food and accommodation (in most cases).

IVS (International Voluntary Service)

Old Hall, East Bergholt
Colchester, Essex CO7 6TQ, England

Tel: +44 (0) 1206 298 215
see: www.gap-year.com

IVS is a membership organisation that 'promotes peace and understanding', and the UK branch of an international organisation called Service Civil International which has links with 40 countries in Europe (including Russia), North Africa (Morocco and Tunisia), North America and Japan. IVS organises short-term (mainly summer) voluntary work projects called international work camps, open to anyone aged 18 or over. Groups of volunteers of different nationalities live and work together for two to four weeks on a community-based project, possibly in conservation, with inner-city children or people with special needs. Students with physical disabilities are encouraged. The project registration fee is £50-£135 which includes food and accommodation during the project.

Kibbutz Representatives

1a Accommodation Road
London NW11 8ED, England

Tel: +44 (0) 20 8458 9235

A kibbutz, for those who don't know, is a farm that operates as a self-contained community in Israel. Kibbutz Representatives is officially part of the kibbutz movement. If you are 18-42 and both physically and mentally fit, KR will organise a place for you either as an individual or as a group. You'll be doing hard manual work, which could be 'light industrial', farming, cooking or working with children for six to eight hours a day. This pays for your board, lodging and laundry. You must apply and be interviewed, and if successful you will be guaranteed a placement. Cost: about £370 including year-long open return air fare and insurance. Minimum stay eight weeks.

Kings World Trust for Children

7 Deepdene, Haslemere
Surrey GU27 1RE
England

Tel: +44 (0) 1428 653504
Fax: +44 (0) 1428 653504
see: www.gap-year.com

The Kings World Trust for Children is a UK-based Children's Charity (formed in 1993) which aims to provide a caring home, an education and skills training for orphaned and homeless children and young people in South India. KWTC has built and manages two Children's

Villages and two Children's Homes in Tamil Nadu State, as well as a couple of rural health clinics, computer and skills workshops, a 32-acre fruit and vegetable farm, a tailoring unit making children's clothes and a hairdressing and beauty salon.

The Trust organises volunteer placements in its own programmes in India to support the Indian staff caring for and teaching the children. Volunteers could expect to get involved with:

- Teaching English in local schools and to the Trust's children (TEFL)
- Organising and coaching sports and games
- Teaching hobbies, music, arts and crafts
- Teaching user skills in computers, carpentry, plumbing and electrics
- Working on the Trust's farm
- Arranging outings and visits for the children
- Maintenance of buildings and construction projects
- Medical duties in clinics (formal qualifications required)

At their interview, volunteers receive a full verbal briefing and a policy handbook on the Trust's work. New volunteers are put in touch with recently returned volunteers so they can find out what to expect when they get out there. On arrival in India, volunteers receive a full briefing and familiarisation and UK-based Trustees are resident in India for six to nine months of the year giving advice and support to volunteers and co-ordinating their activities. The Trust encourages young volunteers to come with friends and gives guidance on health, culture and exploring and travelling around India. The Trust's UK office acts as a point of contact between UK families and volunteers in India, but communication home is also available by phone, fax or e-mail.

Volunteer placements are for one to three months (although extensions are possible). Volunteers live in comfortable accommodation and good food is prepared with strict attention to hygiene and cleanliness.

KWTC offers gappers wanting to volunteer a good cheap option – you only need to raise a minimum of £300 for the Trust and pay £10 a week for food and board. You do have to arrange and pay for your own flights and visa.

L'Arche

GY/03 Freepost BD3209
Keighley
West Yorkshire BD20 9BR, England

Tel: +44 (0) 800 917 1337
Fax: +44 (0) 1535 656426
see: www.gap-year.com

L'Arche (French for 'The Ark') began as a small community in a house in Trosly-Breuil in France more than 30 years ago and is now an international movement with 117 communities in 31 countries. Its aim is to provide local communities – a cluster of houses, usually within walking distance of each other and with access to a workshop – for adults with learning disabilities. The work could be weaving, for example, or making candles. L'Arche is 'shaped and guided by the major Christian denominations', but internationally it is multi-faith, predominantly that of the local area. Volunteer 'assistants' are welcome both for its centres in the UK and abroad, to share life with those who need help to learn. To volunteer abroad you need to contact communities in different countries separately, as they will have different requirements – a list of all L'Arche communities worldwide is available.

Madventurer

Adamson House, 65 Westgate Road
Newcastle upon Tyne NE1 1SG
England

Tel: +44 (0) 191 261 1996
Fax: +44 (0)191 261 9010

Madventurer programmes are flexible and are aimed at gap year students, undergraduates, recent graduates and career breakers. You can work and travel by joining a group or you can go solo.

Mad Group Projects run in rural areas and depart every two months throughout the year to Kenya, Uganda and Tanzania with additional departures every July to Ghana, Peru and Guatemala. Mad has identified five key areas in local communities where group projects can be extremely beneficial: building projects, teaching and coaching opportunities, medical placements, environmental projects and tourism projects. Group Projects cost £1180 for five weeks, this includes all food, accommodation, airport pick-up, transfers to the project site, the full support of your Mad Crew, back-up from Mad HQ in the UK and a £200 donation to project materials.

On a solo project you will be working away from other Madventurers but there will be plenty of opportunity to socialise in the evenings or to travel on a weekend with other Mad people working on different solo projects. There is still the comprehensive support network that Mad offers and you may find yourself sharing a house with another Madventurer in a family environment. As well as the five key areas they get involved in with the group projects, solo projects also offer the opportunity to gain experience in architecture, journalism, media, physiotherapy, care work, law, business and other professional disciplines. Solo projects for up to three months cost £1495 for teaching and £1755 for coaching. Other professions cost £1595 to support, including all food, accommodation, airport pick-up, transfers to the project, the full support of your Mad Coordinator, back-up from Mad HQ in the UK. Additional months cost £295.

Madventurer also offers Combo Expedition, which combines project work with community tourism, allowing you to travel around your

Are you ready for the greatest year of your life?

Inter-Cultural Youth Exchange UK offers young people (aged 18-30) voluntary placements overseas working on social, educational and environmental projects for six months or a year.

For the greatest year of your life visit **www.icye.co.uk** or contact our London office on **020 7681 0983**.

A LOT WILDER THAN IBIZA.

Diving on coral reefs in Jamaica or tracking crocodiles by night in Botswana – these are just two of the 130 conservation research projects that Earthwatch supports worldwide.

Working with us as a volunteer, not only will you have the experience of a lifetime, you'll also help fund our invaluable work to save the world's wildlife.

See the world and give it a future.
Phone us on 01865 318831 for details or visit
www.earthwatch.org/europe

Non-profit making environmental registered charity no. 327017

host country (or countries) and, in return, giving something back to the people. The cost of a Combo Expedition is simply the cost of the Adventure (see Madventurer listing in *Chapter 5: Travel companies*) and Project combined.

Marlborough Brandt Group

1a London Road, Marlborough
Wiltshire SN8 1PH
England

Tel: +44 (0) 1672 514 078
Fax: +44 (0) 1672 514 922

MBG was set up as a link between Marlborough and the village of Gunjur in the Gambia, and has been sending volunteers (from the UK and beyond) to teaching and rural development projects there since 1984. Individual volunteers (you don't have to come from Marlborough) go out for up to six months to the school or to work with TARUD, the local rural development NGO. Selection is by interview; two training weekends are held to prepare volunteers, and there's an induction course on arrival in Gunjur. Costs: about £1500 for the three-month placement and £3000 for the six-month one, all inclusive. One way to 'experience total immersion in African culture'.

MondoChallenge

Galliford Building, Milton Malsor
Northampton NN7 3AB, England

Tel: +44 (0) 1604 858225
Fax: +44 (0) 1604 859323

MondoChallenge has programmes in Nepal, NE India (Darjeeling area), Sri Lanka, Tanzania, Gambia, Kenya and Chile. It is worth noting that they are not just a gap provider as the bulk of their volunteers are post university and career break. But they do accept a select few pre-university gap year candidates each year. Volunteers come from all over the world.

The organisation offers three-month programmes (flexible from two to six months) – mainly teaching small kids in primary schools but there is also some work with street children and in orphanages.

Departure dates are at various times of year and are totally flexible. You make your own travel arrangements. If you want you can spend a little longer by combining two projects – either in the same country or moving on to another country, or even continent!

The cost of around £800 (for three months) doesn't include travel. You also have to pay extra for your food and accommodation, but this is usually with local families at very low cost. MondoChallenge is proud of the fact they put around 15% of their income into local programme development.

Looking for a worthwhile challenge?

Why not spend 10 weeks doing voluntary wildlife research for

GREENFORCE

We organise conservation expeditions around the world.
We need YOU to help us in:
Africa - biodiversity and elephant survey
Amazon - bird mist netting and tree climbing
Fiji, Malaysia and Bahamas - Learn to dive and help to conserve threatened coral reefs.

Full training provided, inc. diver training for marine volunteers. This could be your first step to a career in wildlife conservation. Cost £2,550 ex flight. Call for brochure 0870 770 2646 and visit.

www.greenforce.org

Work on the Wild Side!

L'ARCHE

A life-changing experience

Could you live and work with people who have learning disabilities and open up your mind to new possibilities? Coming to L'Arche for a year is a unique opportunity to use your people skills (and to find some you didn't know you had!). You'll live a simple, shared lifestyle with other assistants and people with learning disabilities, supporting each other in houses, work and therapy projects. In return you will be trained and supported, receiving your own room and free board in a shared house, plus a modest income, holiday time and other benefits.

L'Arche communities are based in Kent, Inverness, Liverpool, Lambeth, Bognor, Brecon, Edinburgh and Preston. They are ecumenical Christian communities, equally welcoming people of other faiths or none, and part of an international federation in 31 countries, founded in 1964 by Jean Vanier.

**L'Arche, GY/03, Freepost BD3209, Keighley BD20 9BR (no stamp required)
Freephone 0800 917 1337   Email: info@larche.org.uk   Fax: 01535 656426
www.larche.org.uk**

A Registered Charity

Muyal Liang Trust

53 Blenheim Crescent
London W11 2EG, England

Tel: +44 (0) 20 7229 4774
see: www.gap-year.com

The Muyal Liang Trust is seeking volunteer teachers for Denjong Pedma Cheoling Academy (DCPA), its school for orphans. The academic year runs from March to December and teachers are required for all subjects as well as English. The school is located in Sikkim, north of Darjeeling. The Indian government restricts foreign visitors to a two-month stay in Sikkim, a sensitive area due to its proximity to the Chinese border. However, permits can be extended for those interested in a longer-term commitment. Teachers will be provided with room and board at Pemayangtse, a 17th century Buddhist monastery in the Himalayan foothills, with magnificent views of Kanchendzonga, the world's third highest mountain. The contact in India is Capt Yapo S Yongda, Muyal Liang Trust, Yongda Hill, Drakchung Dzong, West Sikkim 737113, India. Tel: +91 3595 50656.

Project Trust

The Hebridean Centre, Isle of Coll
Argyll PA78 6TE, Scotland

Tel: +44 (0) 1879 230 444
see: www.gap-year.com

Project Trust offers 12-month placements in over 20 countries across Africa, Latin America, the Middle East, the Caribbean and South and East Asia, departing in August or September. There are also some eight-month placements available on the Winter Programme, departing in January. Projects include teaching English, teaching A level/Higher subjects, work in children's homes, social work, outdoor activities instruction, journalism, conservation and medical projects.

Project Trust places great emphasis on getting the right volunteer in the right project. All applicants attend a five-day selection course at the headquarters on the Isle of Coll and successful candidates return for a five- or six-day briefing and training course in July. Volunteers are expected to raise £3550 from sponsors. This covers selection, training, support overseas, flights, medical insurance, accommodation, food and a small living allowance, and debriefing on return. All volunteers receive ample holiday time to travel and explore the region they are based in. Apply by Christmas 2003 for departure in August 2004.

Quest Overseas

32 Clapham Mansions
Nightingale Lane
London SW4 9AQ, England

Tel: +44 (0) 20 8673 3313
Fax: +44 (0) 20 8673 7623
see: www.gap-year.com

Quest Overseas runs conservation-plus-expedition projects in Africa as well as its projects in South America. Departures are in December,

CORAL CAY CONSERVATION
Expeditions
o Reef & Rainforest
o Community-Based
o Full Training
CORAL CAY
CONSERVATION
"Join our teams of volunteers to survey some of the world's most endangered coral reefs and tropical forests."
FIJI
PHILIPPINES
MALAYSIA
HONDURAS
Tel: ++44 (0) 870 750 0668
Email: info@coralcay.org
real Adventure,
real Science,
real Results
• AWARD WINNING EXPEDITIONS
• 2 WEEK PLUS
• NO EXPERIENCE NECESSARY
OBE David Bellamy
CCC President
www.coralcay.org

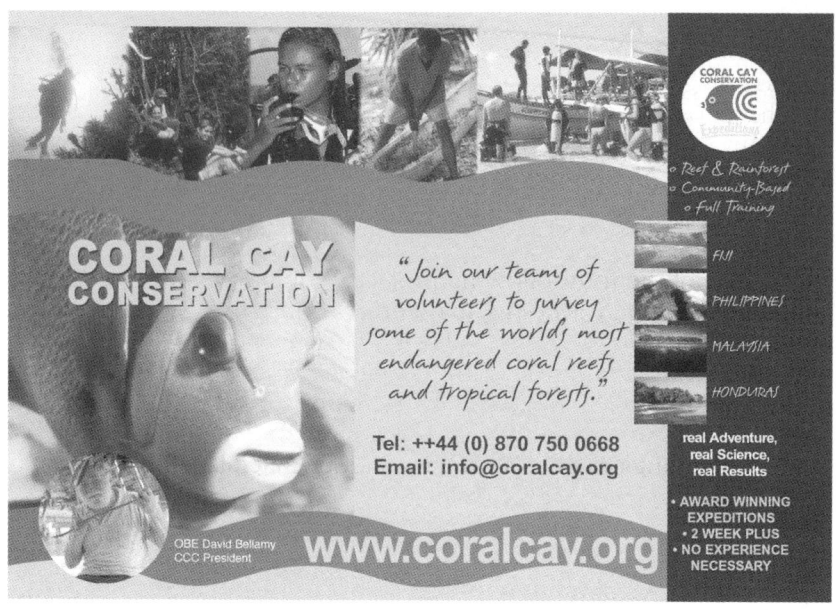

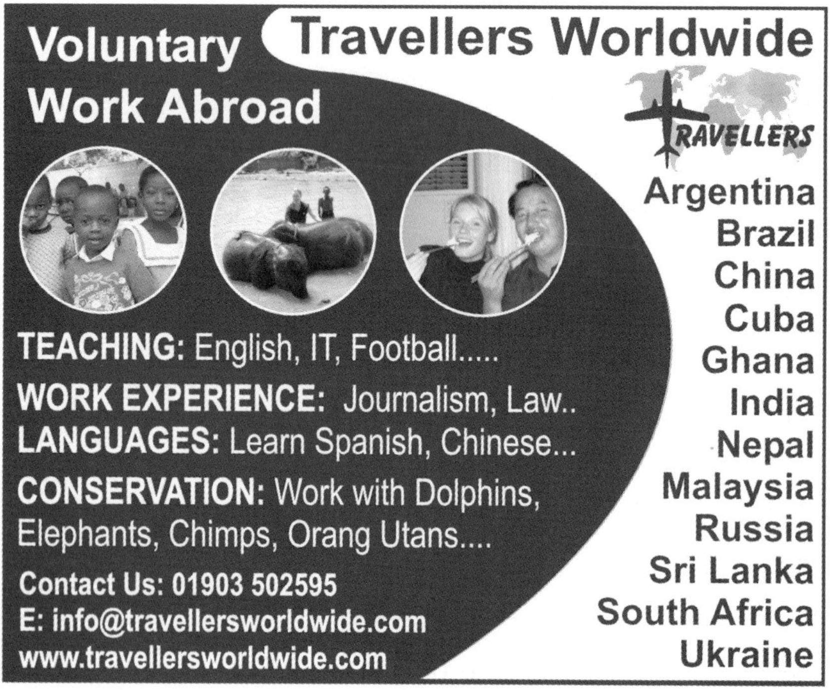
Voluntary
Work Abroad
Travellers Worldwide
TRAVELLERS
TEACHING: English, IT, Football.....
WORK EXPERIENCE: Journalism, Law..
LANGUAGES: Learn Spanish, Chinese...
CONSERVATION: Work with Dolphins, Elephants, Chimps, Orang Utans....
Contact Us: 01903 502595
E: info@travellersworldwide.com
www.travellersworldwide.com
Argentina
Brazil
China
Cuba
Ghana
India
Nepal
Malaysia
Russia
Sri Lanka
South Africa
Ukraine

January, February, March and April. Quest Africa 2003 combines six weeks of community and conservation work (either restoring primary schools in Tanzania or ecological survey work and trail construction on the Lubombo Project in Swaziland) with a six-week expedition through Mozambique, South Africa, Botswana and Zambia.

Quest South America projects work in three phases. Everyone starts with a three-week Spanish language course in either Quito, Ecuador or Sucre, Bolivia. Volunteers spend the next four weeks (in groups of 16) in one of the four following projects (your choice). First, the Villa Maria Children's Project in Lima, Peru, working with children in the poor district. Second, the Santa Lucia Conservation Project in Ecuador, working in a 'cloud forest' (in case you didn't know, that's a high-altitude rainforest). Third, there's the Yachana Rainforest Project, also a conservation project in Ecuador, where you might be maintaining trails or building bridges. Fourth, the Parque Machia project in Bolivia, working in an animal sanctuary looking after confiscated tropical animals before release back into the wild.

Each programme ends with a six-week Andean expedition through Peru, Chile and Bolivia, including Lake Titicaca. Apply as early as possible.

Prices: Africa £2720; South America: £3365 (both excluding voluntary work donations direct to charities, return airfare and insurance).

Raleigh International

Raleigh House
27 Parsons Green Lane
London SW6 4HZ
England

Tel: +44 (0) 20 7371 8585
Fax: +44 (0) 20 7371 5116
see: www.gap-year.com

Raleigh International aims to develop young people through challenging community, environmental and adventure projects, on 10-week expeditions around the word. Destinations include Costa Rica and Nicaragua, Chile, Ghana and Namibia, Belize and Sabah, Malaysia. Applicants not only come from the UK, but also from international countries and the host expedition country itself. The young people, who are also from a variety of different backgrounds, could be involved as part of a year out or as a career break. Applicants (aged 17-25) attend an introduction weekend and then fundraise £3300 for the charity before joining the expedition.

Excellent fundraising support is provided. Included in the fundraising target is a six-month flight ticket to enable travelling independently, medical insurance, training, food and accommodation.

Rempart

1 rue des Guillemites
75004 Paris
France

Tel: +33 (0) 1 42 71 96 55
Fax: +33 (0) 1 42 71 73 00
see: www.gap-year.com

Rempart, a union of conservation associations in France, organises short voluntary work schemes around the world. The projects are all based around restoration and maintenance of historic sites and buildings, from a glamorous French chateaux to a garden in Vietnam.

You need some previous experience and to be prepared to work hard – usually for 30-35 hours per week. Expect to pay about £10 per day to cover food and lodging, depending on where you are placed. Rempart is strictly a French company, so don't expect to be able to organise the trip in English – you'll need to use appropriate language skills wherever you are on your project.

The Right Hand Trust

24 School Street, Wolverhampton
West Midlands WV1 4LF, England
Tel: +44 (0) 1902 428 824

The Right Hand Trust is a Christian organisation which sends volunteers to eight different countries in Africa. Volunteers are usually involved in teaching and social work with another UK volunteer of the same gender, in a rural community.

Training begins in July with an induction course lasting five days. Volunteers then have until Christmas to raise sponsorship (which covers flights, insurance, all training and accommodation). In January there is a cross-cultural training course lasting seven days, followed by the volunteers going to their African countries for a five-day acclimatisation course, after which they commence their teaching, and other posts, until the following August.

Senevolu

Senegal

Tel: +221 550 48 85
Fax: +221 855 71 72

The minimum stay for Senevolu's Volunteer Homestay programme is four weeks, but you can stay as long as a year.

During the first five days volunteers stay at a hostel for an orientation period which includes immersion in the Senegalese culture, language courses (French/Wolof) and excursions in the surroundings of Dakar. Volunteers then move to a host family where they participate in all-day activities: trips, celebrations, ataya *etc*.

From Monday to Friday volunteers work in NGOs (non-governmental organisations), public services, community projects, or primary schools. During the weekend Senevolu organises cultural workshops (African dancing, cooking, djembé, kora, batik *etc*). Senevolu is also happy to organise weekend excursions for groups of five or more.

Smallpeice Trust

74 Upper Holly Walk
Leamington Spa
Warwickshire CV32 4JL, England

Tel: +44 (0) 1926 333200
Fax: +44 (0) 1926 333202
see: www.gap-year.com

The Smallpeice Trust runs the **Smallpeice Engineering Gap Year**, a gap year programme for students who defer their entry to university on an engineering-related degree course.

This pinnacle of engineering gap years uniquely combines study, language, travel and work in Europe:

- three months academic study at a UK university
- one month language tuition at a language school in France, Germany or Spain
- three months work placement in one of nine European countries

The entire programme is arranged and subsidised through The Trust, and starts in September, finishing the following May. The cost per student is £4950, payable in two instalments, which includes all tuition, accommodation, placements, return travel etc.

No other opportunity offers such a firm grounding in engineering, together with personal development, to put students 'head and shoulders' above their peers at university.

SPW (Students Partnership Worldwide)

17 Dean's Yard
London SW1P 3PB
England   Tel: +44 (0) 20 7222 0138

SPW recruits, trains and supports nearly 300 volunteers aged 18-28 abroad each year to work on various projects in partnership with volunteers from the country where the project is run. These divide into two types: Health Education and Environment.

On a Health Education assignment (eight to nine months in Nepal, South Africa, Tanzania or Uganda and four months in India) you won't be replacing a local qualified teacher but giving extra-curricular help with a particlar emphasis on health awareness. For example you could be conducting a workshop on HIV/AIDS prevention, getting young people to perform role plays on teenage pregnancies and holding informal classes on sanitation.

On an Environment project (four to five months in Nepal, Tanzania or Uganda) you could be learning practical methods of dealing with soil

"Raleigh changed my life — the things you see, the people you meet, the sense of achievement, I never dreamt I could do so much with my gap year."

Naomi, Namibia Expedition.

www.raleighinternational.org
020 7371 8585
e-mail: info@raleigh.org.uk

Raleigh International Trust is a registered UK charity No. 1047653

BELIZE   CHILE   COSTA RICA & NICARAGUA   GHANA   MALAYSIA

Learn in the Jungle

Frontier run challenging conservation expeditions for 28 days, 10 weeks or 20 weeks to some of the world's most remote and unexplored areas.

Madagascar Tanzania Vietnam

Conserve and Protect - Take part in an overseas adventure where you will learn new research techniques to help conserve a unique wilderness.

Unique Learning Opportunity - Gain an internationally-recognised BTEC qualification in the wilds of Madagascar, Tanzania and Vietnam.

Escape - with people like you

Visit our website at www.frontier.ac.uk
or contact Gary York for a free information pack:
Tel: +44 (0) 20 7613 2422   E-mail: info@frontier.ac.uk

FRONTIER

www.frontier.ac.uk
A Non-Profit Company

erosion or deforestation prevention and training rural communities to carry them out.

Costs vary but break down something like this: airfare £450-£700; insurance £100-£180; work permit £0-£300; SPW training and support overseas £1600-£2000; SPW support UK £250; total £2400-£3000. Air travel and insurance can be organised independently.

STEN (Save the Earth Network)
PO Box CT 3635
Cantonments-Accra
Ghana
Tel: +233 21 667791
Fax: +233 21 669625

Save the Earth Network finds volunteers placements in Ghana in line with its policy for promoting sustainable development, agro-forestry, environmental conservation, eco-tourism and cultural tourism. Their aim is to help reduce poverty, hunger, malnutrition, disease, illiteracy, drug abuse, unemployment, and environmental degradation whilst offering travellers the most socially responsible, exciting and affordable alternative to mass tourism. You could find yourself teaching English to primary kids, educating local youth on the dangers of drug abuse or planting fruit trees at an agro-forestry farm.

Placements last between one and four months (you can stay longer if you're teaching) and cost between £100 and £175. Accommodation is with local host families and food is mainly Ghanian dishes – this is true immersion in Ghanian culture. The STEN director, Eben Mensak, can be reached by e-mail at ebensten@yahoo.com if you don't want to phone Ghana!

STEP (Short Term Experience Projects)
Latin Link
175 Tower Bridge Road
London SE1 2AB
England
Tel: +44 (0) 20 7939 9000

As part of the missionary society Latin Link, this organisation sends volunteers on projects to Argentina, Bolivia, Brazil, Cuba, Ecuador, Nicaragua, Peru and Spain. There is an orientation weekend in England, training in-country, and debriefing on return. The work is with local churches, building schools, health centres and orphanages or doing evangelical work. There are two projects: the first runs from mid-March to mid-July (four months: £1630), and the second from mid-July to September (six to seven weeks: £1320). You can do both (nearly six months) for £2000. The cost includes airfares, insurance, food, accommodation, a first-aid kit, and equipment. Volunteers must be 18 or over and active members of their local church. Apply by end of November for projects the following spring and May for posts the same year.

visit: www.gap-year.com

VOLUNTARY ORGANISATIONS
Volunteering Abroad

Teaching & Projects Abroad

Gerrard House, Rustington
West Sussex BN16 1AW
England

Tel: +44 (0) 1903 859 911
Fax: +44 (0) 1903 785 779
see: www.gap-year.com

Teaching & Projects Abroad is as an agency which organises voluntary work placements abroad. As its name suggests, many of the work opportunities it offers are in teaching – in such far flung places as China, Ghana, India, Sri Lanka, Mexico, Bolivia, Chile, Russia, Ukraine, Mongolia, Nepal, Peru, Romania, South Africa, Thailand and Togo.

The organisation also offers a variety of other work opportunities – in medicine, veterinary medicine, social work, archaeology, conservation, business and architecture. You could find yourself working with Zing Pong, designer of the Shanghai Opera House. Or you could work in journalism with radio stations in Ghana and Mexico or newspapers in India, Mongolia, Romania and Russia. There is a range of business opportunities in Shanghai, including advertising, human resources, electronics, engineering, IT, accountancy and finance.

The medical placements (in China, India, Ghana, Mexico, Mongolia, Romania and Russia) include anything from dentistry to physiotherapy, and you may even find yourself attending, but definitely not performing, an operation – something to impress medical school with.

VOLUNTEER OVERSEAS
0113 242 6136
for the real intercultural learning experience

AFS, formed in 1947, is the world's leading cultural exchange organisation, represented in 54 countries, and one of the world's largest volunteer based organisations. Next year, over 10,000 participants will join an AFS programme, learn a different language and experience another country's culture by working as a volunteer in a local community.

AFS International Volunteer Programme
- Departing July/Aug 2003 or January/February 2004
- Living with a volunteer host family or in a residential work placement in the community
- Volunteering for 5-6 months in a community service project (areas include health, education, welfare and environment)
- Flights, insurance, preparation and local support provided
- For adults aged over 18 with motivation for the challenge
- Proficiency in another language is not a requirement
- Must be able to contribute towards cost of placement

**Peru • Guatemala • Honduras • Brazil Ecuador
Panama • South Africa and more...**

AFS UK /Leeming House / Vicar Lane / Leeds LS2 7JF
Email: info-unitedkingdom@afs.org   Registered Charity 284174

www.afsuk.org

There's also a conservation placement in Mexico where you can help protect the endangered Olive Ridley Sea Turtle.

Placements start any time and last from as little as one month to as long as a year. Charges range from £995 for three months in Romania to around £1800, and include food, lodging, travel, insurance and local back-up. The organisation holds several open days which give you the opportunity to meet staff and people who have already participated in programmes arranged by Teaching & Projects Abroad.

The Akha Heritage Foundation
Matthew McDaniel, Maesai
Chiangrai, Thailand

Based in northern Thailand, the Akha Heritage Foundation offers volunteering opportunities ranging from one month or less up to one year.

Focus of projects: To assist the Akha Hill tribe peoples with projects to aid clean water, nutrition, human rights, literacy and good governance.

Fees: $450 per month for food, housing and in-country transport; an additional $500 per month for projects in the Akha villages which the volunteer will be conducting with the help of the organization. Volunteers are encouraged to raise funds for these projects if they do not have full funding, and this has been very successful. Some volunteers bring more funding which allows them to do more in the villages – this can be very rewarding.

Volunteers must provide for their health insurance, the air ticket to and from Chiangrai, Thailand and all visas for their stay in Thailand.

The project involves solid, grass roots work and activism at a very close level of community involvement, travelling to villages, working with the Akha on joint projects and living side by side with the Akha communities.

The Leap
Windy Hollow, Sheepdrove
Lambourn, Berkshire RG17 7XA
England

Tel: +44 (0) 870 240 4187
Fax: +44 (0) 1488 685055

The Leap offers placements in some of the most exclusive destinations throughout the world, including Kenya, Tanzania, Uganda, Malawi, Botswana, Namibia, South Africa, Zambia, Seychelles, Zanzibar, India, Sri Lanka, Nepal and Canada. They specialise in placements focused on tourism, combined with a strong emphasis on conservation and community issues. Work can involve assisting in eco-tourism and conservation for the protection, survival and management of wildlife, tribal people and environments. You may also find yourself helping to pro-

Conservation Volunteers for Africa

Conservation Work Placements are available for enthusiastic, self-funding volunteers to spend up to 3 months on Game Reserves in Southern Africa.

Conservation Projects include:
- Game Capture and Relocation (including Darting Elephants and Rhino).
- Predator and Large-Mammal studies.
- Wildlife Rehabilitation and Endangered Species Breeding Projects.
- Dolphin & Whale Research Projects.
- Research & Monitoring Projects involving mammals, birds, reptiles, etc.
- Wildlife Veterinary work.
- Game Ranger Guide Course.

African Conservation Experience
Work on the Wild Side

Tel: 0870 241-5816   e-mail: info@ConservationAfrica.net
Website: www.ConservationAfrica.net

vide activities such as game walks, horse and camel safaris or deep-sea fishing.

All placements are in bush camps, safari lodges, private ranches and boutique hotels, situated in game parks, bush locations, conservation zones and coastal hideaways. Volunteers receive a local living allowance or salary commensurate with local wages. In return they benefit from unique access to the local environment, activities and lifestyle.

To apply, send in your application form and you'll then be sent on a two-day residential 'Familiarisation and Selection Course' in the UK for assessment on suitability and for training/briefing. Each applicant will be carefully selected matching their skills and experience with the hosts' requirements.

Placements last for three months and depart in September, December, March and June or to suit the hosts' seasonal requirements. Placements cost £1950–£2100. In return you can expect: complete supporting travel paperwork, an effective fundraising guide, full local support including 24-hour emergency back-up, full medical, travel and personal effects insurance including air repatriation, a local living allowance or monthly wage, airport pick up and transfer to and from the work placement and full board and accommodation. Cost does not include international flights, visas and independent travel, although The Leap are happy to arrange flights through their partner, Safari Drive Ltd, if you prefer.

The Year Out Group

Queensfield
28 King's Road, Easterton
Wiltshire SN10 4PX, England

Tel: +44 (0) 7980 395789
see: www.gap-year.com

The Year Out Group is an association of leading Year Out organisations that was formed in 1998 to promote the concept and benefits of well-structured year out programmes, to promote models of good practice and to help young people and their advisers in selecting suitable and worthwhile projects. In 2001, the then 23 members of the Group accounted for 18,000 structured year out placements. There are now 28 members (listed below) with several applications in the pipeline

The Group's member organisations provide a wide range of Year Out placements in the UK and overseas that cover courses and cultural exchanges, expeditions, volunteering and structured work placements. All members have agreed to adhere to the Group's Code of Practice (published on the website) and are in the process of developing more detailed operational standards for each of the four sectors mentioned above. The Group's website also contains guidelines for students and advisers. These include questions that potential 'gappers' should ask providing organisations as they look for the programme

VOLUNTARY ORGANISATIONS

that best suits their needs. Year Out Group monitors information published by its members for accuracy.

Year Out Group members are expected to put potential clients and their parents in contact with those that have recently returned. Year Out Group considers it important that these references are taken up at least by telephone and, where possible, by meeting face to face. From October 2002 Group members have agreed to spell out their complaints procedure in their contracts. Year Out Group can advise on making complaints but is not itself able to deal with them. Nor is Year Out Group able to 'police' the 18,000 placements provided by its members but it can take action if any member is shown to be consistently negligent.

There will always be less-than-perfect organisations among members of a trade association and good ones that are not. There are some

small specialist organisations with excellent reputations that cannot afford the membership fees. Whether or not an organisation is a member of Year Out Group, the questions in the student guidelines can be used to advantage.

Year Out Group Membership (January 2003): Academic Year in the USA & Europe; Africa & Asia Venture; Africa Conservation Experience; Art History Abroad; BSES Expeditions; BUNAC; CESA Languages Abroad; Coral Cay Conservation; Council Exchanges; CSV (Community Service Volunteers); Flying Fish; Frontier Conservation; GAP Activity Projects; Gap Challenge/World Challenge Expeditions; Greenforce; i-to-i International Projects; Outreach International; Project Trust; Quest Overseas; Raleigh International; Students Partnership Worldwide; Teaching & Projects Abroad; Travellers Worldwide; Trekforce Expeditions; The International Academy; The Smallpeice Engineering Gap year; The Year in Industry; Year Out Drama.

Time for God

2 Chester House, Pages Lane
Muswell Hill, London N10 1PR
England

Tel: +44 (0) 20 8883 1504
Fax: +44 (0) 20 8365 2471
see: www.gap-year.com

Time for God co-ordinates national and international projects, including youth and community work, homeless and rehabilitation projects *etc* in the UK, USA, Europe, Australia, Ghana *etc*. Start dates are January and September.

Travellers Worldwide

7 Mulberry Close, Ferring
West Sussex BN12 5HY
England

Tel: +44 (0) 1903 700478
Fax: +44 (0) 1903 502595
see: www.gap-year.com

Travellers organises teaching placements in northern and southern India, Nepal, Sri Lanka and South Africa, and has two new projects in China (near Beijing) and Ghana. You could also teach in Russia in either Moscow, St Petersburg, Siberia or in Kiev (where beer is a few pence a litre) in the Ukraine. You usually live with a local family and you don't need formal qualifications – you can teach conversational English or your favourite subject: Maths, Music or whatever it might be.

For 2003 there is a new cultural exchange programme in Cuba, including a Spanish language course. There are also various conservation and work placements in most of these countries. There's no pay, but your food and lodging are free. Prices range from £895 (three months in Moscow) to £1295 (three months in Ghana), both excluding airfares and insurance. Apply any time.

VOLUNTARY ORGANISATIONS
Volunteering Abroad

Trekforce Expeditions

34 Buckingham Palace Road
London SW1W 0RE
England

Tel: +44 (0) 20 7828 2275
Fax: +44 (0) 20 7828 2276
see: www.gap-year.com

Trekforce Expeditions (founded 1990) organise tough eight to 20 week conservation and teaching projects in Central and South America and East Malaysia concentrating on endangered rainforests and working with local communities.

Their extended programmes of four to five months incorporate expedition teamwork, learning new languages and teaching in rural communities, such as the Kelabit of Sarawak or the Spanish and Mayan speaking communities of Belize.

If you are looking for a challenging and rewarding adventure in a summer holiday or after graduation, go and find out more on one of their informal introduction days (apply online or by form). They accept applications throughout the year. Although volunteers are required to fundraise a set target, Trekforce provide extensive help, ideas and support.

UNA Exchange

Temple of Peace
Cathays Park
Cardiff CF10 3AP
Wales

Tel: +44 (0) 29 202 23088
Fax: +44 (0) 29 2066 5557

UNA Exchange has opportunities on a wide range of two to three week International Volunteer Projects in over 60 countries throughout the world, from Armenia to Zambia. These include environmental protection, construction, renovation, organising arts and cultural events, and projects working with disadvantaged children, refugees, and people with special needs.

Projects are hosted by organisations working in the local community and volunteers have many opportunities to meet and engage with local people. You pay for travel and £90-£140 registration fee (depending on the country). Food and accommodation are then provided.

Although most projects are for those aged 18+, there is an increasing number of specialised projects for 15-18 year olds. There are also opportunities for longer term volunteering, on challenging individual placements of up to a year.

Volunteering Abroad **VOLUNTARY ORGANISATIONS**

VAE Kenya

c/o Simon C D Harris (Director)
Bell Lane Cottage, Pudleston
Nr Leominster
Herefordshire HR6 ORE, England

Tel: +44 (0) 1568 750 329
Fax: +44 (0) 1568 750 636

VAE Kenya looks for well motivated school leavers or graduates to become teachers in extremely poor, rural schools, based around the town of Gilgil.

They only place volunteers in schools with a shortage of teachers and resources. Volunteers can assume huge responsibility as they become integrated and live as part of their African community.

VAE Kenya focuses on improving all aspects of education within its schools and is also involved with the local town street-children. Placements last for six months starting in January. The cost of around £3000 covers flights, insurance, salary and accommodation.

VentureCo Worldwide

The Ironyard
64-66 The Market Place, Warwick
Warwickshire CV34 4SD
England

Tel: +44 (0) 1926 411 122
Fax: +44 (0) 1926 411 133
see: www.gap-year.com

VentureCo has two categories of gap year: 'Gap Year' for school leavers and 'Career Gap' for people who have completed their formal education or who are looking for a break in their career.

Volunteering Abroad for school leavers (17½ to 20 years old)

VentureCo runs four-month combination programmes in South America, Central America and Asia. Each Venture combines a language school plus cultural orientation course (three weeks) with a voluntary work placement (four weeks) that leads on to an expedition (eight weeks).

Groups consist of 18 Venturers plus two VentureCo leaders and emphasis is placed on the Venturers taking the initiative. Everyone needs to contribute, through active participation in all three elements, to make the Venture successful.

Programmes in Latin America consist of Inca Venture (Ecuador, Peru, Bolivia and Chile), Maya Venture (Guatemala, Belize, Mexico, Cuba, Dominican Republic and Venezuela) and Patagonia Venture (Peru, Bolivia, Chile, Argentina and Tierra del Fuego). One-to-one Spanish language tuition is provided for the first three weeks. The four-week Aid Projects include working with orphaned children, or volunteering on an Amazon jungle environmental conservation project. The finale

visit: www.gap-year.com

of each Venture is the challenging eight-week expedition that develops team-working and leadership skills.

Himalaya Venture takes place in northern India and Nepal. The three-week Cultural Orientation course in Delhi includes familiarisation with the traditions, food and the railway system of India, as well as instruction in yoga and meditation: basic level Hindi is also taught. The Aid Projects involve assisting the staff of a mobile field clinic in Rajasthan and volunteering on a tiger and wildlife conservation project in Bandavgargh Tiger Sanctuary. The climax to Himalaya Venture is the 19-day trek to Everest Base Camp in Nepal.

Two experienced VentureCo leaders accompany each team, and preparation for the venture gets underway ten weeks before departure from the UK with a build-up weekend. Full in-country expedition training is provided. Planning, leadership and organising roles throughout the Venture are shared amongst the team and each Venturer will lead a leg of the expedition.

All-inclusive prices including international airfares (VentureCo hold ATOL license 5306):

- Maya Venture: £4495
- Inca Venture: £4295
- Patagonia Venture: £4695
- Himalaya Venture: £4175

If you are planning a varied year, for instance a mix of employment, travel and aid work, you may find that one of our Ventures would serve as a valuable building block in your overall gap year plan.

Career Gap: Volunteering Abroad for those over 21

The Career Gap programmes run parallel to the Gap Year programmes, but separately. They are for graduates and people taking a break from their career. The typical range of Venturers' ages is 21 to 35.

Village Educational Project (Kilimanjaro)

c/o Miss Katy Allen MBE, Mint Cottage
Prospect Road, Sevenoaks
Kent TN13 3UA, England   Tel: +44 (0) 1732 459 799

Students teach English to children in rural primary schools in the Marangu region of Mount Kilimanjaro in Tanzania. Cost: about £2000 including airfare but excluding visa, pocket money and insurance. Two weeks pre-departure training is given in Sevenoaks learning some basic Swahili and English teaching skills. School holidays allow time to travel in Tanzania and beyond. With the support of the local community and project workers, you are encouraged to get into village life. Training is in November/December and teaching in Kilimanjaro runs from January to August.

VOLUNTARY ORGANISATIONS

Volunteering Abroad

VSO (Voluntary Service Overseas)
317 Putney Bridge Road
London SW15 2PN
England   Tel: +44 (0) 20 8780 2266

After years of specialising in voluntary work placements for over 21s, VSO has revived its interest in younger volunteers. People aged 18-25 can try for the Youth Action scheme set up by the European Commission: social work placements in Bosnia, Kazakhstan and Russia.

VSO also runs the World Youth Millennium Award Scheme (in partnership with the Prince's Trust and funded by the Millennium Commission), which is a programme for 17-25 year-olds. Volunteers work in a small group for three months in the UK and three months in a developing country, living in pairs with local families and working in pairs with community organisations.

Exchanges start in January, July and October. You are expected to raise £500 in funds, but WYMAS provides funding for participants to cover items including: vaccinations, travel, visas, training, accommodation and pocket money for the six-month exchange period. Contact: Shelagh Savage or Jo Bloxham, Tel: +44 (0) 20 8780 7509.

WWOOF (World Wide Opportunities on Organic Farms)
PO Box 2675
Lewes   Tel: +44 (0) 1273 476 286
East Sussex BN7 1RB   Fax: +44 (0) 1273 476 286
England   see: www.gap-year.com

WWOOF places member volunteers on about 200 organic farms in the UK and many more abroad, on working weekends or longer stays. Interest in organic food production continues to grow. Voluntary work is usually on small farms that cannot afford to take on paid employees but like having volunteers to stay. You work for your board and lodging having paid a £15 (UK) joining fee to WWOOF, who can also introduce you to a long list of WWOOF host farms abroad.

Worldwide Volunteering for Young People
7 North Street Workshops   Tel: +44 (0) 1935 825588
Stoke Sub Hamdon   Fax: +44 (0) 1935 825775
Somerset TA14 6QR, England   see: www.gap-year.com

Worldwide Volunteering publishes the UK's most Authoritative CD-ROM database of volunteering opportunities for 16-25 year olds. The unique software matches volunteers' wishes against the requirements of over 900 organisations with over 250,000 annual placements

visit: www.gap-year.com

VOLUNTARY ORGANISATIONS — *Volunteering Abroad*

throughout the UK and worldwide. Projects last anything from a week to a year and range from those that cost nothing and provide pocket money to those that cost many hundreds of pounds or more. Your school, library or careers centre may have the database or you can find free access points near you on their website. Alternatively contact Worldwide Volunteering at the above address.

Riding the waves

We went to the beach with a group of children, many of whom had never seen the sea before. Since it was in a touristy area I was allowed to swim in a swimsuit, instead of fully clothed.

At first the children were horrified; they'd never before seen anyone reveal themselves so entirely. All 12 of them tried to cover up my 'nudity' using whatever was at hand. I've never felt so naked and unwholesome while clothed in a single piece, granny-like swimsuit.

Deborah, Kings World Trust for Children, 2002

3. Learning Abroad

If you have a thirst for learning but don't want to be stuck at home then your gap year is the ideal opportunity to combine the experience of living in a different culture and studying. You might want to continue learning something that interested you at school – a language perhaps, or history. But 'learning' doesn't have to be purely academic; there are loads of sport 'schools' around the world that cater for all sports and all levels. Or for culture vultures, why not enrol on an art course in Florence or a film course in New York? The opportunities are endless and you can either opt to put your newly-learned skills to use by getting paid work or leave yourself time to travel about.

There is a great variety of types of courses and you should be able to find something to fit your interests, budget and schedule. To make this chapter a bit easier to follow we've split it into section by type: Languages (Language courses, Living with a family, Learn while you earn); Sport; Arts & Culture (Art, Culture, Design & Fashion, Drama); and Spending an academic year abroad. Each section includes a list of organisations that offer relevant gap year programmes or courses or can help you find them.

Languages

Language is part of our everyday lives. We use it constantly to communicate with one another – and yet if we don't speak the same language as another person, it becomes a barrier rather than a bridge. Even if you don't want to study a language academically, being able to speak even the smallest amount of a foreign language opens opportunities.

There's more to a language than just words: most language courses will include local culture, history, geography, religion, customs and current affairs – as well as food and wine. A language also involves more than just translating your own thoughts into someone else's words. A new language brings a whole new way of thinking with it, and therefore a much deeper understanding of the people who shaped it and use it. Why do some languages have no future tense – is there a different way time is conceived? Most people will know that the Icelanders have many different words for 'snow', but did you know that they have 85 words for 'storm'?

Think laterally when you decide where you want to study. Spanish is spoken in many countries around the world, so you could opt for a Spanish course in Brazil, rather than Spain, and then go travelling around South America. Many cities with a particular international

LANGUAGES

Learning Abroad

flavour will offer a variety of language courses: in Brussels, capital of the European Union, courses in other languages such as German, Spanish, Italian or even Russian can be found in a number of institutions throughout the year. As everyone knows, Belgium is partly Dutch/Flemish-speaking and partly French-speaking, so the Belgian Embassy in London will let you have a free list of Flemish or French language schools throughout Belgium.

Belgian Embassy
103 Eaton Square
London NW1 6PU, England
Tel: +44 (0) 20 7470 3700

Be aware though that if you learn a language outside it's original country you may learn a particular dialect that is only spoken there and may be considered inferior by some people (or even not understood) elsewhere, *eg* Spanish in South America, French in Belgium, Canada and Switzerland, German in Austria and Switzerland.

Volunteer placements

There's a whole section in this book about voluntary work abroad (see *Chapter 2: Volunteering Abroad*), whether arranged under the umbrella of a gap year organisation in the UK or independently and directly between the volunteer and the project itself. Some language course organisers also arrange volunteer placements after a language course, which can equip volunteers better for their work, and you can find details on their websites.

Living with a family

If enrolling on a language course sounds too much like school, another way of learning a language is staying with a family as an au pair or tutor (giving, say, English or music lessons to children) and going to part-time classes locally. (See *Chapter 1: Working Abroad*, for more details on au pair work.)

Finding the right place to learn

You can try universities, which often have international summer school centres or courses for foreign students. For those who would prefer to dip their toes in gently, there is the popular network of British Institutes abroad. And there's a plethora of independent language colleges to choose from, either directly or through a language course organiser or agency in the UK. The advantage in dealing with a UK-based organisation is that if something goes wrong, it is easier to get it sorted out within easy reach and under UK law.

Language course organisers, consultancies and agencies will provide advice, book courses and organise your accommodation for you, usually getting their income from the commission they receive from language schools.

Always ask the agency or language school to put you in contact with one or two students who have done the course you have in mind, so that you can get their views of what it's like before you sign up for anything.

Using the internet

As with most subjects the first place to go for extra information on language courses is the internet. Use search engines like **www.freeserve.co.uk**, **www.google.com**, **www.lycos.com**, **www.msn.com** and **www.yahoo.com**. If you're looking for courses abroad and are not a total novice at the language, you could try using search engines specific to the country you want to visit, and typing in keywords in its language.

You can start by looking for specific university websites that you have heard of: for example, the Sorbonne in France. If you key the words 'Chinese language' into a search engine, it will indeed come up with language schools, including ones in China, where you can learn Mandarin or Cantonese. By going to one of the increasing number of websites which give listings of language schools abroad and provide links to their websites you can find a whole lot in one go.

There could be a catch. A college that appears smart on a website may not turn out to be quite so good in real life (maybe it's next to a nuclear reprocessing plant or half the staff are about to leave). College names can also confuse unwitting surfers in other ways: Yale College in Wrexham, Wales, has absolutely no connection with Yale University in the USA for example.

So if you find a suitable college and course on the internet, it is a good idea to check if it's a member of an international language schools association. Alternatively, you can try embassy websites that provide information on language schools in their home country: see links to embassies on *www.gap-year.com*. Or ask the chosen school to provide you with the phone numbers of UK people who have done the course there – as referees.

It's not a good idea to part with money in advance (and certainly not over the internet) without getting references and a written money-back guarantee from schools first. In many cases, terms and conditions of booking can be downloaded from a website.

The following are some international language course websites that we have found:

www.europa-pages.co.uk
www.goabroad.com
www.ialc.org (International Association of Language Centres)
www.languagesabroad.com
www.languageschools.com

Language courses

Courses at language schools abroad can be divided into as many as ten different levels, ranging from tuition for the complete beginner to highly technical or specialised courses at postgraduate level. The usual classification of language classes, however, into 'beginner' or 'basic', 'intermediate' and 'advanced' works well. Within each of these levels there are usually subdivisions, especially in schools large enough to move students from one class to another with ease. When you first phone a school from abroad or send in an application form, you should indicate how good your knowledge of the language is. When you arrive, you may be tested before being allocated to your class, or you may be transferred from your original class to a lower or higher one as soon as they find you are worse or better than expected.

Different schools will use different methods of teaching: if you know that you respond well to one style, check that is what your course offers. Foreign language lessons are often attended by a variety of nationalities so they are almost always conducted in the language you are learning, forcing you to understand and respond without using English. In practice, however, most teachers can revert to English to explain a principle of grammar if a student is really stuck. Sometimes there is a Japanese or Chinese-speaking teacher available to help students for whom learning a European language is a greater challenge.

The smaller the class the better, though the quality of the teaching is most important – at more advanced levels, well-qualified graduate teachers should be available. Language schools and institutes show a mass of information, photographs and maps on their websites, so it's easy to find out if the school is near to other places that interest you, whether it's a city centre or a coastal resort. The admissions staff should be happy to give you references from previous students.

Learning Abroad   **LANGUAGES**

Here we list some of the organisations offering language opportunities to gappers, from formal tuition to 'soaking it up' while you live with a family. We've split the companies according to the languages they offer – some of the larger companies offer several. You'll find the full details of these companies listed up front under the heading 'Multi-languages', and just their contact details under each individual language that they offer.

Multi-languages

AFS Community Projects Overseas

Leeming House, Vicar Lane Tel: +44 (0) 113 242 6136
Leeds LS2 7JF, England see: www.gap-year.com

The AFS Schools Programme (for ages 15-18) offers the opportunity to live abroad for a year, and learn a language through immersion in the way of life. You can choose from 54 countries across South America, Asia and Europe, including Argentina, Paraguay, Venezuela, Hong Kong, Indonesia, Italy, Germany and the USA.

Students live with a volunteer host family as a member of that family, attend a local school, and become involved in the life of their new community. Programmes depart in the summer. What's great about this course is that you learn the language as you go rather than attending classes; AFS reckon you can be a complete beginner when you set off and be really quite fluent in six months.

You will be provided with language kits as part of your preparation as well as taking part in orientation activities before you go. Once abroad you will be well supported by local volunteers.

The programme cost is £3950, which AFS help you to fundraise. The company also offers full or part scholarship opportunities to deserving candidates through their International Diversity Scholarship Fund.

Alliances Abroad

2423 Pennsylvania Avenue NW
Washington DC 20037 Tel: +1 (202) 467 9467
USA Fax: +1 (202) 467 9460

Alliances Abroad offers, language programmes in Costa Rica, France, Italy, Germany, Spain and Mexico and will ensure they find you the best language school available. They supply relevant information on the country you have chosen and provide comprehensive pre-departure support.

visit: www.gap-year.com

LANGUAGES

Learning Abroad

Cactus Language

9 Foundry Street, Brighton
East Sussex BN1 4AT, England

Tel: +44 (0) 1273 687697
Fax: +44 (0) 1273 681412

Residential intensive group and individual courses are available from one week to one year in Europe, Latin America, Asia and Africa with accommodation with host families, in halls of residence or in shared and private apartments. All classes are taught by native teachers, with students from around the world. Multi-destination, work experience and volunteer courses are available worldwide and TEFL (CELTA) courses are offered in England and Spain. Airline tickets can also be arranged (including round-the-world tickets). Full online course search and shopping cart facility.

Caledonia Languages Abroad

The Clockhouse
Bonnington Mill
72 Newhaven Road
Edinburgh EH6 5QG, Scotland

Tel: +44 (0) 131 621 7721/2
Fax: +44 (0) 131 621 7723
see: www.gap-year.com

Caledonia Languages Abroad has been providing tailor-made advice and a personalised booking service for language courses overseas since 1994. Founder/owner Kath Bateman says: "We have travelled to the countries we recommend and are always ready to discuss ideas with gap year students, whether they want to go away for one week or one year." Using 42 language schools around the world, and with a long experience of setting up Volunteer Work too, CLA can organise your course and accommodation and give you practical advice on all aspects of your trip.

Caledonia Languages Abroad can arrange **French** courses in Aix-en-Provence, Bordeaux, Brest, Chambery, Montpellier, Nice or Paris. Nice: from two weeks of 20 group lessons a week at £315 to a four-week combination course of 20 group lessons and five individual lessons for £880. The individual lessons can be focused on specific areas of professional interest, such as business, legal or political French.

You can learn **Spanish** as far away as Cuba, Costa Rica, Bolivia, Ecuador, Mexico or Peru, or in Barcelona, Malaga, San Sebastian or Seville in Spain on Caledonia Languages Abroad courses. In Peru a course in Cusco can be followed by a course in the Sacred Valley of Urubamba, near Inca ruins and trekking routes, or on an island in the middle of Lake Titicaca. Individual lessons cost £200 per week plus accommodation. In Malaga, students can study at the beautiful 'beach-side centre', in a former mansion set in lush gardens beside the beach. This centre is ideally suited for younger students on a budget. Courses are for two or four weeks. Two weeks costs £315 for 40 lessons, and includes accommodation in a student flat.

Caledonia Languages Abroad runs **German** courses in Berlin, Munich or the lively medieval University town of Regensburg in Bavaria. Also available are **Russian** in St Petersburg and **Portuguese** in Lisbon or the Algarve.

Caledonia's **Italian** language school in Siena is in a beautiful building in the oldest part of this walled medieval city. With its bustling, narrow, winding streets and lively student population, Siena is an ideal place to study and absorb culture. Forty lessons over two weeks costs £260. Accommodation with a host family on a half-board basis from £290 for two weeks for a shared room.

CERAN Lingua Internationale
Avenue du Chateau 16
B-4900 SPA, Belgium   Tel: +32 8779 1122

CERAN runs residential language programmes in Dutch, French, German, Japanese and Spanish. Courses are held at various locations throughout the world, and especially in Belgium where the company is based. There are two programmes – a junior programme (ages 18 and under) and an adult programme (ages 19 and over). Both programmes offer intensive tuition, with 'total immersion' in the target language from 8am to 10pm. Courses are run in blocks of one week starting on Sundays, so your course can be as long or short as you want – CERAN generally recommends that you stay for two to three weeks. Prices for junior courses start from just under €1000 (£660) per week, including accommodation; adult courses start at just over €1500 (£990) per week. Japanese is only available on the adult course: a week studying Japanese in Osaka costs ¥180,000-¥220,000 (£934-£1142).

CESA Languages Abroad
CESA House   Tel: +44 (0) 1209 211 800
Pennance Road, Lanner   Fax: +44 (0) 1209 211 830
Cornwall TR16 5TQ, England   see: www.gap-year.com

CESA Languages Abroad is a family company which arranges courses in language colleges in Europe and beyond (Japan and Russia for example), and can offer advice on the most appropriate one for you. Spanish, French, German, Italian and Russian account for 80% of the language courses CESA is asked to arrange.

Of all the languages CESA offers, **Spanish** is most in demand. You can choose from Spanish courses in Costa Rica (San Jose), Ecuador (Quito

Càlédöñiâ
LANGUAGES ABROAD
LANGUAGE LEARNING AND VOLUNTEER WORK ABROAD

Take a language course at one or more of our schools from 2 weeks to 1 year
Selected locations worldwide
Accommodation with host families or in residences or hostels

Spain, France, Germany, Italy, Russia, Portugal, Bolivia, Costa Rica, Mexico, Cuba, Ecuador and Peru

Popular Gap Year Options: Spanish and voluntary work in Bolivia, Costa Rica, Peru or Cuba
French and skiing in Chamonix

Contact us to discuss your plans and ideas for your Gap Year and check our website

www.caledonialanguages.co.uk

Caledonia Languages Abroad. The Clockhouse, Bonnington Mill, 72 Newhaven Road, Edinburgh, EH6 5QG
Tel. (0131)621 772112   Fax. (0131)621 7723   e-mail: courses@caledonialanguages.co.uk

Languages for Life

Why Study Abroad?

It's the only way to really learn effectively. You can concentrate 100% on the language and the structured tuition provided, means you are constantly practising, revising, correcting and expanding your knowledge. Fluency, accuracy and above all confidence are increased enormously.

"The weekend excursions were a brilliant way to meet people and really get a feel for Andalucia. Thank you to everyone at CESA - I really had the time of my life in the amazing city of 'Sevilla'!"
DAISY 18 weeks in Seville

"Mixing with other people from all different parts of the world was the most amazing experience. I now have contacts in Switzerland, Italy and even Israel."
NATALIE 12 weeks in Cannes

"My German improved 100%. It has made me more interested than ever in working with languages. I would recommend it to anyone. A brilliant experience."
GREGORY 8 weeks in Berlin

COUNTRIES COVERED: SPAIN, SOUTH AMERICA, FRANCE, GERMANY, AUSTRIA, ITALY, JAPAN, RUSSIA, MOROCCO, GREECE, PORTUGAL and plenty more...please ask!
QUALIFICATIONS NEEDED: NONE – We cater for linguists AND non-linguists!

www.cesalanguages.com **telephone 01209 211 800**

CESA languages abroad

and Cuenca), and Spain (Granada, Madrid, Malaga, Nerja, Salamanca and Seville – where the oranges come from) for one to six months. Three months tuition plus a flat share in Seville starts at £1770. CESA also runs one-week Easter French and Spanish revision courses (25 lessons) in Nice and Madrid for AS and A2 level students. "We can't provide a cure-all or guarantee to take them up a grade," says CESA director Katherine Brand, "but we give them a chance to immerse themselves in the language for a week."

CESA's **German** courses in Berlin are becoming increasingly popular as the city is now the real capital of Germany in every way. Courses are also run in Cologne, Lindau, Munich (München) and Vienna (Wien), Austria. In Vienna, for example, courses range from 2-24 weeks, with nearly 19 hours a week of tuition for a mixed bunch of nationalities and optional extra classes in the afternoons.

CESA can arrange **Italian** courses of up to 16 weeks in Florence, Rome or Siena. It also runs language crash courses from two weeks to three months long: a two-week French course in Nice (20 lessons of 45 minutes each week) should cost around £725 for tuition and half-board accommodation.

If your language ambitions lie farther afield, CESA also offers courses in **Japanese**, (in Okazaki, near Nagoya), **Russian** (at a language school in St Petersburg) and **Greek** (at a language school in Athens).

CIEE (Council on International Educational Exchange)

52 Poland Street
London W1F 7AB, England

Tel: +44 (0) 20 7478 2020
Fax: +44 (0) 20 7734 7322

CIEE arranges Language Study Abroad programmes with language schools in several countries, offering tuition in flexible blocks (£350 upwards including homestay) in Cuba and Ecuador as well as France, Germany, Italy and Spain.

EF International Languages

74 Roupell Street
London SE1 8SS, England

Tel: +44 (0) 8707 200735
see: www.gap-year.com

On an EF International Language Schools programme you will immerse yourself in the language and culture of some of the world's most exciting cities. Choose from: Nice, Barcelona, Munich, Rome, Quito, St Petersburg or Shanghai. All the schools except the one in Rome are EF owned. Rome is an excellent partner school with the EAQUALS accreditation.

You can study for as little as two weeks (from £620 including accommodation and meals) if you are just looking to brush up, or as long as an Academic Year (from £6250 including flights, accommodation and meals) if you are looking for fluency.

Courses start throughout the year and are open to all levels, from complete beginner to advanced. All courses include accommodation and meals; courses within Europe over 12 weeks also include return flight. In selected locations EF offers work placements and voluntary projects to run in conjunction with the language programme.

Euro Academy

24 Clarendon Place
London SE13 5EY   Tel: +44 (0) 20 8297 0505
England   Fax: +44 (0) 20 8297 0984

Euro Academy has over 30 years' experience in arranging language courses for all ages at all levels at its partner schools throughout Europe and South America. You can study **French** in Paris, Nice, Bordeaux, Tours or Aix-en-Provence; **Spanish** in Spain (Nerja, Benalmadena, Alcala de Henares, San Sebastian, Granada, Madrid, Salamanca, Alicante, Seville, Barcelona, Malaga, El Peurto or Valencia) or South America (Ecuador, Costa Rica, Peru, Brazil or Cuba); **Italian** in Rome, Milan, Florence, Siena or Bologna; **Russian** in St Petersburg; Portuguese in Lisbon or Faro; or **Greek** in Hania (Crete), Athens or Thessaloniki.

Most Euro Academy schools offer courses from one week upwards (some students stay for over six months) for beginners to advanced level students. Courses are flexible and Euro Academy is happy to try to accommodate your needs. They offer one-on-one tuition as well as group language courses.

Type of accommodation varies, catering for all budgets: you can choose from well-appointed student residences, friendly hotels and hostels, or you can opt to live with a host family.

Euro Academy also offers many specialist courses, such as the *Decouverte de la Provence* and *Decouverte de la Cuisine Provencale* courses in Aix-en-Provence which combine language with culture by including a full programme of excursions, wine tasting and cookery lessons. In Malaga students can combine Spanish and dance with Sevillanas and Salsa Lessons. For Art students the Florence school has an 800m² art studio for budding da Vincis. They also offer three Italian and cookery courses. Or if you are facing exam stress, why not try one of their exam revision courses in Bordeaux or Biarritz?

Euro Academy also offers work placements in Europe and the USA and voluntary programmes combined with language in Costa Rica.

Learn Languages Abroad

'Sceilig', Ballymorefinn
Glenasmole
Dublin 24, Ireland

Tel: +353 1 451 1674
Fax: +353 1 451 1636

Learn Languages Abroad is a company that aims to take the guess work out of choosing a language course. They will help you to find the course best suited to your needs – whatever your age or language ability. They work with a number of language schools across Europe, all chosen after extensive research to identify high quality, reasonably priced language schools in excellent locations. Using regular visits and feedback from students they continually monitor the performance of the schools.

They will organise your application to the school and take care of the whole booking process for you. The best bit is that their service is absolutely free (the schools pay them a commission fee if you choose their course).

Courses available range from a week to a full academic year. You can decide upon the intensity – from four hours per day upwards.

Sample prices for a four-week course, including family bed and breakfast accommodation:

French: Paris €1025, Nice €1359, Vichy €1350

Italian: Florence, Rome & Siena €1020

German: Heidelberg €1235

Spanish: Granada €988 (full board), Vitoria & Santander €1286 (half board).

If you want to learn with friends, Learn Languages Abroad can also arrange for special rates for groups of five or more.

Arabic

Arabic is read from right to left. To begin with you need to learn a completely new alphabet, but you can learn a bit of spoken Arabic without mastering the writing.

AFS Community Projects Overseas

Leeming House
Vicar Lane
Leeds LS2 7JF
England

Tel: +44 (0) 113 242 6136
see: www.gap-year.com

For further details see main listing under Multi-languages.

ARABIC/CHINESE

British Council
10 Spring Gardens
London SW1 2BN
England

Tel: +44 (0) 20 7930 8466
see: www.gap-year.com

The British Council in Cairo has courses in Arabic – contact the British Council in London for details.

Embassy of the UAE (Resource Centre)
30 Princes Gate
London SW7, England

Tel: +44 (0) 20 7581 1281

The Embassy of the United Arab Emirates (UAE) in London can send you a list of language institutes, colleges and universities that teach Arabic in the Emirates, particularly Dubai, the city-on-a-creek that combines the heritage of the Middle East with the customs of the West, plus Abu Dhabi and Sharjah.

SOAS (School of Oriental and African Studies)
SOAS Language Centre, University of London
Thornhaugh Street, Russell Square
London WC1H 0XG, England

Tel: +44 (0) 20 7898 4888
see: www.gap-year.com

The SOAS is part of the University of London and can arrange for you to study in an Arabic-speaking country.

Chinese

If you're a take-away sizzling prawn addict, you've probably heard Cantonese, the language of most Chinese people living abroad, from Singapore to Europe and the USA. Cantonese is also spoken widely in the Guangdong and Guangxi provinces of mainland China and in Hong Kong and Macau. But the official language of government, international relations and much education in China is Mandarin, the more formal language most students are advised to learn.

Both languages are 'tonal' (the same sound said in a different tone will change the meaning of a word) and therefore can be quite difficult for English-speakers to learn. The different tonal pronunciation, vowels and consonants effectively turn Mandarin and Cantonese into two different languages, although both use the same written characters.

There's also a third language, Hokkien, which is the language of southern Fujian Province and is related to Taiwanese.

As well as the courses listed below, you can find course information on the internet: **www.webcom/~bamboo/chinese/courses.html**

has an extensive list of courses in Chinese language, literature and civilisation at universities and institutes worldwide, including summer courses, courses in Australia, China, Germany, Portugal, Sweden, Taiwan, Thailand and the UK.

Other websites to try include:
http://asiane.byu.edu/department.html
www.chinapage.com/learnchinese.html

AFS Community Projects Overseas
Leeming House
Vicar Lane
Leeds LS2 7JF   Tel: +44 (0) 113 242 6136
England   see: www.gap-year.com

For further details see main listing under Multi-languages.

EF International Languages
74 Roupell Street
London SE1 8SS   Tel: +44 (0) 8707 200735
England   see: www.gap-year.com

For further details see main listing under Multi-languages.

Dutch

CERAN Lingua Internationale
Avenue du Chateau 16
B-4900 SPA
Belgium   Tel: +32 8779 1122

CERAN runs weekly intensive residential language programmes in Dutch, with 'total immersion' in the language from 8am to 10pm.

Dutch courses are run in Belgium and the Netherlands. A week at Chateau Buitengoed HagenHorst in Holland costs €1695 (£1120) including accommodation. *For further details see main listing under Multi-languages.*

French

There's a busy French community in the UK, a large French Lycée in London and more than one teaching institute run by French nationals, so there are plenty of opportunities to carry on developing your French language skills when you return to the UK.

Belgian Embassy

103 Eaton Square
London SW1 W9B, England
Tel: +44 (0) 20 7470 3700
see: www.gap-year.com

As well as the following organisations, it's worth contacting universities and embassies in France, Belgium, Canada or Switzerland as many of them organise summer language schools for foreign students.

Actilangue

2 rue Alexis Mossa	Tel: +33 (0) 493 96 3384
06000 Nice, France	Fax: +33 (0) 493 443716

Actilangue was established in 1977 by Paul Ceccaldi, the Executive Director. The school building is located in the heart of Nice, near the beach and the famous Promenade des Anglais. The Actilangue language courses are conducted solely in French by experienced instructors. The latest direct teaching methods are applied in a friendly, relaxed atmosphere guaranteeing optimum intensity and maximum individuality.

Placement in the different courses is based on a personal interview and a written test. At all levels, emphasis is placed on the practical use of spoken and written French. The language is learned in realistic situations, reinforced by appropriate background information on the French way of life.

Accommodation is provided with a French family, in a residence for students, in hotels or aparthotels. Actilangue organizes full and half day excursions and makes arrangements for students to participate in group sport outings such as biking, hiking, walking, diving and wind-surfing.

AFS Community Projects Overseas

Leeming House, Vicar Lane	Tel: +44 (0) 113 242 6136
Leeds LS2 7JF, England	see: www.gap-year.com

For further details see main listing under Multi-languages.

Alliance Française

1 Dorset Square
London NW1 6PU
England   Tel: +44 (0) 20 7723 6439

Another well-known centre is the Alliance Française, a non-profit-making organisation funded by a trust. There is a network of Alliances in 138 countries, but the British-based one does not deal with applications to others. However, you can look at the Alliance Française website which has links to or information on Alliances everywhere.

UK teaching centres are spread throughout the country, from Jersey to Glasgow, and many of them regularly run trips to France. These are aimed at giving you a taste of French cuisine and culture as well as the opportunity to improve your language skills. Their two-week trip to Provence (£1330 all inclusive) consists of language activities in the morning and workshops/excursions in the afternoon.

Alliances Abroad
2423 Pennsylvania Avenue NW
Washington DC 20037
USA

Tel: +1 (202) 467 9467
Fax: +1 (202) 467 9460

For further details see main listing under Multi-languages.

BLS French Courses
42 rue Lafaurie de Monbadon
33000 Bordeaux, France

Tel: +33 (0) 556 51 0076

If you like the sound of the Bordeaux area, with its warm, open countryside and vineyards, you could try BLS French Courses, based in the heart of Bordeaux. You will be put up in a modest hotel or, more likely, with a host family, perhaps with another student.

British Institute in Paris
11, rue de Constantine
75007 Paris, France

Tel: +33 1 4411 7373
see: www.gap-year.com

The British Institute in Paris is part of the University of London, and is the only British university institute in continental Europe. It does not run a specific gap year course, but there are courses available covering grammar, translation, and French literature and civilisation which last ten weeks, with between two and eight hours of teaching per week. Course costs depend on the value of the pound – but, roughly speaking, if you do a whole term with eight hours a week tuition, it will cost you around £865.

Cactus Language
9 Foundry Street
Brighton
East Sussex BN1 4AT, England

Tel: +44 (0)1273 687697
Fax: +44 (0)1273 681412

For further details see main listing under Multi-languages.

The Experience Of A Lifetime!

France • Germany • Spain • Italy • Russia • China • South America • Indonesia

Make the most of your Gap Year

EF has a range of exciting opportunities:

- Flexible language courses for all levels, start dates throughout the year
- Gap Year Programme: Learn a language and teach English in two fantastic locations
- Guaranteed language progress so you get more from your travels

Go with an organisation you can trust - EF has 40 years experience in language travel!

www.ef.com   **08707 200 735**
                       gapyear@ef.com

Give yourself
THE BREAK YOU DESERVE:
Come to our idyllic
PROVENCE D'AZUR
to learn French and enjoy true southern hospitality.

Institut E.L.F.C.A.

66 avenue de Toulon
83400 HYERES - France
Tel: (0033) 04-94 65 03 31   Fax: (0033) 04-94 65 81 22
E-mail: elfca@elfca.com   Web: www.elfca.com

Caledonia Languages Abroad

The Clockhouse, Bonnington Mill
72 Newhaven Road
Edinburgh EH6 5QG, Scotland

Tel: +44 (0) 131 621 7721/2
Fax: +44 (0) 131 621 7723
see: www.gap-year.com

For further details see main listing under Multi-languages.

CERAN Lingua Internationale

Avenue du Chateau 16
B-4900 SPA, Belgium

Tel: +32 8779 1122

For further details see main listing under Multi-languages.

CESA Languages Abroad

CESA House
Pennance Road, Lanner
Cornwall TR16 5TQ, England

Tel: +44 (0) 1209 211 800
Fax: +44 (0) 1209 211 830
see: www.gap-year.com

For further details see main listing under Multi-languages.

Challenge Educational Services

101 Lorna Road
Hove
East Sussex BN3 3EL, England

Tel: +44 (0) 1273 220261
Fax: +44 (0) 1273 220376
see: www.gap-year.com

Challenge Educational Services organises **French** courses in collaboration with several French universities (including the world famous Sorbonne University in Paris) and at private language institutes. A full academic year, a single semester (Sep/Oct-Jan or Feb-Jun) or Summer courses are offered at the universities of the Sorbonne, Angers, Nantes, Poitiers and Grenoble. Prices vary from £755 for a four-week summer programme at the Université de Grenoble (20 hours tuition a week) to £4990 for a full academic year at the Université de Poitiers, including tuition and accommodation (staying with a French family costs extra). One semester (1 October to 31 January) at the Université de la Sorbonne, in the heart of left-bank Paris, costs £5390 (including accommodation and 20 hours a week tuition) and summer courses there run from four to eleven weeks (from £1310).

Courses are also available throughout the year at private language schools in Paris, Bordeaux and Antibes lasting from one to 26 weeks. The personal attention, intensive tuition and small class sizes make this type of course ideal for students who have limited time available to study abroad. You can even combine learning French with French gastronomy or fashion.

Challenge also organises a 12-week programme in Paris, combining language tuition with classes at a French Art school. Ideal for those with a reasonable standard of French and at least GCSE Art.

Students wishing to go on the **Lycée Gap Year Programme** must already have a good command of French. You will study the same curriculum as the French students and may be able to sit the Baccalaureat exams provided you reach the required standard.

Tuition is combined with friendly and welcoming host family accommodation. They are also happy to tailor-make courses to suit your individual requirements.

CIEE (Council on International Educational Exchange)

52 Poland Street
London W1F 7AB Tel: +44 (0) 20 7478 2020
England Fax: +44 (0) 20 7734 7322

For further details see main listing under Multi-languages.

EF International Languages

74 Roupell Street
London SE1 8SS Tel: +44 (0) 8707 200735
England see: www.gap-year.com

For further details see main listing under Multi-languages.

ELFCA (Institut d'Enseignement de la Langue Française sur la Côte D'Azur)

66 Avenue de Toulon Tel: +33 (0) 4 9465 0331
83400 Hyères Fax: +33 (0) 4 9465 8122
France see: www.gap-year.com

Spending some time in the Var is a unique experience as it is the real soul of Provence d'Azur, where the inhabitants have managed to hold off the 'concrete invasion' to preserve their sandy beaches, wild coves, flowered islands and Mediterranean forests. Villages have kept their traditional shops, their lively cafés and their boule-grounds under the shade of the trees where everybody is immediately welcomed as part of the group.

Bigger towns, such as Hyères with 55,000 inhabitants, have also kept their provençal authenticity, their architecture and their vividness, still maintaining their weekly markets, with sun-blessed local fruit and vegetables as well as offering all the usual modern entertainments. The inhabitants still take time to enjoy life and are always so proud to introduce their foreign guests to their culture, cuisine and *art de vivre*.

Learning Abroad   **FRENCH**

In a recent French national survey, Hyères was ranked *number one* beach resort, using many criteria such as cleanliness of the sea, climate, surroundings, fun, lodgings, attractions, prices *etc.*

One of the best ways to enter the magic of the region is to take part in a French language course there. The ELFCA institute, located in Hyères on the Mediterranean coast, offers such courses. The school is in smart air-conditioned premises with a restaurant. Accommodation is either in hotels or apartments or, if you want to truly immerse yourself in the French way of life, ELFCA will happily place you with a host family (room and half-board). This is probably the best option as the French are well-known for their cuisine, and those from the southern regions pride themselves on their hospitality and conviviality, so you will be well looked after.

Tuition is in groups or for individuals, 22 to 30 hours a week, with courses ranging from a week at €265 to 22 weeks at €200 per week. Courses last from a week to several months depending on your goals. Students will be able to take the Alliance Française exams on seven dates through the year (ELFCA is recognised as an examination centre by the Alliance Française, so the exams take place at ELFCA's premises), or prepare for the DELF exams.

Euro Academy

24 Clarendon Place	Tel: +44 (0) 20 8297 0505
London SE13 5EY, England	Fax: +44 (0) 20 8297 0984

For further details see main listing under Multi-languages.

Fondation 9

485 Avenue Louise	Tel: + 32 (0) 2 627 52 52
1050 Brussels, Belgium	Fax: + 32 (0) 2 627 51 00

Founded in 1989 by the Université Libre de Bruxelles, the Chamber of Commerce and Industry of Brussels and the city of Brussels, Foundation 9 offers courses on its campus in Brussels with accommodation in the campus halls of residence, with families or in studio flats.

Institut Cunéiforme

3, Rue Maguelone	
34000 Montpellier, France	Tel: +33 4 6706 5690

The Institut Cunéiforme runs intensive courses in Montpellier lasting between two weeks and three months. Accommodation is with local families (although hotels can be arranged on request), and the aim is to immerse you completely in the life of the city. So as well as having French tuition, you can go to classes ranging from cheese to poetry. Visits are organised to local museums, markets and buildings, and Montpellier is an excellent base from which to investigate some wilder pursuits: you can try skiing, snow sports, horse riding, canoeing, trekking and rafting.

Institut Français
17 Queensberry Place
London SW7 2DT
England   Tel: +44 (0) 20 7581 2701

About 6000 students pass through the Institut Français each year – it's the official French government centre of language and culture in London. The Cultural Centre Library at the Institut has a booklet with comprehensive information on language courses in France, *Cours de Français Langue Etrangère* (in French), which lists beginner, intermediate and advanced level courses.

Institut Savoisien

Institut Savoisien d'Etudes Françaises pour Etrangers
Domaine Universitaire de Jacob Bellecombette
BP 1104 – F 73011
Chambery Cedex
France　　　　　　　　　　　　　Tel: +33 4 7975 8414

Among the host of universities in France offering language courses to students from abroad is the Université de Savoie: its language institute offers courses throughout the year. Your level of French is assessed on arrival and you are placed with the appropriate group.

Among the many courses offered, there is a three-week summer course (20 hours per week) costing €490 excluding accommodation. Situated in Chambéry, about 30km from Annecy near the Swiss border with south-east France, the Institut is also the region for ski enthusiasts who prefer to study in winter.

Learn Languages Abroad

'Sceilig'
Ballymorefinn, Glenasmole
Dublin 24　　　　　　　　　　　Tel: +353 1 451 1674
Ireland　　　　　　　　　　　　Fax: +353 1 451 1636

For further details see main listing under Multi-languages.

Lyon Bleu International

3 Grande Rue des Feuillants
69001 Lyon, France　　　　　　　Tel: +33 4 7839 7690

Lyon Bleu International language school is located in a UNESCO-designated World Heritage site in central Lyon. It offers programmes for all levels of French, and teaches for the usual range of recognised French language certificates, including Alliance Française exams.

Guided tours and excursions are arranged and are free to participants of general French classes. There's also a language exchange programme which enables you to meet French people and practise your French.

Point3 Centre de Langues

404 St-Pierre Street, Suite 101, Montréal
Quebec H2Y 2M2, Canada　　　　　Tel: +1 514 840 7228

If you like the idea of learning French in Canada, there's the Point3 language centre in Montréal, Quebec, which promises to limit its class size to ten and runs courses ranging from two to 36 weeks. Culturally one of the liveliest cities in Canada, Montréal is also near the US border and within reach of New York and Boston as well as Toronto, Ottawa and the Niagara Falls. Four weeks' tuition (22 hours per week) costs CAN$924 (£375). Accommodation is charged separately, and prices vary according to where you stay – options include a host family, a student residence or a fully-furnished apartment.

Ski Exp Air

770 Colonel Jones, Ste Foy　　　　　　　　　Tel: +418 654 9071
Quebec City　　　　　　　　　　　　　　　　Fax: +418 654 9071
Canada　　　　　　　　　　　　　　　see: www.gap-year.com

If you would like to add a bit of spice to your language learning why not combine it with a sport course? Ski Exp Air runs courses in Canada, designed to get you a ski/snowboard instructor qualification whilst you improve your French. As the sport course progresses, more and more classes are taught in French and there are weekly French conversation sessions.

You will be based on a college campus in Quebec City where you can mix with French-speaking students. The accommodation has TV/internet facilities and you would have the use of a swimming pool, a gymnasium and tennis, volleyball and badminton courts.

For more in formation about the courses see Ski Exp Air in the *Sport* section later in this chapter.

Vis-A-Vis

2-4 Stoneleigh Park Road, Epsom
Surrey KT19 0QT, England　　　　　Tel: +44 (0) 20 8786 8021

Vis-A-Vis offer French courses in nine locations worldwide including Montréal and Brussels as well as cities throughout France. Prices for Montréal start at £571 for a two-week course (20 hours a week) including half board accommodation with a host family. Various other accommodation options are available, and there is the usual range of course length, level and intensity.

German

Although not as prevalent as French, there is a lively German community in the UK and many courses run by the Goethe Institut, so there are plenty of opportunities to carry on practising your German when you get back. As well as the following organisations it's worth

Learning Abroad

GERMAN

contacting universities in Germany, Austria or Switzerland as many of them organise summer language schools for foreign students.

German Embassy   **23 Belgrave Square**
(Cultural Department)   **London SW1X APZ**
         Tel: +44 (0) 20 7824 1376
         see: www.gap-year.com

German has many very strong dialects (particularly in Austria, Switzerland and much of south Germany), and it is important to bear this in mind if you want to study German academically or use it for business, in which case you really need to be learning and practising Hochdeutsch (standard German).

AFS Community Projects Overseas
Leeming House
Vicar Lane   Tel: +44 (0) 113 242 6136
Leeds LS2 7JF, England   see: www.gap-year.com

For further details see main listing under Multi-languages.

Alliances Abroad
2423 Pennsylvania Avenue NW
Washington DC 20037   Tel: +1 (202) 467 9467
USA   Fax: +1 (202) 467 9460

For further details see main listing under Multi-languages.

BWS Germanlingua
Bayerstr. 13   Tel: +49 (0) 89 599 892 00
80335 Munich, Germany   Fax: +49 (0) 89 599 892 01

BWS Germanlingua, based in Munich and Berlin, prides itself on its high level of teaching and friendly atmosphere. All staff are experienced teachers and classes have a maximum of 12 students.

A standard course (20 lessons per week) starts at €390 for a fortnight; intensive courses (25 lessons per week) range from €450 (for a fortnight) to €6720 for a full year. Individual tuition and specialised courses (*eg* business, hotel and tourism, marketing, banking, law, medicine, music, technology) are also available. Courses lead to various qualifications. You can attend lectures at a local university as a guest.

Cost includes enrolment fee, placement test, course material and certificate, free internet access and three activities per week. You pay extra for accommodation: living with a host family (from €140 per week); a shared student flat (from €120 per week); or an apartment (from €160 per week). BWS offers a comprehensive range of leisure activities and facilities, including dance and art classes, a fitness centre, team sports and bike rental.

Caledonia Languages Abroad
The Clockhouse
Bonnington Mill, 72 Newhaven Road
Edinburgh EH6 5QG, Scotland
Tel: +44 (0) 131 621 7721/2
Fax: +44 (0) 131 621 7723
see: www.gap-year.com

For further details see main listing under Multi-languages.

CERAN Lingua Internationale
Avenue du Chateau 16
B-4900 SPA, Belgium
Tel: +32 8779 1122

For further details see main listing under Multi-languages.

CESA Languages Abroad
CESA House, Pennance Road
Lanner, Cornwall TR16 5TQ
England
Tel: +44 (0) 1209 211 800
Fax: +44 (0) 1209 211 830
see: www.gap-year.com

For further details see main listing under Multi-languages.

CIEE (Council on International Educational Exchange)
52 Poland Street
London W1F 7AB
England
Tel: +44 (0) 20 7478 2020
Fax: +44 (0) 20 7734 7322

For further details see main listing under Multi-languages.

EF International Languages
74 Roupell Street
London SE1 8SS
England
Tel: +44 (0) 8707 200735
see: www.gap-year.com

For further details see main listing under Multi-languages.

German Academic Exchange Service
34 Belgrave Square
London SW1X 8QB, England
Tel: +44 (0) 20 7235 1736

The German Academic Exchange Service is the largest academic exchange service in the world, granting over 60,000 scholarships per year. Its booklet *Sommerkurse in Deutschland* lists summer courses at German universities in language, literature, regional studies, music and other subjects. The list is designed for university students, but there's no reason why gap year students can't apply too.

Goethe Institut

50 Princes Gate, Exhibition Road
London SW7 2PH, England   Tel: +44 (0) 20 7596 4004

The Goethe Institut is probably the best-known international German language school network, with 125 centres in 76 countries. It is a non-profit organisation funded by the German government, and it offers a wide variety of courses as well as having a lending library and multi-media centre in London. It will happily send you information on studying in Germany, including the booklets *Learn German in Germany* and *Sommerkurse in Deutschland*. The former details courses run by the Goethe network in Germany, including some which put more emphasis on sport and leisure activities. You can click through to information about Goethe Institut branches in other countries from its London website. Courses are run all over the world throughout the year. In Germany itself there are 16 course locations including Bonn, where you can, for example, go on a four-week intensive course for €945 (tuition only) or €1355 (single room accommodation included). There's also a three-week summer course aimed specifically at those aged between 18 and 20. It takes place in Berlin and Hersshing and costs €1915 all inclusive.

Learn Languages Abroad

'Sceilig', Ballymorefinn
Glenasmole, Dublin 24   Tel: +353 1 451 1674
Republic of Ireland   Fax: +353 1 451 1636

For further details see main listing under Multi-languages.

Greek

The thoughts of the great philosphers such as Socrates and Aristotle, upon whose ideas the foundations of western values were built, were written in ancient Greek. Democracy, aristocracy, philosophy, pedagogy, and psychology are just some of the many Greek terms that are part of our culture and language. If Homer's epic poem *The Iliad* sounds so bloodcurdlingly beautiful in English, how must it sound in ancient Greek? It is modern Greek, however, which is spoken by ten million Greek citizens and by about seven million others spread

GREEK

around the world. The Centre for the Greek Language website (**www.greeklanguage.gr**) might be a good starting point – it publishes a useful booklet, *Institutions offering Courses of Modern Greek Abroad – with a brief Commentary in Greek*, in electronic format.

AFS Community Projects Overseas

Leeming House, Vicar Lane
Leeds LS2 7JF, England

Tel: +44 (0) 113 242 6136
see: www.gap-year.com

For further details see main listing under Multi-languages.

CESA Languages Abroad

CESA House
Pennance Road, Lanner
Cornwall TR16 5TQ, England

Tel: +44 (0) 1209 211 800
Fax: +44 (0) 1209 211 830
see: www.gap-year.com

For further details see main listing under Multi-languages.

DIKEMES – International Center for Hellenic and Mediterranean Studies

2 Vassileos Constantinou Avenue
GR 11635 Athens, Greece

Tel: +30 210 7560749
Fax: +30 210 7561497

The International Center for Hellenic and Mediterranean Studies is a not-for-profit educational institution which promotes the study of the culture of Greece (ancient, medieval and modern) and the Mediterranean world, addressing university students from North America and Europe, foreign visitors, and the English-speaking community of Greece.

DIKEMES, in collaboration with its North American associate, College Year in Athens, brings more than 300 university students to Athens each year to study Ancient Greek Civilization and the East Mediterranean Area.

A range of university-level summer programmes is also available, including Intensive Modern Greek Language, which attracts participants from Europe and North America.

DIKEMES has now developed continuing education programmes in collaboration with the University of Birmingham, UK in the fields of Archaeology, Ancient History and Byzantine Studies.

Euro Academy

24 Clarendon Place
London SE13 5EY, England

Tel: +44 (0) 20 8297 0505
Fax: +44 (0) 20 8297 0984

For further details see main listing under Multi-languages.

Learning Abroad **GREEK/INDONESIAN/ITALIAN**

Greek Embassy Education Department

1a Holland Park
London W11 3TP
England

Tel: +44 (0) 20 7221 0093
see: www.gap-year.com

Go to the Greek Embassy website to link to the Greek Ministry of Education. Here you can find a list of universities and schools in Athens, Thessalonika, Crete and the Greek islands among other places where modern Greek is taught, in combination with civilisation and culture courses (ancient and modern).

Indonesian

AFS Community Projects Overseas

Leeming House
Vicar Lane
Leeds LS2 7JF
England

Tel: +44 (0) 113 242 6136

see: www.gap-year.com

For further details see main listing under Multi-languages.

Italian

Italy is crowded, noisy and full of mopeds – which is part of what makes it such an exciting place to be. Italian universities like the University of Perugia provide Italian language courses for foreign students, and there's a wide choice of language centres and institutes in big cities. There are language schools in Rome, Venice, Florence and regional towns whose architecture sweeps you effortlessly back to earlier centuries – where you don't need much imagination to see Romeo leaning against a fountain or Juliet waving from a balcony.

The biggest concentration of language schools is in Florence (Firenze), which swarms with students and tourists of all ages almost all year round. If you are there to see the art collections of museums and galleries like the Uffizi (early Renaissance through to Mannerism/Baroque), you may find you have to queue for hours, reserve tickets in advance, and pay fees with few student concessions. But there are cafés and restaurants, evening concerts in churches throughout the city, and for those who want to get away from the the buzzing motorbikes that swarm across the bridges over the Arno, there are the peaceful Boboli gardens. Trains (if they are not on strike) bring Lucca, Siena, Pisa, San Gimignano and Carrara

visit: www.gap-year.com

ITALIAN

(source of Renaissance marble) within easy reach. It's easy to get around the city by bus or rented bike or on foot – it doesn't take much over 20 minutes to walk across the centre of the city.

Schools vary from the very large to very small, each with its own character and range of courses in Italian, Italian culture, history, art, cooking and other subjects. As in language schools across most of Europe, the language is often taught in the morning with extra-curricular activities in the afternoon. If you want to do a course from March onwards it is advisable to get in touch with them at least two months in advance, as courses and accommodation get booked up early in this crowded city.

Most schools can fix you up with accommodation before your trip, either with a family, bed and breakfast, half-board, or renting a studio or flat. If you're part of a small group, you might prefer to arrange accommodation yourself through a local property letting agent, but this can be tricky unless you have someone on the spot to help.

Accademia del Giglio
Via Ghibellina 116
50122 Firenze, Italy
Tel: +39 055 23 02 467
Fax: +39 055 23 02 467

This quiet, small school, several floors up in a building close to the Bargello, takes about 30 students, taught in small classes. Other classes include fresco painting, Italian for business and Italian for hospitality and tourism.

Accademia Italiana
Piazza Pitti 15
50125 Firenze
taly
Tel: +39 055 284 616
Fax: +39 055 284486

An international design, art and language school, the Accademia Italiana puts on summer (one to three months) language courses as well as full-year and longer academic and Masters courses in fashion design, fashion illustration, textile design, interior and furniture design, drawing and painting and others.

AFS Community Projects Overseas
Leeming House
Vicar Lane
Leeds LS2 7JF, England
Tel: +44 (0) 113 242 6136
see: www.gap-year.com

For further details see main listing under Multi-languages.

ITALIAN

Alliances Abroad
2423 Pennsylvania Avenue NW
Washington DC 20037, USA
Tel: +1 (202) 467 9467
Fax: +1 (202) 467 9460

For further details see main listing under Multi-languages.

The British Institute of Florence
Piazza Strozzi 2
1-50123 Firenze
Italy
Tel: +39 (0) 55 2677 8200
Fax: +39 (0) 55 2677 8222
see: www.gap-year.com

The British Institute of Florence was founded in 1917 with the aim of developing cultural understanding between the UK and Italy (particularly Tuscany) through the teaching of their respective languages and cultures and the maintenance in Florence of a library.

Today, the Institute runs a thriving and successful school which offers many courses including Italian from beginner to A level. In 2000, the Institute became affiliated with the University of Bristol enabling it to offer accredited courses including the First and Higher Certificate in Art History.

Other popular cultural courses offered include Tuscan cooking, wine appreciation, opera, Dante, watercolour, life drawing, film appreciation and other aspects of Italian culture.

The Institute also maintains the Harold Acton library, the biggest library of English books (50,000 volumes) in Italy, used by visiting scholars, students and the general public. Every week, the Institute runs a cultural programme consisting of lectures, concerts, recitals and films in the library.

The Italian A level can be taken in one year and course prices range from £95-£2500. The Institute also has a student support and accommodation officer providing help and advice to all students.

Cactus Language
9 Foundry Street, Brighton
East Sussex BN1 4AT, England
Tel: +44 (0)1273 687697
Fax: +44 (0)1273 681412

For further details see main listing under Multi-languages.

Caledonia Languages Abroad
The Clockhouse, Bonnington Mill
72 Newhaven Road
Edinburgh EH6 5QG, Scotland
Tel: +44 (0) 131 621 7721/2
Fax: +44 (0) 131 621 7723
see: www.gap-year.com

For further details see main listing under Multi-languages.

Centro Linguistico Italiano Dante Alighieri
Piazza della Repubblica 5 Tel: +39 (0) 55 21 08 08
Firenze Fax: +39 (0) 55 28 78 28
Italy see: www.gap-year.com

Probably the biggest international language school in Florence, with a sister school in Rome, the Dante Alighieri has expanded rapidly and about 200 students bustle around its building over the Piazza Repubblica. It is 'recognised' by the Italian Ministry of Public Education and some of its courses can be taken as credits for various US and European universities (including Exeter University).

The school has 15 big classrooms with 10-14 students per class and a wide mix of European, American and Asian students, mostly under 30. Like most schools, all teaching is in Italian, though there is a Japanese-speaking teacher on hand. The school can place students in accommodation including shared flats, but will try to avoid placing students with others of the same nationality. There's a very wide variety of language courses at all levels, plus cultural courses such as Italian history, economics, art and music – and if you miss kicking around a football, the CLI Dante Alighieri offers soccer training and matches as part of its extra-curricular activity programme. There's also a baby grand piano and a room for playing musical instruments.

Centro Machiavelli
Piazza Santo Spirito 4 Tel: +39 (0) 55 2396 966
Firenze 50125-I Fax: +39 (0) 55 280 800
Italy see: www.gap-year.com

This is a delightful small language school in the Santo Spirito district of Florence, in a quiet square ten minutes away from the tourist-crammed Ponte Vecchio. You can take your coffee breaks in cafés in this market square where antique carving restorers and craftsmen have workshops, and once a week the square fills up with a bric-a-brac and organic food market.

Apprenticeship courses can be organised in local artists' and artisans' workshops as well as free conversation exchanges with local students. Machiavelli has the normal range of language courses, quite reasonably priced. Happy atmosphere, all ages, with mainly young continental European and some Japanese students.

Centro Studi Europeo (Europass)
Palazzo Guadagni, Piazza Santo Spirito 9
50125 Firenze, Italy Tel: +39 055 213 030

Also in the Piazza Santo Spirito, but in a grander building, Eurocentres Firenze is part of a network of Eurocentres Foundation language schools, with 30 others in Europe, the USA, Canada and Japan. The school is big, airy and light, with a lecture theatre with the beautiful coffered ceiling that you would expect of a palazzo. It takes 150-200 students in the high season and offers a good range of language and cultural courses.

CESA Languages Abroad

CESA House,
Pennance Road, Lanner
Cornwall TR16 5TQ, England

Tel: +44 (0) 1209 211 800
Fax: +44 (0) 1209 211 830
see: www.gap-year.com

For further details see main listing under Multi-languages.

CIEE (Council on International Educational Exchange)

52 Poland Street
London W1F 7AB, England

Tel: +44 (0) 20 7478 2020
Fax: +44 (0) 20 7734 7322

For further details see main listing under Multi-languages.

Euro Academy

24 Clarendon Place
London SE13 5EY, England

Tel: +44 (0) 20 8297 0505
Fax: +44 (0) 20 8297 0984

For further details see main listing under Multi-languages.

Il Sillabo

Via Alberti, 31
52027 San Giovanni
Valdarno (AR), Italy

Tel: + 39 055 9123238
Fax: + 39 055 942439

Il Sillabo is a deliberately small school created by a family. It's small and intimate, offering a relaxed, warm and friendly environment blending language instruction, cultural experiences and companionship.

The school reflects the charm of the Valdarno region of Tuscany, a carefully kept secret on the doorsteps of Firenze (Florence), Siena and Arezzo and within easy reach of the historical, geographical and gastronomic landmarks which have made this part of Italy famous for centuries. The region has managed to stay authentic so you will get a taste of real Tuscany without becoming lost within the throngs of tourists and overwhelmed by the lure of commerce

Il Sillabo offers a wide variety of Italian language courses for all levels, which can be taken alongside additional courses such as cookery, drawing, painting, ceramics and archaeology. It also offers an intensive cultural and social programme which extends well beyond the bounds of San Giovanni and the Valley of the Arno.

Courses start throughout the year. Il Sillabo offers generous discounts for long term enrolment, eg €2079 for the 24-week intensive course instead of €2790. Il Sillabo also helps its students find cheap, convenient accommodation with local host families, in self-contained apartments, on farms or in local hotels. Accommodation in a shared apartment, in a single room for 24 weeks would cost €2040.

Istituto di Lingua e Cultura Italiana Michelangelo
Via Ghibellina 88
50122 Firenze, Italy   Tel: +39 055 240 975

The Michelangelo Institute is more formal than some language schools in Florence. Housed in the 15th-century Palazzo Gherardi close to Michelangelo's house and Florence University, it is open all year round, taking from about 70 students in April to more than 200 in September. Maximum class size is ten. As well as language courses at six levels, there are cultural courses (mainly eight two-hour sessions) on Art History, Literature (Boccaccio, Dante, Petrarch, plus Giacomo Leopardi, Allesandro Manzoni, Pier Paolo Pasolini), Commerce and

Gap Year or New Career?

SHORT & LONG TERM COURSES IN ITALY

- Italian Language
  from beginner to A Level
- History of Art
  short & long term study
- History of Art Year
  First & Higher Certificate
- Italian Culture
  Opera, Dante, Film
- Italian Cooking,
  Life Drawing & Watercolour

www.britishinstitute.it
Piazza Strozzi, 2 - Firenze
phone +39 055 26778200
fax +39 055 26778222
info@britishinstitute.it
Registered Charity 290647

The largest library
of English books in Italy
Fully equipped Study
& Multimedia Resource Centre
Student Support
& Accommodation

Commercial Correspondence, and 'L'Italia oggi', a current affairs course that covers the Italian political system, political parties, north/south issues, the media and EU/Italy relationships.

Istituto Donatello

Via Galliano 1
50144 Firenze, Italy

Tel: +39 055 354 112
Fax: +39 055 355 686

In a very friendly and familial environment you can learn the Italian language as well as learn about Italian art history, cooking, wood carving and theatre. The institute organises accommodation with other students or Italian families.

Italian Cultural Institute (Instituto di Cultura Italiano)

39 Belgrave Square
London SW1X 8NX, England

Tel: +44 (0) 20 7235 1461

The Italian Cultural Institute has a bookshelf brimming with free leaflets on courses of all sorts in Italy (including Italian cookery, musical culture and fashion, for example).

Italian Embassy

N14 3 Kings Yard
London WIK 4EH
England

Tel: +44 (0) 20 7312 2200
See: www.gap-year.com

There's a list of Italian language schools in Italy on the Italian Embassy website.

Learn Languages Abroad

'Sceilig', Ballymorefinn
Glenasmole
Dublin 24
Republic of Ireland

Tel: +353 1 451 1674
Fax: +353 1 451 1636

For further details see main listing under Multi-languages.

Lorenzo de' Medici

Via Faenza 43
Firenze, Italy

Tel: +39 055 287 143 50123

A 15-minute walk from the Piazza del Duomo up winding streets takes you to this language school in via Faenza. The Lorenzo de' Medici's

centro linguistico italiano dante alighieri
school for foreigners in Florence since 1966

The Italian Language Year course in Florence.

A wonderful way to have an incredible experience in one of the most beautiful city in the world.

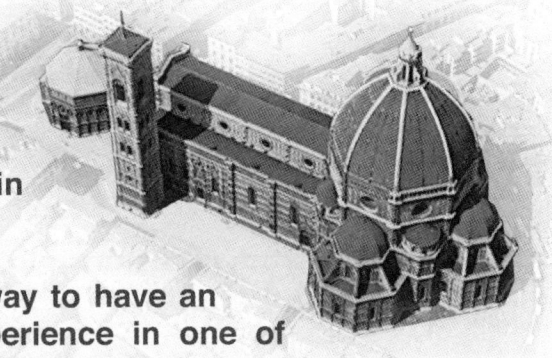

www.clida.it

MACHIAVELLI
Italian Language and Cultural Centre for Foreigners
Piazza S. Spirito 4 - Firenze 50125 - I
tel: (055) 239 6966   fax: (055) 280 800
www.centromachiavelli.it

Italian Language and Culture in Florence

- Group and private tuition at all levels
- Afternoon cultural social program
- Enrolment dates every 2 weeks
- Accommodation booking service
- Additional courses: art history, cooking, music, artisan placements
- Conversation exchanges to meet local university students

intake peaks in spring at about 600 students, with many of them coming from the USA to do cultural courses linked to US university programmes. Its language teaching method is to 'systematically develop the four principal linguistic abilities: speaking, listening, reading and writing.' It also offers the usual combinations of language courses (seven levels) and cultural courses and has a large library in the adjoining San Iacopo di Corbolini church. Also two sparkling professional kitchens where aproned students can be seen making pasta the Italian way.

Scuola Leonardo da Vinci

Via Bufalini 3
50122 Firenze, Italy

Tel: +39 055 261181
Fax: +39 055 294820

Very near the Hospidale and the Piazza del Duomo in the centre of Florence, this happily untidy school offers standard (two to 24 weeks, 20 lessons a week on six ability levels, starting every two weeks, about €570 for four weeks), intensive and intensive plus courses in Italian. Also has schools in Rome (+39 066 889 2513) and Siena (+39 057 724 9097).

Torre di Babele

Via Bixio 74
00185 Roma
Italy

Tel: +39 067008434
Fax: +39 0670497150

Founded in 1984, Torre di Babele is officially authorized by the Italian Ministry of Education and is also a member of ELITE (Excellent Language Institutions Teaching in Europe) and ASILS (Associazione Scuole di Italiano come Lingua Seconda), which guarantee the quality of the teaching and services provided.

Located a few minutes walk from the Colosseum, the school occupies a four-storey building with its own terrace and garden and is easily reached from all parts of the city by public transport.

Courses run all year round and are led by highly-qualified teachers. The school, which is also a teacher training centre, aims to use dynamic teaching methods and stimulating texts in order to incorporate the personal interests of students as well as diverse aspects of Italian life. All courses are taught in small groups (maximum 12), giving students individual attention in a friendly and relaxed atmosphere.

The school offers a rich and interesting extra-curricular programme with guided tours and seminars on art, architecture, cinema, literature, politics, italian cooking and wines. At weekends there are excursions to sites of interest including Pompeii, Naples, Orvieto and Florence.

The school also offers an au-pair service and a free-of-charge interlinguistic exchange with Italian native speakers.

An intensive course (four hours a day for two weeks) costs €310. On request, the school will provide accommodation for students for the duration of their course. Housing is available in private homes, student apartments and hotels. Two weeks' accommodation in a single room costs €207; a double room costs €145. If a student stays for a longer programme there is a refund.

Japanese

A useful resource with information about studying in Japan and many links is **www.aiej.or.jp** run by the association of International Education Japan. Alternatively, the Japan Centre in Piccadilly has an excellent bookshop and is a good starting point for gathering information about Japan. Or if you can get to the Japanese Embassy you can look up a comprehensive guide in its large library called *Japanese Language Institutes* [in Japan]. The library also has material on learning Japanese and stocks Japanese newspapers including the English-language *Japan Times*, which runs information on jobs in Japan. There's also information about studying in Japan on the embassy website, with guidance on the type of visa you will need if you want to teach English as a foreign language or do other types of work there. A student visa normally allows part-time work.

Japan Centre 101-104 **Piccadilly**
London W1V 9LD, England
Tel: +44 (0) 20 7439 8035
www.japancentre.com

Japanese Embassy 101-104 **Piccadilly**
London W1J 7JT, England
Tel: +44 (0) 20 7465 6500
www.embjapan.org.uk

The following organisations offer Japanese language courses:

AFS Community Projects Overseas

Leeming House, Vicar Lane Tel: +44 (0) 113 242 6136
Leeds LS2 7JF, England see: www.gap-year.com

For further details see main listing under Multi-languages.

CERAN Lingua Internationale
Avenue du Chateau 16
B-4900 SPA, Belgium   Tel: +32 8779 1122

For further details see main listing under Multi-languages.

CESA Languages Abroad
CESA House, Pennance Road   Tel: +44 (0) 1209 211 800
Lanner, Cornwall TR16 5TQ   Fax: +44 (0) 1209 211 830
England   see: www.gap-year.com

For further details see main listing under Multi-languages.

Japan Foundation London Language Centre
27 Knightsbridge   Tel: +44 (0) 20 7838 9955
London SW1X 7LY, England   see: www.gap-year.com

The Japan Foundation London Language Centre does not organise courses itself, but it provides a list of Japanese language centres in the UK, for groups, individuals or tailor-made courses at all levels.

SOAS (School of Oriental and African Studies)
SOAS Language Centre, University of London
Thornhaugh Street, , Russell Square   Tel: +44 (0) 20 7898 4888
London WC1H 0XG England   see: www.gap-year.com

The SOAS offers evening classes for beginners. But if you want to study Japanese more seriously there are full-time one-year courses – although these are run in London, once you have successfully passed the three-term course (around £7000!) you are given the chance of a work placement in the Japanese city of Sapporo – famous for holding the 1972 Olympic Games.

Portuguese

Caledonia Languages Abroad
The Clockhouse
Bonnington Mill
72 Newhaven Road   Tel: +44 (0) 131 621 7721/2
Edinburgh EH6 5QG   Fax: +44 (0) 131 621 7723
Scotland   see: www.gap-year.com

For further details see main listing under Multi-languages.

PORTUGUESE

Canning House
2 Belgrave Square
London SW1X 8PJ
England   Tel: +44 (0) 20 7235 2303

The Canning House Education and Cultural Department is, unsurprisingly, in Canning House. It provides information about Latin America, Portugal and Spain. Among various information leaflets (all £4) it publishes a list of universities and language centres offering language courses in these countries, with prices and dates, and another about employment and work experience opportunities for young people in Latin America, Portugal or Spain. This includes organisations and useful contacts for teaching posts, summer jobs, international voluntary work camps and au pair work in each country.

You can use the centre's library, which houses over 60,000 books, to research your trip. Library membership costs £20. Should you be even more interested in matters Portuguese, becoming a member of Canning House (£40 a year, £30 for students) gets you involved in all sorts of London-based Hispanic/Latin events, such as film, poetry readings and talks.

CIAL Centro de Linguas
Av da Republica
41 – 8th Floor
Lisbon 1050-187   Tel: +351 217 940 448
Portugal   Fax: +351 217 960 783

With schools in Lisbon and Faro, CIAL organises courses in Portuguese including group courses with either three hours' tuition (€240 per week) or 6 hours tuition (€432 per week), a two-week teachers training course (€450), individual lessons (€30 per hour) and private groups of two (€45 per hour), as well as specialist courses in Brazilian or African Portuguese.

Accommodation is in private homes at an extra cost of €108 per week, which includes breakfast.

Euro Academy
24 Clarendon Place
London SE13 5EY   Tel: +44 (0) 20 8297 0505
England   Fax: +44 (0) 20 8297 0984

For further details see main listing under Multi-languages.

Russian

AFS Community Projects Overseas
Leeming House, Vicar Lane
Leeds LS2 7JF, England
Tel: +44 (0) 113 242 6136
see: www.gap-year.com

For further details see main listing under Multi-languages.

Caledonia Languages Abroad
The Clockhouse, Bonnington Mill
72 Newhaven Road
Edinburgh EH6 5QG, Scotland
Tel: +44 (0) 131 621 7721/2
Fax: +44 (0) 131 621 7723
see: www.gap-year.com

For further details see main listing under Multi-languages.

CESA Languages Abroad
CESA House
Pennance Road, Lanner
Cornwall TR16 5TQ, England
Tel: +44 (0) 1209 211 800
Fax: +44 (0) 1209 211 830
see: www.gap-year.com

For further details see main listing under Multi-languages.

EF International Languages
74 Roupell Street
London SE1 8SS, England
Tel: +44 (0) 8707 200735
see: www.gap-year.com

For further details see main listing under Multi-languages.

Euro Academy
24 Clarendon Place
London SE13 5E, England
Tel: +44 (0) 20 8297 0505
Fax: +44 (0) 20 8297 0984

For further details see main listing under Multi-languages.

Russian Language Centre of Moscow M V Lomonosov State University
Rooms 3 and 4, Second Floor
Building 9, Khokhlova Str
Moscow State University by M V Lomonosov
Moscow
Russia
Tel: +7 (095) 939-5692
Fax: +7 (095) 939-5692

Founded by Moscow State University in 1990, the Russian Language Centre specialises in providing individual tuition. Courses are held at all levels and range from 12-24 hours per week. The individual nature of the tuition means you can have 'practical' lessons with your tutor, visiting local museums, theatres, exhibitions and cafés.

For a small fee, the centre will provide you with visa support, airport pickup and transfer. Accommodation is either in a hotel on campus (US$16-US$23 per day) or with host families (US$11-US$16 per day). Tuition is billed per 'academic hour' (*ie* 45 minutes), and ranges from US$12 for a one-on-one lesson at a location of your choice to US$4 for a lesson on campus in a group of five to eight. Excursions are arranged to sites of interest including St Petersburg, Irkutsk (lake Baikal) and Petrozavodsk.

The Russian Language Centre
11 Coldbath Square
London EC1R 5HL
England

Tel: +44 (0) 20 7689 5400
see: www.gap-year.com

The Russian Language Centre in London offers a flexible approach to learning this language, with a range of courses available. Courses of any length from two weeks to a year, including summer courses, can be arranged in Russia, at the Grint Educational Centre which used to be part of Pushkin University in Moscow, at Moscow State University or at St Petersburg State University. Accommodation can be arranged for you, either in Soviet-slab type student halls or with a family.

Spanish

Now the UK's second-favourite foreign language at A level, Spanish is the third most widespread language in the world after English and Mandarin Chinese. Over 400 million people in 23 countries are Spanish speakers – Mexico and all central and south America (except Brazil) designate Spanish as their official language. Forms of Spanish can also be heard in Guinea, the Philippines and in Ceuta and Melilla in North Africa. But if you go to a language school inside or outside Spain, you will be learning formal Castilean Spanish – unless you have a burning desire to learn Catalan or Celtic Basque.

Spanish Embassy
Education Department

20 Peel Street
London W8 7PD, England
Tel: +44 (0) 20 7727 2462
Fax: +44 (0) 20 7229 4965

There are a number of universities and schools that, along with the usual lessons in language, offer additional courses to students interested in learning other aspects of the Spanish culture.

SPANISH

Academia de español, Simon Bolivar
Leonidas Plaza 353 y Roca
Quito, Ecuador   Tel: +593 22 504977

The Simon Bolivar Spanish school was established in 1994. The school has grown to become one of the biggest Spanish schools in Ecuador with an average of 40 students per month. Students study there for an average of four weeks. Spanish lessons are offered at the main building in Quito and group lessons are given at centres in the Amazon jungle and on the coast.

Prices are from US$980 to US$1120 for four weeks, including: 20 hours of individual Spanish lessons per week, homestay with private room and three meals, all taxes, airport pickup, unlimited internet usage, all weekdays activities (incl. salsa lessons!) and some teaching materials.

They are located in a quiet residential area of Quito and all host families are located within walking distance of the school.

AFS Community Projects Overseas
Leeming House, Vicar Lane   Tel: +44 (0) 113 242 6136
Leeds LS2 7JF, England   see: www.gap-year.com

For further details see main listing under Multi-languages.

Alliances Abroad
2423 Pennsylvania Avenue NW
Washington DC 20037   Tel: +1 (202) 467 9467
USA   Fax: +1 (202) 467 9460

For further details see main listing under Multi-languages.

Cactus Language
9 Foundry Street, Brighton   Tel: +44 (0)1273 687697
East Sussex BN1 4AT, England   Fax: +44 (0)1273 681412

For further details see main listing under Multi-languages.

Caledonia Languages Abroad
The Clockhouse
Bonnington Mill   Tel: +44 (0) 131 621 7721/2
72 Newhaven Road   Fax: +44 (0) 131 621 7723
Edinburgh EH6 5QG, Scotland   see: www.gap-year.com

For further details see main listing under Multi-languages.

SPANISH

Canning House (HLBC)
2 Belgrave Square
London SW1X 8BJ, England Tel: +44 (0) 20 7235 2303

The Canning House Education and Cultural Department is, unsurprisingly, in Canning House. It provides information about Latin America, Portugal and Spain. Among various information leaflets (all £4) it publishes a list of universities and language centres offering language courses in these countries, with prices and dates, and another about employment and work experience opportunities for young people in Latin America, Portugal or Spain. This includes organisations and useful contacts for teaching posts, summer jobs, international voluntary work camps and au pair work in each country.

You can use the centre's library (with over 60,000 books), to research your trip. Library membership costs £20. Should you be even more interested in matters Spanish, becoming a member of Canning House (£40 a year, £30 for students) gets you involved in all sorts of London-based Hispanic/Latin events, such as film, poetry readings and talks.

CERAN Lingua Internationale
Avenue du Chateau 16
B-4900 SPA, Belgium Tel: +32 8779 1122

For further details see main listing under Multi-languages.

CESA Languages Abroad
CESA House Tel: +44 (0) 1209 211 800
Pennance Road, Lanner Fax: +44 (0) 1209 211 830
Cornwall TR16 5TQ, England see: www.gap-year.com

For further details see main listing under Multi-languages.

CIEE (Council on International Educational Exchange)
52 Poland Street Tel: +44 (0) 20 7478 2020
London W1F 7AB, England Fax: +44 (0) 20 7734 7322

For further details see main listing under Multi-languages.

Cursos Internacionales de la Universidad de Salamanca
Patio de Escuelas Menores
s/n 37008 Salamanca, Spain Tel: +34 923 294 418

The Universidad de Salamanca offers summer courses in subjects like Spanish cookery, Spanish guitar, flamenco dance, and The World of the Bull: a complete guide to Bullfighting.

Don Quijote

PO Box 218, Stoneleigh
Epsom, Surrey KT19 OYF
England

Tel: +44 (0) 20 8786 8081
Fax: +44 (0) 20 8786 8086
see: www.gap-year.com

There are Don Quijote language schools all over Spain as well as in Latin America. In Spain the schools offer courses in Barcelona, Granada, Madrid, Malaga, Salamanca (where you can take a two-week summer course for £389, including staying in a self-catering flat), Seville, Puerto de la Cruz in Tenerife, and Valencia.

In Latin America, which is very popular for gap year Spanish studies (cheaper living costs, better teacher-student ratios and cheap airfares if you're lucky), you can study at a Don Quijote school in Peru and Mexico or other schools in Cuba, Costa Rica, Ecuador or Guatemala. The shortest Don Quijote course in Latin America is two weeks – four hours a day, five days a week in Cuzco for £316 including full-board accommodation. Long courses run for 12-40 weeks. A certificate of attendance is awarded at the end provided you have attended at least 90% of the lessons. Activities and excursions are organised for free time with all courses. Minimum age 18.

Don Quijote also offers Spanish and Activities courses including flamenco dancing, wine tasting, scuba diving, cuisine and literature.

EF International Languages

74 Roupell Street
London SE1 8SS, England

Tel: +44 (0) 8707 200735
see: www.gap-year.com

For further details see main listing under Multi-languages.

Euro Academy

24 Clarendon Place
London SE13 5EY, England

Tel: +44 (0) 20 8297 0505
Fax: +44 (0) 20 8297 0984

For further details see main listing under Multi-languages.

GALA

Woodcote House, 8 Leigh Lane
Farnham, Surrey GU9 8HP, England

Tel: +44 (0) 1252 715 319
Fax: +44 (0) 1252 715 319

GALA acts as an agent for several private language schools in Spain or Latin America. Courses range from two weeks with half-board accommodation in Seville to full nine-month courses. It can also place students in intensive group courses in Ecuador.

Learn Spanish in Spain, Mexico and Peru

- Study in Barcelona, Granada, Madrid, Malaga, Puerto de la Cruz (Tenerife), Salamanca, Seville and Valencia
- Spanish for business, pleasure and exam preparation
- Individual and group tuition
- 2 weeks to 9 months (all levels - all year)
- Host family and student flat accommodation
- Also Cuzco, Peru and Guanajuato, Mexico

Call today for a FREE information pack

Tel: 020 8786 8081
Fax: 020 8786 8086
Email: info@donquijote.co.uk
Website: www.donquijote.org

¿? don Quijote

www.gap-year.com

links to thousands of gap year opportunities

- Work in the UK and abroad
- Sports Courses
- Business skills
- Volunteering
- Travelling
- Languages

A JOHN CATT EDUCATIONAL LIMITED PRODUCT

Hispalingua

General Yague 3
33004 Oviedo
Asturias, Spain   Tel: +34 98 524 3186

Hispalingua in Oviedo offers four- or eight-week summer courses which will leave you with an understanding of the region as well as the Spanish language. It is about three hours by public transport from Bilbao, with its sardine-can Guggenheim museum, and five hours from Madrid.

Instituto Cervantes

326/330 Deansgate
Campfield Avenue Arcade
Manchester M3 4FN, England   Tel: +44 (0) 161 661 4200

Based in Leeds and Manchester, Instituto Cervantes is a Spanish government-funded 'ambassador' for Spanish culture in the UK. Its database provides information about language course locations. Membership of Instituto Cervantes libraries costs £15 and gets you access to Spanish Magazines, Videos, CDs and DVDs.

Instituto Chac-Mool

Privada de la Pradera #108
Colonia Pradera, Cuernavaca
Morelos 62170, Mexico   Tel: +52 (777) 317-1163

Instituto Chac-Mool in Cuernavaca, Mexico offers Spanish immersion courses that include 25 hours of weekly Spanish instruction, culture classes, extra-curricular activities, Sunday excursions, and a homestay with a local Mexican family. It also includes additional hours of optional free private instruction.

All instructors at Instituto Chac-Mool are college graduates, native Spanish speakers, and have been trained for six months in a method that will have students speaking and understanding Spanish quickly. This method emphasizes conversation and stays away from tedious grammar drills. Instituto Chac-Mool is so confident you will learn Spanish quickly that they offer a money back guarantee. Special programmes are also available for medical, business and law enforcement students, contact the institute direct for pricing and more information.

Students of all skill levels can enrol to begin studies any Monday throughout the year and they can study up to 26 weeks. If you mention *The Gap-Year Guidebook*, you will receive discounts on programmes

visit: www.gap-year.com

of four weeks or longer. A four-week programme costs US$1100, (for each additional four-week programme add US$1000). This includes tuition and housing with three daily meals. There is a slightly higher charge if you prefer a private room or study during June and July.

Learn Languages Abroad
'Sceilig', Ballymorefinn
Glenasmole, Dublin 24
Ireland

Tel: +353 1 451 1674
Fax: +353 1 451 1636

For further details see main listing under Multi-languages.

Spanish Study Holidays
67 Ashby Road, Loughborough
Leicestershire LE11 3AA, England

Fax: +44 (0) 1509 260037
Tel: +44 (0) 1509 211 612

Spanish Study Holidays was founded in 1991 by a team of language teachers and offers Spanish courses throughout Spain and central and south America. If you are 16 or over it can put you on courses lasting from one week to nine months, with 12-30 Spanish lessons a week. Courses are run at all levels and weekend excursions are arranged. Accommodation is organised for you in flats, student rooms or with a host family. In Spain, for example, a two-week intensive course in Madrid (20 lessons per week) in self-catering accommodation costs £425; if you stay in a single room, half board with a host family, the course costs £522. The 12-week version of the course costs £1787 (self-catering) or £2380 (host family). Other Spanish course centres include Salamanca, Granada, Seville, Malaga, Madrid, Alicante and Barcelona. Across the Atlantic, courses are run in Bolivia, Costa Rica, Cuba, Ecuador, Guatemala, Mexico and Peru. For example a two-week course in Guatemala (20 lessons per week) costs £349, including tuition and full board with a host family.

Learning while you earn

Now that many gap year students need to save to pay university tuition or perhaps even top-up fees, there is growing demand for gap year courses that can finance themselves. You could be lucky enough to get a place on a programme that offers you free language tuition in exchange for you doing some TEFL work. Alternatively, you may find that you can do a paid job alongside your course or after it has finished. It may be easier to get to know the place you go to and then look for local work yourself, or to earn your money before you leave the UK.

Learning Abroad **LEARN WHILE YOU EARN**

If you're in any country in the European Union, you won't need a work permit. So in Europe, unlike some other parts of the world, it's easier to pick up legitimate work when you get there. But each country will have its own paperwork requirements, so check with the relevant embassy before you go.

Language schools we talked to suggested that you can 'get your feet on the ground' in Europe while you are learning the language, make local contacts, study the local press, and try for a job afterwards – even if it's only bar work or a simple job that doesn't involve being fluent. Don't forget to take a folder of useful documents with you, like copies of your CV, qualifications and references. (See also *Chapter 1: Working abroad*.)

Some language schools will help you find work after your course – they may even have a database. Check this before you book.

EF International Languages

74 Roupell Street
London SE1 8SS
England

Tel: +44 (0) 8707 200735
see: www.gap-year.com

Learn a language, teach English and travel to two fantastic destinations! Choose from Europe (Nice, and Barcelona) South America (Quito, Chile, Mexico, Columbia) China (Various locations), Russia (St Petersburg, Moscow) and North Africa (Casablanca). This ten-month programme starts with a TEFL training course in the UK, is followed by a three-month language course at one of EF's International Languages Schools, and finishes with a six-month placement as an English Teacher in a second destination. Prices start at £5400 and include TEFL course, language programme, accommodation, flights and living allowance on the teaching placement.

En Famille Overseas

4 St Helena Road
Colchester CO3 3BA, England

Tel: +44 (0)1206 546 741
Fax: + 44 (0) 1206 546 740

En Famille Overseas arranges for you to stay with a family in France or Spain as a paying guest. You can attend a suitable language course nearby or have private coaching from your host. Prices start from £200 a week for full board accommodation in Spain, including excursion expenses. Tuition costs are extra – around £12 an hour. You don't have to have language tuition at all: you can use your 'homestay' as a springboard for finding a local job and you can stay with a family for a week to a year, with the board and lodging costs negotiable if you stay more than a month. En Famille usually needs about a month's notice to fix it up.

visit: www.gap-year.com

Interspeak

Stretton Lower Hall, Stretton
South Cheshire SY14 7HS, England   Tel: +44 (0) 1829 250 641

Interspeak organises unpaid work placements in France, Germany and Spain from between one and six months. You pay a registration fee of £80 up front, then a flat fee of £300 for arranging the placement. Interspeak will also organise a family for you to stay with, although you can make your own plans if you prefer. Placement jobs vary widely, but Interspeak says it can find placements in banking, law, marketing, media, hotels and restaurants – citing one student working in a fashion photography studio in France and another for a radio station in Spain.

Smallpeice Trust

74 Upper Holly Walk   Tel: +44 (0) 1926 333200
Leamington Spa   Fax: +44 (0) 1926 333202
Warwickshire CV32 4JL, England   see: www.gap-year.com

The **Smallpeice Engineering Gap Year** provides a unique combination of study, language tuition, travel and work placements in Europe. The importance of languages to engineering can be seen in the growth in the number of degrees that have a language module.

Students will develop their foreign language skills at a school in France, Germany or Spain. To provide the scope of work placements commensurate with this level of course, Smallpeice has established wide-ranging industrial contacts across nine European countries.

The entire programme is arranged and subsidised through The Trust, and starts in September, finishing the following May. The cost per student is £4950, payable in two instalments, which includes all tuition, accommodation, placements, return travel *etc*. No other opportunity offers such a firm grounding in engineering, together with personal development, to put students 'head and shoulders' above their peers at university.

Sport

There are sports courses for all types at all levels, from scuba diving for beginners to advanced ski instructor qualification courses, in pretty much every country in the world. Of course if you manage to get qualified as an instructor you may be able to use it to get a job for the rest of your gap year.

Make sure the course offers the qualifications that will be useful to you and check that the instructors are properly qualified. Most important is to make sure that you have the necessary insurance – take a look at

Learning Abroad **SPORT**

any of the sport websites and you'll find out that accidents do happen (**www.bungeezone.com** is particularly scary) and if you slip whilst up a mountain injuries tend to be a bit more serious – and expensive – than a sprained ankle.

That said, learning a sport abroad is a great way to meet new people, experience the local culture and have a really energetic, fun gap year.

African Sport Experience

PO Box 58, Teignmouth
Devon TQ14 8XW
England

Tel: +44 (0) 870 241 6976
Fax: +44 (0) 1404 811404
see: www.gap-year.com

African Sport Experience organises action sports holidays in South Africa on the Cape Coast. During the four weeks you will receive expert tuition in your favourite sport: golf, scuba diving or even fishing are on offer.

If you choose fishing you could find yourself landing a marlin or tunny while deep sea fishing, fishing off the rocks, in the surf and fly fishing – all with an experienced supervisor who will show you how to collect bait and prepare your catch for eating. You will also get instruction on conservation issues and local species as well as participating in fish tagging for conservation studies.

There is also a vast range of other activities to try: dune boarding down what are reputed to be the highest sand dunes in the world, bogey boarding in the waves, kayaking, hiking through indigenous forests and along coastal trails, horse riding on the beach, mountain biking, 4 x 4 driving, water skiing, parachute jumping or simply a few games of tennis.

Cruising through life

I spent my gap year achieving my Yachtmaster certificate on the winter PCST course at UKSA. Then having got my qualifications, I worked for Sunsail on the beautiful South coast of Cephalonia in Spartia. For the whole summer there I worked as a cruising instructor teaching three-day flotilla courses.

Having a gap year was one of the best decisions I made and I would recommend such an experience to everyone a chance not to be missed!

Emily, who's now at Newcastle Uni

Ale Corte

6A Dale Grove
London N12 8EA, England   Tel: +44 (0) 20 86329829

These clinics are for snowboarders of all levels. They are run by Ale Corte, an experienced snowboarder and instructor who has trained the Argentine National Ski Team and helped compile the techniques and standards used to examine snowboard instructors.

At his clinics you can improve a particular aspect of your technique or progress towards instructor level: you can't actually take the instructor qualifications but you can build up your experience ready for a BASI instructor course or similar.

By using personalised coaching, target building and consistent feedback, the aim is to develop a set of skills, which the snowboarder can use with confidence. The instructor will complete specially prepared tuition appraisal forms and produce video analysis of progress.

Clinics: one or two weeks for a minimum of four people. The package includes accommodation half board, six day lift pass, transfers from airport, six hours day clinic, material assessment and video correction. Price: £850 pp per week. Dates to be confirmed.

Personal tuition: £1500 pp per week.

BASI (British Association of Snowsport Instructors)

Glenmore, Aviemore
Invernesshire PH22 1QU, Scotland
Tel: +44 (0) 1479 861 717
Fax: +44 (0) 1479 861 718

BASI runs a full-time ten-week course for potential instructors (you need to be an experienced skier) from January to April for £4000+. These courses are held in Switzerland, Italy, Andorra and (at a slightly higher price) America. At the end there is an assessment and, if successful, you gain an instructor's licence. BASI advises you to book well ahead.

Bear Creek Outdoor Centre

R R#3 Campbell's Bay
Quebec J0X 1K0
Canada
Tel: +1 819 453 2127
Fax: +1 819 453 2128
see: www.gap-year.com

Bear Creek Outdoor Centre near Canada's national capital of Ottawa offers a ten-week summer programme in outdoor adventure leadership aimed at all levels. You don't need any experience to join the programme, but you must be at least 18 years of age, be able to swim and consider yourself to be in good health.

Whether you choose to work in the growing field of outdoor adventure or just want the skills and knowledge to go out and tackle your own adventure dreams, the training you will receive on this course will give you the confidence and credentials you need.

Nationally (Canadian) and internationally recognised certifications are a major part of the programme and range from kayak instructor to swiftwater rescue technician. Skills are taught in mountain bike guiding, raft guiding, riverboarding, provisioning and backcountry cooking, navigation, group dynamics and leadership.

The team of instructors is highly experienced and you're likely to find yourself being taught to kayak by members of the Canadian Whitewater freestyle team!

The course costs CAN$8000 (about £3700), which includes instruction and certification, transportation from Ottawa, room and board, equipment, accommodation on field trips and personal safety equipment. The price does not include travel to and from Ottawa.

Coral Cay Conservation

The Tower, 13th Floor
125 High Street, Colliers Wood
London SW19 2JG, England

Tel: +44 (0) 870 750 0668
Fax: +44 (0) 870 750 0667
see: www.gap-year.com

Coral Cay Conservation (CCC) is a not-for-profit organisation that sends teams of volunteers to survey some of the world's most endangered coral reefs and tropical forests. Working at the invitation of and in partnership with government bodies, NGOs, local communities and education groups, CCC volunteers have been responsible for the establishment of World Heritage Sites, marine reserves and wildlife sanctuaries.

CCC currently has expeditions in Fiji, the Philippines, Malaysia and Honduras. For the ultimate experience, volunteers can split their time between a marine expedition and a forest expedition: in the Philippines volunteers can dive the fabled Coral Triangle, one of the world's most biodiverse areas of coral reef, and then trek the amazing Negros Rainforest – home to hundreds of endemic mammals, birds and insects!

Although volunteers require no scientific background, applicants must be 16 or over, fit, enthusiastic and hardworking. Combining marine and terrestrial scientific research with international travel and cultural exploration, CCC offers its volunteers a unique career-building opportunity and a once in a lifetime experience. Marine expeditions start at £700 and rainforest expeditions start at £350. Scuba training up to PADI Rescue Diver is provided on location. Costs include Skills Development Training, accommodation and food. Flights not included.

Don Quijote

PO Box 218
Stoneleigh, Epsom
Surrey KT19 OYF, England

Tel: +44 (0) 20 8786 8081
Fax: +44 (0) 20 8786 8086
see: www.gap-year.com

Fancy diving into the Spanish language and into the clear blue Atlantic Ocean? Don Quijote offers a Spanish language/scuba diving package (Beginner or Advanced) in Tenerife.

The Beginners course costs €618 and includes: two weeks intensive Spanish course (four hours a day); five day theory course (two-and-a-half hours a day); two days immersion in swimming pool (four hours a day); three days sea immersion (four hours daily); one day final test with immersion; full insurance against accidents; all equipment; diploma and PADI certificate of Open Water Diving.

The Advanced course costs €588 and includes two weeks intensive Spanish (four hours per day); one deep immersion; one deep immersion from boat; one underwater orientation immersion; one night immersion; one immersion at shipwreck; full insurance against accidents; all equipment; diploma and advanced PADI certificate.

Learning Abroad   **SPORT**

Flying Fish

25 Union Road, Cowes   Tel: +44 (0) 1983 280 641
Isle of Wight PO31 7TW, England   see: www.gap-year.com

Flying Fish runs sailing, surfing, windsurfing and diving gap programmes which lead to professional qualifications and jobs in the sun. For example you can join professional dive training in Australia; go on a work placement in the Mediterranean sailing industry; and do international yacht training in the UK and Australia.

Qualifications include PADI dive awards and RYA Windsurfing Yachting and Dinghy Sailing certificates. A comprehensive training guide is available. Tel (Australia): +61 (0) 2 99 76 6714.

Greenforce

11-15 Betterton Street   Tel: 0870 770 2646 / +44 (0) 20 7470 8888
Covent Garden   Fax: 0870 7702647 / +44 (0) 207 470 8889
London WC2H 9BP, England   see: www.gap-year.com

If you're concerned about the environment and want to do your bit to help preserve what is left of biodiversity on planet Earth then why not become a volunteer researcher on a Greenforce expedition? Greenforce runs a series of ten-week marine and terrestrial expeditions around the world, all of which are based on wildlife conservation. No previous experience is necessary as we train all volunteers from scratch, and marine volunteers get free diver training.

Choose from tracking large mammals in Zambia, investigating the tree canopy of the Amazon rainforest, or diving the coral reefs of the Bahamas, Fiji or Borneo. Whichever project you join you will find a varied and fascinating programme which has a direct impact on conservation in that country. Expedition life can be a challenge – be prepared to live a spartan existence, and to pull your weight in a small, well-organised team. Check out the website for the latest projects.

Neptune's Diving & Sports Center

Km 14.5, Miguel de la Madrid
Manzanillo, Colima,   Tel: +11 52 314 334 3001
28850 Mexico   Fax: +11 52 314 334 3002

Neptune's Diving and Sports Center's internship programme is an intensive programme encompassing classroom, confined water, open water and hands-on learning experience. It is geared to take the novice diver and, with training and actual working experience, turn them into diving professionals. Unlike many other programmes Neptune's allows you to train in two distinct environments: Manzanillo and either Cancun or Cozumel (depending on which course dates you

# Time Out in 2003?

Canada
17th January - 19th March 2003

Travel to the Rockies and qualify as a ski/snowboard instructor

- Powder, free style, terrain park, moguls & race training.
- 6 International accreditations.
- Stay in Kananaskis Mountain Lodge, venue for the 2002 G8 Summit.

AWESOME POWDER

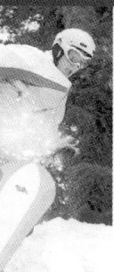

Argentina
29th July - 27th September 2003

SKI & SNOWBOARD Instructor Programme

- Powder, free style, terrain park, moguls & racing training.

Beautiful Argentina & Chile

JUNGLE LEADER
September / October 2003

Travel to Indonesia and qualify as a Jungle Expedition Leader, an open water diver and a day skipper.

- PADI open water diver
- Off shore sailing
- Jungle nights in hammocks
- Natural plunge pools & open fires

IMPROVE YOU CV WITH SKILLS FOR LIFE... NETWORK & MEET NEW EXCITING PEOPLE...

Peak Leaders UK Limited,
Mansfield, Strathmiglo, Fife KY14 7QE
Tel: 01337 860079
www.peakleaders.co.uk

Learning Abroad   **SPORT**

choose). Additionally you will earn both the PADI and NAUI Divemaster qualifications. At each level, you will be building on and perfecting the skills you have learned in the previous programme. Interns must be at least 18 years old, in good physical condition and know how to swim. You must have attended a basic first aid and CPR course (or it can be provided at Neptune's at an additional cost). You will also need to provide a medical clearance for diving dated no more than 30 days prior to attending the course.

The programme is based on two to eight week sessions, and courses are taught in English and Spanish. Beginning with the open water programme, interns are trained in the basic and fundamental aspects of Scuba Diving. The advanced diver programme allows you to build on the initial training, and further experience and master other diving opportunities such as night, deep, wreck, navigation as well as other specialities.

The rescue diver programme helps you master the skills required to perform open water rescues, both on the surface and under water. You will be given training in first aid and CPR, and underwater search and recovery. You then move on to the Divemaster level, the first professional level. At Neptune's you have the added benefit of learning and working in an actual dive shop and you will assist and accompany the staff on dives geared for actual customers. What you learn in the classroom will be practiced in real life. You will also have the opportunity to complete or surpass the minimum number of open water dives required for certification as a Divemaster.

Once you've completed the Divemaster programme you travel to Cancun, Mexico for the Instructor Development Course run at a PADI CDC facility. The IDC is scheduled to correspond with the Instructor Exam which is a requirement for PADI Instructor candidates. Neptune's also conduct the NAUI Instructor Certification Course.

You can start the course at any stage depending on your experience. The complete eight-week course which takes complete novices to Divemaster costs $1600; the nine-day instructor course is an extra $1200. Fees include course training, cost of boat trips, scuba tanks, air fills, weight belts, weights, all the dives required to meet your Divemaster requirements (most interns dive a minimum of 65 dives during the programme) and accommodation.

Nonstopski
1A Bickersteth Road
London SW17 9SE
England

Tel: +44 (0) 20 8772 7852
Fax: +44 (0) 20 8772 7852
see: www.gap-year.com

Nonstopski offers four and 11-week ski and snowboard instructor courses in Fernie, Canada's 'Powder Capital.' Students receive expert tuition from professional coaches in preparation for their international-

Watersports Travel and Instructor Training Courses in South East Asia

Professional Watersports Training Courses are the key to your development as an International Watersports Instructor.

Train on the stunning island of Borocay, enjoying the amazing conditions and high quality tuition. Discover the colourful local culture, making life long friends in a relaxed environment.

Then let us help you get the job of your dreams, working your way around the world.

Diving   Windsurfing   Kitesurfing   Travelling

Agent for ATOL holders

www.ocean-republic.com
T: +44 (0) 1202 469132

Ski & Snowboard
Instructor Training
Queenstown
New Zealand

Ever thought about being a ski or snowboard instructor? Why not come and do just that in Queenstown, New Zealand

11 week program (July—Sept), living in Queenstown, New Zealand, Accommodation, lift pass, skiing 7 days a week, training 3 days a week from New Zealand Ski Examiners, Avalanche awareness course, Heli-Ski/Board trip, evening sessions, video analysis, full exam preparation and the NZSIA (recognized around the world) qualification exam to finish.

For more info
www.skiinstructortraining.co.nz
www.snowboardinstructortraining.co.nz

email
info@skiinstructortraining.co.nz
info@snowboardinstructortraining.co.nz

ly recognised ski (CSIA) and/or snowboard (CASI) instructor qualifications. The course also includes tuition in mountain safety and avalanche awareness, survival skills (a night spent in an igloo up the mountain!) winter first aid, foreign languages, photography, TEFL and cookery.

Weekend trips are arranged to Canadian cities, National Parks, hot springs, cat skiing, other ski resorts and the USA. All abilities are welcome and numbers are limited so early booking is advisable. Situated in the heart of the Rockies, Fernie is the fourth largest ski resort in Canada, rated third in the Best Ski Destinations (CNN.com) and has one of the highest average snowfalls (875cm) in North America providing phenomenal ski conditions.

Ocean Republic

1 The Watertowe, Palmerston Road Tel: +44 (0) 1202 469132
Bournemouth BH1 4HT, England   see: www.gap-year.com

Ocean Republic specialises in training watersports enthusiasts who wish to gain professional qualifications and work in the watersports industry. Instructor qualifications are offered in Diving (PADI), Windsurfing (RYA) and Kitesurfing (IKO and BKSA). The training takes place at their 'intensive training base' on a tropical island in the Philippines, and is run by UK trainers. Courses vary in length from four to 12 weeks depending on the candidates previous experience in a particular discipline. Work experience is available along with Ocean Republic's 'instructor placement programme'.

As well as training candidates, Ocean Republic can organise all-inclusive holidays to their watersports locations in the Philippines with all budgets catered for.

Planet Subzero   Tel: +44 (0) 7905 097 087

Planet Subzero claims to offer a realistic way for gap year students to do a winter season, making sure the experience is more than simply a holiday – their programme includes loads of added extras such as the opportunity to attend avalanche courses, heli-skiing or getting involved in the ski/snowboard competition circuit amongst other things. They cater for everyone from complete beginners through to people who have done several seasons before and provide help, guidance and support at the resorts. They will sometimes even help gappers find work locally if they need it.

It is an opportunity for you to live away from home, immersed in another culture, improve your skiing/boarding, as well as your language skills – the all-round gap year experience. Prices range from £650 for a month to £2200-£2500 for the season (depending on the resort). The company be contacted in France on +33 (0) 679 178 578.

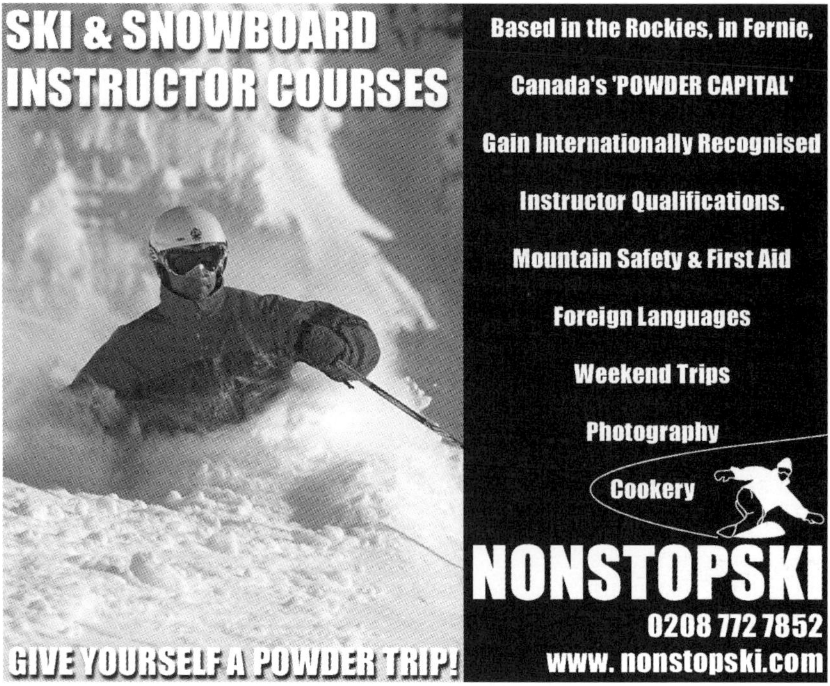

SKI & SNOWBOARD INSTRUCTOR COURSES

Based in the Rockies, in Fernie, Canada's 'POWDER CAPITAL'

Gain Internationally Recognised Instructor Qualifications.

Mountain Safety & First Aid

Foreign Languages

Weekend Trips

Photography

Cookery

NONSTOPSKI
0208 772 7852
www.nonstopski.com

GIVE YOURSELF A POWDER TRIP!

WINTER 2003

BECOME A SKI & OR SNOWBOARD INSTRUCTOR

SKI-EXP-AIR program is aimed first of all to form great skiers and snowboarders.

SKI EXP AIR

www.ski-exp-air.com   e-mail: exp_air@hotmail.com

Learning Abroad **SPORT**

Peak Leaders
Mansfield, Strathmiglo Tel: +44 (0) 1337 860 079
Fife KY14 7QE, Scotland see: www.gap-year.com

Peak Leaders UK is a family run business dedicated to the delivery of quality gap year and time out programmes. Founded in 1998 and incorporated in 2000, the company is based in Scotland.

Winter programmes in Canada, Argentina and New Zealand include ski and snowboard instructor training, mountain safety, first aid, avalanche awareness, language, management and leadership. Summer programmes in Indonesia and Argentina include expedition leadership, mountain and jungle training, diving, sailing, trekking, palaeontology, mountain biking and project work.

Groups are small and programmes are highly structured, leading to certified awards and skills for life. Emphasis is on safety, enjoyment and high grade training. Peak Leaders work with the Year Out Group and promote the FCO 'know before you go' scheme.

Quest Overseas
32 Clapham Mansions Tel: +44 (0) 20 8673 3313
Nightingale Lane Fax: +44 (0) 20 8673 7623
London SW4 9AQ, England see: www.gap-year.com

Quest Overseas runs conservation-plus-expedition projects in Africa as well as its projects in South America. Departures are in December, January, February, March and April. Quest Africa 2003 combines six weeks of community and conservation work (either restoring primary schools in Tanzania or ecological survey work and trail construction on the Lubombo Project in Swaziland) with a six-week expedition through Mozambique, South Africa, Botswana and Zambia. Quest Overseas also offers the PADI Open Water dive course where it is applicable to your chosen programme. *For full details, see their listing in Chapter 2: Volunteering Abroad.*

Ski Exp Air
770 Colonel Jones Tel: +418 654 9071
Ste Foy, Quebec City Fax: +418 654 9071
Canada see: www.gap-year.com

Ski Exp Air courses are designed not only to get you a ski/snowboard instructor qualification, but also to give you the opportunity to improve your French and to get a real taste of Canada. You will be coached in groups of eight or less, and will be on the slopes for least five days a week. Each day students get three hours of instruction and another three hours of training and coaching.

The course begins by preparing and entering you for Level I CSIA (Canadian Ski Instructor Alliance) certification. You will also attend a

SPORT

Learning Abroad

CPR (Cardio-Pulmonary Resuscitation) and first aid course. Upon successful completion of Level I ski or snowboard certification, you can pursue a second certification in the following: Level I ski instructor (CSIA); Level I snowboard instructor (CASI); Level II ski instructor (CSIA); Level II snowboard instructor (CSIA); Level I coaching certificate (CSCF). Having passed your selected discipline, you become a 'ski professional' and you are free to progress even further to more specialised qualifications such as Racing Coach II or Ski Level III.

The company's work experience programme at Stoneham Ski and Snowboard Resort gives you the opportunity to learn about the different aspects of running a winter tourism resort including ski slope maintenance, customer reception, rental shop operations, mountain guiding, wilderness survival and first aid.

All members of staff are fluent in English, so you will be welcomed and taught in English or French during the first few weeks, after which the day-to-day conversation will be more and more in French. There are

AFRICAN SPORT
EXPERIENCE

- ♦ **Golfing with a professional**
- ♦ **Diving - basic and advanced tuition**
- ♦ **Fishing - deep sea, river, rock & surf**

Add to the above:
Kayaking—Boogey Boarding—Water Skiing
Parachuting—Dune Boarding—Power Kiting
Horseriding—Mountain Biking—Coastal Hiking
Deep Sea Cruises—4 x 4 Driving—Tennis
and more

A Sporting Adventure on South Africa's Sunshine Coast

Tel/Fax: 0870 241-6976 www.SportAfrica.org
E-mail: info@SportAfrica.org

Learning Abroad **SPORT**

also weekly French conversation sessions to help you improve your language skills. At weekends there is a variety of cultural and winter sport activities arranged for you, including ice fishing, the Québec Winter Carnival, night skiing, winter wilderness survival/camping and rubber raft sliding at the Village des Sports.

The standard course lasts three months and costs about £5700, excluding insurance and equipment but including flights, full board accommodation, French tutoring, weekend excursions, ski instruction, ski passes, ski examination fees and a year's CSIA or CASI membership fee when you pass your exams.

Ski le Gap
220 Wheeler, Mont-Tremblant
Quebec J8E 1V3, Canada
Tel: +1 819 429 6599
Fax: +1 819 425 7074

Skilegap offers ski and snowboard instructor training courses based at the popular Canadian resort of Tremblant. There are two courses to choose from: the three-month ski/snowboard instructor course and the intensive four-week 'minigap' programme.

The three-month programme prepares you for the level I qualification through tuition in small groups, videos, clinics, seminars, lectures and individualised daily goals. The four-week Minigap is an opportunity to get your instructors qualification at very beginning of season. Be warned – this course is not for beginners! Minigap 2003 will run from November 25 to December 23 and costs £600 including half board accommodation, lift pass, ski/snowboard instruction, Level I ski/snowboard exam fee, transport to and from Dorval airport. The fee does not include airfare, personal medical insurance or equipment.

In your free time you can take part in the activities and trips arranged by Skilegap – including visits to Quebec, Ottawa and Montréal, and an 'outdoor experience' programme which involves cross-country skiing and igloo building. Some students stay on to teach for the Tremblant Ecole de Neige.

Surfing Queensland
13 Durham Cres, Buderim
Qld 4556, Australia
Tel: + 61 075445 4870

Surfing Queensland is affiliated with Surfing Australia nationally and the International Surfing Association, recognised by local, state and national levels of government. They offer education in surf safety/surf awareness, surf instruction for beginners/elite, coaching accreditation, event management amateur/professional and officiating of the same. Their courses are under the NCAS accreditation system. They also employ qualified staff for specific events.

visit: www.gap-year.com

Taupo Bungee

202 Spa Road, PO Box 919
Taupo, New Zealand

Tel: +64 7 377 1135
Fax: +64 7 3771136

To become a Jumpmaster you must be working on a registered bungee site. Normally you start out as a member of the site crew in the office and as you learn you progress up the ladder. If everything goes well, after about 12 months you become a Jump officer helping the Jumpmaster on the platform and learning the ropes, so to speak. After a further six months you get to complete an exam and hopefully you can then be registered as a Jumpmaster. Then the world is your oyster! Most countries recognise the New Zealand registration.

The Ski Instructor Training Co & The Snowboard Instructor Training Co

Queenstown, Otago, New Zealand

see: www.gap-year.com

This is an exciting new venture to train for your ski or snowboard instructor qualification with the New Zealand Snow Sports Instructors Alliance Stage 1 ski or snowboard instructors exam, which is ideal for anyone wanting to break into the ski industry. The 11-week programme, based out of Queenstown, costs around £3200 including accommodation, lift passes, mountain transport, three days a week on-snow training from a New Zealand examiner, evening sessions with the use of video analysis, Heliski/board trip, an off-piste awareness course and the NZSIA Stage One Exam. The organisers are well-qualified – in fact they're examiners for the NZSIA (New Zealand Snow Sports Instructors Alliance). You will need full medical and snow sports insurance cover to be allowed to participate.

UKSA (United Kingdom Sailing Academy)

West Cowes
Isle of Wight
England

Tel: +44 (0) 1983 203014
Fax: +44 (0) 1983 295938
see: www.gap-year.com

The United Kingdom Sailing Academy (UKSA), based in Cowes, trains watersport instructors, professional skippers and crews for yachts. The Academy has modern facilities, including residential accommodation and a fleet of over 300 craft.

Gap year students train with UKSA for six months, in Cowes and Barbados, to become multi-qualified water sport instructors. If you have a yachting background you can complete the Professional Crew and Skipper Training (PCST) course. The comprehensive training is designed to finish just as the major water activity holiday companies are recruiting staff for their summer seasons. The UKSA careers department helps their 'gap graduates' find employment and around 600 companies worldwide recruit directly from them.

Arts & Culture

Attracted to art? Moved by music? Hooked on history? There are some mouth-watering courses across Europe for students interested in art, literature, history and other cultural pleasures.

Art

Soak up the atmosphere while getting your portfolio up to scratch.

Accademia del Giglio
Via Ghibellina 116
50122 Firenze
Italy

Tel: +39 055 23 02 467
Fax: +39 055 23 02 467

This quiet, small school, several floors up in a building close to the Bargello, takes about 30 students, taught in small classes. Other classes include fresco painting, Italian for business and Italian for hospitality and tourism.

Accademia Italiana
Piazza Pitti 15
50125 Firenze
Italy

Tel: +39 055 284 616
Fax: +39 055 284486

An international design, art and language school, the Accademia Italiana puts on summer (one to three months) language courses as well as full-year and longer academic and Masters courses in fashion design, fashion illustration, textile design, interior and furniture design, drawing and painting and others.

Art Under One Roof
Via dei Pandolfini, 46r
50122 Florence
Italy

Tel: +39 055 2478867
Fax: +39 055 2478867

Art Under One Roof is an independent, undergraduate level art institute located in the centre of Renaissance Florence, which specialises in study abroad foundation art programmes. The school follows the North American/English educational structure in an Italian context.

The school has a strict limited enrolment policy of 35 per session and consequently educates its students on a very personal level.

Programmes are bilingual however, from the second month lessons gradually move from primarily English to primarily Italian. Art history is the only course taught exclusively in English. Tuition per term for 2003 is set at €3200.

Challenge Educational Services

101 Lorna Road
Hove
East Sussex BN3 3EL
England

Tel: +44 (0) 1273 220261
Fax: +44 (0) 1273 220376
see: www.gap-year.com

Challenge Educational Services organises **French** courses in collaboration with several French universities (including the world famous Sorbonne University in Paris) and at private language institutes.

Courses are offered at the universities of the Sorbonne, Angers, Nantes, Poitiers and Grenoble and throughout the year at private language schools in Paris, Bordeaux and Antibes. You can combine learning French with French gastronomy or fashion.

Challenge also organises a 12-week programme in Paris, combining language tuition with classes at a French Art school. Ideal for those with a reasonable standard of French and at least GCSE Art.

Tuition is combined with friendly and welcoming host family accommodation. They are also happy to tailor-make courses to suit your individual requirements.

Euro Academy

24 Clarendon Place
London SE13 5EY
England

Tel: +44 (0) 20 8297 0505
Fax: +44 (0) 20 8297 0984

Though mainly a language school, Euro Academy offers many specialist courses which you can combine with language studies such as art in Florence, with use of their 800sqm art studio for budding da Vincis.

Il Sillabo

Via Alberti, 31
52027 San Giovanni
Valdarno (AR)
Italy

Tel: + 39 055 9123238
Fax: + 39 055 942439

See Il Sillabo's listing in the languages (Italian) section.

Learning Abroad   **ARTS & CULTURE**

Steve Outram Crete Photo Tours & Workshops
D Katsifarakis Street
Galatas
Chania 73100
Crete, Greece

Tel: +30 28210 32201
Fax: +30 28210 32201

Professional photographer Steve Outram uses his local knowledge of Zanzibar, Lesvos and Western Crete to show you how to make the most of photographic opportunities and develop your skill as a photographer. These are definitely hands-on workshops and you can expect to spend your days walking a fair distance to get the perfect shot.

You can choose from: Zanzibar (13-26 Sept 2003, price £2355), with exotic Sultan's palaces, Dhow shipbuilders, spice plantations and the mysteries of Stone Town; Lesvos (10-24 Oct, price £1920), a picturesque island in the Aegean Sea, birthplace of the 7th century BC poet Sappho, full of cobblestone streets, Ottoman architecture, Venetian fortresses, ancient monasteries and miraculous icons; or Crete (6-14 May or 30 Sept-8 Oct, price £1245), with its labyrinth of Venetian and Turkish alleyways, Minoan burial chambers, even a carpet weaver at work on his 400-year-old family loom, traditional villages untouched by time, surrounded by the rugged White Mountains, Turkish fountains, bathhouses... the list of photo opportunities is endless.

Note that prices don't include flights or insurance or equipment.

Culture

Culture courses are often included alongside language courses but can be taken on their own by non-linguist gappers.

AFS Community Projects Overseas
Leeming House
Vicar Lane
Leeds LS2 7JF
England

Tel: +44 (0) 113 242 6136
see: www.gap-year.com

The AFS Schools Programme (for ages 15-18) offers the opportunity to live abroad for a year, and learn a language through immersion in the way of life. You can choose from 54 countries across South America, Asia and Europe, including Argentina, Paraguay, Venezuela, Hong Kong, Indonesia, Italy, Germany and the USA.

Students live with a volunteer host family as a member of that family, attend a local school, and become involved in the life of their new

visit: www.gap-year.com

community. Programmes depart in the summer. What's great about this course is that you learn the language as you go rather than attending classes; AFS reckon you can be a complete beginner when you set off and be really quite fluent in six months.

You will be provided with language kits as part of your preparation as well as taking part in orientation activities before you go. Once abroad you will be well supported by local volunteers.

The programme cost is £3950, which they help you to fundraise. AFS also offers full or part scholarship opportunities to deserving candidates through their International Diversity Scholarship Fund.

Art History Abroad (AHA)
26 De Laune Street
London SE17 3UU
England

Tel: +44 (0) 20 7582 8082
see: www.gap-year.com

Art History Abroad (AHA) offers a variety of courses of different lengths. The idea is that you study great art and architecture first hand. You are taught on site in groups of eight (overall party size 24) by

---

STUDY OVERSEAS
0113 242 6136
for the real intercultural learning experience

AFS, formed in 1947, is the world's leading cultural exchange organisation, represented in 54 countries, and one of the world's largest volunteer based organisations. Next year, over 10,000 young people will join an AFS programme, learn a different language and experience another country's culture by studying in high school and living in a local community.

AFS Year Abroad Programme For High School Students
- Departing in August 2003, returning July 2004
- Living with a volunteer host family in the community
- Attending the local high school full-time for one academic year
- Flights, insurance, preparation and local support provided
- For full time students aged 15-18 with school references and enthusiasm for the challenge
- Proficiency in another language is not a requirement
- Must be able to contribute towards cost of placement

Venezuela •Japan • Hong Kong • Indonesia • France • Italy • USA
and more...

AFS UK /Leeming House / Vicar Lane / Leeds LS2 7JF
Email: info-unitedkingdom@afs.org   Registered Charity 284174

www.afsuk.org

experts in their field. AHA's six-week gap year course now runs twice a year: in spring (late January to mid-March) and autumn (late October to mid-December). There is an initial week in London followed by five weeks in Rome, Florence and Venice, with shorter stays in Verona, Siena and Naples.

There's also a shorter course (which can be done either during or after A levels) for two weeks during the summer and covers Rome, Florence and Venice. Also, if you're studying Art History for A level, there is an Easter revision course lasting seven days. Costs range from around £800 for the Easter revision week in Florence through to over £4000 for the six-week gap year course. A scholarship is available for the AHA summer course: the Trenchard Cox Scholarship, awarded for the best pair of 400-word essays on a painting you like and a painting you loathe. Designed for Young NADFAS members. Contact Young NADFAS (National Association of Decorative and Fine Arts Societies) at Tel: +44 (0) 20 7430 0730.

The British Institute of Florence

Piazza Strozzi 2
1-50123 Firenze
Italy

Tel: +39 (0) 55 2677 8200
Fax: +39 (0) 55 2677 8222
see: www.gap-year.com

The British Institute of Florence was founded in 1917 with the aim of developing cultural understanding between the UK and Italy (particularly Tuscany) through the teaching of their respective languages and cultures and the maintenance in Florence of a library.

Today, the Institute runs a thriving and successful school which offers many courses including opera, Dante, film appreciation, Tuscan cooking, wine appreciation, watercolour, life drawing and many other aspects of Italian culture.

Other popular courses offered include Italian language from beginner to A level. In 2000, the Institute became affiliated with the University of Bristol enabling it to offer accredited courses including the First and Upper Certificate in Art History.

The Institute also maintains the Harold Acton library, the biggest library of English books (50,000 volumes) in Italy, used by visiting scholars, students and the general public. Every week, the Institute runs a cultural programme consisting of lectures, concerts, recitals and films in the library.

Many cultural evening lectures and events are held for free whilst course prices range from £95-£2500. The Institute also has a student support and accommodation officer providing help and advice to all students.

ITALY AHA ITALY

A SIX WEEK GAP YEAR COURSE
"3rd November – 15th December 2003 £4,700"
"19th January – 1st March 2004 £4,900"

"The best way to travel in Italy – there is nothing to replace the excitement of first hand knowledge of Art" George Calvocoressi, Spring 1998

Stay in Venice, Florence and Rome (10 days each) Verona, Siena and Naples (3 days) with additional visits to Padua, Vicenza, Bologna, Modena, Pisa, Arezzo, and Orvieto. All teaching on site in small tutor groups of 8. Party size 24.

A structured course of Western Culture: *History, Art History, Theology, Philosophy, Architecture, Literature and Music*. There is always an artist/tutor with the group.

University Admission tutors stress the importance of the personal statement on a UCAS application form. Distinctive and eye-catching 'statements' should include evidence of intellectual horizons beyond your essential curriculum for A levels. AHA Gap Year Courses are known to University Admissions departments and UCAS.

Ask after our Summer Holiday Courses and our Easter A Level Revision Courses

Call NICK ROSS on 020 7582 8082, or write to
AHA, 26 De Laune Street, London SE17 3UU
www.arthistoryabroad.com   email:info@arthistoryabroad.com

EASTER & SUMMER HOLIDAY COURSES
ROME • SIENA • FLORENCE • BOLOGNA • VENICE

Founded 1983

Discover a world of language

in France, Germany & Spain

CHALLENGE Educational Services

Summer Programmes • A Level Revision
Under 18s • Gap Year Programmes
University Programmes • Intensive Short Courses

Challenge Educational Services Ltd,
101 Lorna Road, Hove,
East Sussex, BN3 3EL, England
Fax: +44 (0)1273 220376
e-mail: enquiries@challengeuk.com

Call us now for a free brochure 01273 220261 or visit our website www.challengeuk.com

Challenge Educational Services

101 Lorna Road, Hove
East Sussex BN3 3EL
England

Tel: +44 (0) 1273 220261
Fax: +44 (0) 1273 220376
see: www.gap-year.com

Challenge Educational Services organises **French** courses in collaboration with several French universities (including the world famous Sorbonne University in Paris) and at private language institutes. Courses are offered at the universities of the Sorbonne, Angers, Nantes, Poitiers and Grenoble and courses are also available throughout the year at private language schools in Paris, Bordeaux and Antibes. You can combine learning French with French gastronomy or fashion.

Challenge also organises a 12-week programme in Paris, combining language tuition with classes at a French Art school. Ideal for those with a reasonable standard of French and at least GCSE Art.

Tuition is combined with friendly and welcoming host family accommodation. They are also happy to tailor-make courses to suit your individual requirements.

Cross-Cultural Solutions

47 Potter Avenue, New Rochelle
NY 10801, USA

Tel: +1 914 632 0022
see: www.gap-year.com

Cross-Cultural Solutions offers overseas Volunteer Programmes with a strong emphasis on direct interaction with local people and cultural exchange. Through partnerships with dynamic grassroots organisations working in the areas of education, health care and community development, volunteers experience real immersion in the local culture and have special access to extraordinary people and places rarely seen by the average traveller. Cultural activities such as talks by local guest speakers and excursions to sites of cultural interest all serve to enhance the cultural experience of volunteers.

Cross-Cultural Solutions is setting up a UK information office – see their website for up-to-date details and UK contact information.

DIKEMES – International Center for Hellenic and Mediterranean Studies

2 Vassileos Constantinou Avenue
GR 11635 Athens, Greece

Tel: +30 210 7560749
Fax: +30 210 7561497

The International Center for Hellenic and Mediterranean Studies is a not-for-profit educational institution which promotes the study of the culture of Greece (ancient, medieval and modern) and the Mediterranean world, addressing university students from North America and Europe, foreign visitors, and the English-speaking com-

Cross-Cultural Solutions
AN INTERNATIONAL VOLUNTEER PROGRAM

Volunteer
and see a country from a whole new perspective

Connect with local people, working side-by-side in volunteer placements with our Partner Programs. You will be placed in projects that are locally designed and driven, ensuring that you are involved in sustainable work that's meaningful to the local community. In the afternoons and evenings, you can participate in our Perspectives Programming, which provides you with information and activities to help you achieve a truly realized experience. Free time to travel is also included.

It's your experience.

Our personal program managers, locally based staff and home base structure take care of the details to let it happen.

CONTACT US: 001-914-632-0022
INFO@CROSSCULTURALSOLUTIONS.ORG • WWW.CROSSCULTURALSOLUTIONS.ORG

Programs operate year-round in Brazil, China, Costa Rica, Ghana, India, Peru, Russia, Tanzania and Thailand. Choose between 2-12 weeks. Longer programs can be arranged. Program fees start at $1985 (approx. £1280).

munity of Greece. DIKEMES, in collaboration with its North American associate, College Year in Athens, brings more than 300 university students to Athens each year to study Ancient Greek Civilization and the East Mediterranean Area.

A range of university-level summer programmes, including Intensive Modern Greek Language, which attracts participants from Europe and North America. DIKEMES has now developed continuing education programmes is also available in collaboration with the University of Birmingham, UK in the fields of Archaeology, Ancient History and Byzantine Studies.

Euro Academy
24 Clarendon Place
London SE13 5EY Tel: +44 (0) 20 8297 0505
England Fax: +44 (0) 20 8297 0984

Though mainly a language school, Euro Academy offers many specialist courses such as *Decouverte de la Provence* and *Decouverte de la Cuisine Provençale* courses in Aix-en-Provence which combine language with culture by including a full programme of excursions, wine tasting and cookery lessons. In Malaga students can combine Spanish and dance with Sevillanas and Salsa lessons.

For Art students the Florence school has an 800m^2 art studio for budding da Vincis. They also offer three Italian and cookery courses. Or if you are facing exam stress, why not try one of their exam revision courses in Bordeaux or Biarritz?

Il Sillabo
Via Alberti
31, 52027 San Giovanni Tel: + 39 055 9123238
Valdarno (AR), Italy Fax: + 39 055 942439

See Il Sillabo's listing in the languages (Italian) section.

John Hall Pre-University Course
12 Gainsborough Road
Ipswich Tel: +44 (0) 1473 251 223
Suffolk IP4 2UR Fax: +44 (0) 1473 288 009
England see: www.gap-year.com

Fans of the John Hall Pre-University course, running from January to March, praise its breadth. The course starts with an introductory week in London that includes visits to Agnews (to learn about the art trade),

THE JOHN HALL
PRE-UNIVERSITY COURSE

London VENICE Florence Rome

- entirely different from any other cultural programme in Italy

January to March annually for Students of the Arts and Sciences.

Lectures / on-site visits given by a team of writers, artists, musicians and university lecturers. Art History, Music, Architecture, Conservation, History, Opera, Literature, Design, Cinema.

Visits include Padua, Ravenna, Villas and gardens near Venice, Florence and Rome.

Private visit to the Vatican Museums and Sistine Chapel.

Classes: Life Drawing, Photography, Italian Language.

Information from: The Secretary
12 Gainsborough Road, Ipswich IP4 2UR
Tel: 01473-251223 fax: 01473-288009

www.johnhallpre-university.com

the Richard Rodgers Studios (architecture) and the Saatchi Collection (modern art).

Then a party of about 50 students (almost all on their gap year) travels to Venice for six weeks of visits and lectures, given by nearly 30 different lecturers, on Italian history, European art (from Byzantine through Renaissance to modern), architecture, literature, music, opera (music by local composers Vivaldi and Scarlatti is performed in Venetian churches almost every evening), and Italian cinema. Students can practise life drawing and photography; Italian language lessons are extra.

The group is based in a hotel near the Salute, opposite St Mark's Square. This seven-week course doesn't come cheap (£5470 in 2003), but includes half-board and a one-month vaporetto pass – chugging along Venice's canals is the only alternative to walking. John Hall organises an optional extra week in Florence and five days in Rome.

TASIS, The American School in Switzerland

CH-6926 Montagnola-Lugano Tel: +41 91 960 5151
Switzerland Fax: +41 91 993 2979

The postgraduate year of TASIS, The American School in Switzerland is a challenging, educational experience in Europe for high school graduates who would like an interim year before going to college. Founded in 1956, TASIS is the oldest American boarding school in Europe, with a sister school in England. TASIS is widely recognised as one of the finest schools in Europe.

Each year, the TASIS schools and summer programmes attract over 2400 students representing more than 40 nationalities who share in a caring, family-style international community. The PG Year, established in 1965, enrols a select group of students who wish to participate in a unique educational opportunity, which draws on the academic strengths of TASIS and the cultural resources of Europe.

Design & Fashion

Accademia Italiana

Piazza Pitti 15 Tel: +39 055 284 616
50125 Firenze, Italy Fax: +39 055 284486

The Accademia Italiana is an international design, art and language school. Every year it puts on summer language courses which last from one to three months. Also available are full-year and longer academic and Masters courses in fashion design, fashion illustration, textile design, interior and furniture design, drawing and painting and others.

ARTS & CULTURE   *Learning Abroad*

Drama

Bright Light

3 Fentiman Road   Tel: +44 (0) 20 7582 1582
London SW8 1LD, England   Fax: +44 (0) 20 7582 2379

Bright Light is a not-for-profit organisation that runs gap year drama and education projects in Kenya, Uganda, Tanzania and Ethiopia. You get to learn about East African drama, dance and music as well as teaching African children about Western drama and British culture.

The programme lasts three months and is split into three phases. First you spend time working with African theatre professionals, learning

about traditional African narrative dance and oral literature, as well as helping with performances.

The second phase consists of volunteer teaching in schools. You introduce small groups of children to Western concepts of drama and help them to produce their first play. Finally, you get the chance to produce your own play and then spend time at Lake Naivasha where you can reflect on your experiences. When you return home you may even get the opportunity to workshop your performances at the Old Vic in London.

Tours depart in January and May and cost £2440 including all food, travel, accommodation and insurance.

NYFA (New York Film Academy)

100 East 17th Street
New York NY 10003
USA

Tel: +1 212 674 4300
Fax: +1 212 477 1414

Whether you want to be the next Tarantino, Nick Park or Halle Berry you can hone your film skills at the New York Film Academy. It runs programmes all year round in New York City and at Universal Studios in Hollywood, California as well as Summer workshops at: King's College in London; Princeton University; the Harvard Faculty Club; Disney-MGM Studios, Florida; FEMIS, the French National Film School, Paris; and the ITESM Campus in Mexico City, Mexico.

The programmes offered include four-, six- and eight-week intensive, hands-on filmmaking workshops, 12-week evening classes and the comprehensive One-Year Filmmaking Programme. There's also a one-week Movie Camp ($1500), four-week intensive Acting for Film programme ($2500), four-week 3D Animation programme ($3500 working on the latest equipment) and evening screenwriting workshops during the summer months. There's a good balance of theory and practical.

For the filmmaking courses you'll be expected to write, produce, direct and edit a series of short films. Each film is screened and you 'engage in constructive discussion and critique'. What you learn from the process you put into making the next film, and so on. Teaching standards are high – some of the tutors can even boast an Oscar on their mantlepiece!

Don't worry if you've got no experience – all you need is to be keen and talented. The Academy has an open door policy for applications, but they do expect total commitment. This won't be an easy ride – but it will be the opportunity of a lifetime.

visit: www.gap-year.com

ACADEMIC YEAR ABROAD
Learning Abroad

Spending an academic year abroad

Another way of getting to know a place and its people in depth is to spend a whole year 'living the language and culture' at a foreign school, in Europe, the USA, or even further afield. You could spend the academic year before you go to university in a French Lycée or German Gymnasium, in a school in Spain, or a Spanish-speaking school in Argentina, for example – which still leaves several months free for travel.

European Union   **http://europa.eu.int**

Information on European Community action programmes for education and training is available from the Commission of the European Communities. (The Commission carries out the work of the European Union for its 15 member countries: Austria, Belgium, Denmark, Finland, France, Germany, Greece, Ireland, Italy, Luxembourg, Netherlands, Portugal, Spain, Sweden and the UK).

The most relevant EU education and training programmes are Comenius, ERASMUS, Lingua and Leonardo. The year 2000 was the European Year of Languages, and also the start of a scheme called Europass which provides trainees in any EU country with a 'Europe-wide record of achievement of periods of training undertaken outside the home member state.' So if you are asking questions of a language school in Europe, 'is this course recognised for a Europass?' might be one to try out.

ERASMUS

If you want to spend up to a year abroad at a European university as part of the European Union's ERASMUS scheme, you'll need to have some working knowledge of the relevant language – so a gap year could be the time to start, by studying overseas or in Britain. Information about Erasmus courses is usually given to students in their first year at university: here's a start.

Desiderius Erasmus, as every good European knows, heralded the Reformation with his *Moriae Encomium*. ERASMUS (one of those acronyms where the words were probably made to fit afterwards) stands for EuRopean community Action Scheme for the Mobility of University Students. It's part of a programme called SOCRATES that covers secondary (school) and tertiary (higher) education. To apply, you must be an EU citizen, and when you spend your time abroad, you just continue to pay tuition fees or receive loans or grants as if you were at your university back home. Each university organises its ERASMUS

Learning Abroad **ACADEMIC YEAR ABROAD**

placements – for example, if you look at the web pages for Newcastle University's Socrates Guide, you'll get a good idea of what it's all about: **www.cs.ncl.ac.uk/student.info/Socrates/SocratesGuide.html**

ERASMUS Student Network	**www.esn.org**
EUROPASS	**www.europass-uk.co.uk**
Commission of the European Communities, London	**www.cec.org.uk**

There is also the European Volunteer Service scheme partly funded by the EU which finances voluntary work in EU and Eastern European countries – at no expense and with about £25 a week pocket money. What better way to learn about another country and its language?

Au Pair in America (APIA)

37 Queen's Gate	
London SW7 5HR	Tel: +44 (0) 20 7581 7322
England	see: www.gap-year.com

Don't just live in America for 12 months, be an American student! APIA's **EduCare programme** gives you a taste of US college life. You will be considered a non-degree student and have the freedom to study whatever you like.

Live with an American family and, in exchange for up to 30 hours of childcare, you will receive a $1000 study allowance and a $105 weekly payment plus room and board. A local APIA community counsellor will link you up with other au pairs and EduCare participants in the area and will assist you in selecting and registering for your courses. Most placements are made in late summer and you must be aged 18-26 with a driving licence.

CESA Languages Abroad

CESA House, Pennance Road	Tel: +44 (0) 1209 211 800
Lanner, Cornwall TR16 5TQ	Fax: 01209 211 830
England	see: www.gap-year.com

For further details see main listing under Multi-languages.

Challenge Educational Services

101 Lorna Road, Hove	Tel: +44 (0) 1273 220261
East Sussex BN3 3EL	Fax: 01273 220376
England	see: www.gap-year.com

Challenge Educational Services organises **French** courses in collaboration with several French universities (including the world famous

Sorbonne University in Paris) and at private language institutes. A full academic year, a single semester (Sep/Oct-Jan or Feb-Jun) or Summer courses are offered at the universities of the Sorbonne, Angers, Nantes, Poitiers and Grenoble. A full academic year at the Université de Poitiers costs £4990, including tuition and accommodation (staying with a French family costs extra). One semester (1 October to 31 January) at the Université de la Sorbonne, in the heart of left-bank Paris, costs £5,390 (including accommodation and 20 hours a week tuition).

Students wishing to go on the **Lycée Gap Year Programme** must already have a good command of French. Students will study the same curriculum as the French students and may be able to sit the Baccalaureat exams providing they reach the required standard.

Tuition is combined with friendly and welcoming host family accommodation. They are also happy to tailor-make courses to suit your individual requirements.

English-Speaking Union (ESU)

Dartmouth House
37 Charles St
London W1J 5ED, England

Tel: +44 (0) 20 7529 1550
Fax: +44 (0) 20 7495 6108
See: www.gap-year.com

The English Speaking Union was set up to promote understanding between nations. There is a scholarship scheme for students who would like to spend their gap year studying in a US high school with senior students for two to three terms, or a Canadian school for three terms. Apply well ahead: the closing date for a September start is in mid-January. Apply to the Education Officer at the ESU.

Fulbright Commission

US Educational Advisory Service
62 Doughty Street
London WC1N 2TZ, England

Tel: +44 (0) 20 7404 6994
see: www.gap-year.com

If you want to take a full four-year degree at a US university or college, you will need to start planning at least a year before entry. You need to get in touch with The Fulbright Commission's US Educational Advisory Service (EAS) in London the summer before you want to start a US degree. You will then need to write to US universities, applying for the fall (autumn) term starting at the end of August or beginning of September (application forms available from the university the previous year).

Each October The Fulbright Commission holds a 'College Day' for prospective undergraduates: more than 100 US universities are usually represented. The Fulbright Commission's Beginner's *Guide to Undergraduate Study in the USA* is a good booklet to help get you started.

TASIS, The American School in Switzerland

CH-6926 Montagnola-Lugano
Switzerland
Tel: +41 91 960 5151
Fax: +41 91 993 2979

The post graduate year of TASIS, The American School in Switzerland is a challenging, educational experience in Europe for high school graduates who would like an interim year before going to college. Founded in 1956, TASIS is the oldest American boarding school in Europe, with a sister school in England. TASIS is widely recognised as one of the finest schools in Europe.

Each year, the TASIS schools and summer programmes attract over 2400 students representing more than 40 nationalities who share in a caring, family-style international community. The PG Year, established in 1965, enrols a select group of students who wish to participate in a unique educational opportunity, which draws on the academic strengths of TASIS and the cultural resources of Europe.

The Office of International Education, Iceland

Neshaga 16
107 Reykjavík
Iceland
Tel: +354 525 4311
Fax: +354 525 5850
see: www.gap-year.com

All the universities and colleges co-operate in exchange programmes. ERASMUS (EU programme) is the programme most students participate in. Annually there are around 250 exchange students that visit Iceland, around 150 of whom are from EU member countries.

Don't worry if your Icelandic isn't up to scratch: most institutions offer courses in English and if none are available then you can usually get private tutoring. Information about courses in English can be found on the home pages of the universities and colleges. The number of full-year programmes in English for exchange students is growing every year along with degree programmes in English, in which exchange students can participate.

University of Iceland

The faculty of Natural Sciences offers a one-year course in English for Foreign Students in Earth Sciences. The course covers topics in geology, geography and geophysics. Emphasis is put on aspects of Icelandic geology like volcanic and geothermal activity, glaciers and plate tectonics, as well as physical and human geography. The course is suitable for ERASMUS exchange students from the EU and others wanting to spend a year in Iceland as a part of their university education. A minimum background of one year of undergraduate study in earth sciences is assumed.

The faculties of Social Sciences and Humanities jointly offer courses in Northern Culture providing a general perspective on Icelandic history, society and culture and introducing the Icelandic language to students.

The Icelandic College of Engineering and Technology (ICET)

The Department of Industrial Business Administration offers a one-year programme in English, leading to a BSc degree in International Marketing Management. This programme is open to exchange students. You need to have a diploma in Industrial Business Administration to be considered for this programme.

Bifröst business school

In the spring semester courses are taught in English, and exchange students may study at Bifröst then. During the spring semester, the students complete a project or a dissertation, fulfilling general requirements for similar assignments or a thesis at the final stage of the undergraduate level of education.

Iceland University of Education

To meet the need of incoming exchange students the University offers ten courses taught in English.

The Gap-Year Guidebook 2003/4

TIPS FOR TRAVELLERS

Tips for Travellers

This section covers travel in general: whether you have a pre-arranged voluntary work placement already set up or you're just intending to go with the flow, a read through this chapter should help you plan a problem-free trip. There's lots of practical advice for those who haven't been on long trips abroad before, with information on useful internet sites – take a look at **www.gap-yearshop.com** at the back of the book for kit and accessories you might need to take with you. The next chapter lists travel companies and you'll find useful information about individual countries, including embassy phone numbers in *Appendix 2: Country Info*.

When to go

Before starting university may well be the best time in your life to go abroad – afterwards you might start work which you can't afford to leave because you have bills to pay... then you might get married... then you might have children. After that (although employers' attitudes to career breaks are changing) you may not be able to take more than a few weeks away from all your responsibilities for 20 years or more! That said, an increasing number of people are taking a year out after their degrees: the only general rule is to go for it – the opportunity may not present itself again for some time.

If your finances aren't going to stretch to a year-long round-the-world tour then you're not alone. You could start the year by working (in the UK or abroad) and saving your earnings to pay for your travels.

Money is not the only consideration – you may find other commitments dictate when you can travel. Perhaps you want to fit in retakes, or other courses like learning to drive. And you definitely don't want to have to come back from a sunny beach just to sort out your university entrance.

visit: www.gap-year.com **203**

WHEN TO GO

Tips for Travellers

If you go travelling in the summer straight after A levels – and you haven't got an unconditional offer – you may have to come home in time for the crucial A level results in mid-August to enter clearing. And if you apply for university entrance while on your gap year, you may need to apply before you go travelling and/or return in time to make decisions and sort out all the paperwork.

Life goes on while you're away and you can leave someone reliable and trustworthy in charge of sorting things out for you – especially the official stuff that won't wait. Get someone you really trust to open your post and arrange to talk to them at regular intervals incase something turns up that you need to deal with. But some things you just have to do yourself, so make sure you've done everything important before you go and won't be needed to sign or apply for anything while you're away.

Be prepared

As with most aspects of a gap year, planning ahead is a good idea. The more you know about your destination, the easier your trip will be: India, for example, is unbearably hot in April and May.

Before visiting any country that has recently been politically volatile or could turn into a war zone check the current situation by calling the FCO Travel Advice Unit (Tel: 020 7008 0232/0233) or check on their website, **www.fco.gov.uk** for up-to-date information.

Getting organised

First things first: you'll need a full valid passport in order to go travelling. This may sound obvious but, if you have already got a passport, check it isn't going to run out before your return, or you could have serious trouble getting back into the country. Honestly, it's happened to lots of people – they're so busy worrying about their visas and rucksacks and lists that they forget to check the most basic thing. Some countries don't let you in if your passport has less than six months left to run: check this out first with a travel agent or that country's embassy visa section.

Identity crisis

If you do need to get yourself a passport for the first time, application forms are available from Post Offices. A standard adult ten-year passport costs £33 and you'll need your birth certificate and passport photos. It should take no more than a month from the time you apply to the time you receive your passport, although it's sensible to allow some leaway.

You can send the form direct to the Passport Office or use their 'Check and Send' service (extra £5) at one of the 2300 Post Offices and

PREPARATION

Tips for Travellers

Worldchoice travel agents throughout the UK. The 'Check and Send' service gets your application checked for completeness (including documentation and fee) and given priority by the UK Passport Services (UKPS) – they are usually able to process these applications in two weeks.

If your passport application is urgent you can use the guaranteed same-day (Premium) service or the guaranteed one-week (Fast Track) service. Both services are only available by appointment (phone the UKPS Adviceline on +44 (0) 870 521 0410), and both are expensive (£78 for Premium, £63 for Fast Track). The Premium service is for renewals and amendments only.

This may all seem quite complicated, but the UKPS website, **www.ukps.gov.uk**, is very helpful. It's a good idea to leave a complete photocopy of your passport at home before you go travelling and also to keep a photocopy with you – this can make a lost or stolen passport much easier to cope with.

Passport Agency Globe House,
89 Eccleston Square
London SW1V 1PN
Tel: +44 (0) 870-521 0410
www.ukps.gov.uk

It is useful to join the International Youth Hostels Association (YHA): they run 4500 hostels in over 60 countries offering reasonably priced accommodation. YHA membership for one year costs £13.50 for 18-year-olds and over, and £6.75 for under-18s.

YHA (England & Wales) Dimple Road, Matlock
Derbyshire DE4 3YH
Tel: +44 (0) 870 870 8808
Fax: +44 (0) 1629 592627
www.yha.org.uk
E-mail: customerservices@yha.org.uk

More paper

One bit of advice that may seem glaringly obvious: when you come to Customs and are given stacks of annoying bits of paper, keep them! I was convinced when I was travelling [through Mexico and Belize to Guatemala] that the whole lot were totally irrelevant and chucked them away. It later transpired that one little scrap was my visa and I ended up having to bribe an official at the Guatemalan border to let me in to the country.

Tiff

PREPARATION

Tips for Travellers

An ISIC (International Student Identity Card) costs £7 and is available from STA Travel, either online (**www.statravel.co.uk/c_flights/discountcards.asp**) or by calling +44 (0) 870 1600 599. It identifies you as a student and entitles you to over 900 student discounts in the UK alone. Discounts include everything from museum entrance and restaurant bills to flights and international phonecalls. You also get access to a 24-hour ISIC travel helpline. You qualify for an ISIC if you are in full time education (15 hours per week, 26 weeks per year). If you are on a gap year and have a confirmed place in higher education you are eligible for a card in the calendar year in which you are due to start your higher education place.

If you don't qualify for an ISIC, then the IYTC (International Youth Travel Card, £7) offers similar discounts to anyone under 26, and is available from the same places as an ISIC. Cards are always valid until December: you get the best value if you buy your card in September, since it will then be valid until the end of the following year.

Planning the route

Do you feel lured to a particular area? Latin America? Scandinavia? ...or to a particular climate? Snow? Monsoon? ...or to unexplored territory? Mongolia via the Trans-Siberian Express? ...what about a particular purpose? Surfing? Learning a language? ...or all these ingredients, wrapped up in one journey?

You need to get a framework clear in your mind – or let a cheap round-the-world ticket decide the framework for you. Bear in mind that it's much better (your parents might say essential) to go with a friend, and having contacts lined up along the route is a big help. The more remote a place is, the more useful it is to have company. If you have six months or so to spare, you can arrange travel that takes you all the way round the world, although you may spend more than half your time in one region, like Africa or the USA.

Book now or leave for later?

If you've focusing on one place (rather than going round the world, in which case you usually book a definite route) it's a good idea to plan the main leg of the journey: you can pay for the air, sea or rail ticket out and back in advance but leave the bits in between flexible. Flights inside the USA and between Asian countries with ailing currencies are cheap, for example, and in the CIS (former USSR) they are cheap and scary. However, be sure to research the options thoroughly. For example, flight passes (that is, a number of domestic flights on one ticket in large countries such as Brazil and Mexico) have to be purchased outside the country where they are to be used.

If you've booked a series of flights through a travel agency, you may be able to change the dates directly with the airline when you are abroad, though the route the flight takes usually has to stay the same. Check before you leave how you can alter bookings once you are abroad: you may have to allow 72 hours when making later changes. And you could have to pay for them.

Following the herd

There are well-trodden backpacking routes: through south-east Asia and Australia; across Russia to China and Hong Kong by rail; from the USA to central America; or through Spain and Africa and back to the UK. You may feel that following the same routes everyone else is taking is boring – but there's probably a reason that they've become popular over the recent years – they're interesting, exciting and varied.

If you want to be more explorer than follower of fashion, then why not try countries that have recently opened up to foreign visitors – though they tend to charge a lot for visas (check visa costs through a travel agent, who may be able to arrange it for you).

Obviously avoid danger zones and check with contacts who know a country or the Foreign Office (**www.fco.gov.uk**) before even thinking about getting a visa. The political situation around the world as we go to press is serious stuff and can't be ignored – the point of your gap year travels is to have fun, experience different cultures, meet new people – not to end up in the middle of a war zone with your life in danger. The Foreign Office regularly updates its danger list as new areas of unrest emerge, but it's not and can never be a failsafe, as was illustrated by the Bali bombing in 2002.

Travel guides

There are good travel guides for almost every destination which you can look at before or after you decide where to go and might inspire you to include a certain place. The *Rough Guide* and *Lonely Planet* books are probably the best-known guides and are excellent – whatever your interests, these books will give you relevant information about the places you are going to – as well as copious information on towns, travel routes and budget hotels in the countries they cover.

Insurance

Your insurance needs to be fixed before you go, but it's a far from simple matter. The range of policies is vast – and they all cover different things. The basic things to check if an insurance policy covers are: medical, legal, passport loss, ticket loss, cash loss, luggage, cancellation, missed flights, working abroad, hazardous sports, medical conditions. Also see if they provide a 24-hour helpline.

It is important to make sure that you are covered for the activities you are likely to take part in. Be aware that companies may make a dis-

PREPARATION

tinction between doing a hazardous sport once (*eg* going skiing during your brief trip to the Stubai Glacier) and spending your whole time doing them (*eg* six months intensive skiing in the Rockies). Some insurance policies also have age limits.

Read through the small print carefully and make sure you know what to do if you need to make a claim – most policies will insist that you report a crime to the police (often within a certain time period) and send in the police report with your insurance claim. What you don't want to happen is to have a claim dismissed because you don't have the right paperwork to back it up.

Insurers are unlikely to trip over themselves to pay you money: 'Some [insurers] will do almost anything to avoid paying a claim. Many travel policies impose conditions which are virtually impossible to meet' (*The Sunday Telegraph*, 6 Jan 2002). For example, some policies demand that you report not only theft of items but also loss of items. Fine, but the police are likely to be pretty reluctant to write a crime report because you think you may have accidentally left your camera in the loo! The Foreign Office website, **www.fco.gov.uk/travel**, has a good page about insurance and is worth checking out for advice and links.

Loophole

I went into the yacht club in Sydney harbour and signed on as a crew member on an American yacht – about 40 feet with a crew of five. The skipper was a nuclear submarine captain, a bit of a nutter. We sailed up the coast north from Sydney for about five days and ran into the first reef. One night we attached ourselves to a buoy and we woke up at 3am, smashed against the reef. We scrambled up the mast and as the sun rose we found ourselves lying on the side of the reef with a big hole in the side of the boat.

We were rescued by people from the next door resort island and then we lived it up as shipwrecked mariners for three days. I lost quite a lot of stuff, and things I did get back were soaked in seawater and diesel.

When I put in an insurance claim I got nothing. It turned out that my tourist policy didn't cover me if I worked.

Rupert, Balliol, Oxford University

Already covered?

If you're going abroad on a voluntary work assignment you may find that the organisation arranging it wants you to take a specified insurance policy as part of the total cost.

You may also find you have a 'clash of policies' before you even start looking for the right policy. For example, if your family has already booked you a one-year multi-travel insurance policy to cover travel with the family at other times of the year, you may find you are already covered for loss of life, limb loss, permanent disablement, some medical expenses, theft and so on. These multi-trip policies can be basic as well as quite cheap, and it's essential to check the small print of what the policy covers before you decide whether you need extra cover.

You are very likely to need extra cover if you'll be doing sports or anything dangerous like bungee-jumping. In this case you can start by finding out (through the broker or agent who sold you the policy) if any additional cover can be tacked on to your existing policy, though this can be expensive and most off-the-shelf policies won't do it.

It's a good idea if you can find a policy that doesn't already duplicate what is covered by an existing policy (they don't pay out twice), but some duplication is unavoidable and it's obviously better to be covered twice than not at all.

Medical Insurance

There are reciprocal agreements between EEA (formerly EU) member states to treat each other's medical emergencies free or at a reduced cost, usually where sudden illness or an accident means an immediate operation.

You need to take an E111 ("E one eleven") form with you, which entitles you to free or reduced state medical care while you're in certain countries. They are really simple: pick one up from a post office, fill it in and take it back to the post office to get it stamped. Your E111 lasts you as long as your personal details are still correct – so if you change address, for example, you need to get a new one.

Remember that countries with no health care agreements with the UK include Canada, the USA, India, most of the Far East, the whole of Africa and Latin America. Wherever it happens (especially in the US) a serious illness, broken limb or injury you cause someone else can be very expensive. Insurance for the USA, Canada and the Caribbeans also tends to be even more expensive because of the high medical/legal costs there.

Medical insurance is usually part of an all-in travel policy, costs vary widely by company, destination, activity and level of cover. Make sure you have generous cover for injury or disablement, know what you're covered for and when you've got the policy read the small print care-

visit: www.gap-year.com

Tips for Travellers **PREPARATION**

fully (for example, does it cover transport home if you need an emergency operation that cannot be carried out safely abroad).

Some policies won't cover high risk activities like skiing, snowboarding, bungee jumping *etc* so you'll need to get extra specific cover. If you have a condition that is likely to recur, you may have to declare this when you buy the insurance. Also, check whether the policy covers you for the medical costs if the condition does recur.

Some banks provide cover for holidays paid for using their credit cards, but their policies may not include all the essentials. Banks also offer blanket travel insurance (medical, personal accident, third party liability, theft, loss, cancellation, delay and more). You may be able to get reductions if you have an account with the relevant bank or buy foreign currency through it. Beware of 'free' insurance provided with your ticket. 'Free' can mean 'not very useful'.

Who to choose?

Since travel agents were banned from making you buy their favourite insurance policy as part of a travel package, there has been intense competition between insurance companies. There are now several insurers offering tailor-made insurance policies for gap year students.

Use the web to search for suitable policies. Remember to read all the 'exclusion' clauses. For example, stolen cash, war zones and injuries arising from terrorism are often excluded from a policy.

Here are some of the companies we've found, though we can't guarantee they're the cheapest. All prices were quoted in February 2003.

Boots
Tel: +44 (0) 845 840 2020

£295	12 months worldwide.
£69	Three months in Europe.

These prices are available to those aged between 18-35. Boots offers a 24-hour helpline and covers hazardous sports if arranged by a qualified expert. However, they advise you to call in advance to arrange this.

Down Under Insurance
Tel: +44 (0) 800 393 908

£189	12 months in Australia and New Zealand, with up to 25% of your time spent elsewhere. Covers you for over 60 hazardous sports and for working abroad. Six months cover with the same conditions costs £105.
£57	'Annual Multitrip' – covers a total of 31 days worldwide.
£44	'Annual Multitrip' – covers a total of 31 days in Europe.

visit: www.gap-year.com

Endsleigh

Tel: +44 (0) 1865 245311

£222.83	Single 'Gap Year' worldwide.
£401.09	Couple 'Gap Year' worldwide.
£141.75	Single 'Gap Year' Europe.
£255.15	Couple 'Gap Year' Europe.
£297.10	Single 'Gap Year Plus' worldwide.
£534.78	Couple 'Gap Year Plus' worldwide.
£189	Single 'Gap Year Plus' Europe.
£340.20	Couple 'Gap Year Plus' Europe.

All policies quoted here are for 12 months and are available to those aged 18-35. Sixty sports are covered including canoeing – you can arrange for more to be added. You are also covered for casual work abroad. The 'Couple' policy covers two people travelling together.

Endsleigh are the national student insurer and offer a separate winter sport policy. They also offer various discounts, *eg* 20% off for groups of 10 or more, 50% off for under 18s and 20% off if you don't want your luggage to be covered.

Europ Assistance

Tel: +44 (0) 1444 442 365

£545	12 months worldwide. Dangerous sports need to be arranged in advance.
£400	12 months worldwide excluding the USA, Canada, Bermuda, the Caribbean, Hong King, India and South Africa.
£265	12 months in Europe.

MRL Insurance

Tel: +44 (0) 1737 552 100

£199	12 months worldwide.
£139	6 months worldwide.
£95	6 months in Europe.
£75	4 months in Europe.

Prices above are for the 'backpackers' policy, available to under 35s. Over 80 sports are covered, including white water rafting and parachuting. There's a 24-hour helpline for literally any problem, even if it isn't insurance-related!

Norwich Union/HSBC

Tel: +44 (0) 800 169 4013

£405.35	12 months worldwide; fully comprehensive cover.
£360.30	12 months worldwide excluding the USA, Canada and the Caribbean; fully comprehensive cover.
£513.70	12 months worldwide multitrip; fully comprehensive cover.

Prices above are for the 'youth policy', available to those aged 17-30. Premiums may vary according to pre-existing health conditions. Some hazardous sports (*eg* scuba diving) are covered but others need to be arranged in advance and may cost extra. A winter sports policy is also available, and the company runs a 24-hour helpline.

Options Travel Insurance

Tel: +44 (0) 800 917 1091

£170	12 months worldwide, Silver policy.
£250	12 months worldwide, Gold policy.
£150	12 months Australia and New Zealand, Silver policy (includes 72 hour stop elsewhere).
£165	12 months Australia and New Zealand, Gold policy (includes 72 hour stop elsewhere).

Silver policy gives you legal and medical cover; Gold covers extras such as baggage, as well as some hazardous sports including scuba diving and one bungee jump. The company runs a 24-hour helpline, but does not insure you for medical conditions you are already aware of.

Planet Travel Insurance

Tel: +44 (0) 845 458 4587

£229	'Select' policy (recommended for backpackers). 12 months worldwide, excluding the USA, Canada and the Caribbean.
£424.99	'Comprehensive' policy. 12 months worldwide, excluding the USA, Canada and the Caribbean.
£369	'Select' policy. 12 months in the USA, Canada and the Caribbean.
£475.99	'Comprehensive' policy. 12 months in the USA, Canada and the Caribbean.
£199	12 months in Australia and New Zealand.
£35.99	1 month in the USA, Canada and the Caribbean.

The 'Select' policy covers you for legal, medical, personal accident, luggage, cancellation, repatriation, passport loss, working and 52 haz-

visit: www.gap-year.com

PREPARATION

ardous activities; the 'Comprehensive' policy gives you all this with increased monetary values plus cash loss, missed/delayed departure from the UK and delayed luggage.

If you want to go to America, Canada or the Caribbean you can save money by adding a month's USA, Canada and Caribbean cover to a standard worldwide policy which excludes these countries. Policies can be extended up to two years and the company runs a 24-hour emergency helpline with International Medical Rescue.

STA Travel
Tel: +44 (0) 20 7465 0484

£180	'Backpack' policy. 12 months worldwide, covering medical, legal and cancellation.
£275	'Standard' policy. 12 months worldwide, with higher monetary values and also covering luggage and some hazardous sports including ballooning, abseiling and elephant trekking.
£63	'Backpack' policy covering 6 months in Europe.

A 'Premier' policy is also available covering yet more hazardous activities, including off-piste skiing, sea kayaking and paragliding. The company runs a 24-hour helpline.

24Dr Travel
Tel: +44 (0) 870 740 9260

£135	12 months worldwide excl.uding baggage and cancellation.
£193	12 months worldwide including baggage and cancellation.
£104	12 months worldwide excluding the USA, Canada and the Caribbean, and excluding baggage and cancellation.
£148	12 months worldwide excluding the USA, Canada and the Caribbean, but including baggage and cancellation.
£58	12 months in Europe excluding baggage and cancellation.
£97	12 months in Europe including baggage and cancellation.

These are special rates for under 21s. Policies cover some hazardous sports, including one bungee jump, and white water rafting; others can be added if arranged in advance.

There is also a winter sports policy, covering you for 31 days in Europe for £32 and 31 days in the USA for £56.

What to Take

Start thinking early about what to take with you and write a list – adding to it every time you think of something. Then sit down and rationalise – cross off everything you don't really need. Pack the essentials and enough clothes to see you through – about five changes of clothing should last you for months if you choose carefully. Don't take anything that doesn't match with everything else and stick to materials that are comfortable, hard-wearing, easy to wash and dry and don't crease too much. Make sure you have clothes that are suitable for the climates you are visiting. And relax – you can't prepare for every eventuality if you're living out of a rucksack.

If you do forget to pack something vital try to think imaginatively: if you are in a plane when you realise that you forgot to pack any maps, ask if you can tear the route maps out of the in-flight magazine. That way at least you will know if Chile is on the left or right-hand side of South America.

Religious customs

Women wear long sleeves and cover their legs in Muslim countries: don't wear a bikini top and shorts in city streets. Uncovered flesh, especially female, offends Islam. Similarly in Buddhist countries the head is sacred and so it is unconventional to touch it. Each culture or religion has its own holy 'laws', and casual Anglo-Saxon habits can offend. Do some research first.

Maps, directions and vital information

The most organised people have been known to leave Dover or Heathrow without a single map. Unless you're going trekking you won't need anything too flash: the ones in guidebooks are usually pretty good. A good pocket business diary can be very useful – one that gives international dialling codes, time differences, local currency details, bank opening hours, public holidays and other information.

Take a list with you of essential information like directions to voluntary work postings, key addresses (including your own and other relevant e-mail addresses), medical information, credit card numbers (try to disguise these in case everything gets stolen), passport details, contact numbers in case of loss of travellers cheques and insurance and flight details – and leave a copy with someone at home as well. A contact list of people you know abroad is a good idea, just in case the hostel you booked is full up or you simply want to see a friendly face and have a shower.

WHAT TO TAKE

Tips for Travellers

Another way of keeping safe copies of your vital documents (even if everything you have is lost or stolen) is to scan those documents on to a computer before you leave and send the information on the internet to your e-mail address. This way your details are secure and retrievable wherever you are and however dire your situation. (Remember that if passports or other vital documents get stolen, you have to report all the details to local police.)

Tickets and money

As emphasised already, it's a good idea to leave photocopies of serial numbers of tickets, passports and credit cards at home. It's also worth keeping copies on you, separate from the rest of your valuables, and also one travellers' cheque separate from the others (useful if all the rest get stolen). Waist money pouches worn under clothes are recommended: not the height of fashion, but everyone wears them.

Take widely accepted travellers cheques like those issued by big international banks – but don't make the mistake of taking American Express travellers' cheques to Cuba or any other country on less than friendly terms with the US – and don't carry much cash. Cheques in pounds sterling are widely accepted, but US dollars more so. It is worth recording the numbers of the travellers cheques that you spend, as it helps if you need to replace lost or stolen ones.

If you're travelling in Europe you'll have the convenience of only needing one currency, the Euro, for Austria, Belgium, Finland, France, Germany, Greece, Ireland, Italy, Luxembourg, Portugal, Spain and The Netherlands. This will save you paying commission on changing currencies as you travel round.

Outside the EU member states, it can help to arrive with some local currency in notes and coins. Be careful at foreign exchange shops or kiosks: they often charge extortionate commissions or make the equivalent amount of money on very wide exchange rates.

Credit cards

Essential back-up. Both Visa and Mastercard are useful for getting local currency cash advances, sometimes from a cash dispenser, at banks abroad. You can then use the cash to buy more travellers cheques – safer than walking around with suitcases of money. If you're using your credit card to get money over the counter then you're likely to need some form of ID (eg passport). The problem with a credit card is not losing it or having it stolen – keep a note of the numbers and how to report the loss of the card.

Wiring money

If all else fails and you find yourself stranded with no cash, no travellers cheques and no credit cards, then having money wired to you could be a lifesaver. Two major companies offer this service: MoneyGram (**www.moneygram.com**) and Western Union (**www.westernunion.com**). Both have vast numbers of branches worldwide – MoneyGram has 55,000 in 155 countries and Western Union has 140,000 in 185 countries.

The service allows a friend or relative to transfer money to you almost instantaneously. Once you have persuaded your 'guardian angel' to send you the money, all they have to do is go to the nearest MoneyGram or Western Union, fill in a form and hand over the money (in cash). It is then transferred to the company's branch nearest to you, where you in turn fill in a form and pick it up. Both you and the person sending the money will need ID, and you may be asked security questions.

Kit

Where to buy

Some overseas voluntary organisations (such as SPW) arrange for their students to have discounts at specific shops, like the YHA. The best advice on equipment usually comes from specialist shops, although they may not be the cheapest: these include YHA shops, Blacks, Millets and Camping and Outdoors Centres. Take a look at **www.gap-yearshop.com** for a specialist selling over the internet (see the back of this book).

Rucksacks

Advice from students who have collapsed under the weight of 65- to 70-litre rucksacks: think carefully before buying so big. There is no need to look like a walking sack of coal, sweating under the weight of bottles of shampoo that will take two months to use. Thailand does have shampoo. For hot countries a 30- to 35-litre rucksack (excluding sleeping bag) is usually big enough. In cold countries you are obviously going to need a bigger rucksack, but you can keep bags light by packing clothes made of special lightweight fabrics.

Try not to set off with a totally full bag – you're bound to buy stuff along the way and you don't want to be trekking across the world with a handful of plastic bags. If you really can't resist and end up buying too many souvenirs to carry you can always post them home, but be warned: postage is expensive, so that 'cheap' souvenir could end up costing more than you bargained for. You could always start off with a bigger bag, but remember, the longer you walk the heavier it gets.

Rucksacks that take a sleeping bag at the bottom are popular, and so are ones that open laterally like suitcases so you don't have to pull out all your worldly possessions just to find a pair of socks. You might want to go for one with zips and tiny padlocks for security, but remember that this doesn't give real protection, as a determined thief will happily slash your bag open.

You can get all sorts of trendy attachments such as 'an integral pocket for your hydration bladder' but don't hand over money for stuff you won't need. If you go to a good outdoor store, they should be able to advise you on exactly what you need for your particular trip. Most of these stores have websites with helpful hints and lists of 'essential' items. Best of all talk to someone who's been before and ask them what they wish they'd taken or left at home.

A well-stitched 65-litre rucksack will cost between £60 and £90, and a 35-litre rucksack between £40 and £50, but prices vary greatly. Remember, the most expensive is not necessarily the best – get what is most suitable for your trip.

A must is an extra small day bag or rucksack to carry valuables and things you need in a hurry, as well as bottles of water, guidebooks, camera and so on. You should be able to leave your rucksack in most hostels or guest houses if you are staying for more than a day (most thieves won't be interested in nicking your socks), or in a locker at the train station. ALWAYS take camera, passport, important papers and money with you everywhere, zipped up, preferably out of view.

Footwear

It's worth investing in something comfortable if you're heading off on a long trip. In hot countries, a good pair of sandals is the preferred footwear for many and there's a great range of sports sandals available. They might seem a bit pricey (£30-£70), but a good strong pair will last and be comfortable. If you're going somewhere cheap, you could just pick up a pair out there, but you're likely to be doing a lot more walking than usual – even if you're only sight-seeing – so comfort and durability are important. Blisters can ruin a trip.

Some people like chunky walking boots, others just their trainers, but it's best to get something that won't fall apart when you're halfway up Mount Kilimanjaro. Take more than one pair of comfortable shoes in case they don't last, but don't take too many – they'll be an unnecessary burden, and take up precious space in your rucksack.

Sleeping bags

First, are you sure you even need one? For hot countries you may just want to take a sheet sleeping bag (basically just a sewn-up sheet). If you do take a sleeping bag, think about what you'll be doing. The more active your holiday, the more you need a decent bag; go to a specialist shop where you can get good advice.

Take into account weight and size and the conditions you'll be travelling in – you might want to go for one of those dinky compression sacs that you can use to squash sleeping bags into. Sheet bags are useful, and you can usually rent down bags for treks in, say, Nepal – but don't assume you'll always be able to do this.

For cold countries, you need bulky heat-retaining materials. If you're going to be doing a lot of sleeping outdoors, a roll-mat is probably a good idea too.

The main thing is that you can carry it and that you will be comfortable. No way are you going to have enough energy to look around art galleries, let alone climb Mt Kilimanjaro, if you're not getting any sleep.

Prices vary hugely and you can sometimes find a four-season bag cheaper than a one-season bag – it's mostly down to quality: at the cheaper end expect to pay around £10 for a sheet bag; £30 for a one-season sleeping-bag (suitable to 5°C); £30-40 for a two-season sleeping-bag (suitable to 0°C); £45 for a three-season sleeping-bag (suitable to -5°C). You can pay more than two or three times as much for better gear.

WHAT TO TAKE
Tips for Travellers

First-aid kit

There is no need to take a whole chemist's shop with you. Ask your GP for advice, but useful basics are rehydration sachets (to use after diarrhoea); waterproof plasters; TCP; corn plasters for sore feet; cotton buds; a small pair of straight nail scissors (not to be carried in your hand luggage on the 'plane); safety pins; insect repellent; antiseptic cream; anti-diarrhoea pills (only short term; they stop the diarrhoea temporarily but don't cure you); water sterilisation tablets; and anti-histamine cream.

You can get a medical pack from most chemists or travel shops, by mail order from MASTA (Tel: +44 (0) 113 238 7575; **www.masta.org**). Homeway (see **www.gap-yearshop.com**) also specialises in medical kits for travellers: the contents vary from sting relief, tick removers, blister kits, sun block and rehydration sachets to complete sterile medical packs with needles and syringe kits (in case you think the needle someone might have to inject you with may not be sterile). You can also get dual-voltage mosquito killer plugs, various types of mosquito net, water purification tablets and filters, money pouches, world receiver radios, travel irons and kettles. Not to mention a personal attack alarm. If you take too much kit though, you'll need a removal van to take it with you.

Make sure you read through the Health section later in this chapter and talk to your GP well before you go.

Handy items

The list of useful things to take varies from person to person, but the following are generally considered very helpful: string that can double as a washing line and is handy for putting up mosquito nets; a universal sink plug; a torch; and a padlock and chain to secure your rucksacks on long journeys and double-lock hostel rooms. A penknife with different functions is also extremely useful (remember that since 11 September 2001 you can no longer pack any sharp items in your hand luggage when travelling by 'plane) as are water purifying tablets (if bottled mineral water is available check that the seal is intact). Masking tape has also been recommended to us as a vital piece of survival kit; apparently it's handy for mending slashed rucksacks, sealing ant nests, fixing doors, sticking up mosquito nets...

Cameras

For most people, being able to record their trip is a vital part of the experience. Remember to be very careful to keep cameras and film safe from damage (usually sand and water) and theft. Keep all your negatives in a safe place because most travellers agree there is nothing more gutting than losing either your developed photos or undeveloped films – they're irreplaceable. Getting photos developed as you go along is an option worth considering; it may work out cheaper, and stops you looking at stacks of photos long after taking them and asking yourself "Which mountain is that?" If you are one of those people who considers every new view to be a photo opportunity, then you may not want to carry the extra weight around in your already-heavy rucksack, but you can always post them home either as pics or as undeveloped films. Take a few moments to label them so you know what you're looking at when you get home.

The new APS (Advanced Photo System) films are small and get rid of the need for negatives, as the film can be developed repeatedly. But they are expensive to develop and can be hard or impossible to get hold of in some countries. The APS cameras needed to use them can be expensive, but the cheapest can compete with standard prices.

Of course, the ultimate is the digital camera; you can download your photos and e-mail them home. You can buy quite small digital cameras for as little as £40 – but you need to be sure you can download your pics as they don't tend to be able to store many images at a time.

Health & Safety

Staying healthy

Note: Although we make every effort to be as up-to-date and accurate as possible, the following advice is intended to serve as a guideline only. It is designed to be helpful rather than definitive, and you should **always check with your GP** what you need for your trip, preferably at least eight weeks before going away.

It's not only about which countries you'll be going to, but for how long and to what degree you'll be roughing it: six months in five-bottle-top hostels puts people at higher risk than two weeks in a five-star Mandarin Hotel. Tell your doctor your proposed travel route and the type of activities you will be doing and ask for advice not only about injections and pills needed, but symptoms to look out for and what to do if you suspect you've caught something. Some immunisations are free under the NHS but you may have to pay for the more exotic/rare. Some, like the Hepatitis A vaccine, can be very expensive, but this is not an area to be mean with your money – it really is worth being cautious with your health.

If you are going abroad to do voluntary work, don't assume the organisation will give you medical advice first or even when you get there, though they often do. Find out for yourself, and check if there is a medically-qualified person in or near the institution you are going to

HEALTH & SAFETY

Tips for Travellers

be posted with. People who've been to the relevant country/area are a great source of information.

It is important to keep a record of any treatment, such as courses of antibiotics, that you have when overseas to tell your doctor when you get back. Also be wary of needles and insist on unused ones; it's best if you can see the packet opened in front of you, or you could take a 'sterile kit' (containing needles) with you. Also, many people recommend that you know your blood type before you leave the country, to save time and ensure safety. Your GP might have it on record – if not, a small charge may be made for a blood test.

Some travellers prefer to go to a dedicated travel clinic to get pre-travel health advice. This may be especially worthwhile if your GP/Practice nurse does not see many travellers. British Airways has three travel clinics in London where you can get jabs – call +44 (0) 20 7606 2977 for more information about this service. The Medical Advisory Services for Travellers Abroad (MASTA) has travel clinics around Britain. To find your nearest clinic check the website **www.masta.org** or contact the Location Line (Tel: +44 (0) 1276 685 040).

Bra-less with worms

We were about to go trekking and it looked like I had a huge verruca on my foot, so I wasn't sure if I'd be able to walk. I got it checked out at a clinic in Kathmandu, and as they'd never heard of a verruca, they just decided to chop the dead skin off. I sat there as they sawed and proceeded to pull out a huge sack of worms from inside my foot. The Western doctor said he'd never seen anything like it and he later told me that I must have picked it up from sandflies on a beach in Zanzibar.

While we were trekking I got severe fever which turned out to be typhus contracted from my nits. While I was lying semi-delirious in the lodge, the owner's daughter came into my room and started rummaging under my bed. I was too ill to do anything and I later discovered she'd nicked my bra. I had to trek all the way home bra-less – because being a minimalist trekker I'd only brought one with me.

Catherine

Alternatively you can do your own research and take the information to your doctor or nurse. MASTA has a 'Travellers Health Line' on +44 (0) 906 8224 100. Travellers leave details of their proposed journey to obtain a health brief by first class post. This brief provides information on the recommended vaccines, malaria tablets, disease outbreak information and safety advice. Calls cost 60p/min and last approximately four to five minutes depending on how many countries you request details on.

There are also some websites offering good free advice about vaccinations *etc*:

www.e-med.co.uk
www.fitfortravel.scot.nhs.uk
www.travelhealth.co.uk

For advice on vaccinations, malaria, the latest health news and important political news straight from the Foreign Office visit their website at **www.fco.gov.uk/travel**. Also useful is the Department of Health Freefone Health Information Service (Tel: +44 (0) 800 665 544) and their website: **www.doh.gov.uk/traveladvice**

Make sure you have a sensible first aid kit with you, organise your medical insurance and, if you don't speak the language, have the basic words for medical emergencies written down so you can explain what is wrong.

Accidents/Injuries

Accidents and injuries are the greatest cause of death in young travellers abroad. Alcohol/drug use will increase the risk of these occurring. Travellers to areas with poor medical facilities should take a sterile medical equipment pack with them. As highlighted earlier, make sure that you have good travel insurance that will bring you home if necessary.

AIDS

The HIV virus that causes AIDS is caught from: injections with infected needles; transfusions of infected blood; and unprotected sex with an infected person. It can possibly be caught via cuts – if you have a shave at the barber's, insist on a fresh blade, but it's probably best to avoid the experience altogether. It is NOT caught through everyday contact, insect bites, dirty food or crockery, kissing, coughing or sneezing.

Protect yourself: always use condoms during sex, make sure needles are new (you can take your own sterile pack for medical emergencies), if you need a blood transfusion make sure blood has been

HEALTH & SAFETY

Tips for Travellers

Water needs respect

Water. Seems so simple. Yet if only I had understood how it really can affect the body.

Having decided on joining many like-minded people on an 'adventure of a life time', rather than listen to all the horror stories I wanted to hear about all the amazing places and people I could meet. I didn't want to be bombarded by all the Health and Safety information that doctors and parents give, as it all seemed too serious.

Not only that, it all seemed so expensive at the time, especially when I was scrimping and saving every last penny so I could spend an extra night on that stunning beach I visualised in my mind.

But be warned. I am not alone in the troubles faced when returning. If you survive your entire trip without a doggy stomach then you're one of the few. When I got home, taking into account that it would take a while to adjust back to 'normal living' I made excuses for my general ill health. As time went on my parents and I started to ask questions and saught the help of The Hospital for Tropical Diseases. I was diagnosed with Giardia, a parasite found in water.

How I got it? Simple. Not treating the water properly. Looking back, when travelling you relish the simplicity of living, eating and drinking what and when you like. No one is looking over your shoulder and in this carefree existence you begin to forget the simple rules. All it takes is one lapse, a local ice pop to cool you down in that scorching heat, a lump of ice in your rather warm coke, a sip of someone else's water. In short un-purified water.

And the cost? Well I'm still suffering from the long term effects associated with the parasite and the treatment needed. Not only do I still feel unwell but financially it continues to be very costly. Don't get me wrong, those six months I spent travelling are the best days so far of my life, but, given what I know now, would I change anything? Yes. Simple, I will always treat water with the respect it deserves, which does mean spending money on buying proper equipment to purify water. After all, it's about your long-term health, you don't want to be fighting the after effects like I have been for the last four years: where's the fun in that?

Felicity

visit: www.gap-year.com

screened and don't get a tattoo or piercing until you're back home and can check out the tattoo shop properly. Remember this is a fatal disease and though medical advances are being made there is no preventive vaccination and no cure.

Asthma and allergies

Whether you are an asthmatic or have an allergy to chemicals in the air, food, stings, or antibiotics, ask your GP for advice before you go. You will be able to take some treatments with you.

Chronic conditions

Asthmatics, diabetics, epileptics or those with other conditions should always wear an obvious necklace or bracelet or carry an identity card stating details of their condition. Tragedies do occur due to ignorance, and if you are found unconscious, a label can be a life saver. See **www.medicalert.org.uk** for more information.

You should also keep with you a written record of your medical condition and the proper names (not just trade names) of any medication you are taking. If you are going on an organised trip or volunteering abroad, find out who the responsible person for medical matters is and make sure you fully brief them about your condition.

Contraceptives

If you are on the pill it is advisable to take as many with you as possible. Remember that contraceptives go against some countries' religious beliefs so they may not be as readily available as you might think. Antibiotics, vomiting and diarrhoea may inhibit the absorption of the pill, so use alternative means of contraception until seven days after the illness.

Take condoms with you just in case – even if you are not intending to have sex. However nice and genuine a person seems remember that you don't know who else they've slept with, and they might even pass on an STD (sexually transmitted disease) during unprotected sex without realising it themselves. Keep condoms away from sand, water and sun. If you do buy some condoms abroad, choose a known make and be sure that they haven't been kept in damp, hot or icy conditions.

Dentist

Pretty obvious but often forgotten: get anything you need done to your teeth before you go. Especially worth checking up on are wisdom teeth and fillings – you don't want to spend three months in India with toothache.

Diabetes

Wear an obvious medical alert necklace or bracelet or carry an ID card stating your condition (preferably with a translation into the local language). Take enough insulin for your stay – trying to get insulin in outer Mongolia may be tricky. The problem is that GPs usually only give out three to six months of medication in advance – talk to your doctor early and explain the situation. If you can't get enough for a full year of travelling you will need to be prepared to buy insulin abroad at full price. Ring the BDA (British Diabetic Association) Careline to make sure the brand of insulin you use is available in the particular country you are planning to visit. Your medication must be kept in the passenger area of a plane, not the aircraft hold where it will freeze.

British Diabetic Association   10 **Queen Anne Street**
London W1M 0BD
England
Tel: +44 (0) 20 7323 1531
Careline : +44 (0) 20 7424 1030
E-mail: careline@diabetes.org.uk
www.diabetes.org.uk

The British Diabetic Association produces a general travel information booklet (£2) as well as specific travel packs for about 70 countries. Ring or e-mail the Careline (Mon-Fri 9am-5pm) or check out the website for expert advice and all information for diabetic travellers, including info on travel insurance.

Diarrhoea

By far the most common health problem to affect travellers abroad is travellers' diarrhoea. This is difficult to avoid but it is sensible to do the best you can to prevent problems. High risk food/drinks include untreated tap water, shellfish, unpasteurised dairy products, salads, raw/undercooked meat and fish. Take a kit to deal with the symptoms of travellers' diarrhoea (your doctor or nurse should be able to advise on this). Remember to take plenty of 'safe' drinks if you are ill.

Hepatitis (A&B), Japanese Encephalitis, Meningitis, Polio, Rabies, Tetanus, Tuberculosis, Typhoid, Yellow Fever

Ask your GP for advice on vaccinations/precautions at least six to eight weeks before you go (some may be available on the NHS). Keep a record card on you of what you've had done.

Eyes

If you wear contact lenses you should stock up on cleaning fluid before going, especially if venturing off the beaten track, and be careful what water you use for cleaning; ask your optician for advice. It's also worth making sure you have glasses as a back-up, as it's not always possible to replace lost or broken contacts. If you wear glasses consider taking a spare pair – they don't have to be expensive and you can choose frames that are flexible and durable. Keep them in a hard glasses case in a waterproof (and more to the point, sand-proof) pouch.

Malaria

Caught from the bite of an anopheles mosquito, and mosquitoes are vicious and vindictive. In 2001 there were 2050 reported cases in the UK, according to the figures from the Malaria Reference Laboratory. Highest risk areas are tropical regions like West Africa and Asia. There's no jab, but your GP will give you a course of pills to take.

It may sound obvious, but try to avoid getting bitten as much as possible. Use insect repellent, preferably containing either DEET (diethyl-toluamide), or extract of lemon eucalyptus oil. Keep your arms and legs covered between dusk and dawn and use a 'knockdown' spray to kill any mosquitoes immediately.

Mosquito nets are useful, but they can be hard to put up correctly. It is often worth carrying a little extra string and small bits of wire so that the net can be hung up in rooms that don't have hanging hooks. Ideally the net should be impregnated with an insecticide: you can buy nets that are already treated from specialist shops and travel clinics (see **www.gap-yearshop.com** for a full range). For a long trip, the pills can cost a lot. And some people, particularly on long trips, stop taking their pills, especially if they're not getting bitten much. Don't. Malaria can be fatal.

Your GP, practice nurse or local travel clinic should know which of a variety of anti-malarials is best for you, depending on your medical history (*eg* for epileptics) and the countries you are visiting. Your travel health adviser will also be able to tell you what the symptoms of malaria are, and that you must seek treatment quickly. The combination of paludrine plus chloroquine is recommended for some countries. In areas where the malaria shows significant drug resistance, mefloquine, doxycyline or Malarone will be recommended.

All the anti-malarial tablets have various pros and cons, and some of them have rather significant side-effects. If you are going to try the weekly mefloquine tablets, MASTA recommends that you start the course two to three weeks before departure: this will allow time for side effects to develop and therefore to alter your prescription in time. Malarone is started two days before departure and taken every day until one week after returning from the infected area. Doxycycline can also be started two days before departure and is taken every day until one month after return. For paludrine and chloroquine start the course one week before you leave and continue it for four weeks on your return. Don't think that this means you can leave it until the week before you go – the earlier you see your GP, the better.

As there are a number of different anti-malarials, it's important to make sure you're taking the right variety. Visit your GP or travel clinic a couple of months before you go to discuss the options. It is worth doing a little research of your own before going to your GP or practice nurse. Very occasionally we hear stories of unsuitable drugs being recommended by either a GP, practice nurse, travel agent or pharmacist.

Sunburn

Avoid over-exposure, especially on first arrival in a sunny country, and use sun creams and sun-block frequently. Around 40,500 new cases of skin cancer are reported in Britain every year (of which 5000 are malignant), and it is the second most common cancer in the country. Malignant melanoma is one of the most common cancers among 20-35 year olds. Don't think you're safe if you're spending three months as a skiing instructor, either – snow increases the amount of harmful UVB rays reaching the skin by up to 85%.

Sickness & diarrhoea

You can expect to be a bit ill when you travel just due to different food and an unsettled lifestyle (paracetamol and loo paper will probably be the best things you packed). But if vomiting and/or diarrhoea continue for more than a few days, or you run a fever, have convulsions or breathing difficulties (or any unusual symptoms), get someone to call a doctor straight away. Don't be paranoid about foreign doctors — they do go to medical school.

If the doctor advises being sent home for treatment and you have an insurance policy with a repatriation arrangement, get someone to call the insurance company's headquarters or office in the relevant country for help as soon as possible. If the illness is less urgent a British Embassy or British company operating in that country will usually be able to recommend a good local doctor. If your treatment is not free you should be able to pay by credit card, but check first with your insurers – they may cover the costs upfront. If you do pay yourself, make sure the details are written out on a receipt and keep all bills or receipts so you can claim on your insurance policy when you get home.

Staying safe

Before you do anything or go anywhere, think about the consequences – this isn't about not having a good time, or being boring – it's about getting through your gap year alive and not getting mugged, raped or murdered.

If people hassle you, you can usually crack a joke and move on. If you are offered strange drinks or drugs, be sensible and think about your safety first.

One of the biggest dangers in accepting a drink is that someone can slip in the so-called 'date rape drug' (Rohypnol). It doesn't taste of anything and you won't know you're taking it. Combined with alcohol, it can induce a blackout with memory loss and decrease your resistance, leaving you open to attack. About ten minutes after ingesting the drug, you may feel dizzy and disoriented, simultaneously too hot and too cold, or nauseous. You might have difficulty speaking and moving, and then pass out. Victims have no memory of what happened while under the drug's influence. Another drug that can be used in a similar way is GHB (gamma-hydroxybutrate), also known as 'liquid ecstasy', 'somatomax', 'scoop', or 'grievous bodily harm'.

If someone keeps pestering you with unwanted sexual advances after you have said no, get to somewhere where there are other people within earshot. Only use violence as a last resort – it's not worth fighting back against violent muggers. If someone tries to snatch your bag, throw it at them – it keeps as much space between you and them and puts them off guard, giving you time to get away. Anyway, you'll have wisely hidden any money/passport/tickets in a bag under your clothes. Stick close to other people while you get back to base.

Meeting places

Your first impression of some countries will be the swarm of people that descends on you, hassling you to take a taxi or buy something – at night, it can be quite scary. Remember, anyone can get lost. When you are on the road, don't panic. Always agree meeting places before you go somewhere, and play safe by having a double back-up plan: "If I don't see you outside the Latino Roxy cinema at 1.00, I'll see you at the Lufthansa office at 4.00. Then I'm going back to the hostel." Try looking behind you occasionally.

HEALTH & SAFETY   *Tips for Travellers*

Learning to be safe

Safety courses have been available for business travellers for years – companies are now offering courses specifically designed for gappers. These are by no means boring – you won't be sitting at a desk taking notes!

Expeditionary Advisory Centre
Royal Geographical Society
1 Kensington Gore
London SW7 2 AR, England   Tel: +44 (0) 207591 3000

The Expeditionary Advisory Centre provides information, training and advice to anyone embarking on a scientific or adventurous expedition overseas.

Objective Team
Bragborough Lodge Farm
Braunston, Nr Daventry   Tel: +44 (0) 1788 899 029
Northants NN11 7HA, England   see: www.gap-year.com

Objective Team specialises in providing safety training, including the training of journalists going to war zones.

They offer a unique one-day safety awareness course for gappers and their instructors include ex British Army SAS and intelligence officers. The course is designed to teach you how to recognise, evaluate and so avoid dangerous situations. The course gives advice on how to check the security situation within countries and where to get help if necessary, what to take, how to stay safe whilst travelling and advice on accommodation, changing money and security of possessions.

Also included is a section on medical and first aid, 'how to keep yourself going', and a session at the end of the day 'for girls by girls'.

Courses are held weekly in London and elsewhere on demand.

The Knowledge Gap
Pitt Farmhouse   Tel: +44 (0) 117 974 3217
Chevithorne   Fax: +44 (0) 117 974 3307
Devon EX16 7PU, England   see: www.gap-year.com

The Knowledge Gap has been set up by a group of former SAS soldiers and experienced travellers who have identified a demand amongst students for gaining some practical advice on travel safety prior to embarking upon their gap year.

The tuition offered is provided through a two-and-a-half day residential course based on Exmoor where students will stay in youth hostel accommodation (part of the learning experience) and receive a mixture of indoor and outdoor instruction. The courses are run on

Tips for Travellers — **HEALTH & SAFETY**

Exmoor because, in the majority of cases, it introduces students to an unfamiliar environment.

The course is designed to make you aware of common dangers associated with gap year travel and to demonstrate that these can generally be avoided with a little prior planning and preparation. The course is broken down into useful topic areas:

- *Know yourself:* confidence, control, awareness, respect, responsibility
- *Know where you're going:* politics, law, culture, religion, etiquette, seasons
- *Know who you're going with:* travelling companions
- *Know who you're leaving behind:* family, communication
- *Know how to get there:* tickets, visas, passports
- *Know how to get back:* insurance, embassies
- *Know what to take:* clothing, footwear, essentials, documents, customs
- *Know how to carry it:* rucksacks, daysacks. money belts
- *Know how to live:* accommodation, money, authorities
- *Know your next move:* 'planes, trains, buses, cars, taxis, hitch-hiking, directions
- *Know where you are:* maps, getting un-lost
- *Know your body:* diet, hygiene, common ailments, diseases, altitude
- *Know your instincts*: sensing danger, keeping control
- *Know what to do:* breakdown, emergencies, first aid, self-defence, confrontation, rescue signals
- *Know the risks:* sex, date rape, drugs, alcohol
- *Know the environment:* animals, acts of God.

In no way is the course all theory – it is run on the principle: 'the more you put in, the more you get out' and demands both participation and a sense of humour. It is best to arrive with few assumptions.

Stop thief!

If you have money, a camera or a passport stolen abroad (and the chances of this are high), report the theft immediately to the nearest police station and make sure you have some written record from them giving the date that you did so with all relevant details (some insurance policies will not pay out if you allow more than 24 hours to elapse). Dress smartly (and cover up; going in a bikini is not a good idea) and expect an uphill battle: police in popular budget destinations may have had to deal with hundreds of insurance scams in the past and may not be sympathetic.

Stay polite and calm, but firm. It is very unlikely anyone will catch the thief or get your stuff back – all you need is a record of the police report for your insurance claim. Ask someone back home to notify insurers and post or fax a copy of the police notification home. Many insurers will not pay up for loss or theft unless the police are notified. This also applies if you are involved in any accident likely to result in an insurance claim. Keep records of everything that might be important – better to throw it away later than not to have it when needed.

SAFETY:
boring and a bit obvious, but really important

- Travel in pairs if you can
- Never hitch-hike or accept lifts from strangers
- Avoid badly-lit streets after dark
- Never discuss your own or your family's financial situation with strangers
- Never try unknown substances
- Never carry unopened parcels for people, especially when you fly
- Always let people know where you are going and stay in touch with people back home regularly.
- Don't swim in strong currents or heavy waves: several gap year students have drowned this way
- Check fire exit routes in hostels or other buildings where you plan to stay
- Shake out clothes and shoes before you put them on: snakes, scorpions or allergy-causing plants may have got inside
- If you don't like the look of some of the other people in a hostel, put your bed against the door at night
- Keep windows open if you are in a room with a gas water heater or other source of carbon monoxide to let gases escape if the equipment is faulty

Getting about: Trains, buses, 'planes

Trains
Inter-Railing

If you want to visit a lot of countries, one of the best ways to travel is by train on an Inter-Rail ticket. With Inter-Rail you have the freedom of the rail networks of Europe (and a bit beyond), allowing you to go as you please in 28 countries. From the northern lights of Sweden to the kasbahs of Morocco, you can call all the stops. Inter-Rail takes you from city centre to city centre – avoiding airport hassles, ticket queues and traffic jams, and giving you more time to make the most of your visit.

Overnight trains are available on most major routes, saving on accommodation costs, allowing you to go to sleep in one country and wake up in another! Supplements apply so ask when you book. You will have to pay extra to travel on some express inter-city trains or the Eurostar. Most major stations such as Paris, Brussels, Amsterdam and Rome have washing facilities and left luggage.

Inter-Rail passes are available for both under and over 26s, but you need to have lived in Europe for at least six months. The 12- and 22-day passes allow you to travel across one zone of your choice giving you the chance to explore a particular region of Europe; you can opt for two or three zones with a one month pass; or you can go all out for unlimited travel to as many as 28 countries in Europe, Scandinavia and North Africa.

Inter-Rail divides Europe into eight zones: you can opt to travel in as many zone as you want (see the table below), but your ticket won't include travel in the UK unless you buy it in another country.

Zone A:	Republic of Ireland
Zone B:	Norway, Sweden and Finland
Zone C:	Austria, Denmark, Germany and Switzerland
Zone D:	Croatia, the Czech and Slovak Republics, Hungary and Poland
Zone E:	Belgium, France, Luxembourg, Netherlands
Zone F:	Spain, Portugal, Morocco
Zone G:	Italy, Greece, Turkey, Slovenia (incl. a return sea ticket from Brindisi, Italy, to Patras, Greece)
Zone H:	Bulgaria, Romania, Macedonia and Yugoslavia.

GETTING ABOUT

Tips for Travellers

Inter-Rail Prices			
		Under 26	**Over 26**
Any **1** zone	12 days	£125	£182
Any **1** zone	22 days	£149	£219
Any **2** zones	One month	£195	£275
Any **3** zones	One month	£225	£320
All zones	One month	£265	£379

Prices are valid until 15 December 2003. For further details on how to buy an Inter-Rail pass, visit their website **www.inter-rail.co.uk** *and get £5 off when you book online. Alternatively visit the Travel Centre at 179 Piccadilly, or call +44 (0) 8705 848 848.*

Eurostar

The Eurostar train is a quick, easy and relatively cheap way to get to Europe. You can get from London to Calais for £69, and the trains are comfortable and run frequently. Tickets can be purchased online at **www.eurostar.com**, in an approved travel agency, or at any Eurostar train station.

Trans-Siberian express

If you're looking for a train adventure then you're unlikely to beat the Trans-Siberian Express. It will cost you about £500 for train transport only. On top of this you will need some money for food and drink, visas, air fare *etc*.

The trains can be pretty basic, varying according to which line you're travelling on and which country owns the train. Take a range of clothes – the trains have heating, but it's not always reliable. When the train stops and you get off for a few minutes, it would be worthwhile to have good clothes – you can always buy them from the many traders on board.

On some trains you can opt to upgrade to first class for about an extra $200. This should give you your own cabin with shower, wash basin and more comfort – though you may end up travelling with more English speaking people while the other backpackers and local traders selling leather and woollen goods will all be back in second class.

For China and Mongolia you'll need to have a visa for your passport to allow you into each country. Contact each relevant embassy to find out what type of visa you will need.

It's probably easiest to arrange for all your train tickets, visas and hotel accommodation through a specialist agency, about six months before you leave. This will ensure that you have all your paperwork in order and leave you to enjoy the travelling without the headache of sorting it all out – although it will cost you more to do it this way.

If you travel in late November/December you may freeze into a solid block of ice, but it will be snowing by then and the views will be spectacular. If you go in September it will be warmer and a bit cheaper.

If you want to read up about it before you go, try the *Trans-Siberian Handbook* by Bryn Thomas. It is updated frequently and it has details about the towns you'll be passing through and the timetables. But go to www.trans-siberia.com for the best and most comprehensive information about the Trans-Siberian Express anywhere. It will answer all your questions and give you useful hints. It's run by someone who has personally travelled on the trains, so he knows what he's talking about.

Buses/Coaches

Getting on a bus or coach in a foreign country, especially if you don't speak the language, can be a voyage of discovery in itself. UK bus timetables can be indescipherable, but try one in Patagonia! Get help from a local you trust, hotel/hostel staff, or the local police station if all else fails. In developing countries, locals think nothing of transporting their livestock by public transport, so be prepared to sit next to a chicken!

That said, some buses and coaches can be positively luxurious and they do tend to be cheaper than trains.

Greyhound International

**Greyhound Lines Inc
PO Box 660689
MS490 Dallas
TX 75266-0689, USA
Tel: +1 800 229 9424
www.greyhound.com**

America's legendary bus company Greyhound offers the International Ameripass (from $135 for four days to $437 for 60 days) for routes on the US mainland and selected points in Canada, and there's a separate pass for Canada with some connecting journeys between the two countries. You can travel when you want, but you must show your Ameripass/Canada Pass to a terminal or station ticket agent for validation when you start each journey.

Greyhound buses now have air conditioning, tinted windows and a loo on board, as well as a strict no smoking policy. Greyhound also arranges a 'GoHostelling' package that combines bus travel and hostel accommodation. There's the usual 10% discount for ISIC and Euro 26 ID cardholders. The bus company operates outside America too, with Greyhound Pioneer Australia and Greyhound Coach Lines Africa.

Planes

Travel is one area where the internet has definitely grown up. You can search for ticket information, timetables, prices and special offers whether you're travelling by air, sea, train or bus. In some cases you can book and pay by keying your credit card details into an online order form. Make sure you read the 'Terms and Conditions' to see what you're paying for and whether you can get your money back.

Because the internet gives customers so much information to choose from, travel companies have to compete harder to win your booking. Because it shows you what flexibility is possible (a lot), you could also find your decision-making turned upside down. Instead of planning a round-the-world trip, for example, by deciding on your destinations and then finding the cheapest flight path through them, you could look at the special offers available first, see how far in advance you can book a ticket, and decide what to do with the destinations you've got when you've booked. One of the destinations – for example, a voluntary work assignment beginning in Tanzania in February – may have to be on a fixed date; the others may not.

You can sometimes (but not always) find better ticket bargains by searching the web than by using the phone. As well as bargain one-destination flights the web's a good place to look for round-the-world (RTW) tickets, which are getting cheaper and more flexible for all sorts of reasons, including the formation of alliances between airlines and the speed at which complex route bookings can be made by agents – often using the internet themselves.

The route you have in mind may be different from the samples on offer, but you can usually have one tailor-made for you and the prices you find on the web, with simple maps, can act as a benchmark. Make sure you check out the company making an offer on the web before you use internet booking procedures (does it have a verifiable address and phone number?), and read all the small print in a booking contract before you agree to buy – just as you would outside the virtual world.

Bargain flights

Scheduled airlines often offer discount fares for students under 26, so don't rule them out. Other cheap flights are advertised regularly in the newspapers and on the web (see above). All sorts of travel agents can fix you up with multi-destination tickets, and student travel specialists like STA Travel often know where to find the best deals for gap year students.

Above all, travel is an area where searching the internet for good deals should be top of your list – though it works best for single-destination trips rather than complex travel routes where you have to change several times. Here are some useful websites – the prices are examples we found in February 2003:

Tips for Travellers

GETTING ABOUT

Airline Network — www.airline-network.co.uk

Flight search engine and booking service for low cost scheduled flights.

Sample flight: London to Moscow with BH direct from £157 plus £53.40 tax.

Austravel — www.austravel.net

Combines scheduled and charter flights to produce RTW itineraries. Information about and flights to Australia, New Zealand, Asia and the South Pacific.

Sample flights: London Heathrow to Sydney, Brisbane, Adelaide, Melbourne or Perth from £489. London to Dubai from £379.

Bargain Holidays — www.bargainholidays.co.uk

Not really for students en route to a backpacking trail, but worth a look in case there's a cheap offer that takes you close to where you're heading.

Sample flight: Manchester to Jamaica from £299.

Bridge the World — www.b-t-w.co.uk

Website that gives RTW routes using Quantas/British Airways. For example, the 'Out There & Back' goes from London – Rio de Jeneiro – overland to Buenos Aires – Auckland – overland to Christchurch – Melbourne – overland to Sydney – Bangkok – Hong Kong – overland to Beijing – London from £899.

British Midland — www.flybmi.com

Low cost flights to European destinations.

Sample flights: return flights from Newcastle International to Dusseldorf from £178. Return flight from london Heathrow to Amsterdam from £122.

Buzz — www.buzzaway.com

Lufthansa offshoot: good for cheap flights to European destinations; prices can start at under £10 – in Februaury 2003 Buzz was offering a one-way flight to Amsterdam for £5 plus tax.

GETTING ABOUT

Tips for Travellers

Cheap Flights   www.cheapflights.co.uk

Flights and destinations, special deals, holiday offers, round-the-world tickets, last minute bargains.

Sample 'flight deal of the day' (February 2003): return ticket to Brisbane from Heathrow, £539; London Gatwick to Toronto, £205.

Deckchair.com   www.deckchair.com

Aims to find you the best available fare. Key in where you want to leave from and go to, plus dates and other details, and wait to see what happens! We keyed in London Stansted to Tokyo and found return fares from £415 (Aeroflot Russian Airlines) to £1366 (SAS Scandinavian Airlines).

EasyJet   www.easyjet.co.uk

Easyjet has recently merged with Go to offer even more cheap flights to European destinations with further reductions if you book over the internet. Sample flight: one-way from Luton to Athens, £51.

Flightbookers   www.flightbookers.com

Cheap online flights can be booked from this site. Sample flight: London to Beijing with Air France from £380.

Last Minute   www.lastminute.com

Finds tickets from 24-hours' notice to a few weeks ahead. Negotiates discount flights with various airlines. Sample flight: London to New York return from £129.03 plus £71.70 tax; London Gatwick to Moscow return from £138 plus £40.70 tax.

Last Stop   www.laststop.co.uk

Another site for last-minute bargain holidays.

One World   www.oneworldalliance.com

Alliance between Aer Lingus, American Airlines, BA, Cathay Pacific, Finnair, Iberia, LanChile & Qantas. Their programmes include 'oneworld explorer' and 'circle trip explorer', both of which are good if you want to cover lots of miles and make lots of stopovers. You can do six continents (mixed air and overland travel) for under £1500.

Tips for Travellers — GETTING ABOUT

Ryanair   www.ryanair.com

Low cost airline to European destinations – many outward flights are actually free! – but make sure you check how much the return flight will be.

SkyDeals   www.skydeals.co.uk

Sample flight: London Gatwick to Barbados from £400.

STA Travel
6 Wrights Lane   Tel: +44 (0) 870 160 6070
London W8 6TA, England   www.statravel.co.uk

STA Travel are specialists in travel for students and those under 26, offering low cost flights, accommodation, insurance, gap year travel, overland and adventure tours, ski and snowboard, round-the-world tickets, discount cards, city breaks and international travel help.

They offer students and those under 26 exclusive discounts on travel with quality airlines. Most airline tickets are valid for one year, so it's often impossible to finalise all your plans before you leave the UK. With this in mind STA Travel tickets are designed to offer the greatest possible flexibility. You can usually change your dates of travel and even your route for little cost.

STA Travel have Travel Help branches or agents in over 50 countries worldwide and if you can't get into a local STA Travel branch, then there's a Help Desk telephone service, which provides essential back-up for travellers on the move. With over 400 branches worldwide and well-travelled, experienced staff STA Travel can assist you with all the travel plans for your trip.

Thomas Cook   www.thomascook.com

General travel agent with high street branches offering flights and late deals.

Travelocity   www.travelocity.co.uk

Key in destination and budget and see what Travelocity's search engine finds. Also has destination guide, flight timetables, maps and weather.

Sample flight: London to Hong Kong return with Lufthansa, £300 plus tax.

visit: www.gap-year.com

GETTING ABOUT

Car

Another popular option is to travel (mostly around Europe) by car. It means you can kip in it when necessary, save money on train fares and you don't have to lug your rucksack into cafés.

Make sure you know the motoring regulations of the countries you'll be visiting – they vary from country to country, and **www.gov.uk/driver** is a good place to start looking for them. Check that you are insured to drive abroad and that this is clear on the documentation you carry with you. The AA advises that you carry your vehicle insurance vehicle registration documents and a current tax disc in the car and, of course, take your driving licence with you. If you still have an old paper licence you might want to consider getting it updated to a photo licence before you go, but make sure you leave enough time for this – the DVLNI isn't known for its speedy processing. You can pick up a DL1 form from most Post Offices, your local Vehicle Licencing office or call the DVLNI on +44 (0) 28 7034 1469.

It is also advisable to take an International Driving Permit (IDP) as not all countries accept the British driving licence. In theory you don't need one in any of the EC member states, Iceland, Liechtenstein or Norway, but the AA recommends having an IDP if you intend to drive in any country other than the UK. And as it only costs £4 it's better than getting into trouble and being fined for driving without a valid licence. If you are going to Iraq, Nigeria or Somalia you will need a second, special, IDP (another £4).

An International Driving Permit is valid for 12 months and can be applied for up to three months in advance. Applying is easy – The AA and RAC issue the permits – you must be over 18 and hold a current UK driving licence. You'll need to fill in a form and provide your UK driving licence, passport and a recent passport-sized photo of yourself, which you can take to a participating Post Office or post them to the AA or RAC (see below for address), allowing at least ten working days. Both the AA and RAC websites have loads of info about the permit and driving abroad in general, and you can even download the application form.

It's a good idea to put your car in for a service a couple of weeks before you leave and, unless you're a mechanic, it is worth getting breakdown cover specifically for your trip abroad with any of the major recovery companies such as the AA, RAC or Green Flag. If you end up stuck on the side of the road it could end up an expensive experience.

The RAC recommends taking a first aid kit, fire extinguisher, warning triangle, headlamp beam reflectors and spare lamp bulbs. These are all required by law in many countries and make sense anyway.

The Automobile Association Fanum House
Erskine
Renfrewshire PA8 6BW, England
Tel (IDP): +44 (0) 800 55 00 55
(Other motoring enquiries): +44 (0) 8705 500 600
www.theaa.com

The RAC Motoring Services
Travel Administration
PO Box 1500
Bristol BS99 2LH, England
Tel (IDP): +44 (0) 800 550055
(Other motoring enquiries): +44 (0) 906 471740
www.rac.co.uk

Ships

If you want to get to the continent, then taking a ferry across to France or Belgium can be cheap – but why not sail free as a working crew member on ships? Contact head offices of shipping companies to find out the procedures before you leave the UK and find out how to book a passage from a foreign port.

A useful book on this subject is *Working on Cruise Ships*, Price £9.99 (plus £1.50 p&p), published by Vacation Work Abroad, 9 Park End Street, Oxford OX1 1HJ, Tel: +44 (0) 1865 241 978, Fax: +44 (0) 1865 790 885.

Bicycles

Of course, if you're feeling hyper-energetic, you could cycle around the place. This is really popular in north Europe, especially Holland, where the ground tends to be flatter. Most travel agents would be able to point you in the right direction, or you can just rely on hiring bikes while you are out there – make sure you understand the rules of the road.

Florence by Bike

Via San Zanobi 120-121
50129 Firenze
Italy

Tel: +39 055 488 992
see: www.gap-year.com

Florence by Bike is a well-organised bike rental company operating in Tuscany. To see what they offer, take a look at their impressive website.

Accommodation

Hostels are to backpackers what eggs are to bacon, and there are masses to choose from. How safe they are (from fire, flood, drugs, prostitution, theft, rip-off scams *etc*) obviously varies widely and gappers often rely on *Rough Guide* or *Lonely Planet* guidebooks or the word-of-mouth recommendations from other backpackers to find a suitable one. Check out **www.hostelworld.com** for hostels pretty much anywhere.

No-one expects five-star conditions and most backpackers don't care too much about the usual drawbacks (from cockroaches to back-breaking beds) as long it's cheap – most hostels would have to double their prices to conform to rigorous health and safety regulations.

Use your common sense and always check where the fire exits are when arriving at a hostel – it's too late to look if there's already a fire and you're trying to get out if the building. This may sound odd, but don't have a bath without some ventilation – faulty water heaters give off lethal and undetectable carbon monoxide fumes and will kill you without you realising it as you fall gently to sleep, never to wake up again. Use your instincts – if you the think the hostel's dodgy or simply not up to scratch, go and find another one.

Keeping in touch: phone, e-mail, snail mail

Spare a thought for those you're leaving behind – friends as well as family. Not only will they be worried about your safety, but they may actually be interested in your travels – most are probably jealous and wish they could go too.

You might find your parents are panic-stricken at the thought of you going off into the wide world without them, especially if you are travelling under your own steam rather than on an organised project. Their way of showing they care may be to treat you like you're six years old again – they can't help it – humour them. Try to reach a compromise about how often you will get in touch with them – once a fortnight seems reasonable.

It's not just about keeping them happy: make sure you tell them where you are and where you are going – that way if something does happen to you, at least they know where to start looking. Backpackers do go missing, climbers have accidents, trekkers get lost; at least if someone is concerned by you not getting in touch when expected they can then alert the police. Of course if you don't stick to what you agreed, don't be surprised if the international police come looking for you.

On the receiving end

You probably can't wait to get away, but you'll be surprised how homesickness can creep up on you when you're thousands of miles away. Getting letters or e-mails can be a great pick-me-up if you're feeling homesick, weary or lonely, so distribute your address widely to friends and family before you go in order to ensure a steady supply of mail. If you're not able to leave behind an exact address then you can have letters sent to the local Poste Restante, often at a main post office, and collect them from there. Also, parcels do usually get through, but don't send anything valuable.

Phone

Use a credit card if you can. If you walk into any international hotel you should be able to use a Visa or Mastercard to pay for an international phone call, but watch out for overcharging. Or you can reverse the charges: if the international operator doesn't understand, try using the American term 'collect call'.

One alternative is to take a chargecard with you. This avoids having to get to grips with local phonecards, operators who don't speak your language and having enough local currency coins to feed the payphone. If you do a search on the internet you will find various offers and schemes – check what you're getting before you give your credit card details. We've detailed a couple of the more well-known companies below – but you may be able to find a better deal elsewhere.

You can use BT's *Chargecard* to phone home from abroad from any phone – just call the operator and quote your pin number. The calls are charged to your BT phone account back home and are itemised on the bill; weekly limits can be set in advance. There are different types of Chargecard accounts you can set up, including limiting card use to one number or a set of numbers. For further details on BT Chargecards call: Freephone +44 (0) 800 345 144.

Alpha Telecom's *Global Calling Service* is designed for anyone wishing to save money on international phone calls when calling from abroad – especially from hotels, payphones and mobile telephones. Alpha's international calling network can be used from more than 60 countries (check there's one in your destination country) by dialling a freephone access number and then entering a unique Alpha account number and PIN. This account works in the opposite way to the BT Chargecard in that you pay for your account up front and then use the card until your credit is used up. You can check your account at any time over the phone and top it up from your credit card.

visit: www.gap-year.com

Mobiles

If you're one of those people who needs to be attached to your mobile day and night, you'll probably want to take it with you. Make sure you've set up your account to allow you to make and receive calls and text messages in all the countries you'll be travelling to (and e-mails if you've got a WAP phone).

Try to limit use of your mobile to emergencies – they usually cost a fortune to run abroad as you pay for all the incoming calls at international rates too. It's worth insuring the handset as mobile theft is common and if it's the latest model, try not to flash it around

But don't rule out using your mobile phone as gap year kit; it might save your life if you break your leg half way up a mountain and need to call for help (make sure you keep the battery charged).

Snail mail

Aerogrammes are a cheap way of writing from most countries. Registering letters usually costs only a few pence (or equivalent) from third world countries, and is definitely worthwhile. Postcards are quick, cheap and easy – though not very private.

E-mail

Really useful technologies are rare, but e-mailing is one of them. What's more, you can now send e-mails free from almost any web-connected computer to almost any other, using services like Hotmail. These are usually free because they are being paid for by advertising or telephone line rental charges. All you do is get the free e-mail website up on a computer screen before you leave the UK and key in your registration details to get a free account. Then, if you can get to a cybercafé or internet kiosk in an airport, hotel, university, office or home when you're abroad you can simply log in to your mailbox (remember your 'User ID' and password if these are part of the package) and receive messages or send them back home.

It beats picture postcards for speed, and you can write much more. If you're a techie with a digital camera and access to computer equipment, you can send your photos 10,000 miles home as e-mail attachments minutes after you've taken them. Here are some free e-mail providers we found:

www.altavista.com   www.postmaster.co.uk
www.excite.co.uk   www.talk21.co.uk
www.hotmail.com   www.yahoo.co.uk

Hotmail is the best known of these, although in practice there is little difference between the services. Most give the opportunity to redirect mail from other e-mail addresses, so you don't need to worry about telling everyone what your new e-mail address is. A BT or other UK service will give you the comfort of communications back-up at home, where someone can sort things out for you if you leave them your password and contract details.

If you think getting to a cybercafé is going to be hard there are always WAP phones (you need to register your e-mail address before you leave). Air Mail (**www.airmail.co.uk**) will forward e-mails to you as text messages on your mobile, and you can send e-mails by simply sending them a text message which they will forward as an e-mail. Check their website for their up-to-date tariff. In practice, however, if there are no internet facilities in the area then the chances are there won't be a mobile phone signal either, and you may have to resort to more traditional methods of communication.

Having said that, thousands of cybercafés now sprinkle the globe, and even nuns in Bolivia have got wired up to the Net, so you'll probably find somewhere that you can e-mail home from at some point. This has got to be the quickest and most reliable way to communicate.

Going it alone

I began my travels with two guys I had previously shared a flat with at university – the idea of five months away on my own didn't really appeal. However, I hadn't realised how difficult and essential it is to find someone who is truly compatible to travel with. Although great friends at home, things can be very different when you head off. The differences in priorities and ideas about travel soon became clear once we were on the road. Their concerns about accommodation, food and transport soon took priority. Not being very fussy myself, this was quite hard.

After a month of travelling with the others I decided it wasn't for me, and a week or so later I was a solo traveller and much happier for it. With only myself to please things became much easier and more fun. I could make the decisions as to how long to stay in places, and when to leave.

Being on your own encourages you to interact more with strangers and, in turn, you become more approachable and so you learn more about the local culture and way of life through the local people. This can lead to unexpected experiences such as being invited to stay. One of my best experiences so far has to be visiting one of the villages in Fiji where I attended a church service after which I went for lunch with one of the families in the village. I learnt so much more and developed a much greater appreciation for the place than in all my time spent with my own country folk. The local people were extremely enthusiastic about showing me their country and making sure I had a good time. Having photos of these people will be more memorable as they are my own personal experiences as opposed to the same as everyone else's.

Although you have to be slightly more careful travelling on your own and it isn't suited to everyone or indeed every country, I have found it much more rewarding and would have no reservations about planning a trip on my own again. The others still don't understand why I like travelling alone and wouldn't dream of doing it themselves. They have carried on together and are having a great time; it just wasn't for me. Fortunately we are still really good friends and haven't fallen out – it was just a difference in priorities, which weren't considered fully before we left. Things such as budget, what type of accommodation you want and personal objectives really need to be thought out carefully, if you can't find anyone who shares your priorities then go it alone. I have not been lonely once since I've been away, as I've met so many people doing the same things along the way.

Jodie

5 Travel Companies

Travel agents and tour organisers

The names of exotic travel agents can be found in advertisements in the national daily and Sunday newspapers. Voodoo Ventures, say, may promise three weeks of throbbing thrills in Haiti. Make sure you get references and talk to a gapper who has been on their gap year before you hand over hard cash or sign up for anything.

If you're not sure about a company you can contact the Year Out Group and see if they're a member or if the YOG have heard of them – **www.yearoutgroup.org**, Tel: +44 (0) 7980 395 789.

As gap years become more popular and so become big business, more travel companies are offering travel deals specifically aimed at gappers. The following travel companies are just some of the ones we found that are used to dealing with independent travellers and students:

AAHA Adventure Trekking & Expedition

PO Box 12205
Kathmandu
Nepal

Tel: +977 1 357135
Fax: +977 1 357135
see: www.gap-year.com

Nepal-based AAHA is a government-licensed trekking and touring company specialising in nature, culture, adventure and tailor-made programmes for travel in Nepal, Tibet, Bhutan and India.

The company offers trekking, mountaineering, climbing, mountain flights, jungle safaris, river rafting, hiking, sightseeing, hot air ballooning, mountain biking and various tours including: pilgrimage, cultural, religious, anthropological, and buddhist. It is also happy to organise your hotel reservations and all domestic and international air ticketing and land transport.

Importantly, AAHA is committed to the preservation of the environment, the safeguarding of ecological balance, and the emancipation and economic advancement of women in more remote parts of the country.

AAHA prides itself on its customer service and promises to "definitely put every ounce of effort to make your holiday a remarkable memory, an unforgettable one forever!"

African Conservation Experience

Applications Department
PO Box 9706
Solihull
West Midlands B91 3FF Tel: 0870 241 5816 (UK only)
England see: www.gap-year.com

ACE is run by Rob Harris, who lived in South Africa for 35 years and knows its game reserves well. He has links with some 20 game and nature reserves in the southern African bush where he places volunteers, and is sending out 200+ a year to Botswana, Namibia, South Africa and Zimbabwe.

Work can involve game capture and tagging, game counts, habit observation, checking game fences, anti-poaching patrols, controlled burning and everyday reserve maintenance. You could be living in a thatched rondavel or sharing a house with other staff. Fees range from an average £2500 for four-week placements (lowest £1795 for four weeks in the Kaggakamma reserve) to an average £3500 for 12-week placements, and cover flights, transfers, accommodation and food. No pocket money. If you want to phone or fax from abroad, use this number: +44 1404 811404

African Sport Experience

PO Box 58, Teignmouth Tel: +44 (0) 870 241 6976
Devon TQ14 8XW Fax: +44 (0) 1404 811404
England see: www.gap-year.com

African Sport Experience organises action sports holidays in South Africa on the Eastern Cape. During the four weeks you will receive expert tuition in your favourite sport: golf, diving or even fishing are on offer.

If you choose fishing you could find yourself landing a marlin or tunny whilst deep-sea fishing, fishing off the rocks, in the surf and salt water or fly fishing – all with an experienced supervisor, who will show you how to collect bait and prepare your catch for eating. You'll also get instruction on conservation issues and local species as well as participating in fish tagging for conservation studies. Plus there is a vast range of other activities to try: dune boarding down what are reputedly the highest sand dunes in the world, bogey boarding in the waves, kayaking, hiking through indigenous forest and along coastal trails, horse-riding on the beach, mountain biking, 4 x 4 driving, water skiing, parachute jumping or simply a few games of tennis.

AFS Community Projects Overseas

Leeming House
Vicar Lane
Leeds LS2 7JF
England

Tel: +44 (0) 113 242 6136
see: www.gap-year.com

AFS has a Schools Programme (don't let the name put you off) for ages 15-18 giving you the opportunity to live abroad for a year and learn about a country's culture and language through immersion in its way of life. You can choose from 54 countries across South America, Asia and Europe, including Argentina, Paraguay, Venezuela, Hong Kong, Indonesia, Italy, Germany and the USA.

Students live with a volunteer host family as a member of that family, attend a local school, and become involved in community life. Programmes depart in the summer. You'll be provided with language kits as part of your preparation as well as taking part in orientation activities before you go. Once abroad you will be well supported by local volunteers.

The programme cost is £3950, which AFS help you to fundraise. The company also offers full or part scholarship opportunities to deserving candidates through their International Diversity Scholarship Fund.

Alliances Abroad

2423 Pennsylvania Avenue NW
Washington DC 20037
USA

Tel: +1 (202) 467 9467
Fax: +1 (202) 467 9460

If you're looking for something a bit different, tailored to your needs, time frame, budget, skills, interests *etc*, Alliances Abroad will design a customized programme for you or your group. Their vast range of packages include teaching English (in China or Spain); internships and work placements in the US; working in rural Australia on a ranch or farm; volunteer placements in Costa Rica (environment and national parks), South Africa (helping out zoologists and vets), Hawaii (organic farm work); Venezuela (adventure, language and volunteering).

Their experienced staff will help you with all of your travel needs, including travel arrangements, recommendations on what to do while abroad, visa/work permit procurement, airport transfers and all that other organisational stuff. Most of their programmes offer guaranteed placement before departure, airport pickup, local orientation and full-time support before, during and after the programme.

COMPANIES: B – C

Bridge the World
45-47 Chalk Farm Road, Camden
London NW1 8AJ, England
Tel: +44 (0) 870 444 7474
see: www.gap-year.com

Organises tailor-made RTW trips and has experience with gap year travellers. If you're interested in visiting Australia, there's a 'wine and canapé' meeting on the first Thursday of every other month at their West End office (4 Regent Place, London W1B 5EA) giving you the chance to discuss your plans with consultants. Phone in advance as places are limited.

CTS Travel
44 Goodge Street
London W1, England
Tel: +44 (0) 20 7290 0620

Student travel specialists offering adventure tours, worldwide flights, budget accommodation, rail and coach passes and student travel cards, insurance, budget car rental and lots of other travel stuff. Can also be contacted at University College London, 25 Gordon Street, London WC1 and at the University of Westminster, 35 Marylebone Road, London NW1.

Encounter

2001 Camp Green
Debenham, Stowmarket
Suffolk IP14 6LA, England

Tel: +44 (0) 1728 862222
Fax: +44 (0) 1728 861127

Encounter organises overland trips in groups of 8-23 people, usually with a wide spread of nationalities. Your main mode of transport is a truck, which you could ride all the way from London to Cape Town or even to Kathmandu via Nairobi. Trips last between two and 26 weeks and are also run to South America. It's mainly camping, with hostel stays in big centres. There are also shorter tours like the six-day trek in Borneo. You can book from the UK or when you're out there.

Exodus Travels

9 Weir Road
London SW12 0LT, England

Tel: +44 (0) 20 8675 5550
Fax: +44 (0) 20 8673 0779

Exodus organises adventure trips for groups of between eight and 22 people. Their tours range from one-week multi-activity holidays in Europe to overland expeditions across Africa, Asia, South America and Australia, as well as treks to most of the world's great mountain ranges. Brochure hotline: +44 (0) 20 8673 0859

Goaway

Tel: +44 (0) 20 7224 7070
Fax: (0) 20 7224 5353

Visit India with its population of over one billion people and diversity like you've never seen before – to the point where it's often described as more like a continent than a country. Wherever you go, north, south, east or west, you'll come across a vast array of different people, different customs, different religions and different languages. India is enriched with history, culture, wildlife and artistic scenery and it is these aspects that draw so many visitors to her lands year on year.

Specialist tour operator Goaway offers flexibility for those who want to travel to India. Your journey will begin when you arrive in Goa where you can relax or from where you can travel northwards taking in many famous historical and religious sights along the way.

You can use your journey to take in many of the must-see places of the world. Some of the most popular sights include the Taj Mahal in Agra, the beaches in Goa, wildlife parks of Kerala, the Himalaya mountains, Dharmsala – and you might even catch a glimpse of Bollywood stars in Mumbai.

visit: www.gap-year.com

COMPANIES: G

Travel Companies

Greyhound International

Greyhound Lines Inc
PO Box 660689
MS490 Dallas
TX 75266-0689, USA   Tel: +1 800 229 9424

America's legendary bus company Greyhound offers the International Ameripass (from $135 for four days to $437 for 60 days) for routes on the US mainland and selected points in Canada, and there's a separate pass for Canada with some connecting journeys between the two countries. You can travel when you want, but you must show your Ameripass/Canada Pass to a terminal or station ticket agent for validation when you start each journey.

Greyhound buses now have air conditioning, tinted windows and a loo on board as well as a strict no smoking policy. Greyhound also arranges a 'GoHostelling' package that combines bus travel and hostel accommodation. There's the usual 10% discount for ISIC and Euro 26 ID cardholders. The bus company operates outside America too, with Greyhound Pioneer Australia and Greyhound Coach Lines Africa.

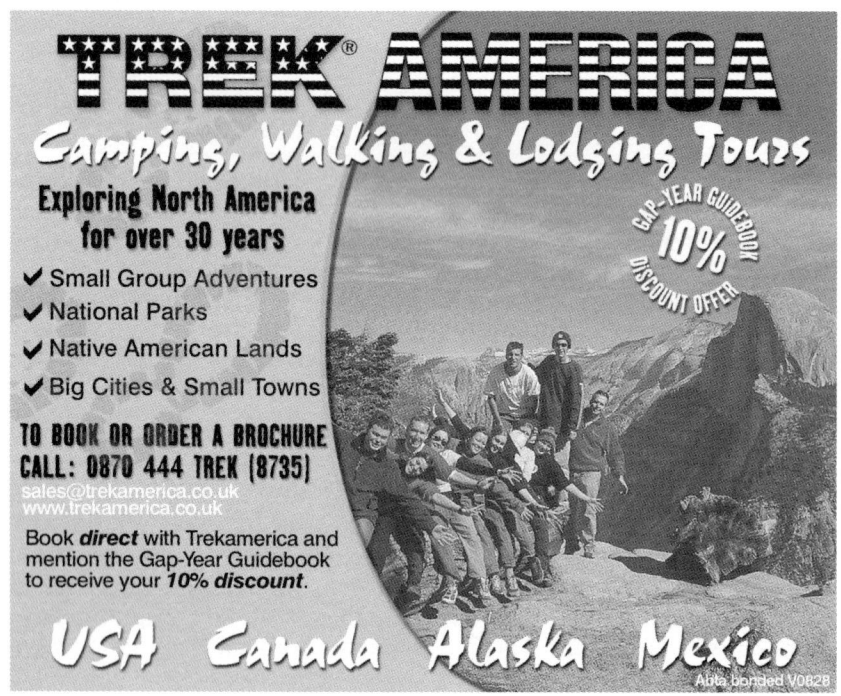

Journey Latin America

12/13 Heathfield Terrace
London W4 4JE, England

Tel: +44 (0) 20 8747 3108
Fax: +44 (0) 20 8742 1312

JLA is the UK's major specialist in travel to Latin America. Its 'Open-Jaw' transatlantic tickets permit you to fly into one country and out of another. Airpasses can be arranged throughout the continent to cut out long, potentially dangerous bus routes. The Mercosur airpass allows you to travel economically within Argentina, Brazil, Uruguay, Paraguay and Chile. Price is calculated by mileage – so, for example, Rio – Iguacu – Buenos Aires – Montevideo – Asuncion – Sao Paulo covers 3200 miles, costing $345.

Madventurer

Adamson House
65 Westgate Road
Newcastle upon Tyne NE1 1SG
England

Tel: +44 (0) 191 261 1996
Fax: +44 (0)191 261 9010

Madventurer programmes are flexible and are aimed at gap year students, undergraduates, recent graduates and career breakers.

As a Madventurer you will visit some amazing places, meet interesting people and take part in a range of thrilling activities. You will travel on a fully-equipped 4x4 overland vehicle, which by its very nature is fun and challenging. You will work as part of a team, sharing the fun, exhilarating and arduous experiences. Overlanding allows you to explore those out-of-the-way places that you would otherwise not be able to reach safely on your own.

Each adventure group has two expedition leaders who are fully trained mechanics and have a wealth of travelling experience in Africa and Latin America, which they are happy to pass on.

You will participate in daily tasks such as setting up the camp and shopping for fresh supplies in local markets. The overland vehicle has a tape deck stereo, coolbox for drinks, tarps that can be rolled up for all round viewing, a truck expedition medical kit, a global positioning system, truck spares and all the camping and cooking equipment.

There is an exciting range of adventures to choose from, including the Gorilla Trek Safari which lasts for 22 days taking you through Kenya and Uganda, and the Andes to Amazon adventure, following in the footsteps of the Incas by hiking to the mysterious ruins of Machu Picchu. After such breathtaking and exhilarating experiences, there will be plenty of time to relax, socialise and soak up the sun.

Madventurer also offers Combo Expedition, which combines project work (see Madventurer listing in *Chapter 2: Volunteering abroad*) with community tourism, allowing you to truly experience your host country (or countries) and, in return, give something back to the people. Each group project lasts for between four to five weeks and solo projects can last from between three months and one year. The cost of a Combo Expedition is simply the cost of the Adventure and Project combined.

Mountain Beach Activity Holidays
13 Church Street
Ruddington
Nottingham
Nottinghamshire NG11 6HA   Tel: +44 (0) 115 921 5065
England   Fax: +44 (0) 1159 216 182

One company offering mountain biking holidays (with first-aid trained guides) is Mountain Beach Activity Holidays. With holidays in Greece, Portugal, Costa Rica, Brazil, Chile, Mexico, New Zealand, Scotland, Canada or France, it aims to 'emphasise the holiday element, rather than an enforced regime, and ensure a great experience.'

Most of the bikers are 20-somethings. Prices vary: from two weeks in Greece for £549 (excl. flights) to two weeks in Costa Rica for £1495 (excl. flights). Bike hire and shared accommodation included. Insurance extra.

Peak Leaders
Mansfield
Strathmiglo
Fife KY14 7QE   Tel: +44 (0) 1337 860 079
Scotland   see: www.gap-year.com

Peak Leaders UK is a family-run business dedicated to the delivery of quality gap year and time out programmes. Founded in 1998 and incorporated in 2000, the company is based in Scotland.

Winter programmes in Canada, Argentina and New Zealand include ski and snowboard instructor training, mountain safety, first aid, avalanche awareness, language, management and leadership. Summer programmes in Indonesia and Argentina include expedition leadership, mountain and jungle training, diving, sailing, trekking, palaeontology, mountain biking and project work.

Groups are small and programmes are highly structured, leading to certified awards and skills for life. Emphasis is on safety, enjoyment and high grade training. Peak Leaders work with the Year Out Group and promotes the FCO 'know before you go' scheme.

Phoenix Expeditions
College Farm, Far Street
Wymeswold
Leicestershire LE12 6TZ, England

Tel: +44 (0) 1509 881818
Fax: +44 (0) 1509 881822

Specialises in safaris and expeditions in Africa, Turkey and the Middle East. Trips range from 18 days to 20 weeks. Sample trip: Zimbabwe to the Cape, via Botswana and Namibia, 32 days, from £385 plus kitty. Extras like quad biking, white water rafting and bungee jumping cost a bit more.

Senevolu

Senegal

Tel: +221 550 48 85
Fax: +221 855 71 72
see: www.gap-year.com

The minimum duration of Senevolu's Cultural Homestay programme is three weeks, but you can stay as long as a year. During the first five days you will stay at a hostel for an orientation period. This orientation includes immersion in the Senegalese culture, language courses (French/Wolof) and excursions in the surroundings of Dakar. You will then move to a host family where you'll participate in all-day activities: trips, celebrations, ataya *etc*.

From Monday to Thursday Senevolu organises cultural workshops (two sessions each day of two hours each). You can choose from the following activities: djembé, danse, kora and batik (African dyeworks). During the weekends Senevolu can organise excursions for groups of five people or more.

STA Travel
6 Wrights Lane
London W8 6TA, England

Tel: +44 (0) 870 160 6070
see: www.gap-year.com

STA Travel are specialists in travel for students and those under 26, offering low cost flights, accommodation, insurance, gap year travel, overland and adventure tours, ski and snowboard, round-the-world tickets, discount cards, city breaks and international travel help.

They offer students and those under 26 exclusive discounts on travel with quality airlines. Most airline tickets are valid for one year, so it's often impossible to finalise all your plans before you leave the UK. With this in mind STA Travel tickets are designed to offer the greatest possible flexibility. You can usually change your dates of travel and even your route for little cost.

STA Travel have Travel Help branches or agents in over 50 countries worldwide and if you can't get into a local STA Travel branch, then there is a Help Desk telephone service, which provides essential backup for travellers on the move. With over 400 branches worldwide and well-travelled, experienced staff STA Travel can assist you with all the travel plans for your trip.

STEN (Save the Earth Network)
PO Box CT 3635　　　　　　　　　　Tel: +233 21 667791
Cantonments-Accra, Ghana　　　　　Fax: +233 21 669625

STEN organises eco-tourism programmes in Ghana in conjunction with a network of tour operators there. The trips, in small groups led by a guide, include hiking, river rafting and canoeing, mountaineering, villages and beaches, culture and photo tours, traditional stories, historic sites, traditional drumming and dances, traditional houses, trekking, touring environmental conservation projects, animal sanctuaries and nature tourism. Accommodation is with local host families or in hotels. The cost of $140 a week includes a room and board – usually Ghanaian dishes – but doesn't cover transport or health insurance. The STEN director, Eben Mensak, can be reached by e-mail at ebensten@yahoo.com if you don't want to phone Ghana!

Trailfinders
215 Kensington High Street
London W8 6BD, England　　　　　　Tel: +44 (0) 20 7937 1234

Trailfinders has four offices in London and six others around the country. They offer a one-stop service for independent travellers – including visa and medical arrangements. It is more expensive to get your vaccinations done here rather than with your GP but the service is much more efficient. You don't need to make an appointment, but try to avoid lunch time if you can as this is the busiest time. The London Travel Clinic is at 194 Kensington High Street (Tel: +44 (0) 20 7938 3999) and is open Fri-Wed, 9am to 5pm, Thursday 9am to 6pm and Saturday 10am to 5.15pm.

For flight information, call +44 (0) 20 7937 1234 (European flights); +44 (0) 20 7937 5400 (Transatlantic flights); +44 (0) 20 7938 3939 (Long-haul flights); +44 (0) 20 7938 3848 (Visa and Passport Service).

TrekAmerica
4 Waterperry Court
Middleton Road, Banbury　　　　　Tel: +44 (0) 870 444 8735
Oxfordshire OX16 4QG　　　　　　　Fax: +44 (0) 1295 257 399
England　　　　　　　　　　　　　　see: www.gap-year.com

Get the most out of your gap year experience – TrekAmerica offers you more of North America for less money! Sit back, relax and let your tour leader do all the driving, taking you where buses and trains don't go – the National Parks, Indian Lands and out-of-the-way small towns. They will also take the worry out of booking accommodation in the big cities and can offer a local's knowledge of the best places to eat, drink and party.

By sharing travelling expenses, preparing group meals, camping in the great outdoors and offering optional activities TrekAmerica allows you to stretch your budget and maximize your fun by doing and seeing more than the typical backpacker.

To get your 10% discount, you must book *direct* (not through a travel agent) with TrekAmerica and mention *The Gap-Year Guidebook* – see above for their contact details.

Trekforce Expeditions

34 Buckingham Palace Road
London SW1W 0RE
England

Tel: +44 (0) 20 7828 2275
Fax: +44 (0) 20 7828 2276
see: www.gap-year.com

Trekforce Expeditions (founded 1990) organise tough eight to 20 week conservation and teaching projects in Central and South America and East Malaysia concentrating on endangered rainforests and working with local communities.

Their extended programmes of four to five months incorporate expedition teamwork, learning new languages and teaching in rural communities, such as the Kelabit of Sarawak or the Spanish and Mayan speaking communities of Belize.

If you are looking for a challenging and rewarding adventure in a summer holiday or after graduation, go and find out more on one of their informal introduction days (apply online or by form). They accept applications throughout the year. Although volunteers are required to fundraise a set target, Trekforce provide extensive help, ideas and support.

Truck Africa

Wissett Place, Norwich Road
Halesworth, Suffolk IP19 8HY
England

Tel: +44 (0) 1509 881509
Fax: +44 (0) 1986 874114

Organises long haul adventure camping safaris for people aged 18-30. For example, the 'Trans Africa' trip lasts five months and travels from the UK to Tanzania, via (amongst other places) Marrakesh, the beaches of the Ivory Coast, the stilted villages of Benin, the Rift Valley lakes of Kenya and the Serengeti National Park.

The trip costs £2100 per person (plus £550 kitty money), which works out as £129 per week. Trips leave in October. Their UK agent is Phoenix Expeditions (Tel: +44 (0) 1509 881818).

COMPANIES: W

World Challenge Expeditions

Black Arrow House
2 Chandos Road
London NW10 6NF, England

Tel: +44 (0) 20 8728 7272
Fax: +44 (0) 20 8961 1551
see: www.gap-year.com

World Challenge Expeditions has been organising placements and expeditions to some of the most remote and culturally diverse places on Earth for over 15 years. Their progressive programmes give you the opportunity to participate in a physical adventure that teaches invaluable life skills and introduces you to wider cultures and the genuine challenge of life survival.

World Challenge Expeditions runs the following programmes:

Team Challenge: the opportunity to plan and lead your own one-month or six-week expedition to the developing world, to East Africa, the Andes and Amazon, Borneo, India and the Himalayas or Central America. Accompanied by a highly-qualified and experienced Expedition Leader, you'll be trekking in some of the most amazing scenery in the world and completing worthwhile project work.

First Challenge: offers students a range of eight- and fourteen-day expeditions including First Challenge Learning to Lead, designed specifically to develop leadership potential in students aged 18-20. Under the discreet guidance of a highly-qualified leader you will be responsible for planning and leading your own adventurous journey to Morocco, Poland, Romania and Andalucia.

It's a jungle out there

When working and living in the jungle, one becomes accustomed to the everyday appearance of a vast array of interesting creatures.

With the resident iguana enjoying the comforts of our roof, frequent visits to Terry the tarantula on the way to work as well as daily attacks by the army of coatis, it was certainly an educational experience. The Scarlet Macaws overhead and Blue Morph butterflies passing by provided a slightly more attractive and colourful side to the life of the jungle. However, none of these encounters prepared us for a visit from a 3 metre long Boa Constrictor, who decided to make himself comfortable behind our sofa!

Jo, Raleigh International in Costa Rica and Nicaragua, 2003

Your Gap Year in the UK

Business Skills

If you have your A levels sorted out (and perhaps a place on an overseas voluntary work project) the next thing to go for is work to pay for the rest of your year off. You might have some wonderful, highly sought after skills (see Chapter 1 about working as a sports instructor) or you could look for basic temporary work like shelf-stacking in supermarkets. Alternatively, you could get yourself trained up in order to find better-paid office work.

The skills most modern offices need are based on information technology, so here is some advice on training and a list of colleges that run short courses in basic computer and office skills. These skills will always come in useful and you can make good money working as an office temp.

You may be eligible for Job Seekers' Allowance or other benefits whilst you are training (**www.thesite.org.uk/newdeal/**).

Skills for work

What business skills do you really need to learn between school and university? The short answer is – just enough to get you work. In fact, you may not need training at all. If you work as a barman, waiter or shop assistant you should get trained on the job. But if you want to earn enough to travel widely in the shortest possible time, there is nothing to beat competence with computers. If you can type fast and accurately into a database, write HTML (hypertext mark-up language) or SQL or design website graphics, your chances of earning good money are high.

"We have quite a lot of 18-year-olds, coming through us," says Louise Billington of Henderson Recruitment. "We send them out to work and six months later they're different people – except for some who can't cope with work, or can't get out of bed. Most stay in a job for three or four months and save themselves a few thousand to go abroad with. We can help them if they're bright and based in London. The most important thing they need is 40-45 wpm touch-typing. You can teach yourself this with a computer package but if you're trying to teach yourself it's tempting to go off and watch *Neighbours* in the middle, or cheat. That's no good if you go into an agency for a job – you'll be tested on your skills and you'll need to understand how to format documents as well. A good telephone manner and knowledge of Microsoft Office software (Access, Excel, Powerpoint and Word) are a big help. And it helps to take the stud out of your nose."

SKILLS FOR WORK　　　　　　　　　　　　　　　　*Business Skills*

Work experience asap

Whatever your approach to finding jobs in your gap year, it's a good idea to get some work experience under your belt before you leave school. Experience is just as important as a qualification – sometimes more so – and it gets you over the chicken-and-egg hurdle: you apply for a first job; the employer asks what work experience you've had; you say none: the employer says he can't take you on without experience; you ask how you can get experience if no-one will let you get it; then you go home and shout at the cat and eat too much chocolate.

But don't give up. Most schools organise work experience placements (maybe for one or two weeks in the holidays). If yours doesn't, it's worth getting the best short-term job you can in a school holiday before you get bogged down in A level revision, even if it does not pay well. You can use contacts of families and friends, the local newspaper or you can search the web (see Chapter 8: Work in the UK and the list of gap year employers). Work experience before leaving school can be just as important as a business skills qualification, because if your work experience boss thinks you're good, he or she will probably give your prospective gap year employer a glowing reference.

Qualifications – who needs them?

It depends what you're supposed to be qualified to do. If you apply for a job where you need to type fluently in Portuguese, and you are neither Portuguese nor have lived in Portugal, you will probably have to show qualifications to prove your skills. But for everyday office skills (touch-typing; producing word-processed documents quickly, neatly and accurately; operating photocopiers; using laser printers and fax machines; e-mailing), you might find a sensible employer who is prepared to try you out rather than ask for bundles of paper qualifications. "More important than any paper qualification is that your typing speed and accuracy are strong enough to take you through the tests which agencies will ask you to undertake. Practice is vital in building up your speeds but don't despair, if you don't reach the magic 45 words per minute in the test, there may be other options available which will help you build up your speeds while you are working," says James Reed, Chief Executive, Reed Employment Services.

For many busy employers in small and medium-sized companies, it's easier to take you on for a few days on trial than check up on an array of confusing qualifications. With internet skills, you can demonstrate your abilities by referring an employer to your website.

Can you do IT?

Computer work can be dull, but if you are numerate, literate, efficient and can type information into computers accurately and fast then you can get good pay.

You may need more IT (information technology) training, but you don't have to huddle over a keyboard for months before looking for a job (colleges used to take nine months to teach what some can now accomplish in one month). Nor do you have to pay four-figure sums to learn – you can do day or evening courses at a local FE college for less than £100 and practise your word-processing at home. Public libraries also have computer training and practice areas and offer courses where you can learn computer and internet skills in your spare time.

IT is firmly on the school curriculum, and many gap year students are already familiar (sometimes expert) with the wordprocessing, database, spreadsheet and web packages used by business. This basic training, however, may need to be combined with what colleges call 'communications skills', and (as computer and internet use become more prevalent and more complicated) some extra training designed to stop you fouling everything up when you arrive at your first job.

Colleges and other business skills training centres have cottoned on to the fact that gap year students looking for work want to get good qualifications quickly, flexibly and at a reasonable price. In some cases this may mean getting an exam certificate only to confirm self-taught skills. But students are likely to have to enrol for at least part of a course to take the necessary tests, and that usually means applying in advance and paying some course fees. Check out enrolment, attendance, notice and other conditions with colleges well in advance.

Basics: touch typing

The best place to start is to learn to touch-type at least as fast as 40 words per minute. That's usually enough to get you a job and you will get faster with practice – something that's unlikely to happen if you type with two fingers.

Option one is to try teaching yourself by buying a do-it-yourself touch-typing book or kit, making up qwerty keyboard templates to hang in front of you, and making sure you don't look down at the real keyboard as you type. This can result in a lot of spilt coffee.

Option two, also DIY, is to download from the internet a touch-typing computer package like Mavis Beacon. But you need to be self-disciplined to make yourself stick to the regime.

Option three is to go on a touch-typing course: if time and money are short then a course that takes you from scratch to 20 wpm (the stage at which you don't have to look at the keys) is enough. You should then be able to get yourself up to 40 wpm by practising at home.

Timing your training

If you can fit in a short business skills course (which means mainly IT skills) before the end of the autumn, you will have qualifications when you look for work before Christmas.

CHOOSING A COURSE

At the end of this chapter is a list of colleges and training centres which offer short, flexible and/or modular courses that lead to qualifications with certificates and are, in most cases, reasonable value. We have included as many as we can fit in: there are many more. (Many of these colleges offer a plethora of other courses – like aromatherapy, bee-keeping or journalism – which are great ways of passing time but are unlikely to lead to a gap year job.)

Choosing the right course

Finding the right level

Most computer (and other business skills) courses are divided into different levels of ability. With many different companies producing these courses and examining them, people can't be sure that, say, a Level 1 Word Processing course from Pitman Training is better or worse than one produced by OCR. Here's how City & Guilds, who award over a million certificates a year, define the levels of their qualifications (which continue up to Level 7):

Level 1: introductory awards for those new to the area covering routine tasks or basic knowledge and understanding.

Level 2: qualifications for those with some knowledge of and ability in the area which acknowledge individual responsibility.

Level 3: qualifications that recognise complex work involving supervisory ability.

So if you reckon you're up to Level 2 already, you might find you don't have to pay to learn the Level 1 stuff all over again.

Which college?

Some colleges run language courses (not necessarily for A level retakes) and two- or three-term secretarial courses as well as short business skills courses, so you can choose what you want to do.

You can phone for prospectuses, or check them out on the web for key details about fees, hours and equipment before you go, and arrange a visit. It's also important to ask the college whether it has links with recruitment agencies or employers who can give you a job. The biggest and best-known are not necessarily the best value or the most fun to go to, though their qualifications may be better recognised by employers. Find out first.

Which qualifications?

Oxford, Cambridge and RSA Exams (OCR)

"RSA qualifications are well-known and widely respected by employers – RSA Stage III in typing is an assurance that you have reached over 45 words a minute" says James Reed, Chief Executive, Reed

Employment Services. As well as typing courses, OCR also offer the following well-known RSA CLAIT (Computer Literacy & Information Technology) and IBT (Integrated Business Technology) computer courses, which are useful for getting temp work and for building up your business and IT skills:

- **RSA CLAIT Stage I** includes: word processing, spreadsheets, databases, accounting and graphical representation of data, computer-aided design, desktop publishing and online communications.
- **RSA IBT Stage II** includes WP, database, spreadsheets, graphics and integration.
- **RSA IBT Stage III** includes: interrogating/manipulating existing data. You need good WP or DTP skills to produce a publication and an automated presentation.
- **RSA Text Processing Diploma** includes: word processing and medical WP, audio-transcription, medical transcription, mailmerge and shorthand.

NVQs and SVQs

NVQs (National Vocational Qualifications) or SVQs (Scottish Vocational Qualifications) are not usually the best training for gap year work. They take a full year and test 'competencies' (the ability to do a particular task). The courses involve training or learning on-the-job at work, so to get an NVQ/SVQ, you normally need to have a job first, and by the time you've got your qualification your gap year is nearly over.

There are, of course, exceptions to this rule. According to careers advisers, it is possible to take one or two modules of an NVQ/SVQ and come away with certificates. And those who really know what type of career they want to get into can get started with an NVQ. For example, if you are interested in a sport-related vocation, Levels 1-2 Sport, Recreation and Allied Occupations may well be of interest.

Fees

You may be happy to pay extra for a good reputation and pleasant surroundings, but how much? Check that VAT and all extras are included in the figure given to you. Work out how many hours a week of teaching you are getting for your money. Some 'full-time' courses run for very short hours or don't specify the hours their students are taught – saying only that they are 'flexible'. And don't forget to check under what circumstances you can change a booking or get a refund.

Teaching hours vary from course to course. Students need a lot of practice time, and complex equipment means that even practice sessions need some supervision – but you are paying for teaching as well as tapes. If you are left in front of a PC and told to follow the instruction manual, what are you going to do if you get locked into an unknown sequence and no-one is there to show you how to get out?

Find out first how much time experienced teachers will spend with you; and second, how much supervised or unsupervised time you can have to practise.

Equipment

Make sure you know what equipment you will be using on the course. Course prospectuses do not specify to colleges what hardware or software they should use to teach you. Learning how to construct a database, for example, at Level 1, does not require the latest expensive upgrade. Colleges may make you pay through the nose for using the most recent software, while learning the basics from an earlier version will teach you everything you need to know.

On the other hand, employers attach great importance to software brands, so if you haven't been trained to use a widely-used package, you may have to sell your skills harder to a prospective employer. Colleges prefer training a novice to retraining someone in a new product, so don't be put off if you feel you're clueless. If you have done information technology at school, find out what new things you will be learning.

Job prospects

Does the college keep records of where its leavers work afterwards? How many people who finished the last course got a job? Does the college have links with employment agencies? Ask these questions before you choose. And if they say they can find you a job when you qualify, make them put it in writing.

Rates of pay

Rates for computer skills vary according to which software applications and programming languages you can use. If you are good but not experienced, try the pages of *Guardian Online* (with *The Guardian* newspaper on Thursdays). Those with more than a year's experience can do even better. "If you know how to make up a presentation in PowerPoint on a Mac or a PC with Windows you could earn £12-14 an hour, and people who can operate Quark XPress are getting £12-£15 an hour," says Cara Ostryn of Aquent Partners in London. "HTML skills are worth £15-20 an hour," adds the Internet division's Steve Hudson, "but you do need to be able to deal with designers who are in a flap and telling you to move things over by two pixels pretty quickly." Some freelancers earn more than £20 an hour for creating interactive web pages using Flash, Java or Photoshop.

Note: keep copies of any certificates you do get and take them abroad when you travel if you plan to look for work.

Colleges

Over the next pages you'll find a list of colleges from all over the country which run intensive business skills courses. It is only an indicator of what's available, not a guarantee of quality. We're happy to hear from (and reports about) any training centres that offer short courses in office skills.

KEY

Size of college:
L	Large, 100+ full-time students
M	Medium, 50-100
S	Small, 0-50

Course types:
I	intensive, usually 12 weeks or less
Md	modular, can be arranged to cover the course specifications at own pace
Flex	Mix of tuition and practice time with flexible timing
Cert	Lead to recognised certificated qualifications
DIY	One or two modules studied at college/training centre. Student can enter exam for individual elements or full set of modules including ones that have been self-taught

Course contents:
WP	Word processing (document formatting, layout, typing, saving, filing, mailmerge, printing, storing)
TT	Touch-typing (computer keyboard speed training to 40wpm)
DB	Databases (construction, entry, access, calculation, manipulation, printing)
SS	Spreadsheets (construction, entry, access, calculation, manipulation, printing)
EM	E-mail (sending, receiving, forwarding, address lists, attachments, filing, sorting, retrieving, security)
Web	Web design (basic HTML tags, formatting, creating hyperlinks, inserting images, structuring websites, using FTP)

visit: www.gap-year.com

ENGLAND

Bedfordshire

Barnfield College (FE)
Rotherham Avenue, Luton
Bedfordshire LU1 5PP
Tel: 01582 569 700

L / Flex, Cert
WP, TT, DB, SS, EM, WB

Birmingham

Bournville College of Further Education
Bristol Road South, Northfield
Birmingham B31 2AJ
Tel: 0121 483 1000
www.bournville.ac.uk

L / Flex, Cert
WP, TT, DB, SS

Bristol

City of Bristol College
College Green Centre
St George's Road,
Bristol BS1 5UA
Tel: 0117 904 5000
www.cityofbristol.ac.uk

L / Flex, Cert, DIY
WP, TT, DB, SS, EM, WB

Emma Hall Business & Secretarial College
7 Duchess Road, Clifton
Bristol B58 2LA
Tel: 0117 973 4783

S / Flex, Cert, DIY
WP, TT, DB, SS, EM

Soundwell College (FE)
St Stephens Road, Kingswood
Bristol BS16 4RL
Tel: 0117 967 5101
www.soundwell.ac.uk

L / Flex, Cert
WP, TT, DB, SS, EM, WB

Cambridgeshire

Huntingdonshire Regional College
California Road,
Huntingdon
Cambridgeshire PE18 7BL
Tel: 01480 379 100
www.huntingdon.ac.uk

L / Flex, Cert, DIY
WP, TT, DB, SS, EM, WB

Business Skills **COLLEGES**

Isle College
Ramnoth Road, Wisbech
Cambridgeshire PE13 0HY
Tel: 01945 582 561

L / Flex, Cert, DIY
WP, TT, DB, SS, EM

Peterborough Regional College
Park Crescent, Peterborough
Cambridgeshire PE1 4DZ
Tel: 01733 767 366

L / Flex, Cert, DIY
WP, TT, DB, SS, EM, WB

Cheshire

Newton Secretarial School
12L Saltney House
Chesterbank Business Park
River Lane, Saltney
Chester, Cheshire CH4 8SL
Tel: 01244 681 814 / 01244 537265

S / I, Flex, Cert, DIY
WP, TT

South Trafford College
Manchester Road, West Timperley
Altrincham, Cheshire WA14 5PQ
Tel: 0161 952 4600
www.stcoll.ac.uk

L / Flex, Cert, DIY
WP, TT, DB, SS, EM, WB

Cleveland

Redcar & Cleveland College
Corporation Road, Redcar
Cleveland TS10 1EZ
Tel: 01642 473 132
www.cleveland.ac.uk

L / Flex, Cert, DIY
WP, DB, SS, EM, WB

Cornwall

Cornwall College
Trevensen Road, Cornwall TR15 3RD
Tel: 01209 611 611
www.cornwall.ac.uk

L / Flex, Cert, DIY
WP, TT, DB, SS, EM, WB

Penwith College
St Clare Street, Penzance
Cornwall TR18 2SA
Tel: 01736 335 000
www.penwith.ac.uk

L / Web, Flex, Cert
WP, TT, DB, SS, EM

Derbyshire

Mackworth College

Prince Charles Avenue, Mackworth	L / Flex, Cert, DIY
Derbyshire DE22 4LR	WP, TT, DB, SS, EM, WB
Tel: 01209 611 611	
www.mackworth.ac.uk	

Devon

Plymouth College of Further Education

King's Road, Devonport	L / Flex, Cert, DIY
Plymouth, Devon PL1 5QG	WP, TT, DB, SS, EM, WB
Tel: 01752 305 300	
www.pcfe.ac.uk	

Dorset

Broadlands Training

121a Old Christchurch Road	S / Flex, Cert, DIY
Bournemouth	WP, TT, DB, SS, EM
Dorset BH8 0AL	
Tel: 01202 552 161	

Essex

Havering College

Ardleigh Green Road	L / Flex, Cert
Hornchurch, Essex RM11 2LL	WP, TT, DB, SS, EM, WB
Tel: 01708 455 011	
www.havering-college.ac.uk	

South-East Essex College (F&HE)

Carnovan Road	L / Flex, Cert
Southend, Essex	WP, TT, DB, SS
Tel: 01702 200 400	
www.se-essex-college.ac.uk	

Thurrock & Basildon College (FE)

Woodview Gray	L / Flex, Cert
Essex RM16 2YR	WP, TT, DB, SS, EM, WB
Tel: 01375 371 199	
www.thurrock.ac.uk	

Gloucestershire

Hartpury College
Hartpury House, Hartpury, Gloucester	L / Flex, Cert
Gloucestershire GL19 3BE	WP, DB, SS, EM, WB
Tel: 01452 702 132	
www.hartpury.ac.uk	

Hampshire

Cricklade College
Charlton Road, Andover	L / Flex, Cert, Split
Hampshire SP10 1EJ	WP, TT, DB, SS, EM, WB
Tel: 01264 363 311	
www.cricklade.ac.uk	

Havant College (FE)
New Road, Havant	L / Flex, Cert
Hampshire PO9 1QL	WP, TT, DB, SS, EM, WB
Tel: 023 9238 3131	
www.havant.ac.uk	

Highbury College
Dovercourt Road, Cosham	L / Flex, Cert, DIY
Portsmouth, Hampshire PO6 2SA	WP, TT, DB, SS, EM, WB
Tel: 023 9238 3131	

South Downs College
College Road, Waterlooville	L / Flex, Cert
Hampshire PO7 8AA	WP, TT, DB, SS, EM, WB
Tel: 023 9279 7979	
www.southdowns.ac.uk	

Sparsholt College
Winchester, Hampshire SO21 2NF	L / Cert
Tel: 01962 776 441	WP, DB, SS, EM
www.sparsholt.ac.uk	

Herefordshire

Herefordshire College of Art & Design
Folly Lane, Hereford	L
Herefordshire HR1 1LT	WB
Tel: 01432 273 359	
www.hereford-art-col.ac.uk	

Hertfordshire

Barnet College

Wood Street, Barnet Hertfordshire EN5 4AZ Tel: 020 8440 8300 / 020 8440 6321 www.barnet.ac.uk	L / Flex, Cert, Md, I WP, DB, SS

Kent

Bromley College of F&HE

Rookery Lane, Bromley Kent BR2 8HE Tel: 020 8295 7000 www.bromley.ac.uk	L / Flex, Cert WP, DB, SS, EM, WB

Mid-Kent College of F&HE

Horsted Centre Maidstone Road, Chatham Kent ME5 9UQ Tel: 01634 830 633	L / Flex, Cert, DIY WP, DB, SS, EM, WB

Orpington College

The Walnuts, Orpington Kent BR6 0TE Tel: 01689 899 700 www.orpington.ac.uk	L / Flex, Cert, DIY WP, TT, DB, SS, EM, WB

West Kent College (FE)

Brook Street Tonbridge Kent TN9 2PW Tel: 01732 771 415 www.wkc.ac.uk	L / Flex, Cert, DIY WP, TT, DB, SS, EM

Lancashire

Accrington & Rossendale College

Sandy Lane Centre Sandy Lane Accrington Lancashire BB5 2AW Tel: 01254 354 095 www.accross.ac.uk	L / Flex, Cert, DIY WP, TT, DB, SS, EM, WB

Leicestershire

Leicester College (FE)

Freeman's Park Campus Aylestone Road Leicester, Leicestershire LE2 7LW Tel: 0116 224 2000 www.leicestercollege.ac.uk	L / Flex, Cert, DIY WP, TT, DB, SS, EM, WB

Lincolnshire

Boston College

Skirbeck Road, Boston Lincolnshire PE21 6JF Tel: 01205 313 252 www.boston.ac.uk	L / Flex, Cert, DIY WP, DB, SS, EM

Grantham College (FE)

Stonebridge Road, Grantham Lincolnshire NG31 9AP Tel: 01476 400 200 www.grantham.ac.uk	L / Flex, Cert, DIY WP, TT, DB, SS, EM, WB

London

City College

University House 55 East Road London N1 6AH Tel: 020 7253 1133 www.citycollege.ac.uk	L / Flex, Cert, DIY WP, TT, DB, SS, EM, WB

Computer Skills Centre

20/21 Jockeys Fields London WC1R 4BW Tel: 020 7404 3636 www.computerskillscentres.com	S / Md, Flex, Cert, DIY WP, TT, DB, SS, EM, WB

Enfield College (FE)

73 Hertford Road, Enfield London EN3 5HA Tel: 020 8443 3434 www.enfield.ac.uk	L / Flex, Cert, DIY WP, TT, DB, SS, EM, WB

visit: www.gap-year.com

COLLEGES

Institut Français

17 Queensberry Place, London SW7 2DT Tel: 020 7581 2701 www.institut-francais.org.uk	L / Flex, Cert

Merton Adult College

Whatley Avenue, London SW20 Tel: 020 8543 9292 www.mertonadultcollege.ac.uk	L / Flex, Cert, DIY WP, DB, SS, EM, WB

Pitmans Training Centre

288 Regent Street, London W1R 5HE Tel: 020 242 4590 www.pitmantraining.com	M / Flex, Cert, DIY WP, TT, DB, SS, EM, WB

Queen's Business & Secretarial College

24 Queensberry Place, London SW7 2DS Tel: 020 7589 8583 www.qbsc.ac.uk	L / I, Cert WP, TT, DB, SS, EM

After university, graduates are facing increasing competition for jobs and employers can afford to favour those with the most extensive portfolio of relevant work experience. Well-organised students will begin to build this portfolio during their gap year and continue throughout the long vacations during their time at university.

Exotic travel plans require financing, which means most gap year students will need to find a job. Many, however, do not appreciate just how important that job can be for their future careers.

Taking an intensive course at Queen's can equip students with the IT and business skills they need to gain this experience and to help boost finances during vacations. Fast keyboarding and good computer skills are also an obvious advantage at university. In addition, job-search skills are an integral part of all courses at Queen's. Students are given a thorough training in preparing a CV, writing covering letters, interview technique and the importance of personal presentation.

St James's & Lucie Clayton College

4 Wetherby Gardens, London SW5 OJN Tel: 020 7373 3852 Fax: 020 7370 3303 www.sjlccollege.co.uk	M / I, Md, Flex, Cert WP, TT, DB, SS, EM

St James's & Lucie Clayton College offers a number of courses for gap year students. The One Term Gap Course, offered in September, January and April covers three essential areas: commercial IT with keyboard training, practical business studies and personal development (ranging from interview techniques to self-defence). Short intensive touch typing and IT courses start every Monday and last from one to six weeks and prove particularly popular with male gap year students.

The College's associated recruitment consultancy can help to find temporary assignments which can offer attractive rates of pay.

Manchester
Manchester College of Arts & Technology (FE)

Ashton Old Road, Openshaw	L / Flex, Cert, DIY
Manchester M11 2WH	WP, TT, DB, SS, EM, WB
Tel: 0800 068 8585	
www.mancat.ac.uk	

Merseyside
Knowsley Community College

Rupert Road, Ruby	Flex, Cert, DIY
Merseyside L36 9TD	WP, TT, DB, SS, EM, WB
Tel: 0151 477 5700	
www.merseyworld.cam/kcc	

Middlesex
Stanmore College (FE)

Elm Park, Stanmore	L / Flex, Cert, DIY
Middlesex HA7 4BQ	WP, TT, DB, SS, WB
Tel: 020 8420 7700	
www.stanmore.ac.uk	

West Thames College (FE)

London Road, Isleworth	L / Flex, Cert, DIY
Middlesex TW7 4HS	WP, TT, DB, SS, EM, WB
Tel: 020 8326 2000	
www.west-thames.ac.uk	

Norfolk
Great Yarmouth College

Southtown, Great Yarmouth	L / Flex, Cert, DIY
Norfolk NR31 0ED	WP, TT, DB, SS, EM, WB
Tel: 01493 655 261	

QUEEN'S
BUSINESS TRAINING

Essential IT & Business Skills
including Marketing, PR and Advertising

For Gap Year Students & School Leavers
• *for temping* • *university* • *your career*

Temping gives you valuable work experience while funding other projects.

At *university* fast typing and good IT skills are a real asset.

Whatever *your career* good IT skills are essential.

4/6/12 week intensive courses • 2 and 3 term career training courses

020 7589 8583
www.qbsc.ac.uk

Queens Business & Secretarial College, South Kensington, London

GAP YEAR COURSE

The ideal Gap Year...

- **Learn**
- **Earn** *and then*
- **Sunburn!**

12 week course that gives you the work skills to make the most of your Gap Year

Oxford Media & Business School

Full details: **01865 240963**
Rose Place, Oxford OX1 1SB Web: www.oxfordbusiness.co.uk

College of West Anglia

Tennyson Avenue, King's Lynn	L / Flex, Cert, DIY
Norfolk PE30 2QW	WP, TT, DB, SS, EM, WB
Tel: 01553 761 144	
www.col-westanglia.ac.uk	

Nottinghamshire

Broxtowe College (F&HE)

High Road, Chigwell, Nottingham	L / Flex, Cert, DIY
Nottinghamshire NG9 4AH	WP, TT, DB, SS, EM, WB
Tel: 0115 917 5252	
www.broxtowe.ac.uk	

Oxfordshire

Abingdon College

Northcourt Road, Abingdon	Flex, Cert
Oxfordshire OX14 1NN	WP, TT, DB, SS, EM
Tel: 01235 555 585	
www.abingdoncollege.ac.uk	

Oxford Media & Business School

Rose Place, Oxford	Flex, Cert
Oxfordshire OX1 1SB	WP, TT, DB, SS, EM, WB
Tel: 01865 240 963	
www.oxfordbusiness.co.uk	

Oxford Media & Business School offers three-month gap year 'Life Skills' courses starting three times a year: January, July and September. The gap year 'Life Skills' course is designed to help you make the most of your gap year: first, it will give you an early taste of a university style environment, so when the time comes to start your degree you'll quickly feel at home. Second, the course will give you useful training in key 'Life Skills' such as the use of the latest IT software – invaluable both for later degree submissions and for earning useful extra cash for the rest of your gap year. Finally, it will actually help you find well-paid gap year temping work through the OMBS Careers Direct placement bureau – great for your CV and great for funding your gap year travelling.

Shropshire

Shrewsbury College of Arts & Technology

London Road	Flex, Cert, DIY
Shrewsbury, Shropshire SY2 6PR	WP, TT, DB, SS, EM, WB
Tel: 01743 342342	

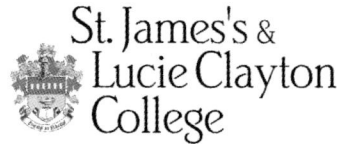

St. James's & Lucie Clayton College

Executive Business & Secretarial Courses in Your Gap Year

One Term Gap Course

- In-depth IT training, a grounding in Media subjects & Teeline shorthand
- Tutor led, excellent results
- Emphasis on confidence building & careers advice
- Associated Recruitment Consultancy
- Commercial language options
- Courses start in January, April & September

Short, Intensive Touch Typing & IT Courses

- Up to date MS Office packages
- Courses start every Monday; from two to six weeks

Fun Summer Courses

- One to two week Image Courses including Make-up & Style, Confidence & Interview Techniques

Please contact us for a prospectus

St. James's & Lucie Clayton College, 4 Wetherby Gardens, London SW5 0JN
Tel: **020 7373 3852** · Fax: **020 7370 3303** · Email: **information@sjlccollege.co.uk**

www.sjlccollege.co.uk

Somerset

Bridgewater College

Bath Road	L / Flex, Cert, DIY
Bridgewater	WP, TT, DB, SS, EM, WB
Somerset TA6 4PZ	
Tel: 01278 455464	
www.bridgewater.ac.uk	

Cannington College (FE)

Cannington	L / Flex, Cert, DIY
Bridgwater	WP, TT, DB, SS, EM
Somerset TA5 2LS	
Tel: 01278 65500	

Staffordshire

Cannock Chase Technical College

The Green, Cannock	L / Flex, Cert, DIY
Staffordshire WS11 1UE	WP, TT, DB, SS, EM, WB
Tel: 01543 462 200	
www.cannock.ac.uk	

Rodbaston College (F&HE)

Rodbaston, Penkridge	L / Flex, Cert, DIY
Staffordshire ST19 5PH	WP, DB, SS, EM, WB
Tel: 01785 712 209	
www.rodbaston.ac.uk	

Suffolk

Leiston Training Centre (FE)

47 High Street	S / Flex, Cert, DIY
Leiston	WP, TT, DB, SS, EM, WB
Suffolk IP6 4E	
Tel: 01728 831 464	

Rendlesham Training Centre (FE)

Building 164	S / Flex, Cert, DIY
AIA Rendlesham	WP, TT, DB, SS, EM, WB
Woodbridge	
Suffolk IP12 2TW	
Tel: 01394 461 438	

visit: www.gap-year.com

Surrey

Guildford College of Further and Higher Education

Stoke Park
Guildford
Surrey GU1 1EZ
Tel: 01483 448 500
www.guildford.ac.uk

Flex, Cert
WP, DB, SS, WB

Guildford Secretarial & Business College

16-19 Chapel Street
Guildford
Surrey GU1 3UL
Tel: 01483 564 885
www.g-s-c.co.uk

Flex, Cert, DIY
WP, TT, DB, SS, EM, WB

Merton College

Morden Park, London Road
Morden, Surrey SM4 5QX
Tel: 020 8408 6500
www.merton.ac.uk

L / I, Flex, Cert
WP, TT, DB, SS, EM, WB

Nescot

Reigate Road, Ewell
Epsom, Surrey KT17 3DS
Tel: 020 8394 3038
www.nescot.ac.uk

L / Flex, Cert, DIY
WP, TT, DB, SS, EM, WB

East Sussex

Brighton and Hove College

Medina House
41 Medina VillasHove
East Sussex BN3 2RP
www.bhcollege.org

M / Flex, Cert
WP, TT, DB, SS, EM, WB
Tel: 01273 772577

Plumpton College

Ditchling Road
Plumpton
Nr Lewes
East Sussex BN1 3AE
Tel: 01273 890 454
www.plumpton.ac.uk

L / Flex, Cert
WP, DB, SS, EM, WB

West Sussex
Crawley College (FE)
College Road
Crawley
West Sussex RH10 1NR
Tel: 01293 442205
www.crawley-college.ac.uk

L / Flex, Cert, DIY
WP, TT, DB, SS

Tyne & Wear
Newcastle College
Rye Hill Campus,
Scotswood Road
Newcastle-upon-Tyne NE4 7SA
Tel: 0191 200 4000
www.ncl-coll.ac.uk

L / Flex, Cert, DIY
WP, TT, DB, SS, EM, WB

Warwickshire
Stratford-upon-Avon College (FE)
The Willows North, Alcester Road
Stratford-upon-Avon, Warwickshire CV37 0QR
Tel: 01789 266 245
www.strat-avon.ac.uk

L / Flex, Cert
WP, DB, SS, EM

Warwickshire College
Warwick New Road, Leamington Spa
Warwickshire CV32 6PG
Tel: 01926 318 000
www.warkscol.ac.uk

L / Flex, Cert, DIY
WP, TT, DB, SS, EM

West Midlands
Coventry Technical College (FE)
Butts, Coventry
West Midlands CV1 3GO
Tel: 02476 526700

L / Flex, Cert, DIY
WP, TT, DB, SS, EM, WB

Dudley College
The Broadway, Dudley
West Midlands DY1 4AS
Tel: 01384 363 000
www.dudleycol.ac.uk

L / Flex, Cert, DIY
WP, TT, DB, SS

COLLEGES
Business Skills

Wiltshire

Lackham College
Lacock, Nr Chippenham	L / Flex, Cert, DIY
Wiltshire SN15 2NY	WP, DB, SS, EM
Tel: 01249 466 800	
www.lackham.ac.uk	

Salisbury College
Southampton Road	L / Flex, Cert, DIY
Salisbury, Wiltshire SP1 2LW	WP, DB, SS, EM, WB
Tel: 01722 344 344	
www.saled.com	

Worcestershire

Evesham College
Cheltenham Road, Evesham	L / Flex, Cert, DIY
Worcestershire WR11 6LP	WP, DB, SS, EM, WB
Tel: 01386 712 600	
www.evesham.ac.uk	

East Yorkshire

Bishop Burton College
Bishop Burton	L / Cert
Beverley	WP, DB, SS, EM, WB
East Yorkshire HU17 8QG	
Tel: 01964 553 000	
www.bishopburton.ac.uk	

Hull College
Queen's Gardens Site	L / Flex, Cert
Hull, East Yorkshire HU1 3DG	WP, TT, DB, SS
Tel: 01482 329 943	
www.hull-college.ac.uk	

North Yorkshire

Selby College (FE)
Abbott's Road	L / Flex, Cert, DIY
Selby	WP, TT, DB, SS, EM, WB
North Yorkshire YO8 8AT	
Tel: 01757 211 000	
www.selbycollege.co.uk	

visit: www.gap-year.com

Business Skills

COLLEGES

West Yorkshire

Dewsbury College
Halifax Road, Dewsbury West Yorkshire WF13 7AS Tel: 01924 436 221 www.dewsbury.ac.uk	L / Flex, Cert, DIY WP, DB, SS, EM, WB

Park Lane College (FE)
Park Lane, Leeds West Yorkshire LS3 1AA Tel: 0113 216 2020 www.parklanecoll.ac.uk	L / Flex, Cert, DIY WP, TT, DB, SS, EM, WB

Shipley College (FE)
Exhibition Road, Bradford West Yorkshire BD18 3JW Tel: 01274 757 222	L / Flex, Cert, DIY WP, TT, DB, SS, EM, WB

Westfield College of FE
Margaret Street Wakefield West Yorkshire WF1 2DH Tel: 01924 789 789 www.wakcoll.ac.uk	L / Flex, Cert, DIY WP, TT, DB, SS, EM, WB

NORTHERN IRELAND

County Down

East Down Institute of Further and Higher Education
Market Street, Downpatrick County Down BT30 6ND Northern Ireland Tel: 01396 615 815	L / Flex, Cert, DIY WP, TT, SS, EM

Londonderry

North West Institute of F&HE
Strand Road Londonderry BT48 7BY Northern Ireland Tel: 028 7126 6711 www.nwifhe.ac.uk	L / Flex, Cert, DIY WP, TT, DB, SS, EM

visit: www.gap-year.com

SCOTLAND

West Lothian

West Lothian College (FE)

Marjoribanks St, Bathgate	Flex, Cert, DIY
West Lothian EN48 1QS, Scotland	WP, TT, DB, SS, EM, WB
Tel: 01506 634 300	

WALES

Denbighshire

Coleg Llysfasi

Ruthin, Denbighshire LU5 2LB	Flex, Cert, DIY
Wales	WP, TT, DB, SS, EM, WB
Tel: 01978 790 263	
www.llysfasi.ac.uk	

Pembrokeshire

Pembrokeshire College (FE)

Haverfordwest	L / Flex, Cert
Pembrokeshire SA61 1SZ, Wales	WP, TT, DB, SS, EM, WB
Tel: 0800 716 236	
www.pembrokeshire.ac.uk	

I did the gap year course at OMBS to earn some money to finance my gap year travels to Australia.

Learning to touch type was also invaluable. I had always been fascinated by people that could sit there, staring at the screen, while their fingers swept across the keyboard in a flurry of digits. Once I'd completed the course I was a lot more confident about using a computer, and I too could type whilst staring at the screen.

I got a temporary job at a company that makes computer games. My job wasn't glamorous: I typed up letters, I answered the phone and I sent mail, but I did enjoy myself nonetheless. When I left two weeks later I had a big fat cheque in my pocket and a grin on my face

Since then the skills I learnt have been invaluable to my university career in that I can set up my essays the way I want them to look; graphs *etc* for projects look the way I want them to look; and I can get all my essays typed up so much quicker because I don't have to look at the keyboard.

Ellie

 # Extra Skills

Frustrated that hardly anything you were taught at school seemed relevant to your life? Why not use your gap year to learn new skills that you choose yourself – you can make them as useful as you want.

Archaeology

Are you an avid watcher of *Time Team* or fascinated by the Sutton Hoo treasure? Would you love to find an ancient relic? You could get yourself on an actual archaeological dig.

Archaeology Abroad
Institute of Archaeology, University College
31-34 Gordon Square
London WC1H 0PY   Fax: 0207 383 2572

For info on digs abroad try the *Archaeology Abroad* bulletin and web pages.

Council for British Archaeology
Bowes Morrell House   Tel: 01904 671 417
111 Walmgate, York   Fax: 01904 671 384
Yorkshire YO1 9WA   www.britarch.ac.uk

The Council for British Archaeology is a good starting point for general archaeological information. They also have a magazine called *British Archaeology* (**www.britarch.ac.uk/ba/ba.html**), which comes out six times a year and contains *CBA Briefing* (from the Council of British Archaeology), with information about events and courses, as well as digs where volunteers are needed.

Museum of London
London Wall   Tel: 020 7814 5777
London EC2Y 5HN   www.museumoflondon.org.uk

The Museum of London runs four archaeology courses from September to March and one from April to July ('Field archaeology and the Roman-British period in southern Britain'). These run on one evening a week (with a break at Christmas and Easter), and cost £166 (student discounts available) for the whole course.

Art

If you're seriously interested in painting, sculpting or other artistic subjects, but don't know if you want to carry it through to a full degree, there is the useful option of a one-year art foundation course, available from a wide variety of art colleges. A foundation course at art college doesn't count towards an art degree in the sense that you can then skip the first year of your three-year degree course.

However, art colleges say that with competition for undergraduate places based on the volume and standard of work in a candidate's 'entry portfolio', having a portfolio from your foundation course puts you at a natural advantage. Course providers also advise against specialising in one discipline, say sculpture, before covering the more wide-ranging syllabus of a foundation course.

Blake College
162 New Cavendish Street
London W1W 6YS

Tel: 020 7636 0658
www.blake.ac.uk

Camberwell College of Arts
Peckham Road
London SE5 8UF

Tel: 020 7514 6302
www.camb.linst.ac.uk

Cardiff School of Art and Design
University of Wales Institute
Cardiff
Llandaff Campus
Western Avenue
Cardiff CS5 2YB
Wales

Tel: 02920 416 291
www.uwic.ac.uk/csad

Central Saint Martins
Southampton Row
London WC1B 4AP

Tel: 020 7514 7000
www.csm.linst.ac.uk

Chelsea College of Art and Design
Manresa Road
London SW3 6LS

Tel: 020 7514 7750
www.chel.linst.ac.uk

Heatherley School of Art

80 Upcerne Road, Chelsea　　　　　Tel: 020 7351 6945
London SW10 0SH　　　　　　　　www.heatherleys.org

The Heatherley School of Art in Chelsea runs a full-time one-year foundation/portfolio course and other courses include a two-year diploma in portraiture, art A level (one-year intensive course), print-making, watercolour/pastel, general drawing and painting, life drawing, oil painting and figurative sculpture. There are plenty of Saturday and evening classes too, for those who have to toil through daylight hours during the week.

Slade School of Fine Art (Summer School)

University College
Gower Street　　　　　　　　　　Tel: 020 7679 7772
London WC1E 6BT　　　　　　　　www.ucl.ac.uk/slade

Three hundred people go each year to summer schools at the Slade School of Fine Art, where the 12 separate courses vary from one to ten weeks and span all art forms. There's a ten-week summer Alternative Foundation Course which consists of an intense six-day week where the students are given their own space and have regular tuition from Slade tutors. Accommodation is available in the halls of residence at an extra cost but the basic course is £2500. For those with an interest in theatre, there's a two-week course on Designing Theatre Space (£525).

Wimbledon School of Art

　　　　　　　　　　　　　　　　Tel: 020 8408 5000
Merton Hall Road　　　　　　　　Fax: 020 8408 5050
London SW19 3QA　　　　　　　　www.wimbledon.ac.uk

Cookery

You probably spend more than 500 hours a year eating, but can you cook? There are really two types of cookery courses for gappers: basic skills and how to earn money.

The basic skills courses are for those who want to be able to feed themselves more than baked beans or packet soup. These courses can take you from boiling water through to quite a reasonable level – you may not be able to cook for a dinner party of 12, but you should leave being able to cook a variety of tasty meals without poisoning anyone. Cheap and cheerful cookery courses (standard, ethnic, exotic) can be found at

COOKERY *Extra Skills*

day or evening classes at local colleges of further education. Usually the fees are low but you have to pay for ingredients.

The second type of course is aimed at teaching you the skills needed to work as a cook during your gap year. Working as a cook in ski resorts, on yachts in the Caribbean or in villas in Tuscany or the South of France not only allows you to see the world, but pays you while you see it.

"The majority of those who want to work after doing our Essential Cookery course do find cooking work," says Hilary McFarland from Cookery at the Grange. "What's involved in being a chalet cook depends on what a ski company or employer wants. Usually the day starts with cooked breakfast for the ski party, then possibly a packed lunch, tea and cake when hungry skiers get back, possibly canapés later, and a three- or four-course supper. The food does need more than the usual amount of carbohydrate." That doesn't mean dropping a large pile of pasta on a plate. Ski companies expect high standards and may ask for sample menus when you apply for chalet cooking jobs. Sometimes the menus are decided in advance and the shopping done locally by someone else; sometimes the cook has to do the shopping. Perhaps surprisingly, ski companies and agencies rarely ask about language skills – the cooks seem to manage without. See *Chapter 1: Working Abroad* for ideas on making use of your new skills.

COOKERY

Aldeburgh Cookery School
84 High Street, Aldeburgh
Suffolk IP15 5AB   Tel: 01728 454 039

Courses range from one to five days and cover a range of themes, from shellfish and pacific cuisine to exotic spices.

Annette Gibbons Cookery
Ostle House, Mawbray
Maryport
Cumbria CA15 6QS   Tel: 01900 881 356

Annette Gibbons offers a one-day How to Cope at University cookery course. In the morning she demonstrates how to cook a nutritious lunch, then you sit down to eat it, and afterwards you learn how to shop and eat wisely and cheaply.

Cookery at The Grange
The Grange, Whatley   Tel: 01373 836 579
Frome, Somerset BA11 3JU   see: www.gap-year.com

Cookery at the Grange in Somerset offers an intensive residential cookery course, using organic foods and working in kitchens round a farmhouse courtyard. You won't be turning rabbits into *lapin au deux moutardes*, but all the bread is home baked. A popular student course is The Essential Cookery Course, which runs for four weeks, starting eight times a year. It costs £2290-£2690 (depending on the time of year) and this includes accommodation in twin-bedded rooms. The Grange also has a one-week chalet course where students can cook typical chalet-style menus and learn about running a chalet (£650).

Cookery School at Little Portland Street
15B Little Portland Street
London W1W 8BW   Tel: 020 7631 4590

Cookery School at Little Portland Street is a new arrival on the London cookery scene. Their aim is to turn out confident, inspired cooks rather than restaurant chefs. Students taking part in their courses will learn cooking skills to stand them in good stead at university and beyond.

Courses specially tailored for university and pre-university students are run during the summer holidays. They also run a range of classes suitable for all ages and levels of experience. If you are a novice, go along to their Saturday beginners course (£210 for six weeks) where you will learn how to roast chicken, bake bread, assemble delicious salads and whip up simple cakes amongst other things.

LE CORDON BLEU

THE WORLD'S MOST FAMOUS NAME IN THE CULINARY ARTS

- 'ESSENTIALS' COURSE FOR GAP YEAR STUDENTS
  IDEAL FOR SKI CHALET AND YACHT WORK.

- FAMOUS DIPLOMAS FOR CUISINE
  AND PÂTISSERIE IN JUST 30 WEEKS.

- FABULOUS GOURMET SESSIONS
  TO SUIT ALL TASTES AND ABILITIES

Le Cordon Bleu, 114 Marylebone Lane, London W1U 2HH
Tel: 020-7935 3503   Fax: 020-7935 7621
Internet: www.cordonbleu.edu   E-mail: london@cordonbleu.edu

---

*Learn to cook with confidence on the intensive
four-week Essential Cookery Course
or the one-week Chalet Course*

COOKERY AT THE GRANGE

- *Excellent practical courses*
- *Enthusiastic professional tuition*
- *Ideal for those wanting to work in chalets
  or galleys or for families at home or abroad*

The Grange, Whatley, Frome, Somerset BA11 3JU
Tel/Fax: 01373-836579

www.cookery-grange.co.uk • info@cookery-grange.co.uk

Extra Skills **COOKERY**

For students who can already cook and would like to learn something new, their evening classes cover a range of specialist areas of cooking such as soufflés and sushi (£40 per class including a light supper and wine). And if you plan to cook that traditional student staple, pasta, when you get to university, why not learn how to make fresh pasta yourself!

The school's principal, Rosalind Rathouse, has many years' experience both as a professional cook and a study skills tutor for A level and university students. Her teaching approach is practical and fun – starting with simple techniques and showing how to develop these into a range of delicious menus.

All classes are held in their custom-designed premises in central London. Little Portland Street is two minutes from Oxford Circus and within walking distance of some of London's best shops, bars and restaurants.

Cutting Edge Food & Wine School
Hackwood Farm, Robertsbridge
East Sussex TN32 5ER
Tel: 01580 881 281
and 07900 583 150

Based in a 16th century farmhouse at Robertsbridge vineyard, Cutting Edge offers a range of cookery courses in modern kitchens. The foundation course provides a practical introduction to subjects like 'healthy eating on a budget', 'hygiene' and 'cooking for friends'. The chalet cooking course gives you tips on cooking for groups, shopping, storage and quantities, and helps you develop a wide repertoire of recipes. You will be taught in small groups (maximum ten) by Tom Kime, who has an excellent reputation and who cooked for Jamie Oliver's wedding! Courses last a week (Mon-Fri) and cost £349 including accommodation, meals and all equipment. The chalet course can be extended to two weeks, costing £649.

Edinburgh School of Food and Wine
The Coach House, Newliston
Edinburgh EH29 9EB
Scotland
Tel: 0131 333 5001
Fax: 0131 333 5041

Jill Davidson's School offers courses for aspiring cooks of all levels from basic to cordon bleu. The school is set in an idyllic country location and is the only cookery school in Scotland to be accredited by the British Accreditation Council.

Courses of particular interest to gappers are the Certificate Course – five-week Intensive which is geared towards chalet work and the one-week Survival Certificated Course, ideally suited to those leaving home for the first time. Both courses are designed to develop students' culinary ability through a combination of demonstration and practical sessions in a friendly professional environment.

visit: www.gap-year.com

LEITHS

SCHOOL OF FOOD AND WINE

Tel: 020 7229 0177
21 St Alban's Grove London W8 5BP
email: info@leiths.com   www.leiths.com

Diploma or Certificate Courses

Gap Year Courses

Holiday Courses

Saturday Cookery Mornings

Cookery and Wine Evening Classes

Corporate Events

LEITHS LIST
AGENCY FOR COOKS

Tel: 01225 722983   email: list@leiths.com

The Certificate Course – five-week Intensive is a practical 'hands on' cookery course and provides the opportunity to learn fundamental skills that will last a lifetime. The School works closely with both large and small companies within the travel and tourism market and can offer a personal introduction to agents and ski companies based in Scotland, England and Europe.

There are many opportunities to work freelance and previous students have found work in ski chalets, directors' dining rooms, yachts and shooting and fishing lodges, to name a few examples.

Course fees vary in price from £70.50 for a day to £365 for the one-week Survival Certificated Course or £2500 for the Certificate – five-week Intensive Course.

Kilbury Manor Cookery Course
Colston Road, Buckfastleigh
Devon TQ11 0LN   Tel: 01364 644079

Established for over seven years, Kilbury Manor offers personally designed and intensive short courses, for a maximum of four people throughout the year. The courses are always designed to suit individual needs, including chalet and crew cooks, and cater for all ranges of ability: professional as well as amateur cooks are welcomed.

Kilbury Manor can arrange extended programmes and can cover an amazing amount in a short space of time: they reckon their five-day course will cover all requirements for chalet and crew cooks and more!

Courses cost £325 (one-on-one) for a two-day course with 12 hours tuition per day; £225 per person for two people and £200 per person for three people. The cost of the course is fully inclusive of accommodation, food, notes and recipes *etc*. Kilbury Manor is happy to supply references. Contact the school for their full range of courses and prices.

Le Cordon Bleu
114 Marylebone Lane   Tel: 0800 980 3503
London W1U 2HH   see: www.gap-year.com

Le Cordon Bleu has courses ranging from their famous diplomas in 'Cuisine and Pâtisserie', to the shorter Gourmet Sessions featuring regional French cuisine, fusion, pâtisserie *a la carte* and bread baking. They also run an intensive version of their standard ten-week professional programme, allowing students to study on a fast track system. The Essentials Course is geared to gap year students. It is full time, and runs over four weeks, including a trip to Paris. The price is £1940 and includes the minimum uniform required, although students can purchase further items if they want. Contact the institute for brochures covering all their courses.

COOKERY

Extra Skills

Leiths School of Food & Wine

21 St Alban's Grove
London W8 5BP

Tel: 020 7229 0177
Fax: 020 7937 5257
see: www.gap-year.com

Leiths runs a four-week Foundation Course (£1860) starting in mid-July, five days a week. The most popular gap year courses, useful for chalet-people-to-be, are the three-month Beginner's Certificate in Food and Wine (£4150, September to December) and the Basic Certificate in Practical Cookery (£1860, four weeks, full-time from August), which include the professional exam qualifications required by some ski companies.

Leiths also runs evening classes for beginners (£475 for ten lessons) and intermediate/advanced (£478), as well as one-week beginners' courses (£490) twice a year at Christmas and Easter. Attached to the school is Leiths List, which finds its leavers cooking jobs in ski chalets in Europe, for family summer holidays in Cornwall, or for parties in London.

TANTE MARIE
· SCHOOL OF COOKERY ·

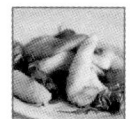
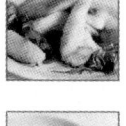

Cordon Bleu Certificate
11 weeks Internationally recognised qualification.
IDEAL FOR WORK IN SKI CHALETS AND ON YACHTS.

Essential Skills Course
4 weeks. Learn many of the essential skills to cook with confidence. Helpful in securing short term employment.

Beginners Course
1 or 2 weeks. An excellent course to inspire an interest in good food and to learn basic cookery skills.

call **01483 726957** or visit **www.tantemarie.co.uk**

Tante Marie School of Cookery Limited
Woodham House, Carlton Road, Woking, Surrey GU21 4HF Fax: 01483 724173 info@tantemarie.co.uk

Tante Marie
Woodham House
Carlton Road,
Woking
Surrey GU21 4HF

Tel: 01483 726957
Fax: 01483 724173
see: www.gap-year.com

Tante Marie School of Cookery is the UK's largest independent cookery school and offers a variety of courses suitable for gap year students.

The 11-week certificate course provides an internationally recognised qualification and is particularly suitable for students who wish to work the ski and yacht season. This course starts each September, January and April (£4050). The four-week Essential Skills Course (£1700) offers a good grounding in cookery and is recognised by some ski and leisure companies recruiting temporary staff. Courses run throughout the year.

For the absolute beginner, the one- or two-week Beginners' Course (£450 and £750 respectively) runs in July.

The Murray School of Cookery
Glenbervie House
Holt Pound
Farnham
Surrey GU10 4LE

Tel: 01420 23049
Fax: 01420 23049

The Murray School of Cookery offers two courses for gappers: the Cookery Certificate Course and the Chalet Chef Course.

The Cookery Certificate Course is an intensive four-week course that covers all the skills required for catering for small groups or for first-class home entertaining – ideal for anyone wanting to work on luxury yachts, at premier ski chalets or at small restaurants and hotels. The course costs £1200, which does not cover accommodation.

The Chalet Chef Course is a one-week course designed in conjunction with major ski operators and teaches students how to prepare typical recipes ideal for catered ski chalets. Successful students also have access to the Murray School of Cookery database of ski companies and any job vacancies they know about. The course covers menu planning, accounting, hygiene and other knowledge needed to be a successful chalet host. The course is non-residential and costs £395 per person including all ingredients and equipment. There is B&B accommodation at Glenbervie House for £25 per night or the school will provide a list of other B&B accommodation available locally.

Drama

You want to be an actor? Your parents may be quaking in the background, telling you it's insecure and you'll never know where your next pay packet's coming from. Well, one way to find out if you really can make it in acting (or if you're more suited to being a barrister or a bricklayer) is to try a drama course in your gap year.

Oxford School of Drama

Sansomes Farm Studios Tel: 01993 812883
Woodstock Fax: 01993 811220
Oxford, Oxfordshire OX20 1ER see: www.gap-year.com

The Oxford School of Drama runs a six month Foundation Course for students over the age of 17. The course runs from September to March so you can take it during your gap year and still have time to spend working or travelling.

Classes include acting technique, movement, voice, music, film, stage management and stage fighting – giving you a real feel for life

at drama school. Entry is purely by audition, so if you enjoy performing but haven't taken exams in Drama or English you can still apply.

Foundation Course graduates have gone on to train at leading drama schools including the Royal Academy of Dramatic Art, the London Academy of Music and Dramatic Art, the Guildford School of Acting, further courses at the Oxford School of Drama and to study at Oxford, Cambridge and other leading universities.

RADA (Royal Academy of Dramatic Art)

62-64 Gower Street
London WC1E 6ED

Tel: 020 7636 7076
Fax: 020 7323 3865

This legendary drama college runs summer school courses and not all of them are for people who have already played King Lear in ten different styles. No audition is needed for the RADA Summer School (July-Aug) with its four weeks of intensive 'Shakespeare-based' workshops. There's also a two-week practical theatre set design course (£630) in July where you will design the scenery and costumes for a Shakespeare play. RADA Technical courses run open days throughout the academic year where you are welcome to see work in progress and meet staff and students.

Stratford-upon-Avon College

Stratford-upon-Avon
Warwickshire CV37 9QR

Tel: 01789 266245

Stratford-upon-Avon College runs a Year Out Drama Course. You have the option to take Theatre Studies A level, or you can just do it for fun: the drama equivalent of an art foundation course. The course includes acting, directing, design, costume, performance, voice work, movement, text study and theatre trips, and at least one leaver has gone on to work for the Royal Shakespeare Company.

Driving

There are two reasons to learn to drive: first, unless you're intending to live in an inner city indefinitely, you'll need a driver's licence to get a job; secondly, it will give you independence and you won't have to rely on everyone else (especially your parents) to give you lifts everywhere. Even though you might not be able to afford the insurance right now, let alone an actual car, your gap year is an ideal time to take driving lessons.

visit: www.gap-year.com

DRIVING

Extra Skills

The test comes in two parts, theory and practical: and you need to pass the theory test before you apply for the practical one. However, you can start learning practical driving before you take the theory part, but to do that you need a provisional driving licence, which now comes with a photocard. You need to complete driving licence application form D1 and photocard application form D750 (available from most post offices). Send the form, the fee of £29 and original documentation confirming your identity such as your passport or birth certificate (make sure you keep a photocopy) and a passport sized colour photograph to the DVLA. You also need to check that you are insured for damage to yourself, other cars or other people, and if you are practising in the family car, your parents will have to add cover for you on their insurance.

Theory test

The theory test is a 40-minute touch-screen test where you have to get 30 out of 35 multiple-choice questions right. You don't have to answer the questions in turn and the computer shows how much time you have left. You can have 15 minutes practice before you start the test

visit: www.gap-year.com

properly. If you have special needs you can get extra time for the test – ask for this when you book it.

Since November 2002, the theory test has also included a hazard test, in which you are shown a number of video clips filmed from a car, each containing one or more developing hazards. You have to indicate as soon as you see a hazard developing which may result in the driver taking some action, such as changing speed or direction. The sooner a response is made the higher the score.

Test results and feedback information are given within half-an-hour of finishing. The test fee is £15.50. Your driving school, instructor or local test centre should have an application form, although you can book your test over the phone (0870 0101 372) or online at DSA Online booking.

Practical test

You have two years to pass the practical test once you have passed the theory part. The practical test will cost £36.75, unless you choose to have it in the evening or on Saturday in which case the cost will increase to £48. You can book the practical test in the same way as the theory test. The bad news is that the tests are tough and it's quite common to fail twice or more before a pass. The practical test requires candidates to drive on faster roads than before – you'll need to negotiate a dual carriageway as well as a suburban road. You'll fail if you commit more than 15 driving faults. Once you pass your practical test, you can exchange your provisional licence for a full licence for £12.

Instructors

Of course some unqualified instructors (including parents) are experienced and competent, as are many small driving schools – but some checking out is a good idea if a driving school is not a well-known name. You can make sure that it is registered with the Driving Standards Agency and the instructor is qualified. AA and BSM charges can be used as a benchmark if you're trying other schools.

AA (Automobile Association)

Tel: 0800 587 0087
www.theaa.co.uk

Routes you to an AA centre near you. Website has lots of useful information on driving in the UK and abroad, with breakdown, insurance and other services.

BSM (British School of Motoring)

Tel: 08457 276 276
www.bsm.co.uk

Driving Standards Agency

Tel: 0870 010 1372
www.driving-tests.co.uk

Information on theory and practical driving tests, fees and other relevant information. Also has a driving test booking service.

DVLA (Driver and Vehicle Licencing Agency)

Tel: 0870 240 0009
www.dvla.gov.uk

RAC (Royal Automobile Club)

Tel: 0800 55 00 55
www.rac.co.uk

The RAC website has lots of useful information on driving in the UK and abroad, with breakdown, insurance and other services.

Languages

According to the latest statistics from HESA (Higher Education Statistics Agency), studying languages may help your chances of employment – just under 60% of students who graduated in 2002 with a language degree (first degree) went straight into a job.

Even if the job you are applying for doesn't require them, employers are often impressed by language skills. With the growth of the internet, most companies like to think of themselves as having international potential at the very least.

If you didn't enjoy language classes at school, that shouldn't necessarily put you off. College courses and evening classes are totally different – or at least they should be. If in doubt ask to speak to the tutor or to someone who has already been on the course before you sign up.

And even if you don't aspire to learn enough to be able to use your linguistic skills in a job, you could still take conversation classes so you can speak a bit of the language when you go abroad on your holidays. It is amazing what a sense of achievement and self confidence you can get when you manage to communicate the simplest things to a local in their own language: simply ordering a meal or buying stamps for your postcards home.

The best way to improve your language skills is to practice speaking, preferably to a native speaker in their country. But if you don't have the time or the money to go abroad yet, don't worry. There are plenty

Extra Skills **LANGUAGES**

of places in the UK to learn a wide variety of languages, from Spanish to Somali. We've listed some language institutions below, but also find out what language courses your local college offers, and what evening classes there are locally.

Alliance Française
1 Dorset Square, London NW1 6PU   Tel: 020 7723 6439

One well-known centre is the Alliance Française, a non-profit-making organisation funded by a trust. There is a network of Alliances in 138 countries, but the British-based one does not deal with applications to others. However, you can look at the Alliance Française website which has links to or information on Alliances everywhere. Teaching centres are spread throughout the country, from Jersey to Glasgow, and courses range from intensive to evening classes. For example, a two-week intensive course in London costs £220 and gets you 15 hours' tuition per week (Mon-Fri, 10am-1pm).

Goethe Institut
50 Princes Gate, Exhibition Road
London SW7 2PH   Tel: 020 7596 4004

The Goethe Institut is probably the best-known international German language school network, with 125 centres in 76 countries. It is a non-profit organisation funded by the German government, and it offers a wide variety of courses as well as having a lending library and multi-media centre. Courses in London cater for all levels and include two-and-a-half-week intensive courses. Typical prices are £345 for the intensive German course (Mon-Fri 9am-1pm), or £245 for the General German Language course (52 lessons: three a week spread over one semester of 17 weeks).

Institut Français
17 Queensberry Place, London SW7 2DT   Tel: 020 7581 2701

About 6000 students pass through the Institut Français each year – it's the official French government centre of language and culture in London. The institute's courses are mainly in the evening and at weekends, but there is also an intensive French course which runs over two weeks with 30 hours' tuition. Courses are held at all levels and most cost £230, with a £30 discount if you book early. As well as conversation and grammar classes, there is a mind-boggling range of cultural courses, from news and current affairs to philosophy; from history and politics to French cartoons.

visit: www.gap-year.com

LANGUAGES

Extra Skills

Instituto Cervantes
326/330 Deansgate
Campfield Avenue Arcade
Manchester M3 4FN   Tel: 0161 661 4200

Based in Leeds and Manchester, Instituto Cervantes is a Spanish government-funded 'ambassador' for Spanish culture in the UK. Its database provides information about language course locations. The Instituto, with 37 branches in 24 countries, runs its own Spanish courses throughout the academic year in Leeds and Manchester. As well as learning the language, Instituto Cervantes can really immerse you in Spanish culture – there are dance courses (flamenco, tango, salsa), guitar courses and regular 'Spanish evenings' with talks and music. The 10-week flamenco course (two hours per week) in Manchester costs £95; the ten-week guitar course costs £120. Membership of Instituto Cervantes libraries costs £15 and gets you access to Spanish magazines, videos, CDs and DVDs.

Russian Language Centre
11 Coldbath Square   Tel: 020 7689 5400
London EC1R 5HL   see: www.gap-year.com

The Russian Language Centre in London offers a flexible approach to learning this language, with a range of courses available: standard, accelerated and private. The classes run in the evenings and a term's Standard course (one evening a week, mostly business people, so you may not be reading Turgenev) costs £275.

SOAS (School of Oriental and African Studies)
SOAS Language Centre, University of London
Thornhaugh Street, Russell Square   Tel: 020 7898 4888
London WC1H 0XG   see: www.gap-year.com

The SOAS (part of the University of London) runs courses for all levels in Arabic language, culture and civilization. Courses range from one-year full-time to Saturday and evening classes. SOAS students have free access to a huge library and resources room. There are also chances to go out to study in an Arabic-speaking country.

SOAS also offers a wide range of other languages including from **Africa**: Afrikaans, Amharic, Hausa, Shona, Somali, Swahili, Twi, Yoruba and Zulu; **Near and Middle East**: Arabic, Hebrew, Kurdish, Persian, Turkish; **Asia**: Bengali, Burmese, Chinese, Gujarati, Hindi, Indonesian, Japanese, Korean, Malay, Nepali, Punjabi, Sanskrit, Tamil, Thai, Urdu, Vietnamese. On one of its other courses you could try your hand at exquisite Chinese calligraphy.

Extra Skills **LANGUAGES**

A word in your ear...

The unserious way, but a good method on long journeys if you have a Walkman, is to buy an audio language course on cassette or CD.

There are loads of different companies to choose from, ranging from extensive courses that are really quite expensive down to the cheaper beginner's level with mostly useful phrases and an emphasis on pronunciation. One of our researchers used a German course on CD and found it helped for buying tickets, getting around and for understanding what was going on. Most courses come with a course or phrase book. The advantage of an audio course over a stand alone book is that you can hear what you should sound like.

You should find a good variety at your local library, bookshop or of course on a web-based bookstore (like **www.amazon.co.uk**).

BBC Education

Orders c/o BBC Languages
PO Box 234
Wetherby
West Yorks LS23 7EU   Tel: 01937 541001

The BBC Education department produces the *Get by in...* language tapes in many languages. These courses are around £12 and consist of one or two cassettes plus a course/phrase book, which you can take with you when you go. They are available at most bookshops

Online learning

Companies offering languages courses have cottoned on to the fact that many of us are welded semi-permanently to our computers.

You can now get very comprehensive language courses on CD-ROM which include booklets or pages that can be printed off. The better ones use voice recognition as well, so you can practise your pronunciation. These can also be found in book stores.

The internet itself is also a good source of language material. There are many courses, some with free access, some that need a very healthy credit card. If all you want is a basic start, then take a look at **www.bbc.co.uk/education/languages/** which offers you the choice of beginner's French, German and Spanish complete with vocab lists to download, all for free.

As well as courses, there are translation services, vocab lists and topical forums – just do a web search and see how many sites come up. Lots of them are free.

| MUSIC | Extra Skills |

Practice makes perfect

When you need to practise, find out if there are any native speakers living in your town – you could arrange your own language and cultural evenings. Terrestrial TV stations run some language learning programmes, usually late at night. If you have satellite or cable TV you can also watch foreign shows – though this can be a bit frustrating if you're a beginner. It's best to video the programmes so you can replay any bits that you didn't understand the first time round. Once you're getting a bit more advanced then you can try tuning your radio in to foreign speech-based shows.

Champs-Elysées   Tel 0800-833 257

If you already have a fair grasp of a language, the best way to prevent rustiness is to continue hearing or speaking it. Champs-Elysées produces monthly or bimonthly tapes (in French, German, Spanish and Italian) that sound like authentic radio shows from the relevant countries. This is a good way to keep up to date with current affairs in your chosen country, as well as keeping up your listening and understanding skills. Subjects are wide-ranging, and there's something to interest everyone. The tapes have been well-received by teachers and reviewers, but are a bit expensive for the average gap year student. It costs extra for the glossy booklet containing a transcript of the programme and help with vocabulary.

Music

Perhaps you always wanted to learn the saxophone, but never quite got 'round to it? Now would be an ideal time to start. If you're interested, your best bet is to find a good private tutor. Word of mouth is the best recommendation, but some teachers advertise in local papers, and you could also try an online search engine like Musicians' Friend (**www.musiciansfriend.co.uk**).

If you already play an instrument, you could broaden your experience by going on a residential course or summer school. These are available for many different ability levels, although they tend to be quite pricey. There are a number of websites dedicated to music that will list courses (try **www.excel-ability.com/Music/**) . Here are a few of the courses we've heard about.

Lake District Senior Summer School

Stricklandgate House   Tel: 01539 724441
92 Stricklandgate, Kendal   Fax: 01539 741882
Cumbria LA9 4PU   see: www.gap-year.com

Ensemble-based course for string players and pianists intending to pursue careers as professional musicians. Coaching given by top instrumentalists and ensembles. Runs from 2-13 August, costing £495, which includes tickets to events at the Lake District Summer Music Festival.

London Music School

131 Wapping High Street
London E1W 3NG

Tel: 020 7265-0284
see: www.gap-year.com

The London Music School offers a six-month Diploma in Music Technology, open to anyone with musical ability aged 17 or over, starting in April. On this course, in their own words, 'you can perfect your digital groove'. In other words, you could play your tunes on a keyboard and learn how to convert these 'musical strands' digitally (using MIDI technology) into anything from a full orchestral symphony to a club mix.

The six-month course costs £2820 plus a £125 registration fee, but if you're strapped for cash they might give you a discount. The course explores professional recording and you get to use a 24-track studio.

The North London Piano School

78 Warwick Avenue, Edgeware
Middlesex HA8 8UJ

Tel: 0208 958 5206
see: www.gap-year.com

The Residential Summer Course at Queenswood, Potters Bar runs in August, costing from £450.

The Oxford Flute Summer School

9 Pinehurst
Horsham
West Sussex RH12 2DL

Tel: 01403 259 463
Fax: 01403240610
see: www.gap-year.com

Runs from mid-August, costing from £430. Offers several levels of tuition to suit your standard.

Choirs and orchestras

Another option is to join a choir or an orchestra. Many orchestras have their own choruses, and these are generally not too difficult to get in to, provided you're a good sight-reader, have sung in a choir before and can commit yourself for long enough.

There's not usually any pay for singing, but it's great fun, brings an occasional recording fee, and you could just be lucky enough to go on tour. Big choirs tend to be particularly keen to recruit tenors and basses. Try **www.colcanto.co.uk/BCN/home.htm** for a very thorough list of choirs in the UK.

MUSIC

Extra Skills

If you're planning to spend at least six months in another country, you can find out a lot about joining a chorus there by using the web. If you're using an internet search engine, it obviously helps to key in the local language term, like *orchestre symphonique* to find out about a possible orchestra in France, Canada or other French-speaking countries.

If you want to join an orchestra, you could find it a bit more tricky, although it depends what instrument you play. Once you've left school, you're up against much stiffer competition for places. You may still qualify to play in your local youth orchestra, but if not, then use the internet to find which ensembles are based in your area, and phone them up to find out if there are any opportunities for you. Orchestra Net (**www.orchestranet.co.uk**) and UK Amateur Orchestras (**www.amateurorchestras.org.uk**) might be good starting points.

Photography

There are lots of photography courses available, from landscape photography to studio work. Don't fool yourself that a photography course is going to get you a job and earn you pots of money, but there's nothing to stop you enjoying photography as a hobby or sideline.

Royal Photographic Society

The Octagon,
Milson Street
Bath BA1 1DN

Tel: 01225 462 841
www.rps.org

The Royal Photographic Society holds photography courses all through the year, mostly at weekends, for all standards. The price for a weekend course ranges from £79 for the basic beginners' course to £130 for the more advanced.

Sport

After all that studying maybe all you want to do is get out there and do something. If you're the energetic type and hate the thought of spending your gap year stuck behind a desk, why not get active and do some sport?

There are sports courses for all types at all levels, from scuba diving for beginners to advanced ski instructor qualification courses. Of course if you manage to get an instructor's qualification you may be able to use it to get a job (see *Chapter 1: Working Abroad*)

If you hated sport at school, try giving it another chance during your gap year – you may be surprised how much you like it.

X-rated

If you want a real adrenelin rush, go for one of the extreme sports like BASE jumping, street luge or skyboarding. BASE refers to the four types of launching points: Buildings, Antennas, Spans (bridges) and Earth (cliffs and waterfalls). One of the features of BASE jumping is that launch heights are comparatively low, giving you little time to open your specially-designed parachute. This is a sport that takes skill and bravery!

Street luge is where you lie on a narrow aluminium rail and race down a street with no brakes. Skyboarding is basically a combination of skydiving and snowboarding – you throw yourself out of a plane wearing a parachute and perform acrobatic stunts on a board.

Or if you like company when you're battling against the elements, then you could get involved in adventure racing: teams race each other across rugged terrain without using anything with a motor, for example skiing, hiking, sea kayaking. Team members have to stay together throughout the race. Raid Gauloises (five-person teams, two weeks, five stages, half the teams don't finish!) and Eco-Challenge (ten days, 600km, several stages and an environmental project) are the two most well-known adventure race events.

The annual X Games feature a wide range of extreme sports and take place during one week in summer (including aggressive in-line skating) and another week in winter (including mountain bike racing on snow). Check out their website **http://expn.go.com/** for the full details.

If you want to get wet, then try diving, kayaking, sailing, surfing, water polo, windsurfing, or whitewater rafting.

And if those don't appeal then there's always abseiling, badminton, baseball, basketball, bungee jumping, cavediving, cricket, fencing, football, golf, gymnastics, hang gliding, hockey, horse riding, ice hockey, ice skating, jet skiing, motor racing, mountain biking, mountain boarding, netball, parachuting, polo, rock climbing, rowing, rugby, running, skateboarding, skating, ski jumping, skiing, skydiving, skysurfing, snooker, snow mobiling, snowboarding, squash, stock car racing, tennis or trampolining!

If the sport you are interested in isn't listed below then try contacting the relevant national association (*eg* the LTA for tennis) and asking them for a list of course providers.

BERSA (British Elastic Rope Sports Association)

33a Canal Street
Oxford
Oxfordshire OX2 6BQ

Tel: 01865 311 179
Fax: 01865 426007
see: www.gap-year.com

Not for people who lie about their weight – if you say you're lighter than you are... splat! Bungee-jumping is still a very scary sport, but regulations set up by BERSA have made it safer, and you need to check that any jump site you consider is certified by BERSA before you take the plunge. The chances are that you will bungee-jump from a crane any height from 150 feet upwards (apparently the biggest crane in England is 325 feet high) and it will cost you around £50. Many sites offer a reduced rate on your second jump. Remember as you leap off that what you are doing is jumping from very high up with an enlarged elastic band tied to your feet.

Britannia Sailing Schools

Tel: +44 (0) 1473 787019
Fax: +44 (0) 1473 787018
see: www.gap-year.com

Britannia Sailing is a well-established company on the east coast offering all aspects of sailing instruction and yacht charter. It is approved by the Royal Yachting Association and teaches the full RYA syllabus. Based at Shotley Marina near Ipswich, they are perfectly placed to take full advantage of all that the east coast has to offer the yachtsman – the sheltered and uncrowded waters offer good sailing with many idyllic anchorages. If you want to travel further afield, the coasts of France, Belgium and The Netherlands are all within a day's sail.

They offer first class facilities; the practical courses take place on spacious and modern yachts and the theory courses are taught in their dedicated classroom within the marina. Instructors are trained to the highest standards and selected for their personality as well as their sailing ability.

British Mountaineering Council

177-179 Burton Road
West Didsbury
Manchester M20 2BB

Tel: 0870 010 4878
Fax: 0161 445 4500
see: www.gap-year.com

The British Mountaineering Council is the representative body that exists to protect the freedoms and promote the interests of climbers, hillwalkers and mountaineers, including ski-mountaineers.

The BMC can help you with technical and medical advice, training and finding climbing centres and clubs. It supports over 50 expeditions a year and runs a wide range of international meets. Its excellent website is full of relevant and helpful information.

British Offshore Sailing School – BOSS

Hamble Point Marina, School Lane
Hamble
Hampshire SO31 4NB

Tel: 023 8045 7733
Fax: 023 8045 6744
see: www.gap-year.com

BOSS offers complete 5-day and weekend RYA shore-based and practical training courses from Hamble Point Marina. If your aim is to get a job in the marine industry, BOSS run a 'Fastrak' course – intensive professional sail-training course which takes you from beginner to Yachtmaster in just 18 weeks.

Bungeezone

see: www.gap-year.com

Bungee-jumping associations worldwide.

Commodore Yachting

Commodore House, 63 The Hillway
Portchester, Hampshire PO16 8BP

Tel: 023 9279 3421
see: www.gap-year.com

Based at Haslar Marina in the Solent, Commodore Yachting offers sailing courses from 'the basic competent crew' to the more experienced 'Yachtmaster Offshore'. Practical course sizes are kept to a maximum of five students on eight-berth yachts, which allows for a good level of individual training.

Devon & West Yacht School

Tel: 01803 883718
see: www.gap-year.com

RYA approved sail training from Competent Crew to Yachtmaster. Practical courses cost £310 per person; theory courses also available.

Extra Skills   SPORT

Kiteboarding UK
                                                      Tel: 01502 512768

Kiteboarding UK offer kiteboarding lessons on their council-approved training area at Kesslingland beach near Lowestoft. Two types of lesson are availiable: Land based (£60) and water based (£90).

Lawn Tennis Association (Coaching Dept)
The Queen's Club
West Kensington   Tel: 020 7381 7000
London W1H 9EG   see: www.gap-year.com

The LTA runs coaching courses with three levels of qualification: Development, Club and Performance, all running for 14 days over five months. Before you start any of these you need to do the two-day Tennis Assistants course (£55). The Development Course takes you to a level where you can get coaching jobs (though some employers will expect you to be a 'Licenced Coach').

After the Development Course the LTA will tell you about employment opportunities, and on the LTA website there's a list of UK tennis clubs you can apply to, or where you can advertise your brilliance as a coach to less brilliant players.

London Scuba Diving School
Rabys Barn, New Chapel Road   Tel: 0700 027 2822
Lingfield, Surrey RH7 6LE   see: www.gap-year.com

Anyone into scuba knows you can book a holiday abroad and take scuba diving lessons when you get there, renting the kit as you learn. (Make sure your instructor is qualified.) But it may be safer to train in the UK first – then you can get the most from your holiday trying out (and improving) your scuba skills. The London Scuba Diving School walks you underwater on the floors of swimming pools in Battersea and Bayswater and arranges one-week diving holidays in the Red Sea where divers can explore the wreck of the merchant ship Dunraven (sunk in 1876). Diving limit 30 metres. Accommodation is in a 13-cabin cruiser where night dives are possible. Prices £600-£700.

National Mountaineering Centre
Plas-y-Brenin, Capel Curig
Bettws-y-Coed, Gwynedd LL24 OET   Tel: 01690 720 214
Wales   see: www.gap-year.com

For those hoping to reach dizzy heights, the National Mountaineering Centre at Bettws-y-Coed offers a vast range of activities and courses.

visit: www.gap-year.com

There are 170 courses in Wales, Scotland and the Swiss Alps priced from £99 upwards.

The recommended course for those wanting to gain experience in all outdoor pursuits is the week-long multi-activity course. Priced at £310, it includes indoor climbing, skiing, kayaking, navigation and mountain walking as well as accommodation for the week. Alternatively there's a weekend course priced at £145.

Suffolk Sailing

Unit 75, Claydon Business Park
Gipping Road
Great Blakenham
Ipswich
Suffolk IP6 0NL

Tel: 01473 833010
Fax: 01473 833020
see: www.gap-year.com

Although mainly suppliers of sailing safety equipment, Suffolk Sailing does offer a one-day RYA/DOT Basic Sea Survival Course for Small Craft.

The course includes:

- Preparation for sea survival – survival, difficulties and requirements; equipment available; training drills; actions prior to abandonment.
- Practical wet drill – liferaft launching, boarding, survival whilst in water; capsize drill; final abandonment.
- Principles of survival – protection in both hot and cold conditions; location; water rationing and collection; food rationing; survival craft ailments.
- Lifejackets and liferafts – life jacket design, construction, wearing and use; safety harness design and use; liferaft standards, design, launching, equipment; actions taken whilst in liferaft.
- Search and rescue – rescue by helicopter; coastguard, SAR organisation.

Sunsail

The Port House
Port Solent
Portsmouth
Hampshire PO6 4TH

Tel: 023 9222 2224
Fax: 023 9221 9827
see: www.gap-year.com

Sunsail offers the full range of RYA yacht courses as well as their own teaching programmes. Their instructors are RYA qualified. They have bases in the UK, the Canaries and Thailand.

Extra Skills **SPORT**

UKSA (United Kingdom Sailing Academy)

West Cowes
Isle of Wight

Tel: 01983 203014
Fax: 01983 295938
see: www.gap-year.com

The United Kingdom Sailing Academy (UKSA), based in Cowes, trains watersport instructors, professional skippers and crews for yachts. The Academy has modern facilities, including residential accommodation and a fleet of over 300 craft.

Gap year students train with UKSA for six months, in Cowes and Barbados, to become multi-qualified water sport instructors. The comprehensive training is designed to finish just as the major water-activity holiday companies are recruiting staff for their summer seasons. Six hundred companies worldwide recruit directly through the Academy. The UKSA careers department helps their 'Gap graduates' to find employment for the second six months of their year. If you have a yachting background you can complete the Professional Crew and Skipper Training (PCST) course in the first six months, before seeking employment for the rest of the year.

These qualifications gained during your gap year last from two to four years. You can use your qualifications to find further employment in the international holiday market in future university vacations.

 # Working in the UK

Why work?

Isn't this supposed to be a year off?...

Yes, but there are different reasons why you might consider getting a job for part of your gap year: to save up for travelling later; to raise funds for a voluntary placement; to save up in advance for university; to get useful career experience. If what you need is cash and fast, be prepared to do something tedious and mindless – but don't spend all of your gap year doing it. If, however, this is a career move, be prepared to get paid a pittance! It's useful to remember when working out a timetable that some casual work is seasonal: there are more jobs in stores at Christmas, for example, and of course on farms in the summer.

Funding for the fun

If you need to pay for your gap year travel, it's easy to make the assumption that you will be able to pick up jobs as you travel to pay for your gap year. Maybe you will, but it's a bit of a gamble and you could end up having to come home early. That's one of several reasons why many gap year students prefer to look for paid work in the UK before they start voluntary work or freewheeling travel abroad.

One way to finance travel is to look for an employer who will place you on a special gap year work scheme and pay you enough for travel afterwards (see Gap Year Employers later in this chapter). Another increasingly popular move is to look for a summer camp, language school or agency that introduces you to a job after the course or placement it is offering you. Find out first whether it's paid.

One way to plan a gap year is to set a target to finance something you want to do – like earning £4000 in different jobs after leaving school to pay for a place on an overseas project and a few months' travel.

Earning for the learning

Unless your parents are loaded and generous, you're a dotcom millionaire or you're a genius funded by NASA, you're going to find university leaves you seriously in debt. One way to get ahead is to save up some money in advance, say £1000, perhaps at the end of your gap year.

visit: www.gap-year.com

Getting your foot in the door

Another reason for working during your gap year is less about money and more about getting some relevant experience to add to your CV, especially if you're planning a career in the media.

There are professions where it really does help to know the right people. More than anything else, employers want to see hard evidence that you are dedicated to the career, not just acting on a whim, before they invest their time and money in you. Telling them you're "really interested" isn't going to impress, but a CV with relevant work experience (or a portfolio of articles you've had published if you want to be a journalist, for example) will make them sit up and listen. So how do you get a job to get the experience to get a job? Yes, this is the original Catch 22 situation.

Don't be put off; perseverance pays. Smaller local TV and radio stations or a local newspaper may let you 'help out' – you're likely to get little or no pay, but you might feel it's worth investing the time now to get ahead of the competition. And if you can use your gap year to gain relevant experience it will help you get your foot in the door. Who knows – if you prove yourself it might even earn you the chance of a 'proper' job once you've graduated.

Finding a job

School careers advisers are usually happy to advise and will have a mine of information to hand. Much of it is now on computers: recruitment on the internet has begun to take off. There should also be relevant books at school, at local public libraries and at more than 100 local authority careers offices – these act as centres for advice and training as well as employment agencies.

Advertisements

Companies often don't advertise for staff until they're desperate, so the first good candidate often gets a job. Act quickly. Buy your local newspaper or magazine as soon as a new edition comes out on the news stand; be the first to get on the telephone; ask only essential questions; speak clearly and take down necessary directions to get to the place where you may be recruited. Most national newspaper advertising is for full-time 'permanent' jobs, so it's usually quicker to try local newspapers and specialist trade magazines. Don't give up – if the first 21 advertisers turn you down for their jobs, the 22nd may just say "yes".

Contacts, CV and follow-up

Many jobs are filled by personal contact before being advertised: it is no surprise that students sometimes have to pull strings hard to get interesting paid work. Use every family connection or friend-of-a-friend that you can muster.

Try contacts first: if you want to get a foot in the door in television, for example, by manning the phone in a studio, make sure you go and see your best friend's second cousin who works in TV. You can ask for advice and names and addresses, make notes of what the expert friend tells you and act on the advice. Don't wait for something to happen, make it happen!

You can use a home or school computer to produce a spotless and well-organised CV. Remember to include all *relevant* skills, work experience and other achievements (money raised for charity, successful stint selling hand-made hats as a Young Enterprise marketing director). Experience with computers (especially website work) will score highly (see *Chapter 6: Business Skills*), and if you want to show off technical skills like website design, suggest the employer looks at your website – get a friend to check it first for spelling mistakes. These days most employers are happy to receive your CV as an e-mail attachment but make sure your computer doesn't have a virus – crashing the company's computer system won't get you the job.

When you've sent off your CV, whether it's to a contact, to a company simply on spec or in response to an advertisement, make sure to follow it up. Also follow any advice a contact gives you: if they suggest you ring studios A and B, say, and speak to X and Y at the end of July after you have sent them each your CV with a covering letter, then do exactly that. Never be afraid to persist or try a 'passing visit' to a potential employer, unless it's a big company whose security staff won't let you in without an appointment. Small companies are more relaxed: there may be no job now, but if you impressed them, they may remember you when they need to recruit someone later.

Be informed. Do you know about sound studio mixing equipment? Or engineering widgets? Read the trade magazines before you meet someone for a job interview, because even knowing a bit about the business will make them feel happier about employing you. Even more importantly, find out about the company – check out their website or ask to be sent a company brochure. This should also give you some ideas for questions to ask at interview.

Employment agencies

There are two types, the public Job Centres (with local authority careers centres) and the private employment agencies. These used to be very different, with the state-owned employment centres known for

visit: www.gap-year.com

low-wage, hard-labour jobs (work on building sites, lifting crates of beer, cleaning offices at 5am), while the private agencies specialised in office jobs. Now the difference is not so clear-cut.

Everyone knows the names of the office work agencies with branch networks: Brook Street Bureau, Reed Employment and others. If you have the skills covered in *Chapter 6: Business Skills*, you should have an instant passport to office work through one of these agencies. The work may be boring, but the company could be fun, and computer-literate work tends to be well paid. Try local agencies first, look smart, and take every certificate and reference you can lay your hands on, including evidence of work experience – even if it was only a week working in the family business.

Gap year specialists

If you would like to get a work placement from a gap year specialist, a good starting point is The Year Out Group, an association of organisations formed to promote the concept and benefits of well-structured year out programmes and to help people select suitable and worthwhile projects. The Group's member organisations provide a wide range of year out placements in UK and overseas including structured work placements.

Year Out Group members are expected to put potential clients and their parents in contact with those who have recently returned. Year Out Group considers it important that these references are taken up at least by telephone and, where possible, by meeting face to face.

Year Out Group Membership (February 2003): Academic Year in the USA & Europe; Africa & Asia Venture; Africa Conservation Experience; Art History Abroad; BSES Expeditions; BUNAC; CESA Languages Abroad; Coral Cay Conservation; Council Exchanges; CSV (Community Service Volunteers); Flying Fish; Frontier Conservation; GAP Activity Projects; Gap Challenge/World Challenge Expeditions; Greenforce; i-to-i International Projects; Outreach International; Project Trust; Quest Overseas; Raleigh International; Students Partnership Worldwide; Teaching & Projects Abroad; Travellers Worldwide; Trekforce Expeditions; The International Academy; The Smallpeice Engineering Gap year; The Year in Industry; Year Out Drama.

The Year Out Group   **Queensfield, 28 King's Road
Easterton, Wiltshire SN10 4PX
Tel: 07980 395789
see:** www.gap-year.com

Job surfing

Some of the major job agencies, and many smaller ones, now have websites. You don't get the personal touch from a website that you do by going into a local branch and getting advice or registering face-to-face, but recruitment websites are really useful if you know what you want to do and you have a 'skills profile' that one of their customers is looking for. Some of them are aimed at graduates and students, others at a general audience, others at specific areas of work (IT, for example). Here are a few to start with:

www.activate.co.uk
www.excite.co.uk
www.fish4jobs.co.uk
www.ft.com
www.gradunet.co.uk
www.hotel-recruit.com
www.jobserve.com
www.jobstelegraph.co.uk
www.jobsunlimited.co.uk

www.milkround.co.uk
www.monster.com
www.peoplebank.com
www.reed.co.uk
www.search.co.uk
www.stepstone.com
www.studentrecruitment.com
www.uk.careers.yahoo.com

If you're interested in working for a particular company, take a look at its website – the bigger firms usually have a recruitment page.

On spec

If contacts, advertisements, agencies or the internet all fail there is always DIY job-hunting. Just walk into shops and restaurants to ask about casual work or use a phone directory (*eg* Yellow Pages) to phone businesses (art galleries, department stores, zoos...) and ask what is available. Ring up, ask to speak to the personnel manager, and ask if and when they have jobs available and how you should apply. If they ask you to write in, you can do it after the call. If you go in, make sure you look smart.

Opportunities in the big professional firms are not always well-publicised. Temporary jobs (except agency-filled ones) are often filled by personal contact. If you have a burning desire to work for an architects or lawyers firm, for example, and you find nothing advertised, you could try phoning through a list to ask if work is available. If you can't find a professional directory in your library, try the professional trade association. Most have lists of their member firms.

The Institute of Chartered Accountants Student Recruitment Office in Milton Keynes produces a free national list of firms with training vacancies called *Guide to Training Vacancies*.

Institute of Chartered Accountants

**Student Recruitment Office
Gloucester House, 399 Silbury Blvd.
Central Milton Keynes MK9 2HL
Tel: 01908 248 108
www.icaew.co.uk**

Interviews

All your hard work has paid off and now you've been invited in for an interview – this is your chance to shine and make sure you persuade them that the only sensible thing to do is give you the job. Get family or teachers to give you practice job interviews so you have answers ready for those big questions like "What can you bring to this company?" or "What are your strengths and weaknesses?" Be positive. Above all when you talk to employers, show interest, sound sensible and show that you are bright, but not rude or arrogant. Never run down previous employers or your school or teachers. Interviewers will expect you to be rude about them behind their backs too.

You are not expected to turn up dressed like a member of the Royal Family, but T-shirts and trainers are likely to ruin your chances with all but the most modern of bosses. Nerd clothes, however, don't matter much in a dotcom company. If you've got the talent, you'll be in faster than you can say 'WAP'.

If you don't get the job, better luck next time. It may just be that the next person had slightly more relevant qualifications or more experience – that's life. Think of it as good practice for the next one.

Accepting the job

If a job is offered, make sure you know the terms: what type of work, how much per hour pay, if lunch breaks are included, hours of work, how and when you will get paid and whether you will have tax deducted or not. If you think you could get injured on the job, say, by heavy lifting, check also that you are covered by your own insurance policies, although the employer may be technically liable for damages.

Money, money, money

So you got the job, you've put in the hours and you are just waiting for the cash to roll in...

Pay, tax and National Insurance

You can expect to be paid in cash for casual labour, by cheque (weekly or monthly) in a small company and by bank transfer in a large one. Always keep the payslip that goes with your pay, along with your own records of what you earn (including payments for casual labour) during the tax year: from 6 April one year to 5 April the next. You need to ask your employer for a P46 form when you start your first job and a P45 form when you leave (which you take to your next employer).

If you are out of education for a year you are not treated as a normal taxpayer. So you can earn up to £4615 a year tax free (this is the personal allowance for the tax year 2002/2003 and will be reviewed in April '03). If you end the year having earned less than this but have had tax deducted during the year, you can claim a rebate from the Inland Revenue.

Unless you're self-employed, you also start to pay National Insurance (NI, a contribution to the country's health and social welfare system) on anything you earn when you get to £89 a week. So if you are employed on the PAYE (Pay As You Earn) system you will find NI money has been deducted from your pay, as well as tax. Always keep a note somewhere safe of your NI number – you'll need it quite often in life.

If you're not a gap year student (for example if you are still at school, college or university) and you are doing casual work in your holidays the rules are different. You need to ask your employer for a P38(S) form, on which you declare that you are in full-time education and that you will not be earning more than £4615 during the tax year.

If you have any questions about tax or National Insurance take a look at the IR website or give them a call – they are surprisingly helpful and nice. The general helpline is open Monday to Friday, 8.30am to 5.00pm.

Inland Revenue   **General Helpline: 020 7667 4001**
www.inlandrevenue.gov.uk

Minimum wages, maximum hours

If you are over 18 the government has set a minimum wage that your employer can pay you. Workers aged 18-21 must be paid at least £3.60 per hour. If you are 22 or older you are entitled to at least £4.20 per hour except during the first six months in a new job with a new employer and if you are receiving accredited training.

To check on how the National Minimum Wage applies to you, use the TIGER interactive website or phone the National Minimum Wage Helpline on 0845 6000 678. This is also the number to ring if you think you are being underpaid and want to complain. All complaints about underpayment of the National Minimum Wage are treated in the strictest confidence.

There is also a law on working hours which the UK has had to put into force to comply with European Union legislation. This says that (with some exemptions for specific professions) no employee should be expected to work more than 48 hours a week. Good employers do give you time off 'in lieu' if you occasionally have to work more than 48 hours a week. Others take no notice, piling a 60-hour-a-week workload on you. This is against the law and, unless you like working a 12-hour day, they must stop. You are also entitled to four weeks paid leave per year, a day off each week and an in-work rest break if the working day is longer than six hours.

Gap year employers

Over the next few pages we list companies that either have specific gap year employment policies or that we think are worth contacting. We've split them into three groups: arts festivals, seasonal work and general employers. This isn't a comprehensive list, so it's still worth checking the internet and your local companies (in the Yellow Pages, for example).

Arts festivals

Whether musical, literary or dramatic, there are loads of festivals taking place up and down the country every year. You need to apply as early as possible, as there aren't that many placements. Satellite organisations spring up around core festivals, so if you are unsuccessful at first, try to be transferred to another department. The work can be paid or on a voluntary basis. Short-term work, including catering and stewarding, is available mainly during the summer. Recruitment often starts on a local level, so check the local papers and job agencies.

Facilities Management Catering Ltd.

FMC are the official Caterers to The Championships, Wimbledon.

If you are a keen, enthusiastic, hard working individual and would like to work at **THE** most prestigious sporting event of the year, From Saturday 21st June until Sunday 6th July 2003

Then call us **NOW** for an application pack.

FMC Ltd.,
Church Road,
Wimbledon
SW19 5AE

Tel: 020 8947 7430
Fax: 020 8944 6362
Email: resourcing@fmccatering.co.uk
Website: www.fmccatering.co.uk

Brecon Jazz Festival
Festival Office, The Watton
Brecon, Powys LD3 7EF
Wales

Tel: 01874 625 557
see: www.gap-year.com

This mid-Wales town turns into New Orleans in August every year as jazz bands and singers from all over the world congregate to share their syncopated rhythm.

Brighton Literary Festival
12A Pavilion Buildings
Castle Square
Brighton, East Sussex BN1 4EE

see: www.gap-year.com

Volunteer posts in the education and press office departments during the festival in May.

Cheltenham Festivals
Cheltenham Town Hall
Imperial Square
Cheltenham, Gloucester GL50 1QA

Tel: 01242 263 494
see: www.gap-year.com

This company runs festivals throughout the year, including jazz, science, music, folk, fringe and literary events. There are usually a number of placements available, although they tend to be unpaid. Check out their website for details about each festival and who to contact.

Edinburgh International Festival
The Hub, Castlehill
Edinburgh EH 2NE
Scotland

Tel: 0131 473 2099
Fax: 0131 473 2002
see: www.gap-year.com

Big and long-established late summer festival that has managed to stay cutting-edge. Paid employment is available in the centre's press office, front of house, box office, shop and café. Applications by post.

Facilities Management Catering
Church Road
Wimbledon
London SW19 5AE

Tel: 020 8947 7430
Fax: 020 8944 6362
see: www.gap-year.com

The official caterers to the Wimbledon Tennis Championships, FMC employ keen, hard-working gappers from mid-June to early July. Contact the company for an application pack.

EMPLOYERS: SEASONAL

Hay Festival
General Manager Administration
The Drill Hall
25 Lion Street
Hay-on-Wye HR3 5AD

Tel: 01497 821217
Fax: 01497 821066
see: www.gap-year.com

One of the most famous literary festivals in the UK. Most departments take on extra workers for festival fortnight, including stewards, extra staff for the box-office and the bookshop and six interns. Accommodation and food are provided.

Seasonal work

Seasonal work covers a wide variety of jobs including working with kids on summer camps and farm work. Although seasonal work doesn't tend to give you 'career experience' it can pay quite well and it doesn't last all year so you get time to do something else.

The following companies offer seasonal work – and you could also take a look at **www.studentrecruitment.com**, a web-based recruitment service specifically for seasonal farm work.

Acorn Adventure
22 Worcester Road
Stourbridge
West Midlands DY8 1AN

Tel: 01384 446057

Acorn Adventure runs adventure holiday camps based in nine centres in France, Italy, Spain and the UK – their main customers are school groups. They operate from April until September and have a good range of rewarding positions available, employing approximately 300 staff annually.

Pay starts from National Minimum Wage in the UK with additional qualification bonuses and returning staff bonuses. As an example of pay in European centres, a BCU Level 3 Canoe Coach would be expected to earn an average of £140 per week with food and accommodation included.

Acorn offers comprehensive training packages, including National Governing Body qualifications as well as free uniform and free travel. If you're looking for fun, hard work, qualifications, training, friendships, experience, travel, adventure, challenge and reward then get in touch with the Recruitment and Training Department.

Camp Beaumont

The Old Rectory
Beeston Regis
Norfolk NR27 9NG

Tel: 01263 823000
Fax: 01263 823002

You may remember going to Camp Beaumont summer camps as a teenager. Well, now you can go back and work there. There are seven day camps around London and the home counties and six residential sites around the country. There's also one camp in France, for which a TEFL qualification is useful (see *Chapter 1: Working Abroad*). Jobs last for five to eight weeks during the summer holidays: recruiting continues until late June. Basic pay starts at £144 a week, but varies depending on experience and qualifications. The contact numbers for Camp Beaumont's Beaumont House office are: Tel: 01603 284280, Fax: 01603 284250.

Facilities Management Catering Ltd

Church Road
Wimbledon
London SW19 5AE

Tel: 020 8947 7430
Fax: 020 8944 6362
see: www.gap-year.com

The official caterers to the Wimbledon Tennis Championships, FMC employ keen, hard-working gappers from mid-June to early July. Contact the company for an application pack.

PGL

PGL Recruitment Team
Alton Court
Penyard Lane
Ross-on-Wye
Herefordshire HR9 5GL

Tel: 01989 767 833
Fax: 01989 767 760

PGL runs activity holidays and courses for children. Each year the company employs over 2000 young people to work as instructors, group leaders and support staff at its centres in the UK, France and Spain. Positions are available between February and October each year. Ideally you should be able to start before May and be able to commit for a minimum of eight weeks. You must also be over 18 years of age. You will receive full board and accommodation in addition to £60-£90 per week, depending on your role.

To work as an instructor or group leader you should have relevant experience. You don't need to be qualified as PGL provides training programmes to help staff gain the necessary skills and qualifications.

General companies

In this section we list the businesses and organisations offering special schemes for those taking a gap year, possibly in partnership with a gap year organisation. Alongside these are other companies providing paid work and a miscellany of additional companies, large and small, just to show you what's available. The contact details we've listed are not necessarily company headquarters, but the best places to apply to.

If you're a science or engineering student and you'd like to do a one-year placement, try the Year in Industry.

Abbey National

For jobs in branches check the local press or ask your local branch about short term employment opportunities. For advertised vacancies, contact Customer Services for an application form. Abbey has a recruitment section on its website.

Alliance & Leicester

Graduate Recruitment
Customer Services Centre
3rd Floor, Building 4, Narborough
Leicester, Leicestershire LE9 5XX

A&L can't guarantee work but it will keep your CV on file in case a project comes up that needs extra staff, usually at the Narborough customer services centre.

Anne Havercroft Schools Appointment Service

23 Peters Close
Prestwood
Buckinghamshire HP16 9ET

Tel: 01494 863027
Fax: 0494 864122

The Anne Havercroft Schools Appointment Service is a recruitment agency for pastoral staff: residential nurses, matrons and houseparents. It can also find placements for gap year students as games assistants or at boarding schools. There is no appointment no fee – you can register for free.

Arcadia Group plc

For jobs in branches (Burton Menswear, Dorothy Perkins, Evans, Hawkshead, Principles, Racing Green, Topshop/Man), apply directly to your local branch.

Bank of Scotland

Their Vacation Placement scheme is run every year in different divisions of the bank from June to September. To apply, send your CV and a letter by December to one of the following addresses:
Personal Banking: Director of Human Resources, Bank of Scotland, Cherrybank, Perth PH2 0NG
Business Banking: Director of HR, Bank of Scotland, Capital House, Queens Park Road, Chester CH38 7AW
Corporate Banking: Director of HR, Bank of Scotland, The Mound, Edinburgh EH1 1YZ
IT Centre: Director of HR, Bank of Scotland, 2 Bankhead Crossway North, Edinburgh EH11 4EF

BDO Stoy Hayward
8 Baker Street
London W1M 1DA   Tel: 020 7486 5888

A firm of chartered accountants, BDO Stoy Hayward has several gap year vacancies in the London office. Successful applicants will be employed as an audit assistant within one of the general business groups. Most placements run for nine months from September to May, but shorter placements can also be arranged. Some of the other offices across the UK also take applications for gap year placements. Applicants should contact the office they are interested in directly for more information. National office details can be found in its graduate brochure or website.

Bierrum and Partners
Bierrum House
High Street
Houghton Regis, Nr Dunstable   Tel: 01582 845 745
Bedfordshire LU5 5BJ   Fax: 01582 845 746

A civil engineering firm which takes one gap year student a year through YINI. Contact them direct for other short-term work.

Blue Circle Industries
Group Personnel Manager
84 Eccleston Square
London SW1V 1PX

Possibility of some clerical/WP/DB/DTP work for a few weeks. Send a CV and brief covering letter.

EMPLOYERS: GENERAL

Boots

Recruitment of post-GCSE and A level students with a view to long-term employment in the company for which full training is given. However, eight-week vacation placements are offered to university students. Contact your local store and ask about temporary employment opportunities.

BP Amoco
Recruitment Adviser, Britannic House
1 Finsbury Circus, London EC2M 7BA

Eight-week placements are offered to generalists in their penultimate year and vacation or one-year placements to technologists in their second and third years.

Getting the experience

After finishing my A levels I wanted a break before starting my degree. I see a gap year as an excellent opportunity to gain work experience, travel and earn money to support myself at university.

During my placement, here at PricewaterhouseCoopers, I am being treated like a graduate joiner, given real responsibility and am learning a huge amount about the finance and business world. I am also developing more confidence as well as my communication and teamworking skills. The intensive induction training and tremendous support I am receiving from my colleagues helped me integrate into the firm and I feel very much part of the team.

After my six month placement finishes I'll be helping to run a summer camp for young children before travelling around the world. So when I start university I will have had some incredible work experience, made dozens of new friends and had a kick-start to my future career!

Dhruv
Gap Year Student,
joined PricewaterhouseCoopers in October 2001

Cadbury Schweppes

25 Berkeley Square
London W1J 6HB

Tel: 020 7409 1313
Fax: 020 7830 5200

Cadbury Schweppes places people on work experience in response to specific business needs. Contact the business units direct.

Carlton Communications

Personnel Manager
101 St Martin's Lane
London WC2N 4AZ

Holding company for Carlton Television. There are few opportunities and they are inundated with applications, so preference is given to those who specifically want a career in TV. Apply in writing.

Corus Group

Graduate Recruitment
Ashorne Hill Management College
Leamington Spa, Warwickshire CV33 9PY   Tel: 01926 488 029

Corus Group (merger of British Steel and Koninklijke Hoogevens) takes on a small number of gap year students intending to study mainly engineering/scientific courses with a view to possible undergraduate sponsorship. The gap year is spent working in a department related to your forthcoming course. Apply in writing to the Graduate Co-ordinator at your nearest Corus business or the above address.

Demos

The Mezzanine, Elizabeth House
39 York Road
London SE1 7NQ

Tel: 020 7401 5330

Independent research institute, specialising in research into public policy issues. Occasional vacation work available. Send CV and letter.

EMI Group

4 Tenterden Street, Hanover Square
London W1A 2AY

Tel: 020 7355 4848

Short term employment is made available according to company demand. Contact individual businesses such as EMI Music International (Tel: 020 7467 2000) or EMI Records UK (Tel: 020 7605 5000).

visit: www.gap-year.com

EMPLOYERS: GENERAL

Foreign Office
see: www.gap-year.com

As a member of the Diplomatic Service, you could be doing political or economic work in their embassy in Moscow, helping companies export their products, or consular work in Hanoi. See their website for more about careers and opportunities in the Diplomatic Service.

Great Universal Stores (GUS)
Human Resources Department
One Stanhope Gate
London W1K 1AF   Tel: 020 7495 0070

Advice is to write early, stating your preferred area of work (such as customer services, merchandise, IT, marketing, personnel). For speculative applications send CV and letter.

Halifax plc
Trinity Road, Halifax, West Yorkshire HX1 2RG

For temporary vacation work contact regional offices.

HSBC

Hongkong & Shanghai Banking Corporation may have vacancies at regional branches. Check the local press or ask your local branch about short term employment opportunities. Posts generally arise on an *ad hoc* basis.

IBM UK Ltd
Student Employment Officer
Recruitment Department
PO Box 4, North Harbour
PortsmoutH, Hampshire PO5 3AU   Tel: 01705 426 426

IBM aims to take at least 50 gap year students into its UK pre-university employment programme. Most successful candidates have at least two As and a B at A level and many jobs require aptitudes found in those planning to read subjects like computing, engineering and science.

The programme opens in September: apply as early as you can in spring 2003 for September 2003 places. Students are asked their preference for locations, and the most strongly technical placements are in Warwick and Hursley, near Winchester. Some students return to IBM in vacations afterwards and on graduation.

IMI plc
PO Box 216
Witton
Birmingham B6 7BA　　　　　　　　　　　　Tel: 0121 356 4848

IMI operates a global graduate development programme and offers vacation work from June to September to penultimate year engineering (mechanical, electrical or manufacturing) students leading to possible sponsorship through the final year at university.

Johnson & Johnson

Manufacturer of hospital products, with a factory in Yorkshire. Possible places are subject to availability and advertised in the national press.

Kingswood Study Centres
Overstrand Hall
Overstrand
Norfolk NR27 OJJ　　　　　　　　　　　　Tel: 01263 579 157

This company works at the same residential schools as Camp Beaumont – in Stafford, Norfolk, Devon, north Wales and the Isle of Wight, as well as in France. It offers contracts for eight months to three years. Pay for the first year is only £250 a month, but you get full board as well. No qualifications or experience are needed (although they may be useful), but you must want to work with children.

Land Securities
5 Strand
London WC2N 5AF　　　　　　　　　　　　Tel: 020 7413 9000

Although Land Securities doesn't offer placements to pre-university gappers, graduates who have taken a year out are looked on favourably for recruitment. Enquiries to the Personnel Department.

London Electricity
Templar House
81-87 High Holborn
London WC1V 6NV　　　　　　　　　　　　Tel: 0207 242 9050

Industrial placements are available for undergraduates as part of their course, but only for those budding engineers among you. Apply by post with a CV to the Personnel Division.

visit: www.gap-year.com

Nortel Networks
The Resourcing Organisation
Maidenhead Office Park, Westacott Way
Maidenhead, Berkshire SL6 3QH   Tel: 01628 432000

Operates through the Year in Industry Scheme, but also welcomes speculative applications from gap year students. Send CV and letter.

Norwich Union
PO Box 4, Surrey Street
Norwich, Norfolk NR1 3NG   Tel: 0800 092 9561

Short-term contract opportunities still exist at (former) CGU sites across the UK. Contact their local branch, or, for specific interest areas (*eg* statistics, human resources, marketing) contact The Resourcing Manager at the above address.

Outdoor Trust
Windy Gyle, Belford   Tel: 01668 213 289
Northumberland NE70 7QE   see: www.gap-year.com

The Outdoor Trust is a registered charity based in north Northumberland that organises outdoor pursuits for schools, individuals, youth groups and management training. It has a residential centre as well as a watersports base at Beadnell for windsurfing, sea-kayaking and sailing. Other activities include climbing, abseiling, hill walking and canoeing.

There's work for volunteers and paid trainees; jobs depend on qualifications. Pay isn't excessive at £30+.

---

www.gap-year.com

links to thousands of gap year opportunities

- Sports Courses
- Business skills
- Volunteering
- Travelling
- Languages
- Work in the UK and abroad

P&O Cruises
Personnel Department
Richmond House
Terminus Terrace
Southampton
Hampshire SO14 3PN

There's no official gap year placement scheme run by P&O Cruises, but it's worth contacting them if you're interested in working your way to your destination on board ship. Some cruises only hire over-21s (because of American drinking laws).

Powergen
Westwood Way
Westwood Business Park
Coventry
West Midlands CV4 8LG   Tel: 02476 424 723

Powergen offers sandwich placements for undergraduates as well as occasional summer vacancies. For speculative applications contact the personnel department at head office (Coventry), stating whereabouts in the country you would like to work and they will refer you to the relevant manager.

PricewaterhouseCoopers
Southwark Towers
32 London Bridge Street   Tel: 0808 100 1500
London SE1 9SY   see: www.gap-year.com

The PricewaterhouseCoopers Gap Year Programme is open to high calibre students who are taking some time out between school and university. Their six month programme runs from September to March and offers a real opportunity to experience life in the world's largest professional services firm. You'll need a strong academic record, excellent interpersonal skills and the ability to work as part of a team.

Reuters
85 Fleet Street
London EC4P 4AJ

Gap year placements for university students are much sought after because Reuters organises real projects aimed at moving the business forward. Opportunities range across the whole company: from general to business to technical and to journalism. Reuters takes around 30 students a year.

Go to their website to read about the company and choose the opportunities in which they are interested at the website, looking specifically at Interns & Placements. The opportunities are generally skills based (*eg* telephone skills, databases), but the application procedure is clear and easy. It should be followed carefully, as applications which do not conform will be ignored.

Rolls-Royce plc
PO Box 31, Derby
Derbyshire DE24 8B

Two forms of placements are available, vacation trainee and industrial trainee. For the vacation trainee attachments are available in engineering, marketing and commercial, procurement, human resources and logistics. Ten weeks are spent in a department relevant to the course being studied. Training takes place during the summer vacation before the final academic year at university. Students complete an individual project or contribute to a major piece of work in the department. Industrial trainee placements usually take place during the final industrial training period of a sandwich course. The number of attachments depends on business requirements.

Twelve month placements in finance usually include three attachments within the company. Attachments last 6-12 months and trainees may have to undertake one major project in one department. For application form contact the Company Recruitment Officer.

Royal & SunAlliance
Personnel Department,
St Mark's Court, Chart Way
Horsham, West Sussex RH12 1XL   Tel: 01403 232323

Gap year students are taken on according to business needs. Send a CV and letter stating what experience you wish to gain.

Royal Bank of Scotland
PO Box 31
42 St Andrew's Square
Edinburgh EH2 2YE, Scotland   Tel: 0131 556 8555

Vacation work is available. Contact the personnel department of your local branch or Head Office at the above address.

Scottish Courage Brewing

Production Personnel Director
John Courage House
1 Broadway Park
South Gyle, Edinburgh EH12 9GQ
Scotland

Recruiting is done locally on an *ad hoc* basis. Write in for work placements specifically in production.

Tesco

There are numerous job opportunities in Tesco stores throughout the UK. Ask in a store near you for more details about the jobs on offer.

Thorn UK

Baird House
Arlington Business Park
Theale
Reading
Berkshire RG7 4SA   Tel: 01734 306030

Possibility of some vacancies, though opportunities are limited. Speculative letters to the Human Resources Department.

Transco

31 Homer Road
Solihull
West Midlands B91 3LT   Tel: 0121 626 4431

See Year in Industry

Unilever

This highly decentralised business has summer placements available for penultimate-year undergraduates. Advice to gap year students is to approach some of the largest subsidiaries: Bird's Eye Walls, Walton-on-Thames, Surrey; Lever UK, Kingston upon Thames, Surrey. 'It is my opinion that graduates who have taken a year out at the age of 21 are more likely to do much more daring and ambitious things in that year out – all of which contribute to their personal development,' says Dr M J Duffell, former Head of Graduate Recruitment, National Personnel Department.

GAP YEAR PROGRAMME.

PricewaterhouseCoopers is the world's largest professional services organisation. What you'll also find is that we're a very different organisation - an organisation with a unique diversity of people and opportunities and a supportive culture that recognises you as an individual.

Our Gap Year Programme is for high-calibre students who are taking time out between school and university. The programme gives you a chance to do the job for real, which means real responsibility and real work. During your 6 month placement, you will develop a range of new skills whilst gaining a valuable insight into the world of professional services.

If you are interested in starting your career with PricewaterhouseCoopers, and have a strong academic record, well-developed interpersonal skills and a variety of external interests, then call **freephone 0808 100 1500** or alternatively **tel: +44 (0) 121 265 5852** for a brochure. **Apply online** or send your completed application form (obtainable from your careers service, our website or the above numbers), to the address on the form.

Please quote SIDP031002.

www.pwcglobal.com/uk/sidp/

PricewaterhouseCoopers refers to the UK firm of PricewaterhouseCoopers and to other member firms of the worldwide PricewaterhouseCoopers organisation.

Unipart
Unipart House, Cowley
Oxford, Oxfordshire OX4 2PG

Speculative applications for Unipart's Year in Industry project should be sent to DCM Human Resources.

United Biscuits
Human Resources
Hayes Park, Hayes End Road
Hayes, Middlesex UB4 8EE   Tel: 020 8234 5000

Although there are no gap year placements, sandwich (degree) students should contact the Graduate Resourcing Department for an updated list of placements.

Whitbread
Whitbread Court
PO Box 777, Dunstable LU5 5XE

Contact restaurants and pubs individually for holiday work.

WPP Group Plc
Programme Co-ordinator
27 Farm Street, London W1X 6RD   Tel: 020 7408 2204

WPP Group is a leading communications services group. Through its member companies, the group offers clients advertising, media, information and consultancy, public relations and public affairs, promotions, direct marketing and other specialist communications.

WPP has developed the WPP Fellowship programme for graduates, to develop high-calibre management and talent with work experience across, and understanding of, a range of marketing disciplines. WPP is looking for gappers who are resourceful, committed to marketing, intellectually curious and will take a rigorous and creative approach to problem solving.

Year in Industry
University of Manchester, Simon Building   Tel: 0161 275 4396
Oxford Road   Fax: 0161 275 4396
Manchester M13 9PL   see: www.gap-year.com

YINI places 18- and 19-year-olds with industry in their gap year before they begin a university course and aims to match students to companies according to their interests and career plans. More than 250 companies take part, ranging from multinationals to small enterprises.

YINI offers quality, paid, real and challenging work in a UK company, backed by on-the-job training in practical skills, management training and a personal mentor support scheme. The scheme is almost exclusively for pre-university students and usually runs from August to July. About 90% are expected to return to industry after graduation. You receive a salary within the range of £8k-£11k (some companies pay more).

"Today's students must develop the skills employers seek and find ways to stand out from the crowd," says Brian Tripp, chief executive of the Engineering Development Trust, which administers EES (England) and the Year in Industry scheme. He maintains that a year in industry gives students some idea of what industry is really about and allows industrialists to benefit from "some of the best innovative young brains in the country". Tripp himself spent 20 years in industry, with years of experience in petrochemicals and precision engineering.

You need to apply early in your final sixth form year at about the same time as you apply for university entrance, but you can generally defer university entrance until after you get your YINI place.

Yorkshire Water
PO Box 52
Bradford BD3 7YD   Tel: 01274 692 060

Individual enquiries about work experience should be made to the number above. Most of the 'opportunities' are unpaid, but there can be paid placements, depending on current projects.

 Volunteering in the UK

At the risk of sounding all 'worthy', it is important to spend at least some of your gap year doing something for the benefit of others. You will get both a satisfying sense of achievement and an opportunity to learn about other people as well as a lot about yourself.

Don't feel that to do anything really worthwhile you have to go abroad – there are many deserving cases right on your doorstep. You might also find that if you do voluntary work close to home it will make you more involved in your own community.

Although the definition for 'voluntary work' is strictly-speaking work that you're not paid for, voluntary schemes (especially the government-inspired ones) will often pay you some 'pocket money' and may also give you free meals and accommodation. Each scheme varies in what it provides – there are no rules. The point is that these are not 'jobs'; what you will be doing is altruistic: helping someone or a specific cause, usually a charity, whether you're working directly with children with special needs or doing the office filing for a charity.

Volunteering can also be an opportunity to gain relevant work experience. If you know, for example, that you want a career in retail, a stint with Oxfam will teach you a lot. Many charity shops recognise this and offer training. Or perhaps you could find yourself helping develop a charity's website.

Below we list the contact details of a number of charities and organisations that are grateful for volunteers – go to **www.gap-year.com** for a direct link to their websites and e-mails. If you can't find anything that interests you here, then there are a number of organisations which place people with other charities or with a wide national network of their own – an internet search should give you a good list.

The following websites provide useful links and information about volunteering:

www.do-it.org.uk
www.namss.org.uk
www.ncvo-vol.org.uk
www.timebank.org.uk
www.vois.org.uk

A week with the National Trust

I had no confidence and was carrying a lot of frustration. I wanted a change and new people around me. The Worldwide Volunteering database let me say what kind of work I was looking for and offered projects in Britain and overseas with hundreds of organisations. I was able to contact several but settled on the National Trust.

For a week during May I was treated to beautiful countryside and the most enthusiastic people I have ever met. Right from the start they really wanted to bond and made a big effort to do so. The brochure description never quite prepares you for the huge wave of energy that you get from doing the tasks. On the day that we attempted dry-stone walling the rain came down in sheets, and even getting a stone from the field made me feel a lot of pride.

In Cumbria, although the most demanding task was dry-stone walling, it certainly took less time than clearing a lake of poisonous weed! I enjoyed my week so much that I volunteered for a second week in Wales. Wherever you go on a National Trust placement there will always be thousands of rhododendrons to clear. We were set to work to create an opening in the forest.

As you have probably guessed from the enthusiasm with which I write I have a lot of interest in the environment. That is why I have chosen to take a National Diploma in Countryside Management at college in September. This will mean that I have some theory and a bit of practical over two years. So for me the Worldwide Volunteering database has led to two incredible weeks and a new direction in my life with a two year college course starting soon.

Voluntary Organisations

Barnabas Trust
Carroty Wood
Higham Lane
Tonbridge
Kent TN11 9QX

Tel: 01732 366 766
Fax: 01732 366 767
www.barnabas.org.uk

Opportunities are available to assist in the practical running of their centres.

Break
Residential Volunteers' Co-ordinator
1 Montague Road
Sheringham
Norfolk NR26 8LN

Tel: 01263 822161
Fax: 01263 822181
www.break-charity.org

Break runs two residential holiday/respite centres in Norfolk, offering mentally and physically disabled people week-long holiday breaks.

BTCV
36 St Mary's Street
Wallingford
Oxfordshire OX10 0EU

Tel: 01491 821 600
Fax: 01491 839 646
www.btcv.org

BTCV runs working holidays doing conservation work in England, Wales, Scotland and Northern Ireland. The conservation holidays last from two days to two weeks, and can involve dry-stone walling, creating anti-erosion defences or general upkeep of natural features. Accommodation varies according to the project (usually a youth hostel) and the cost ranges from £45-£90 a week. Training courses are available.

To get experience of publicity, administration and fundraising work you can go along to your local BTCV office and volunteer. BTCV provided more than 3000 volunteer placements for 16- to 24-year-olds under the Millennium Volunteer Programme last year and will be involved again this year.

BTCV Scotland

Balallan House
24 Allan Park
Stirling FK8 2QG, Scotland

Tel: 01786 479697
Fax: 01786 465359
www.btcv.org.uk

BTCV Scotland provides all-year-round environmental volunteering opportunities for over 6000 people a year. Depending on the amount of time you have to give you could go on one of their many conservation holidays across Scotland, get involved in running one of their Green Gyms, join a Volunteer Officer programme, assist their renowned 'Action Recycle' projects, help organise and run a National Environmental Skills training programme or become a Biodiversity Action Team member.

Many volunteers use their experiences with BTCV Scotland as a means of gaining full-time employment in the environmental sector; others simply want to 'give something back', meet like-minded friends; and, of course, have fun. No skills are required, just an interest in the environment and people and an energy to help BTCV help others. BTCV operates across the whole of Scotland, provides expenses for all regular volunteers, and accommodation for those working from their Inverness office.

Camphill Communities in the UK

William Morris House, Stonehouse
Gloucestershire GL10 3SH

Tel: 07941 360039
Fax: 01453 825807

Camphill is a worldwide network of communities (schools, colleges or adult centres) dedicated to work and life with children, adolescents or adults with developmental and other disabilities. The first such community – Camphill Rudolf Steiner School in Scotland – was founded in 1940 by the child psychiatrist Karl Koenig. The insights of the Austrian philosopher and innovator Rudolf Steiner provide a basis for pedagogical and therapeutic approaches, socio/economic forms and the cultural and spiritual creativity of the communities.

Life and work as a volunteer/co-worker in Camphill communities is demanding, diverse and rich. As a co-worker you need to be physically and emotionally healthy. Flexibility, openness and a serious willingness to work with developmentally disabled children or adults and other co-workers are essential. Co-workers are role models for those in their care, and a high level of maturity and judgement will be expected from you at all times. The safety and well-being, both physical and mental, of your companions is of primary importance, therefore the consumption of alcohol, as well as excessive smoking is strongly discouraged. Room, board, and pocket money for personal needs are all provided.

As a member of a household, you will be taking part in all domestic tasks. You will be responsible for direct care activities for the companions in your household as needed. Depending on the nature of your community – school, college or adult centre – you will participate in classroom and therapy support, vocational and/or workshop activities. You will also support the companions in their life skills and recreational activities.

Most communities ask that co-workers commit themselves for at least one full year. Induction and orientation courses are offered to first-timers, providing a basic introduction to the guidance of people with special needs, to Camphill life and anthroposophy.

Most Camphill communities are keen to have committed gap year students join them for a year, although some centres specify a minimum age of 19 or 20 years. If you are interested in spending your gap year with them, please visit their website for more information and contact details for specific communities. Their site also carries a list of current vacancies in the various UK communities.

Careforce

35 Elm Road
New Malden
Surrey KT3 3HB

Tel: 020 8942 3331
Fax: 020 8942 3331
www.careforce.co.uk

Each year Careforce recruits Christians aged 18 to 25 and places them throughout the UK for their gap years starting in early September. Placements are at churches and community projects in England, Scotland, Northern Ireland and Wales:

- The churches are interdenominational, active, outward-looking, evangelical and are moving into their communities in loving service and relevant outreach. They are in urban, rural and suburban situations.

- The projects are serving the most vulnerable people including those with addiction and learning disabilities, the elderly and the homeless.

Careforce volunteers serve for 11 to 12 months and receive full support from those on their placement and from Careforce staff. There are no fees to pay and full board and lodging is provided together with a small weekly allowance. Training is given on site and through central Careforce courses and there is peer support from groups of other volunteers.

Applications from within the UK can be made until 31 August each year. The closing date for applications from outside the UK is 28 February.

Central Scotland Countryside Trust

Hillhouseridge, Shottskirk Road
Shotts ML7 4JS, Scotland

Tel: 01501 822 015
www.csct.co.uk

CSCT organises volunteers to help with ecological improvements in Central Scotland. Work includes fence repairing and path building.

> VOLUNTARY ORGANISATIONS

Volunteering in the UK

The Centre for Alternative Technology

Machynlleth
Powys SY20 9AZ
Wales

Tel: 01654 705 951
Fax: 01654 702782
www.cat.org.uk

The Centre for Alternative Technology (CAT) has welcomed volunteers for a number of years, during which time they have contributed much to the vitality and running of the organisation. In addition to the one-week 'short term volunteer' programme, which runs throughout the summer, there is also a 'long term volunteer' (LTV) programme. Several departments take on a full time LTV for a period of six months during which the volunteer will assist with the everyday running of the department, have the opportunity to learn new skills and develop a work-related project. Anyone can apply to be an LTV but those with specific skills and experience to offer are more likely to be taken on. At present CAT takes on LTVs in biology, building, engineering, gardening, information, media, publications and site maintenance.

There are limited places for LTVs to stay on the CAT site as part of Site Community; some volunteers stay on site whilst the rest find accommodation locally. All CAT volunteers are entirely self-funding for the duration of their stay: organic, vegetarian staff lunches are provided and travel expenses paid to those living off site.

All prospective LTVs are invited to come for a 'trial week' before they can be accepted for a longer placement. This tried and tested system seems to work well for both parties. Applications should be addressed to the department you would like to volunteer for and be in the form of a CV with an accompanying covering letter.

Children's Country Holidays Fund

Holiday Project Manager, CCHF
42-43 Lower Marsh
London SE1 7RG

Tel: 020 7928 6522
Fax: 020 7401 3961
www.childrenholidays-cchf.org

The Children's Country Holidays Fund (registered charity number 206958) provides holidays for London children who have no other chance of a holiday. Volunteers are required to be activity holiday camp supervisors in the summer school holidays. The holidays are a week long, residential and incorporate a wide range of activities to provide a fun, safe and memorable holiday for 32 children aged 8-12. Supervisors are responsible for the care, welfare and entertainment of four children within a larger group of 32, under an experienced leader and deputy. Training is provided and all travel, board and accommodation costs are met.

Children's Trust
Tadworth Court
Tadworth
Surrey KT20 5RU

Tel: 01737 365000
Fax: 01737 365001
www.thechildrenstrust.org.uk

Residential centre for about 80 severely disabled children, currently expanding. Volunteers would help with the day-to-day needs of the children.

Churchtown Outdoor Adventure Centre
Churchtown
Lanlivery
Bodmin
Cornwall PL30 5BT

Tel: 01208 872 148
Fax: 01208 873 377
www.wft.org.uk

The Churchtown Outdoor Adventure Centre is an activity holiday centre for people of all ages, many disabled. Volunteers get pocket money and board, with a minimum stay of one month. They will help out with looking after the visitors and with activities.

CSV (Community Service Volunteers)
237 Pentonville Road
London N1 9NJ

Tel: 0800 374 991
Fax: 020 7837 9318
www.csv.org.uk

CSV, a registered charity, matches a full-time volunteer placement to every volunteer who applies. Volunteers must be aged 16+ (or 18+ if you are from outside the UK) and able live away from home for between four and 12 months. Over the past decade over 21,000 young people have taken part, supporting people who need help in a social care or community setting. Volunteers receive free accommodation, food and travel plus a weekly allowance of £27. No minimum qualifications or previous experience are needed; just enthusiasm and commitment.

Environmental Task Force

Tel: 0845 606 2626
www.thesite.org/newdeal

Part of the Government's New Deal for people aged 18-24, this scheme offers the opportunity to work on an environmental project for six months. While you're on the scheme you may still be entitled to the Job Seekers' Allowance, as well as a grant of up to £400 and travel expenses.

VOLUNTARY ORGANISATIONS — *Volunteering in the UK*

Friends of The Earth

26-28 Underwood Street
London N1 7JQ

Tel: 020 7490 1555
Fax: 020 7490 0881
www.foe.co.uk

Friends of The Earth welcomes volunteers at their head office in London, or at any of their regional offices.

Go to **www.foe.co.uk/press_for_change/volunteer** to apply online. Work may involve administrative work – from helping with mailouts and press cuttings to research and information gathering. Wherever possible, they aim to identify specific roles providing an opportunity for the development and acquisition of skills.

HiPACT

PO Box 770, York House
Empire Way, Wembley
Fax: 0208 900 0330
Middlesex HA9 0PA

Tel: 0208 900 1221
http://hipact.sentral.co.uk

HiPACT is an association of British Universities which aims to widen participation in higher education. It offers opportunities to volunteer both

---

INDEPENDENT LIVING ALTERNATIVES — LOOKING FOR SOMETHING DIFFERENT?

ILA is looking for volunteers, with four months to spare, to enable disabled people to live independently. No experience is necessary as all training and on-going support is provided; you must be 18+ and have an empathy with the philosophy of ILA. You will work on average 4 days per week and receive £63.50 living expenses and accommodation. A placement with ILA is a chance for you to meet new people and try new things. You will gain a direct insight into disability and work experience which may help you to find employment in the future and you'll have plenty of free time to see London!

Independent Living Alternatives, Trafalgar house, Grenville Place, London, NW7 3SA
tel/fax: 00 44 (0)20 8906 9265
email to: mail@I-L-A.fsnet.co.uk   web: www.I-L-A.fsnet.co.uk

Charity Registration No: 802198

in the UK and abroad. In the UK you could help at one of the summer schools run each year at various universities throughout the country.

The summer schools are attended by students from schools that rarely send their pupils on to higher education – they are designed to build confidence and give information. As a current undergraduate or recent graduate, you could help lead workshops on career choice, self-confidence or overcoming difficulties.

ILA (Independent Living Alternatives)

Trafalgar House
Grenville Place
London NW7 3SA

Tel: 020 8906 9265
Fax: 020 8906 9265
www.I-L-A.fsnet.co.uk

ILA is a charity run for the disabled by people with direct experience of disability. It provides full-time personal assistants to disabled people who want to live in their own homes, and also relevant advocacy, counselling and information. ILA needs full-time volunteers with four months to spare to work as personal assistants, providing physical support – such as helping someone to get out of bed, get dressed, have a wash and do practical things like cooking, shopping and housework. No experience is necessary but personal assistants must be over 18. The work averages four days a week and you get a living allowance (£63.50 a week) for food, travel and leisure, plus free accommodation.

L'Arche

10 Briggate
Silsden, Keighley
West Yorkshire BD20 9JT

Tel: 0800 917 1337
Fax: 01535 656426
www.larche.org.uk

L'Arche (French for 'The Ark') began as a small community in a house in Trosly-Breuil in France more than 30 years ago and is now an international movement with 117 communities in 31 countries. Its aim is to provide local communities – a cluster of houses, usually within walking distance of each other and with access to a workshop – for adults with learning disabilities. The work could be weaving, for example, or making candles. L'Arche is 'shaped and guided by the major Christian denominations', but internationally it is multi-faith, predominantly that of the local area. Volunteer 'assistants' are welcome both for its centres in the UK and abroad, to share life with those who need help to learn. To volunteer abroad you need to contact communities in different countries separately, as they will have different requirements – a list of all L'Arche communities worldwide is available.

Millennium Volunteer Programme

MV Unit, DfES, Room 4　　　　　　　Tel: 0800 085 1624
Moorfoot, Sheffield S1 4PQ　　www.millenniumvolunteers.gov.uk

Despite its slightly out-of-date name, the Millennium Volunteer Programme is still going strong. Launched in 1999, it's for people aged 16-24. The idea is that you volunteer your time to help others, doing something you enjoy. If you complete 200 hours of work, you get an Award of Excellence.

The National Trust for Scotland

Wemyss House, 28 Charlotte Square　　Tel: 0131 243 9300
Edinburgh EH2 4ET　　　　　　　　　　Fax: 0131 243 9301
Scotland　　　　　　　　　　　　　　　www.nts.org.uk

A conservation charity that protects and promotes Scotland's natural and cultural heritage for present and future generations to enjoy.

New Deal

Information Line: 0845 606 2626
www.thesite.org.uk/newdeal

As part of its New Deal project, the government runs a Work in the Voluntary Sector scheme which allows you to work for a voluntary organisation whilst still being able to claim Job Seekers' Allowance. There's a similar scheme for working on an environmental project for six months.

NSPCC

42 Curtain Road　　　　　　　　　　Tel: 020 7596 3700
London EC2A 3NH　　　　　　　　　　www.nspcc.org.uk

NSPCC volunteers can either do (primarily) fundraising work in their local area (see your local branch for details), or office work at head office in London.

Ockenden International

Constitution Hill　　　　　　　　　　Tel: 01483 772012
Woking, Surrey GU22 7UU　　　　　　www.ockenden.org.uk

Want to read all the papers and all the websites about refugees on a regular basis? Fancy trying to convince journalists to cover an angle on refugee events?

Ockenden International, set up in 1951, are based in Woking, 25mins from Waterloo. They have evolved into a specialist agency that deals with overseas refugees, delivering long-term development solutions. They are secular, non-political and work in some of the harshest environments in the world, primarily in Africa, Asia and the Middle East. They also have programmes in Uganda, Sudan, Cambodia.

They rely on volunteers, and in return try to treat them as equal to paid members of staff by offering training, (internal and external) travel expenses and interesting and necessary tasks. In return they ask for commitment and enthusiasm. Hours and type of placement vary. At time of going to press they were looking for a communications officer (minimum of one day per week for at least six months, or two days per week for three months.

The sort of things you might be doing include: research tasks for communications, including country profiles and facts; admin tasks relating to communications *eg* checking internet sites for news related to countries and refugees; keeping abreast of current affairs and informing the communications manager of important developments and changes; keeping the news board up-to-date; making regular phone calls to journalists to follow up on coverage, photos *etc*; choosing photos for stories and liaising with journalists on national TV and radio; mature and responsible dealing with celebrities including letter writing, maintaining relationships and research; researching for campaigns.

This is a great opportunity for anyone who wants to develop their research skills, or who may be interested in a media or marketing career, but you will need a genuine interest in current affairs.

Outdoor Trust

Windy Gyle, Belford
Northumberland NE70 7QE

Tel: 01668 213 289
www.outdoortrust.co.uk

The Outdoor Trust is a registered charity based in north Northumberland that organises outdoor pursuits for schools, individuals, youth groups and management training programmes. It has a residential centre as well as a watersports base at Beadnell for windsurfing, sea-kayaking and sailing. Other activities include climbing, abseiling, hill walking and canoeing. Work for volunteers and paid trainees; jobs depend on qualifications. Pay isn't excessive at £30+. Call Tracy on 01668 213 289 for more information.

Pax Christi

Christian Peace Education Centre
St Joseph, Watford Way
London NW4 4TY

Tel: 020 8203 4884
Fax: 020 8203 5234
www.pci.ngonet.be

An international movement involved with efforts in the fields of demilitarisation, human rights, ecology, development and economic justice.

They are active on four continents, but volunteers in England will mostly be doing office work.

Rainforest Concern

27 Lansdowne Crescent
London W11 2NS

Tel: 020 7229 2093
www.rainforest.org.uk

Rainforest Concern has office work placements in London to help in the fundraising department. Ideally volunteers should be able to work for longer than two months. Rainforest Concern also runs a scheme with Quest Overseas sending volunteers to projects in Ecuador and Costa Rica to help in the construction of rainforest corridors.

Rempart

1 rue des Guillemites
75004 Paris
France

Tel: +33 (0) 1 42 71 96 55
Fax: +33 (0) 1 42 71 73 00
www.rempart.com

Rempart, a union of conservation associations in France, organises short voluntary work schemes around the world, including in the UK. The projects are all based around restoration and maintenance of historic sites and buildings, from the glamour of castles in Dumfries to the more practical historic pathways in Wales.

You need some previous experience and to be prepared to work hard – usually for 30-35 hours per week. Expect to pay about £10 per day to cover food and lodging, depending on where you are placed. Rempart is strictly a French company, so don't expect to be able to organise the trip in English.

RSPB (Royal Society for the Protection of Birds)

The Lodge
Sandy
Bedfordshire SG19 2DL

Tel: 01767 680 551
Fax: 01767 683262
www.rspb.org.uk

Operating on 31 reserves around England, Scotland and Wales, the RSPB Residential Voluntary Wardening Scheme provides the opportunity to gain practical experience of the day-to-day management of an RSPB reserve by living and working on the reserve as a volunteer.

The work varies from season to season, and from reserve to reserve, but can include practical management tasks, work with visitors, survey/monitoring work or habitat management. Ornithological knowledge is less important than enthusiasm, an interest in conservation and a willingness to work as part of a team.

Anyone over 18 (16 on some reserves) is eligible to take part. Bookings are made by the week, Saturday to Saturday. Volunteers need to organise and pay for their own travel to and from the reserve, and to provide and cover the cost of their own food during their stay. The RSPB will provide accommodation free of charge.

SHAD

Wandsworth
5 Bedford Hill
London SW12 9ET

Tel: 020 8875 6095
Fax: 020 8673 2118
www.shad.org.uk

SHAD needs volunteers to help disabled adults with everyday tasks. Accommodation is provided for volunteers and SHAD asks for a commitment of at least three months. There are many branches of the SHAD charity – look on the net for the one nearest you.

The Shaftesbury Society

Burton Hill School
Malmesbury
Wiltshire SN16 0EG

Tel: 01666 822 685
Fax: 01666 826 022
www.shaftesburysoc.org.uk

Provides care and education services for people with physical and learning disabilities, and support for people who are disadvantaged or on a low income.

Tent City

Milfields Road, Hackney
London E5 0AR
(sae needed)

Tel: 020 8743 5708
www.tentcity.co.uk

Volunteers needed to work in reception and help to maintain this London campsite.

The Blackie / Great George's Community Cultural Project

Great George Street
Liverpool L1 5EW

Tel: 0151 709 5109
Fax: 0151 709 4822
www.theblackie.org.uk

The Blackie is one of Britain's longest running cultural community projects. Residential or non-residential volunteers can get involved in bringing all aspects of the arts to the local community though games, workshops and many other activities.

visit: www.gap-year.com

The Monkey Sanctuary
Murrayton, Nr Looe
Cornwall PL13 1NZ

Tel: 01503 262 532
www.monkeysanctuary.org

The Monkey Sanctuary provides a home to a colony of Amazonian woolly monkeys and rescued ex-pets. Volunteers help all year round, making monkey food, cleaning enclosures, helping serve the public in the summer and maintenance and other projects in the winter. Volunteers do not work directly with the monkeys.

Placements are for two to four weeks. Volunteers may stay as guests if they are over 18 and are asked to make a voluntary donation to the Monkey Sanctuary Trust.

The Oxford Centre for Enablement
Nuffield Orthopaedic Centre NHS Trust
Windmill Road, Headington
Oxford, Oxfordshire OX3 7LD

Tel: 01865 227600
Fax: 01865 737260

The Oxford Centre for Enablement cares for both the assessment and management of clients with recent neurological disability as well as those with longer term disability. Volunteers are needed at the centre to help with creative activities, gardening, table games, story groups, computers and cooking as well as outings, and also to help on holidays, usually two per year.

Applicants of all nationalities are welcome although clear and fluent English is essential as the centre's clients may have communication problems. You must be over 19 and fit, healthy and patient. Those who go on the holidays will be away for a week but helpers at the centre will be required on occasional days for an indefinite period.

On the holidays, accommodation and travel are paid for by the centre but a small donation towards food costs would be appreciated. No accommodation is provided at the centre.

The Simon Community
PO Box 1187
London NW5 4HW

Tel: 020 7485 6639
Fax: 020 7482 6305
www.waterloo.com/simon/

The Simon Community is a partnership of homeless people and volunteers living and working with London's street homeless. We need full time residential volunteers all year round. This is a real challenge which offers work experience in many areas, especially if you intend to work professionally with people in the future. Volunteers need to be 19+, and to commit for between three months to two years. Pocket money, time off, paid leave and training provided.

Volunteering in the UK **VOLUNTARY ORGANISATIONS**

The Year Out Group

Queensfield
28 King's Road
Easterton
Wiltshire SN10 4PX

Tel: 07980 395789
www.yearoutgroup.org

The Year Out Group is an association of leading year out organisations that was formed in 1998 to promote the concept and benefits of well-structured year out programmes, to promote models of good practice and to help young people and their advisers in selecting suitable and worthwhile projects. In 2001, the then 23 members of the Group accounted for 18,000 structured year out placements. There are now 28 members (listed below) with several applications in the pipeline

The Group's member organisations provide a wide range of year out placements in UK and overseas that cover courses and cultural exchanges, expeditions, volunteering and structured work placements. All members have agreed to adhere to the Group's Code of Practice (published on the website) and are in the process of developing more detailed operational standards for each of the four sectors mentioned above. The Group's website also contains guidelines for students and advisers. These include questions that potential 'gappers' should ask providing organisations as they look for the programme that best suits their needs. Year Out Group monitors information published by its members for accuracy.

Year Out Group members are expected to put potential clients and their parents in contact with those that have recently returned. Year Out Group considers it important that these references are taken up at least by telephone and, where possible, by meeting face to face. From October 2002 Group members have agreed to spell out their complaints procedure in their contracts. Year Out Group can advise on making complaints but is not itself able to deal with complaints. Nor is Year Out Group able to 'police' the 18,000 placements provided by its members – but it can take action if any member is shown to be consistently negligent.

There will always be less-than-perfect organisations among members of a trade association and good ones that are not. There are some small specialist organisations with excellent reputations that cannot afford the membership fees. Whether or not an organisation is a member of Year Out Group, the questions in the student guidelines can be used to advantage.

Year Out Group Membership (February 2003): Academic Year in the USA & Europe; Africa & Asia Venture; Africa Conservation Experience;

visit: www.gap-year.com

VOLUNTARY ORGANISATIONS

Art History Abroad; BSES Expeditions; BUNAC; CESA Languages Abroad; Coral Cay Conservation; Council Exchanges; CSV (Community Service Volunteers); Flying Fish; Frontier Conservation; GAP Activity Projects; Gap Challenge/World Challenge Expeditions; Greenforce; i-to-i International Projects; Outreach International; Project Trust; Quest Overseas; Raleigh International; Students Partnership Worldwide; Teaching & Projects Abroad; Travellers Worldwide; Trekforce Expeditions; The International Academy; The Smallpeice Engineering Gap year; The Year in Industry; Year Out Drama.

Time for God

2 Chester House
Pages Lane
Muswell Hill
London N10 1PR

Tel: 020 8883 1504
Fax: 020 8365 2471
www.timeforgod.org.uk

Time for God co-ordinates national and international projects, including youth and community work, homeless and rehabilitation projects *etc* in the UK, USA, Europe, Australia, Ghana *etc*. Start dates are January and September.

UNICEF
(United Nations Childrens Fund)

55 Lincoln's Inn Fields
London WC2A 3NB

Tel: 020 7405 5592
www.unicef.org.uk

UNICEF normally has two or three volunteers working in its main office at one time, and local offices will always need help: apply to them direct. The organisation campaigns and sets up initiatives to promote better health, education and sanitation for children around the world.

Volunteer Development England

New Oxford House
16 Waterloo Street
Birmingham B2 5UG

Tel: 0121 633 4555
Fax: 0121 633 4043
www.vde.org.uk

VDE can put people in touch with their local volunteer bureau, which matches people wanting to volunteer with local and national voluntary or community groups that are looking for help. Contact the address above, your nearest volunteer bureau or take a look at their website. Length of work depends on the individual's interests and commitments, and the requirements of the charities involved. Necessary expenses of volunteering will be met.

Volunteer Reading Help

Charity House 38, 14-15 Perseverance Works
Kingsland Road
London E2 8DD

Tel: 0870 77 44 300
www.volunteer-reading-help.co.uk

VRH is a national charity that helps primary school children who find reading a struggle. Training takes six hours and volunteers work with the same children every week, giving at least an hour of their time.

Whizz-Kidz

1 Warwick Row
London SW1 5ER

Tel: 020 7233 6600
www.whizz-kidz.org.uk

Whizz-Kidz aims to improve the lives of disabled under-18s by providing wheelchairs, trikes, walking aids and so on.

Winged Fellowship Trust

Angel House, 20-32 Pentonville Road
London N1 9XD

Tel: 020 7833 2594
www.wft.org.uk

Runs five separate centres around the country, providing holiday and respite opportunities for people with disabilities and their carers. Volunteers are welcomed and needed, and will receive accommodation and board. No experience is necessary. Usual placements are for one or two weeks, but longer placements can be arranged, especially at a new centre offering outdoor pursuits, where specialist training is provided.

Worldwide Volunteering for Young People

7 North Street Workshops
Stoke Sub Hamdon
Somerset TA14 6QR

Tel: 01935 825588
Fax: 01935 825775
www.wwv.org.uk

Worldwide Volunteering publishes the UK's most authoritative CD-ROM database of volunteering opportunities for 16-25 year olds. The unique software matches volunteers' wishes against the requirements of over 900 organisations with over 250,000 annual placements throughout the UK and worldwide.

Projects last anything from a week to a year and range from those that cost nothing and provide pocket money to those that cost many hundreds of pounds or more.

Your school, library or careers centre may have the database or you can find free access points near you on their website. Alternatively contact Worldwide Volunteering at the above address.

Young People's Trust for the Environment and Nature Conservation

8 Leapale Road
Guildford
Surrey GU1 4JX

Tel: 01483 539 600
www.yptenc.org.uk

Provides free lectures and information on the environment to local schools in Surrey, Dorset and the Lake District. Also runs the Young Environmentalist of the Year Awards (YEYA), the Barclaycard Livingland Awards and the Millennium Living for the Future Awards.

Youth Hostel Association

Trevelyan House
Dimple Road
Matlock
Derbyshire DE4 3YH

Tel: 0870 870 8808
Fax: 01629 592627
www.yha.org.uk

You might think of Youth Hostels as just a cheap place to stay while travelling, but the YHA is primarily an education charity with a mission statement to help all, especially young people of limited means, to a greater love and care of the countryside, particularly by providing hostels or other simple accommodation for them on their travels. The YHA has 230 Youth Hostels around the country and needs volunteers to help with running them and maintaining the local environment and paths, as well as fundraising. If you would like to volunteer, contact the YHA at the above telephone number.

Appendices

Choosing a tutorial college

Standards vary and it's best to check out two or three colleges before you choose. Here are some things to check before you decide:

- Does the college get results? For the last few years *The Daily Telegraph* has regularly published a table in early September giving the average A level retake grade improvements at tutorial colleges.
- Does the college have a good reputation? Get references from former students – the college should be happy to supply you with contact names.
- Has the college been inspected by the Department for Education and Skills (DfES) or an independent body such as BAC (the British Accreditation Council for Independent Further and Higher Education) or CIFE (the Council for Independent Further Education)?
- Does the college teach the right subjects?
- Does the college teach the same syllabus (*eg* OCR/French) that you studied at school?
- What time of year are the courses run? (this affects what you can do during the rest your year out).
- Who will be teaching you? Check their qualifications and how familiar they are with the syllabus.
- Is the place up-to-date? near transport? does it have quiet study rooms and good facilities?
- What does it cost? What are the hourly rates?
- What do get for your money? How many hours of group teaching each week and how many one-to-one tutorials?

MEDICINE? DENTISTRY? VETERINARY SCIENCE?

Choose....

CAMBRIDGE TUTORS COLLEGE, CROYDON

Cambridge Tutors College

If you plan to enter a competitive degree course and would like to use your gap year to re-take A-levels....talk to us. Hundreds of students have benefited from our specialist science teaching over the past 20 years. This dynamic community of 270 young people is offered superb individual support. Teaching takes place in small groups and each subject is tested on a weekly basis under exam conditions.

Make your future happen - contact:

Nicki Rigby (Admissions)
Cambridge Tutors College
Water Tower Hill
Croydon
Surrey
CR0 5SX

Tel: 020 8688 5284/7363
Fax: 020 8686 9220
e-mail: admin@ctc.ac.uk
website: http://www.ctc.ac.uk

Affiliate Member

Retakes

There are several reasons why you might find yourself considering retakes: maybe because your grades are too low to meet a conditional offer (and the university won't negotiate with you to admit you on lower grades), or because illness interfered with exams, for example.

But beware, getting better grades second time round doesn't guarantee you a university place – often unis will demand even higher grades if it's taken you two bites at the cherry (unless of course you've got a really good excuse, like illness).

Grade appeals

The A level marking scandal in 2002 has left many people wondering just how much we can trust exam results. If you really think you've been done down by a tired exam marker, a misleading or misprinted question or some other factor, you can appeal against your result.

You appeal first to the examination board that set the exam, and if you don't think the adjudication is just, you can go on to appeal to the Examination Appeals Board (EAB). Be warned: this process takes a long time and there's no guarantee the appeal will go your way.

Retake timing

Now that modular A levels are firmly entrenched you may be able to retake the modules you did badly in while you are still at school instead of having to retake them in your year out.

Unfortunately for some gap year students, the rules on AS/A level module retakes are being changed. In the past it was easier to raise A level grades by resitting just one or two modules. That way, you could get the necessary qualifications for university entrance without re-learning an entire two-year syllabus.

Keeping quiet about the first result and retaking a module more than once to upgrade was also possible until the universities began to ask for information about previous results to be declared. So now you need to make sure your chosen university course doesn't set higher entry grades for exams taken at a second sitting. And under the new A level system, retaking a module more than once is no longer allowed.

In some cases you may find that when you retake a certain exam you have to change exam board – this can be a problem in some subjects (*eg* languages with set texts) and you may therefore have to resit your A levels a whole year after the original exams, which can seriously disrupt your gap year. Check with your exam board as early as you can.

Tutorial colleges like to keep students working on A levels for a full year. That keeps the college full and tutors paid. But many agree that the best thing is to get resits over before work already done is forgotten. So the best timing, if you are academically confident and want to enjoy your gap year, is to go to a tutorial college in September and resit the whole exam or the relevant modules in January – if sittings are available then.

visit: www.gap-year.com

Languages

If you have only language AS levels, A2 levels or A levels to retake, there are several options:

- Take an extra course or stay in the country of the relevant language and return to revise for a summer resit, choosing the same exam board (courses abroad, however, are not usually geared to A level texts).
- Check with tutorial colleges how much of your syllabus module or modules (the chosen literature texts are crucial) overlap with those of other exam boards. This may give you the chance to switch exam boards and do a quick retake in January.
- Cram for as long as necessary at a specialist language college. Some British tutorial colleges and language course organisers have links with teaching centres in France so it's worth checking this out before signing on.

Retake results

Those who sit A level retakes in January and get the grades needed for a chosen place will not have to wait until August for that place to be confirmed. Examining boards will feed the result directly into UCAS so you will know your place has been clinched. A technicality, but comforting for gap year students who want to go away.

And don't forget that if you have a firm choice conditional offer and you make the grades asked for, the university can't back out. It has an obligation to admit you.

A level examining boards

There are five A level examining boards: AQA (Assessment and Qualifications Alliance), Edexcel, OCR (Oxford, Cambridge & RSA), Northern Ireland (CCEA) and Wales (WJEC). All these boards now provide their exam timetables on the internet about nine months in advance: we've provided their details below, along with those of other exam-related organisations.

AQA (Assessment and Qualifications Alliance)

Stag Hill House
Guildford
Surrey GU2 7XJ

Tel: 01483 506506
www.aqa.org.uk

CCEA (Northern Ireland Council for the Curriculum, Examinations and Assessment)

Clarendon Dock
29 Clarendon Road
Belfast BT1 3BG
N Ireland

Tel: 028 9026 1200
www.ccea.org.uk

EAB (Examination Appeals Board)

83 Piccadilly
London W1J 8QA

Tel: 020 7509 5995
www.theeab.org.uk

This is the final court of appeal for exam grades. You only go to the EAB if an appeal to the relevant examination board for your exam paper has failed. The EAB website has a notice board showing when appeals are going to be heard.

RETAKES

EDEXCEL
Stewart House
32 Russell Square
London WC1B 5DN

Tel: 0870 240 9800
www.edexcel.org.uk

IBO (International Baccalaureate Organisation)
Route des Morillons 15
CH-1218 Grand-Saconnex
Geneva
Switzerland

Tel: +41 22 791 7740
www.ibo.org

Central body for the development, administration and assessment of the International Baccalaureate Diploma Programme.

OCR (Oxford, Cambridge & RSA Examinations)
1 Regent Street
Cambridge
Cambridgeshire CB2 1GG

Tel: 01223 553 311
www.ocr.org.uk

QCA (Qualifications and Curriculum Authority)
83 Piccadilly
London W1J 8QA

Tel: 020 7509 5555
www.qca.org

The QCA is the body that (along with the Qualifications, Curriculum and Assessment Authority for Wales: ACCAC) approves all syllabuses and monitors exams (grading standards, for example).

You can get some basic explanations of the new A level system on its website, though much QCA information is aimed at teachers rather than those who are going to sit the exams.

SQA (Scottish Qualifications Authority)
Hanover House
24 Douglas Street
Glasgow G2 7NQ
Scotland

Tel: 0141 242 2214
www.sqa.org.uk

Central body for the development and assessment of Scottish qualifications, including Standard Grade, Highers, Advanced Highers, HNCs, HNDs and SVQs.

WJEC (Welsh Joint Education Committee)
245 Western Avenue
Cardiff CF5 2YX
Wales

Tel: 029 2026 5000
www.wjec.co.uk

Colleges accredited by BAC and CIFE

The following independent sixth-form and tutorial colleges offering A level tuition (one-year, two-year, complete retakes, modular retakes or intensive coaching) are recognised by the British Accreditation Council (BAC, Tel: 020 7233 3468, **www.the-bac.org**) and/or the Council for Independent Further Education (CIFE, Tel: 020 8767 8666, **www.cife.org.uk**). Of course a college can have a good reputation and acheive excellent results without accreditation.

Abacus College (Oxford)	BAC	Tel: 01865 240 111
The Abbey College (Malvern)	BAC	Tel: 01684 892 300
Abbey College Birmingham	BAC	Tel: 0121 236 7474
Abbey College Cambridge	BAC	Tel: 01223 578 280
Abbey College London (W2)	BAC	Tel: 020 7229 5928
Abbey College Manchester	BAC	Tel: 0161 236 6836
Albany College (London, NW4)	BAC/CIFE	Tel: 020 8202 5965
Ashbourne Independent Sixth Form College, (London W8)	BAC/CIFE	Tel: 020 7937 3858
Bales College (London W10)	BAC/CIFE	Tel: 020 8960 5899
Basil Paterson Tutorial College (Edinburgh)	BAC	Tel: 0131 556 7695
Bath Academy (Bath)	BAC	Tel: 01225 334 577
Bellerbys College (Hove)	BAC/CIFE	Tel: 01273 723 911
Bosworth Independent College (Northampton)	BAC/CIFE	Tel: 01604 239 995
Brooke House College (Market Harborough)	BAC/CIFE	Tel: 01858 462 452
Cambridge Arts and Sciences (Cambridge)	BAC	Tel: 01223 314 431

Appendix 1A — BAC/CIFE COLLEGES

College	Accreditation	Telephone
Cambridge Centre for Sixth Form Studies (Cambridge)	CIFE	Tel: 01223 716 890
Cambridge Seminars (Cambridge)	BAC	Tel: 01223 313 464
Cambridge Tutors College (Croydon)	BAC/CIFE	Tel: 020 8688 5284 see: www.gap-year.com
College of International Education, Oxford	BAC	Tel: 01865 202 238
Cherwell College (Oxford)	BAC/CIFE	Tel: 01865 242 670
Collingham (London SW5)	BAC/CIFE	Tel: 020 7244 7414
Concord College (Shrewsbury)	CIFE	Tel: 01694 731 631
CRTS International College (London N17)	BAC	Tel: 020 8801 0371
David Game College (London W11)	BAC	Tel: 020 7221 6665
Davies, Laing & Dick (London W2)	BAC	Tel: 020 7727 2797
Dean College (London N7)	BAC	Tel: 020 7281 4461
Duff-Miller Sixth Form College (London SW7)	BAC/CIFE	Tel: 020 7225 0577
Exeter Tutorial College (Exeter)	BAC/CIFE	Tel: 01392 278 101
Harrogate Tutorial College (Harrogate)	BAC/CIFE	Tel: 01423 501 041
Holborn College (London SE7)	BAC	Tel: 020 7385 3377
Interlink College of Technology (London E15)	BAC	Tel: 020 8522 0622
Irwin College (Leicester)	BAC/CIFE	Tel: 01162 552 648
Islamic College for Advanced Studies (London NW10)	BAC	Tel: 020 845 9993
Kings School, Oxford	BAC	Tel: 01865 711 829
Lansdowne College (London W8)	BAC/CIFE	Tel: 020 7616 4400

BAC/CIFE COLLEGES

Appendix 1A

London School of Management (London W5)	BAC	Tel: 020 8567 4355
Mander Portman Woodward (Birmingham)	BAC/CIFE	Tel: 0121 454 9637
Mander Portman Woodward (Cambridge)	BAC/CIFE	Tel: 01223 350 158
Mander Portman Woodward (London SW7)	BAC/CIFE	Tel: 020 7835 1355
Modes Study Centre (Oxford)	BAC/CIFE	Tel: 01865 249 349
Oxford Tutorial College (Oxford)	BAC/CIFE	Tel: 01865 793 333
Padworth College (Nr Reading)	BAC/CIFE	Tel: 0118 983 2645
Rochester Independent College (Rochester)	BAC	Tel: 01634 828 115
St Andrew's (Cambridge)	BAC	Tel: 01223 360 040
St Clare's (Oxford)	BAC/CIFE	Tel: 01865 552 031
Stafford House College (Canterbury)	BAC	Tel: 01227 866 540
Surrey College (Guildford)	BAC/CIFE	Tel: 01483 565887
The Tuition Centre (London NW4)	BAC	Tel: 020 8203 5025
Wentworth Tutorial College (London NW11)	BAC	Tel: 020 8458 8524

# 1B Applying to University

The number of students who took up university and college places in Autumn 2002 was the highest ever. According to provisional UCAS figures (at 9 October 2002), the number of applicants increased by 1.8 % from 451,467 in 2001 to 459,395 in 2002, and the number of accepted applicants increased by 2.8% from 355,765 to 365,897.

You may make the decision to take a year off well in advance. Many students have already chosen to defer university entrance because there are things they would like to use the time to do. For 2002 entry, 39,706 applicants made at least one application for deferred entry. Some students choose not to apply at all until after they get their A level grades.

Other students find themselves taking a gap year on shorter notice. For example, they may take a year off because their A level grades are not what they had expected – either too low to win the university place they accepted, or high enough to win them a place at a better university than the ones they applied to. Whatever the reason, the result is a gap year.

Application process

UCAS is the world's largest central admissions service for higher education. UCAS handles applications to all universities (except the Open University) as well as to most other institutions offering higher education courses. Applications to Oxford, Cambridge and for all professional qualifications leading to a career in medicine, dentistry and veterinary science/medicine are also handled by UCAS, although the application deadlines are earlier than for other courses.

UCAS

Rosehill
New Barn Lane
Cheltenham GL52 3LZ

Tel: 01242 227788
Minicom: 01242 544942
www.ucas.com
enquiries@ucas.ac.uk

UCAS is a registered charity and a private company, funded by the fees paid to it by students when they send in their UCAS applications. Fees from applicants account for about 31% of UCAS's income, and fees from universities make up some 35% of its income.

UCAS also offers a distribution service to companies who wish to send promotional material to students. UCAS handles the distribution itself and does not pass on your personal details, which remain confidential. If you prefer not to receive this kind of material however, make sure that you tick the box in section 6 of your UCAS form.

You can apply for six different courses at any UCAS institution, except for medical courses A100, A101, A103, A104, A106, dentistry courses A200, A203, A204, A205, A206 and veterinary science courses D100, D101 for which you can make just four choices. If you are using the 'two-track' application procedure for art and design courses you can use up to three of your choices in Route B. If you are applying for art and design through Route B, you can still only apply to a maximum of six choices overall. The different combinations that you can use are listed on the UCAS website. You can hold on to two of the offers you get: one 'firm (first) choice' and one 'insurance (second choice) place'. So you may have to be cautious about the courses you pitch for.

Electronic and online application

The Electronic Application System (EAS) allows applicants to fill in their application forms on a PC at their school, college, local careers service, or even at home. You can't use EAS to apply on an individual basis – applications must be submitted to UCAS through a teacher or careers adviser, either via the internet or by floppy disk.

New to UCAS this is year is a secure, web-based application system called **apply**. Each school, college, careers agency or British Council Office that has registered with UCAS to use **apply** appoints a co-ordinator who manages the way **apply** is used. For students, registering to the new system takes about 15 minutes and costs nothing. Once a student has registered, they are given a username and are asked to choose a password and one further secret piece of information that they will need to use each time they want to access their application forms. Applicants can use this new system anywhere that has access to the web. The new service works in tandem with the UCAS course search and applicant enquiry services. Check out the UCAS website **www.ucas.com** for more information.

EAS is the easiest way to apply because the software automatically checks the data and alerts you to possible errors. Common mistakes such as incorrect course codes are quickly discovered. Processing times are much shorter too and UCAS hopes that soon most applications will be made this way.

A level results

A level results come out in mid August. Depending on your grades one of the following will happen:

- Firm (first) choice uni writes to confirm offer of a place
- Insurance (second choice) uni writes to confirm offer of a place
- Clearance
- Retakes

Before you make any decisions make sure you know all the angles: retakes may be the only way for you to get to university, but most universities will demand even higher results the second time round. "We expect slightly higher requirements if you don't get good enough grades in one A level attempt," says Glasgow University. For its 2002 Classics degree course, for example, you would have needed B,B,C, but that goes up to B,B,B for retakes.

Qualifications tariff

The tariff system was introduced in 2002 to give admissions tutors a way to compare the various qualifications including the Advanced Higher in Scotland, GNVQ as a Vocational A level, AS and A2. UCAS reckons the new system will better reflect the marks required to achieve each grade. UCAS is keen to encourage more universities to use the new tariffs to make the application system more uniform across the country. But at the moment many admissions tutors are sticking to what they know and understand: good A level grades.

UCAS plans to widen the tariff in future to include points scores for the International Baccalaureate, BTEC National qualifications and the Irish School Leaving Certificate. Here's how the different qualifications shape up:

Appendix 1B

APPLYING TO UNIVERSITY

QUALIFICATION	GRADE	POINT SCORE
A2, Scottish Advanced Higher and Vocational A level*	A	120
	B	100
	C	80
	D	60
	E	40
AS Level and Vocational AS level	A	60
	B	50
	C	40
	D	30
	E	20
Scottish Higher	A	72
	B	60
	C	48

Vocational A level Double Award points are double those of Vocational A level

Points are also awarded for Key Skills, Scottish Intermediate, Standard Grade, Core Skills and the CACHE (Council for Awards in Children's Care and Education) Diploma. For 2004 entry onwards, music examinations from grades 6-8 will also be included in the system. For full details on the tariff project and the 'Tariff Calculator' see the UCAS website, **www.ucas.co.uk/candq/tariff.**

Key dates

The autumn term is when final-year sixth-formers usually begin to apply for university and college places through the UCAS system though some super-organised schools and students start preparations in the summer of Lower Sixth.

The *UCAS Directory* lists all courses and institutions and is available free to schools, (on the web or CD-ROM), or individuals can order one from UCAS for £6. Information about application for university places appears in the guide *How to Apply*, which is sent to you automatically when you send for an application form.

- University open days organised from spring each year.
- *UCAS Directory* and *How to Apply* available from June 2003 until September 2004.
- UCAS application forms for 2004 entry available from August 2003.
- Applications for 2004 entry which include either Oxford or Cambridge choices or Medicine courses: A100, A101, A103, A104, A106, Dentistry courses: A200, A203, A204, A205, A206 and Veterinary Science courses: D100, D101 should be returned to UCAS by 15 October 2003.
- Other applications for 2004 entry (except Route B applications for art and design courses: see *How to Apply*) should be returned to UCAS between 1 September 2003 and 15 January 2004.
- If you are sending in a paper application form, you will receive an acknowledgement card from UCAS as soon as the form is received. This does not mean that your application has been processed – this happens later when you are sent an acknowledgement letter stating your choices and application number. If there seems to be a mistake, call UCAS immediately, quoting your application number.

visit: www.gap-year.com

- Universities and colleges start to notify UCAS of their decisions for 2004 entry after October 2003. Applicants receive decisions via UCAS (interview, unconditional offer, conditional offer or unsuccessful application).
- You should reply to offers as soon as you receive all your university decisions from UCAS.
- UCAS has two main deadlines. 15 January is the initial closing date. Applications received after 15 January are marked 'late'. 30 June is the final closing date. After 30 June, the university or college you have applied to does not guarantee that it will consider your application. Applications received after this date go straight into Clearing.
- A level results will be published on Thursday, 14 August 2003.
- Note that UCAS advises that applicants should confirm their acceptance of an offer of a university place as quickly as possible.
- After the A level results are released, UCAS will automatically send out Clearing Entry forms (CEFs) to applicants who have missed their grades, who have not received offers earlier in the year, who have declined all offers made to them, who have applied 'late' (see above), or who haven't found a place using Extra.
- A list of vacancies for degrees and HNDs is published on the UCAS website at **www.ucas.com** as soon as results are released. This online vacancy service is updated several times a day. Vacancy listings are also published in *The Independent* and the *Daily Mirror* from A level results day.
- Clearing closes at the end of September.

Deferred entry, rescheduled entry or late application?

There are three ways to apply for university if you want to take a gap year. The safest is usually to apply for deferred entry. The problem is that not all courses accept deferred entry candidates especially if demand for a course is high. Some courses will have a set number of places allocated for those taking a gap year, but these are usually limited so competition is even higher! Our advice is to talk to the admissions office before making a decision about taking a gap year.

Deferred entry

- Check first with the appropriate department of the university you want to go to that they are happy to take students after a gap year. If it's a popular course, preference may go to the current year applications.
- On the front of the UCAS form there is a specific 'Defer entry' column in the key 'Applications' section. Write 'D' in the 'Defer entry' box for all (or some) of the courses you apply for, having checked that they will still be available a year later. Talk to your teachers first and follow instructions in *How to Apply*.
- If you are planning to take a gap year, you will need to explain why in the Personal Statement (section 10) of the UCAS form. You need to convince the university that a year off will make you a better applicant, so give an outline of what you plan to do and why.
- Send your completed application to UCAS, like any other student applying for entry without taking a gap year. Those who do so well before 15 January deadline, however, may be among the first to start receiving replies (via UCAS). You will get a call for selection interview(s), a rejection or an offer which is conditional on getting specific A level grades or total point score.

NOTE: Some academics are not happy with deferred entry because it could be nearly two years before you reach higher education. During that time a course may have changed, or you may have changed. So your application may be looked on unfavourably without you knowing why. Many university departments are in favour of a gap year but they are not all in favour of deferred entry. If they interview you in November 2002 for a place in October 2004 it will be 23 months before they see you again. Check it out with the university department first.

Rescheduled entry

This is when you apply for a place for the coming university year, not the one after. Then, after A level results, if you have won a place at the university of your choice, you can negotiate directly with that university as an individual about deferring your entry for another year. If they say yes, you will receive a 'changed entry date confirmation letter'. You must reply to UCAS within seven days to accept the place, using the form that is attached to the letter. If the university says no, you have the option of taking your insurance place or starting the application process all over again.

NOTE: Some admissions tutors say that to give up a place on a popular course is risky, because the university will not be happy after you have messed them about. Others say that if a course has over-recruited, your deferral will be welcome.

Post A level applications

If you take A levels in June 2003 and do not send in a UCAS application before the end of the cycle, you should apply – between 1 September and 15 January – for entry in the following year.

Universities don't favour people who do not apply through UCAS, then ring up at the last minute to try to get a place on a course. It can play havoc with the targets they set to fund the places they offer. Universities lose financially if they 'under-shoot' or 'overshoot' the predicted number of students on a specific course.

Faculty check: all subjects

If you want to take a gap year, remember (before you apply) to contact the appropriate department or faculty at the university you would like to go to, and find out if they approve of gap years or not. Prepare a good case for it before you phone. It is advisable to do this even if you're an absolutely outstanding candidate, because on some courses a year off is considered a definite disadvantage. This is usually the case where a degree course is very long or requires a large amount of remembered technical knowledge at the start.

Art and design

Applying through UCAS to your chosen college of Art and Design involves applying by two different routes (Route A and Route B). You must make your Route A application by 15 January and your Route B application between 1 January and 24 March. Route B applications are restricted to just three choices. When you send off your UCAS form with your Route A choices, remember to indicate that you intend to apply through Route B as well, so that UCAS will send you further documentation.

Medicine, dentistry and veterinary science

If you hope to pursue a career in medicine, dentistry or veterinary science, you can use four of your possible six choices when applying for the following courses:

Medical courses: A100, A101, A103, A104, A106
Dentistry courses: A200, A203, A204, A205, A206
Veterinary Science courses: D100, D101

Don't forget that UCAS must receive ALL applications for these courses by 15 October.

visit: www.gap-year.com

Foundation degrees

As if qualifications weren't complicated enough already, with GNVQs, GCSEs, AS levels, A2 levels, HNDs, Diplomas and undergraduate and postgraduate degrees, the government has now introduced a new Foundation Degree. The Foundation Degree (not to be confused with a foundation year), which started in autumn 2001, is a two-year 'vocational' degree – in other words, a degree in work-related subjects like computing or business studies rather than purely academic subjects. Students (of any age) do work experience as part of the course, and the degree will be convertible to an honours degree by adding further study afterwards. This makes getting a degree more flexible, and adds another opportunity to take a gap year – you could take a Foundation Degree, then have a gap year, then restart studies later to convert it into a full Honours Degree.

Financing your studies

Under the student support scheme introduced in 1998, government support for undergraduates now comes only in the form of loans, through the Student Loans Company (Tel: 0800 40 50 10 Web: **www.slc.co.uk**). You start repaying the loan once you've graduated, when your income reaches £10,000 or more gross (before you've paid tax).

Applications are made through your Local Education Authority (LEA) and should be made early (certainly before July). How much you get depends on your circumstances. 75% of the maximum loan is available to all eligible students regardless of any other income they have. Your LEA will assess whether you get any of the other 25% according to your income and your family's income.

The maximum amount of loan that you can get in 2003/04 is:

- ♦ £4000 for students living away from home
- ♦ £4930 for students in London and living away from home
- ♦ £3165 for students living at home

Useful reading

Student Loans: Guidance on Terms and Conditions

Financial Support for Higher Education Students in 2003/04

Both booklets are available from your LEA, **www.dfes.gov.uk/studentsupport** (Forms and Guides page) or by calling 0800 731 9133.

Bursaries, scholarships and sponsorship

Although the number of fully-sponsored degrees on offer from the public or private sector declined in the 1990s, many organisations still offer sponsorship to students to study for a degree. Nowadays this is sometimes on condition that they join the sponsoring company or institution for a period when they graduate. The Army is one example from the public sector (Tel: 01980 618 181).

If you're looking for sponsorship, The Year in Industry improves your chances and removes the need to write endless letters (Tel: 0161 275 4396), or you may be interested in the offer from the Smallpeice Trust (Tel: 01926 333200).

1c Universities in the UK

The University of Aberdeen	Tel: 01224 272 000 www.abdn.ac.uk
University of Abertay Dundee	Tel: 01382 308 000 www.abertay.ac.uk
Anglia Polytechnic University	Tel: 01245 493 131 www.anglia.ac.uk
Aston University	Tel: 0121 359 3611 www.aston.ac.uk
University of Bath	Tel: 01225 826 826 www.bath.ac.uk
University of Birmingham	Tel: 0121 414 3344 www.bham.ac.uk
Bolton Institute	Tel: 01204 900 600 www.bolton.ac.uk
Bournemouth University	Tel: 01202 524 111 www.bournemouth.ac.uk
University of Bradford	Tel: 01274 733 466 www.brad.ac.uk
University of Brighton	Tel: 01273 600 900 www.brighton.ac.uk
University of Bristol	Tel: 0117 928 9000 www.bristol.ac.uk
Brunel University, West London	Tel: 01895 274 000 www.brunel.ac.uk
University of Buckingham	Tel: 01280 814 080 www.buckingham.ac.uk
Buckingham Chilterns University College	Tel: 0800 056 5660 www.bcuc.ac.uk
University of Cambridge	Tel: 01223 337 733 www.cam.ac.uk
University of Central England in Birmingham	Tel: 0121 331 5000 www.uce.ac.uk

UNIVERSITIES IN THE UK

Appendix 1C

University of Central Lancashire	Tel: 01772 201 201 www.uclan.ac.uk
City University	Tel: 020 7040 5060 www.city.ac.uk
Coventry University	Tel: 02476 631 313 www.coventry.ac.uk
Cranfield University	Tel: 01234 750 111 www.cranfield.ac.uk
De Montfort University	Tel: 01162 551 551 www.dmu.ac.uk
♦ **De Montfort University – Bedford**	Tel: 01234 351 966
♦ **De Montfort University – Leicester**	Tel: 01162 551 551
♦ **De Montfort University – Milton Keynes**	Tel: 01908 695 511
University of Derby	Tel: 01332 622 222 www.derby.ac.uk
The University of Dundee	Tel: 01382 223 181 www.dundee.ac.uk
University of Durham	Tel: 0191 374 2000 www.dur.ac.uk
University of East Anglia	Tel: 01603 456 161 www.uea.ac.uk
University of East Anglia – University College Suffolk	Tel: 01473 255 885 www.suffolk.ac.uk
University of East London	Tel: 020 8590 7722 www.uel.ac.uk
University of Edinburgh	Tel: 0131 650 1000 www.ed.ac.uk
University of Essex	Tel: 01206 873 333 www.essex.ac.uk
European Business School, London	Tel: 020 7487 7505 www.ebs.london.ac.uk
University of Exeter	Tel: 01392 263 263 www.exeter.ac.uk
University of Glamorgan	Tel: 0800 716 925 www.glam.ac.uk
The University of Glasgow	Tel: 0141 339 8855 www.gla.ac.uk
Glasgow Caledonian University	Tel: 0141 331 3000 www.gcal.ac.uk

Appendix 1C — UNIVERSITIES IN THE UK

University of Gloucestershire	Tel: 01242 532 700 www.chelt.ac.uk
The University of Greenwich	Tel: 020 8331 8000 www.gre.ac.uk
Heriot-Watt University	Tel: 0131 449 5111 www.hw.ac.uk
University of Hertfordshire	Tel: 01707 284 000 www.herts.ac.uk
The University of Huddersfield	Tel: 01484 422 288 www.hud.ac.uk
The University of Hull	Tel: 01482 346 311 www.hull.ac.uk
Keele University	Tel: 01782 621 111 www.keele.ac.uk
The University of Kent at Canterbury	Tel: 01227 764 000 www.ukc.ac.uk
Kingston University	Tel: 020 8547 2000 www.kingston.ac.uk
Lancaster University	Tel: 01524 65201 www.lancs.ac.uk
The University of Leeds	Tel: 0113 243 1751 www.leeds.ac.uk
Leeds Metropolitan University	Tel: 0113 283 2600 www.lmu.ac.uk
University of Leicester	Tel: 0116 252 2522 www.le.ac.uk
University of Lincoln	Tel: 01482 440 550 www.lincoln.ac.uk
University of Liverpool	Tel: 0151 794 2000 www.liv.ac.uk
Liverpool Hope University College	Tel: 0151 291 3000 www.livhope.ac.uk
Liverpool Institute for Performing Arts	Tel: 0151 330 3000 www.lipa.ac.uk
Liverpool John Moores University	Tel: 0151 231 2121 www.cwis.livjm.ac.uk

UNIVERSITIES IN THE UK

University of London   Tel: 020 7862 8004
(contact colleges directly)   www.lon.ac.uk

- **Birkbeck College**   Tel: 020 7631 6000   www.bbk.ac.uk
- **British Institute in Paris**   Tel: +33 1 44 11 73 73   www.bip.lon.ac.uk
- **Courtauld Institute of Art**   Tel: 020 77848 2777   www.courtauld.ac.uk
- **Goldsmith's College**   Tel: 020 7919 7171   www.goldsmiths.ac.uk
- **The Guy's, King's and St Thomas' School of Medicine**   Tel: 020 7848 6971   www.kcl.ac.uk/depsta/medicine
- **Heythrop College**   Tel: 020 7795 6600   www.heythrop.ac.uk
- **Imperial College at Wye**   Tel: 020 758 95111   www.wye.ac.uk
- **Imperial College of Medicine**   Tel: 020 7589 5111   www.med.ic.ac.uk
- **Imperial College of Science, Technology and Medicine**   Tel: 020 7589 5111   www.ic.ac.uk
- **Institute of Education**   Tel: 020 7612 6000   www.ioe.ac.uk
- **King's College London**   Tel: 020 7836 5454   www.kcl.ac.uk
- **London Business School**   Tel: 020 7262 5050   www.lbs.ac.uk
- **London School of Economics and Political Science**   Tel: 020 7405 7686   www.lse.ac.uk
- **London School of Hygiene and Tropical Medicine**   Tel: 020 7636 8636   www.lshtm.ac.uk
- **London School of Jewish Studies**   Tel: 020 8203 6427   www.lsjs.ac.uk
- **Queen Mary, University of London**   Tel: 020 7882 7882   www.qmw.ac.uk
- **Royal Academy of Music**   Tel: 020 7873 7373   www.ram.ac.uk
- **Royal Free and University College Medical School**   Tel: 020 7679 2000   www.rfc.ucl.ac.uk
- **Royal Holloway, University of London**   Tel: 01784 434 455   www.rhul.ac.uk
- **The Royal Veterinary College**   Tel: 020 7468 5000   www.rvc.ac.uk
- **School of Oriental and African Studies**   Tel: 020 7637 2388   www.soas.ac.uk
- **School of Pharmacy**   Tel: 020 7753 5800   www.ulsop.ac.uk

Appendix 1C — UNIVERSITIES IN THE UK

- ♦ School of Slavonic and East European Studies — Tel: 020 7636 8000 — www.ssees.ac.uk
- ♦ St Bartholomew's and The Royal School of Medicine and Dentistry — Tel: 020 7377 7747 — www.mds.qmw.ac.uk
- ♦ St George's Hospital Medical School — Tel: 020 8672 9944 — www.sghms.ac.uk
- ♦ University College London — Tel: 020 7387 7050 — www.ucl.ac.uk

University	Contact
London Guildhall University	Tel: 020 7320 1000 — www.lgu.ac.uk
Loughborough University	Tel: 01509 263 171 — www.lboro.ac.uk
University of Luton	Tel: 01582 734 111 — www.luton.ac.uk
The University of Manchester	Tel: 0161 275 2000 — www.man.ac.uk
University of Manchester Institute of Science and Technology (UMIST)	Tel: 0161 236 3311 — www.umist.ac.uk
Manchester Metropolitan University	Tel: 0161 247 2000 — www.mmu.ac.uk
Middlesex University	Tel: 020 8362 5000 — www.mdx.ac.uk
Napier University	Tel: 0131 444 2266 — www.napier.ac.uk
University of Newcastle	Tel: 0191 222 6000 — www.ncl.ac.uk
University of North London	Tel: 020 7607 2789 — www.unl.ac.uk
University of Northumbria at Newcastle	Tel: 0191 232 6002 — www.unn.ac.uk
University of Nottingham	Tel: 0115 951 5151 — www.nott.ac.uk
The Nottingham Trent University	Tel: 0115 941 8418 — www.ntu.ac.uk
The Open University	Tel: 01908 274 066 — www.open.ac.uk
University of Oxford	Tel: 01865 270 000 — www.ox.ac.uk
Oxford Brookes University	Tel: 01865 741 111 — www.brookes.ac.uk

visit: www.gap-year.com

UNIVERSITIES IN THE UK

Appendix 1C

University of Paisley	Tel: 0141 848 3000 www.paisley.ac.uk
University of Plymouth	Tel: 01752 600 600 www.plymouth.ac.uk
University of Portsmouth	Tel: 02392 876 543 www.port.ac.uk
Queen Margaret University College	Tel: 0131 317 3000 www.qmuc.ac.uk
Queen's University of Belfast	Tel: 028 9024 5133 www.qub.ac.uk
The University of Reading	Tel: 01189 875 123 www.rdg.ac.uk
The Robert Gordon University	Tel: 01224 262 000 www.rgu.ac.uk
Royal College of Art	Tel: 020 7590 4444 www.rca.ac.uk
Royal College of Music	Tel: 020 7589 3643 www.rcm.ac.uk
The University of Salford	Tel: 0161 295 5000 www.salford.ac.uk
University of Sheffield	Tel: 0114 222 2000 www.shef.ac.uk
Sheffield Hallam University	Tel: 0114 225 5555 www.shu.ac.uk
South Bank University	Tel: 020 7928 8989 www.sbu.ac.uk
University of Southampton	Tel: 023 8059 5000 www.soton.ac.uk
University of St Andrews	Tel: 01334 476 161 www.st-andrews.ac.uk
Staffordshire University	Tel: 01782 294 000 www.staffs.ac.uk
University of Stirling	Tel: 01786 473 171 www.stir.ac.uk
University of Strathclyde	Tel: 0141 552 4400 www.strath.ac.uk
University of Sunderland	Tel: 0191 515 2000 www.sunderland.ac.uk
University of Surrey	Tel: 01483 300 800 www.surrey.ac.uk

Appendix 1C **UNIVERSITIES IN THE UK**

University of Surrey Roehampton	Tel: 020 8392 3000 www.roehampton.ac.uk
University of Sussex	Tel: 01273 606 755 www.sussex.ac.uk
University of Teesside	Tel: 01642 218 121 www.tees.ac.uk
Thames Valley University	Tel: 020 8579 5000 www.tvu.ac.uk
Trinity College of Music	Tel: 020 8305 3888 www.tcm.ac.uk
University of Ulster	Tel: 08 700 400 700 www.ulst.ac.uk
University of Wales (contact colleges directly)	Tel: 029 2038 2656 www.wales.ac.uk
♦ **The University of Wales, Aberystwyth**	Tel: 01970 623 111 www.aber.ac.uk
♦ **University of Wales, Bangor**	Tel: 01248 351 151 www.bangor.ac.uk
♦ **Cardiff University**	Tel: 029 2087 4000 www.cardiff.ac.uk
♦ **University of Wales Institute, Cardiff**	Tel: 029 2050 6070 www.uwic.ac.uk
♦ **University of Wales, Lampeter**	Tel: 01570 422 351 www.lamp.ac.uk
♦ **University of Wales College of Medicine**	Tel: 029 2074 7747 www.uwcm.ac.uk
♦ **University of Wales College, Newport**	Tel: 01633 430 088 www.newport.ac.uk
♦ **University of Wales, Swansea**	Tel: 01792 205 678 www.swansea.ac.uk
University of Warwick	Tel: 02476 523 523 www.warwick.ac.uk
University of the West of England, Bristol	Tel: 0117 965 6261 www.uwe.ac.uk
University of Westminster	Tel: 020 7911 5000 www.wmin.ac.uk
University of Wolverhampton	Tel: 01902 321 000 www.wlv.ac.uk
University of York	Tel: 01904 430 000 www.york.ac.uk

visit: www.gap-year.com

Country info

Once you have chosen where you want to go, whether one country or a dozen, do some research. It would be a shame to travel to the other side of the world and then miss what it has to offer. There are loads of websites giving interesting and useful factual advice (weather, geographical, political, economic) as well as those that are more touristy.

Foreign Office warnings

It is worth bearing in mind that the economic and political situations change rapidly in many countries, so check with the Foreign and Commonwealth Office that the country is still safe to travel to before you go. There's a link to their website on www.gap-year.com. Travel advice for individual countries is updated regularly on the FCO Travel Advice page.

It is important to look at the lists of specific areas to avoid either completely, or unless on essential business. There are many of these and they can change suddenly.

It is also advisable to note the phone numbers of all British embassies and consulates in areas where you may be travelling in case you need to contact them for help.

Telephone or e-mail home regularly to save your family a lot of worry and British embassies a lot of wasted time. Just to give you a taste, the following pages contain data for individual countries: the FCO warnings given here were correct at time of going to press in February 2003.

Afghanistan

- ◆ Population: 26.8 million ◆ Capital: Kabul
- ◆ Currency: Afghani
- ◆ Language: Pushtu, Dari, Persian
- ◆ Religion: Muslim

After the events of September 11 and subsequent military action, Afghanistan remains extremely dangerous and out of bounds.

The FCO advises against all travel to all areas except Kabul.

Albania

- ◆ Population: 3.5 million
- ◆ Capital: Tirana
- ◆ Currency: New Lek ◆ Language: Albanian
- ◆ Religion: Muslim, Albanian Orthodox, Roman Catholic
- ◆ British Embassy: +355 4 2 34973/4/5

Though most visits to Albania are trouble-free the FCO is currently advising against all travel in the north east border areas between Albania and Kosovo. Parts of the land route between Albania and Kosovo are in poor condition, and the threat remains from gangs of armed criminals in the far north.

The FCO advises against all travel to the following areas: North East Border areas between Albania & Kosovo.

Algeria

- Population: 31.7 million ◆ Capital: Algiers ◆ Currency: Dinar
- Language: Arabic, French ◆ Religion: Muslim
- British Embassy: +213 21 230068

The FCO advises against travel to this country except on essential business.

Andorra

- Population: 68,000 ◆ Capital: Andorra la Vella
- Language: Catalan, Spanish, French ◆ Religion: Roman Catholic
- British Consulate: +376 839840; +34 3 419 9044 (Consumer and Consular enquiries)

Angola

- Population: 10.3 million ◆ Capital: Luanda ◆ Currency: Kwanza
- Language: Portuguese, Bantu
- Religion: indigenous beliefs, Roman Catholic, Protestant
- British Embassy: +244 2 334582/3; +244 2 392991

The FCO advises against travel to this country except on essential business.

Antigua and Barbuda

- Population: 67,000 ◆ Capital: St John's ◆ Language: English
- Religion: Anglican, Roman Catholic
- British High Commission: +268 462 0008/9; +268 463 0010

Argentina

- Population: 37.3 million ◆ Capital: Buenos Aires ◆ Currency: Peso
- Language: Spanish, English, Italian, German, French
- Religion: Roman Catholic ◆ British Embassy: +54 11 4808 2200

The country is at the moment going through a period of severe economic hardship and political change. Looting of shops has resulted from the conditions of social unrest, and some sporadic violence has occurred. The FCO is not warning against travel to Argentina, but recommends that visitors avoid demonstrations and public gatherings and keep up to date with all the latest events. Demonstrations have so far centred on the area of Plaza de Mayo and Congreso. Banking conditions remain difficult, and the FCO advises visitors to carry several methods of payment including a credit card and sufficient US dollars in cash.

Armenia

- Population: 3.4 million ◆ Capital: Yerevan ◆ Currency: Dram
- Language: Armenian ◆ Religion: Armenian Orthodox
- British Embassy: +374 1 543 822/832

Australia

- Population: 19.5 million ◆ Capital: Canberra ◆ Currency: Australian Dollar
- Language: English ◆ Religion: Anglican, Roman Catholic
- British High Commission: +61 (2) 6270 6666

Appendix 2   **COUNTRY INFO**

Austria
- Population: 8.1 million ◆ Capital: Vienna ◆ Currency: Euro
- Language: German ◆ Religion: Roman Catholic, Protestant
- British Embassy Tel: +43 1 716130; +43 1 716130

Hapsburg baroque and fattening cakes.

Azerbaijan
- Population: 7.8 million ◆ Capital: Baku ◆ Currency: Manat
- Language: Azerbaijani Turkic, Russian, Armenian
- Religion: Shi'a Muslim, Russian Orthodox, Armenian Orthodox
- British Embassy: +99 412 975188/89/90

The FCO advises against all travel to the following areas: western region of Nagorno-Karabakh and the militarily occupied area surrounding itwestern region of Nagorno-Karabakh and the militarily occupied area surrounding it.

Bahamas
- Population: 295,000 ◆ Capital: Nassau ◆ Currency: Bahamian Dollar
- Language: English ◆ Religion: Baptist, Anglican, Roman Catholic
- British Embassy: +1 242 325 7471

One of several warm tax havens around the Caribbean.

Bahrain
- Population: 640,000 ◆ Capital: Manama ◆ Currency: Bahrain Dinar
- Language: Arabic, English ◆ Religion: Shi'a Muslim
- British Embassy: +973 574 100; +973 574 167 (Information Hot-Line); +973 960 0274 (Emergency Number)

Bangladesh
- Population: 131 million ◆ Capital: Dhaka ◆ Currency: Taka
- Language: Bangla, English ◆ Religion: Muslim, Hindu
- British Embassy: +880 2 882 2705

Barbados
- Population: 275,000 ◆ Capital: Bridgetown ◆ Currency: Barbados Dollar
- Language: English
- Religion: Anglican, Methodist, Pentecostal, Roman Catholic
- British Embassy: +1 246 430 7800

Most densely populated of the Caribbean West Indies Islands. Restaurants, bars, nightclubs, big waves (Atlantic coast), cricket, sugar plantation houses (*eg* St Nicholas Abbey), fig-trees and luminous plants (Andromeda Gardens).

Belarus
- Population: 10.3 million ◆ Capital: Minsk ◆ Currency: Belorussian Ruble
- Language: Belorussian ◆ Religion: Orthodox
- British Embassy: +375 172 105920/1; +375 172 292310 (Visa and Consular - recorded information)

Minsk, where the first British diplomat to arrive after the collapse of the Soviet Union had to spend three weeks finding a typewriter. Should be easier now.

visit: www.gap-year.com

Belgium

- Population: 10.2 million ◆ Capital: Brussels ◆ Currency: Euro
- Language: Flemish and French
- Religion: Roman Catholic ◆ British Embassy: +32 2 287 6211

Emergency numbers for the police are 101; medical services 100; from a mobile phone 112. Mostly very flat. Mussels, frites and beer (hundreds of local brews), lots of well-behaved eurocrats, international lawyers and consultants. Take normal sensible precautions to avoid the usual city dangers of mugging, bag-snatching and pickpocketing. Danger spots are reported to be the main railway stations in Brussels and on the underground, buses and trams, particularly in the vicinity of Rondpoint Schuman (the EU quarter).

Belize

- Population: 256,000 ◆ Capital: Belmopan ◆ Currency: Belize Dollar
- Language: English, Creole, Spanish ◆ Religion: Roman Catholic, Protestant
- British High Commission: +501 822 2146

Warm, wet and tropical, this is where many gap year students have been diving to map endangered coral reefs (the Belize Barrier Reef).

Benin

- Population: 6.5 million
- Capital: Porto-Novo (official), Cotonou (de facto)
- Currency: Franc CFA (Communaute Financiere Africaine)
- Language: French, Fon Yoruba
- Religion: indigenous beliefs, Muslim, Christian
- Community Liaison Officer in Cotonou, for consular emergencies only. Otherwise refer to British Embassy staff in Nigeria: +229 3012 74

Bhutan

- Population: 2 million ◆ Capital: Thimphu ◆ Currency: Ngultrum
- Language: Dzongkha ◆ Religion: Buddhist, Hindu

Difficult to get in to Bhutan, because of restrictions on the number of tourists who can enter the country. Great if you have contacts inside the country who can invite you in.

Bolivia

- Population: 8.3 million ◆ Capital: La Paz ◆ Currency: Boliviano
- Language: Spanish, Quechua ◆ Religion: Roman Catholic
- British Embassy: +591 2 2433424

Beautiful mountainous country, fabulous climate, but here are a few warnings (which are no less than for many other countries in South America). Pickpocketing, especially on buses or in crowded areas, is fairly common: most thieves work in teams to distract their victims. Recently incidents in La Paz have reflected a trend towards aggressive crimes against foreigners, including slashing bags or pockets with knives and choke-holding the victim until unconscious or pouring substances over the victim's clothing – then, while pretending to help clean the mess, carrying out a robbery. Visitors travelling alone overland are advised to be extremely vigilant. Tourists travelling around Rurrenabaque are strongly advised to use only the services of registered travel agencies. All tourist guides are required by law to hold an identity card. Travellers off the beaten track, particularly in coca-growing areas, such as the Chapare, should exercise particu-

Appendix 2   **COUNTRY INFO**

lar caution especially when carrying cameras or binoculars. The altitude in La Paz and other parts of Bolivia can cause problems for travellers. Visitors who suffer from diabetes, heart or chest complaints should consult a doctor before travelling. Alcohol should be avoided before and shortly after arrival. Drink lots of water. Visitors should carry a photocopy of their passport. Long-term visitors should register with the British embassy.

Bosnia-Herzegovina

- Population: approx 3.9 million ◆ Capital: Sarajevo ◆ Currency: Dinar
- Language: Serbian, Croatian, Bosnian
- Religion: Muslim, Orthodox, Catholic, Protestant
- British Embassy in Sarajevo Tel: +387 33 204 781/2/3; +387 33 204 781/2/3

One of the several parts of former Yugoslavia which have been splintered by war to become independent nations. British citizens don't need visas to enter Bosnia and Herzegovina. Some major credit cards can now be used to obtain cash from some banks in Sarajevo, but only during office hours (there are no ATMs), and the number of businesses accepting credit cards is still very limited. Medical facilities are limited. Take great care when travelling outside main towns and cities, especially in winter, and drivers should keep to the main roads and not stray off-road as large areas of the country are still mined. Avoid long-distance driving at night. British visitors who intend to stay in Bosnia and Herzegovina for an extended period of time should register at the British embassy.

Botswana

- Population: 1.5 million ◆ Capital: Gaborone ◆ Currency: Pula
- Language: Setswana, English ◆ Religion: Christian, indigenous beliefs
- British High Commission: +267 395 2481

Brazil

- Population: 174 million ◆ Capital: Brasilia ◆ Currency: Real
- Language: Portuguese ◆ Religion: Roman Catholic
- British Embassy in Brasilia (other offices elsewhere): +55 61 225 2710

Brunei Darussalam

- Population: 344,000 ◆ Capital: Bandar Seri Begawan
- Currency: Brunei Dollar ◆ Language: Malay, English, Chinese
- Religion: Muslim, Buddhist, Christian
- British High Commission: +673 2 226001

Bulgaria

- Population: 7.7 million ◆ Capital: Sofia ◆ Currency: Lev
- Language: Bulgarian ◆ Religion: Orthodox, Muslim
- British Embassy: +359 2 933 9222

Burkina Faso

- Population: 12.2 million ◆ Capital: Ouagadougou
- Currency: Franc CFA (Communaute Financiere Africaine)
- Language: French, tribal languages
- Religion: Muslim, Christian, indigenous beliefs
- British Honorary Consulate: +226 30 73 23

visit: www.gap-year.com

Burundi

- Population: 6.2 million ◆ Capital: Bujumbura ◆ Currency: Burundi Franc
- Language: Kirundi, French, Swahili
- Religion: Roman Catholic, Protestant, indigenous beliefs
- British Embassy - refer to Kigali, Rwanda

Current advice from the FCO advises against all travel to Burundi, with rebel groups operating throughout much of the country, and the security situation unstable.

Cambodia

- Population: 12 million ◆ Capital: Phnom Penh ◆ Currency: Riel
- Language: Khmer, French, English ◆ Religion: Buddhist
- British Embassy: +855 23 427124; +855 23 428295

Once a kingdom, then a French colony, and in the 1980s a dictatorship under Pol Pot and the Khmer Rouge. Site of Angkhor Wat temple. You can go safely to parts of Cambodia but areas are still dicey - check with the FCO before you travel.

Cameroon

- Population: 15.8 million ◆ Capital: Yaounde ◆ Currency: Franc CFA
- Language: French, English
- Religion: indigenous beliefs, Christian, Muslim
- British High Commission: +237 222 05 45; +237 222 07 96

Canada

- Population: 31.5 million ◆ Capital: Ottawa ◆ Currency: Canadian Dollar
- Language: English, French ◆ Religion: Roman Catholic, United Church
- British High Commission in Ottawa
  (further offices elsewhere): +1 613 237 1530

Cape Verde

- Population: 405,000 ◆ Capital: Praia ◆ Currency: Cape Verdean Escudo
- Language: Portuguese, Creole
- Religion: Roman Catholic, indigenous beliefs
- British Consulate for emergencies only (on Sao Vincente): +238 32 66 25/26/27

Central African Republic

- Population: 3.5 million ◆ Capital: Bangui ◆ Currency: Franc CFA
- Language: French, Sangho, Arabic
- Religion: indigenous beliefs, Protestant, Roman Catholic, Muslim
- Refer to the British High Commission in Cameroon

The FCO advises against all travel to this country.

Chad

- Population: 8.7 million ◆ Capital: N'Djamena ◆ Currency: Franc CFA
- Language: French, Arabic, tribal languages
- Religion: Muslim, Christian, traditional beliefs
- British Embassy - refer to the
  British High Commission in Cameroon: +235 841 1102

The FCO advises against all travel to the following areas: the Borkou-Ennedi-Tibesti provinces.

Appendix 2 **COUNTRY INFO**

China

- Population: 1.27 billion ♦ Capital: Beijing ♦ Currency: Yuan
- Language: Putonghua, Cantonese
- Religion: officially atheist (though the traditional religion contains elements of Confucianism, Taoism and Buddhism), Muslim, Christian
- British Embassy: +86 10 6532 1961

Colombia

- Population: 40 million ♦ Capital: Bogota ♦ Currency: Columbian Peso
- Language: Spanish ♦ Religion: Roman Catholic
- British Embassy: +57 1 317 6690; +57 1 317 6310/21

The FCO advises against all travel to the following areas: all Provinces of Choco, Putumayo, Meta and Caqueta and to rural areas of Antioquia, Cauca, Narino and Norte de Santander Provinces.

Comoros

- Population: 600,000 ♦ Capital: Moroni ♦ Currency: Franc CFA
- Language: French, Arabic ♦ Religion: Sunni Muslim, Roman Catholic
- British Consulate: +269 733182

Congo

- Population: 2.9 million ♦ Capital: Brazzaville ♦ Currency: Franc CFA
- Language: French, Lingala, Kikongo ♦ Religion: Christian, Animist, Muslim
- British Honorary Consulate: +242 44904

The FCO advises against all travel to the following areas: Brazzaville and Pointe Noire.

Congo, Democratic Republic of the

- Population: 53.6 million ♦ Capital: Kinshasa
- Currency: Congolese Franc
- Language: French, Swahili, Lingala, traditional languages
- Religion: Roman Catholic, Protestant, Muslim, indigenous beliefs
- British Embassy: +243 98 169100; +243 98 169 200

The FCO advises against all travel to the following areas: Outside Kinshasa and the government-controlled town of Lubumbashi.

Costa Rica

- Population: 3.7 million ♦ Capital: San Jose ♦ Currency: Colon
- Language: Spanish ♦ Religion: Roman Catholic
- British Embassy: +506 258 2025

Cote D'Ivoire

- Population: 16 million
- Capital: Yamoussoukro (official) Abidjan (administrative)
- Currency: Franc CFA ♦ Language: French, African languages
- Religion: indigenous beliefs, Muslim, Christian
- British Embassy in Abidjan: +225 20300800

The FCO advises against all travel to this country.

Croatia

- Population: 4.3 million ◆ Capital: Zagreb
- Currency: Kuna ◆ Language: Croation, Serbian, Bosnian
- Religion: Catholic, Orthodox, Slavic Muslim, Protestant
- British Embassy: +385 1 6009 100; +385 1 6009 122 (Visa and Consular)

Cuba

- Population: 11 million ◆ Capital: Havana ◆ Currency: Peso
- Language: Spanish ◆ Religion: Roman Catholic
- British Embassy: +53 7 204 1771

Cyprus

- Population: 764,000 ◆ Capital: Nicosia
- Currency: Cyprus Pound
- Language: Greek, Turkish, English
- Religion: Greek Orthodox, Sunni Muslim
- British High Commission: +357 22 861100

Czech Republic

- Population: 10.3 million ◆ Capital: Prague
- Currency: Koruna
- Language: Czech ◆ Religion: Roman Catholic, Protestant, Orthodox
- British Embassy: +420 2 5740 2111

Most visits to the Czech Republic are trouble-free, but there's been a rise in petty theft and beware of bogus plain clothes policemen who may ask to see your foreign currency and passport. If approached, don't show your money but offer instead to go to the nearest police station. New entry procedures to the Czech Republic for nationals of some non-visa countries were introduced on 1 January 2000. Though not directed at British citizens, these caused some uncertainty and delays at points of entry. Make sure your passport is valid and in a presentable state (British nationals with passports in a poor condition have been refused entry to the Czech Republic before now). Carry ID at all times and keep a photocopy of your passport. Travellers are advised to use major taxi companies. It is not possible to change Scottish or Northern Irish banknotes. Visitors to the forested areas should seek medical advice about immunisation against tick-borne encephalitis. Prague is a beautiful and exciting city, and other areas of the country remain relatively untouched by tourists.

Denmark

- Population: 5.4 million ◆ Capital: Copenhagen
- Currency: Krone ◆ Language: Danish
- Religion: Evangelical Lutheran, Protestant, Roman Catholic
- British Embassy: +45 35 44 52 00

Home of Legoland.

Djibouti

- Population: 461,000 ◆ Capital: Djibouti ◆ Currency: Djibouti Franc
- Language: Arabic, French, Afar, Somali ◆ Religion: Muslim, Christian
- British Consulate: +253 3 85007

Dominica

- Population: 70,000 ◆ Capital: Roseau ◆ Currency: East Caribbean Dollar
- Language: English, French ◆ Religion: Roman Catholic, Protestant
- British High Commission: +246 430 7800

Dominican Republic

- Population: 8.5 million ◆ Capital: Santo Domingo
- Currency: Dominican Peso ◆ Language: Spanish
- Religion: Roman Catholic ◆ British Embassy: +1 809 472 7111

Ecuador

- Population: 13.2 million ◆ Capital: Quito ◆ Currency: Sucre
- Language: Spanish, Quechua ◆ Religion: Roman Catholic
- British Embassy: +593 2 2970 800/1

The FCO advises against all travel to the following areas: northern border areas with Colombia, particularly Sucumbios, Orellana and Napo Provinces.

The FCO advises against travel to the following areas except on essential business: the highland areas surrounding Quito only.

Egypt

- Population: 69.5 million ◆ Capital: Cairo ◆ Currency: Egyptian Pound
- Language: Arabic ◆ Religion: Muslim, Christian
- British Embassy: +20 2 794 0850/2/8

El Salvador

- Population: 6.2 million ◆ Capital: San Salvador ◆ Currency: Colon
- Language: Spanish ◆ Religion: Roman Catholic
- British Embassy: +503 209 6000

Equatorial Guinea

- Population: 486,000 ◆ Capital: Malabo ◆ Currency: Franc CFA
- Language: Spanish, French, pidgin English
- Religion: Roman Catholic, Protestant
- The British Ambassador to Equatorial Guinea is based in Cameroon

Estonia

- Population: 1.4 million ◆ Capital: Tallinn ◆ Currency: Kroon
- Language: Estonian, Russian, Finnish ◆ Religion: Lutheran, Orthodox
- British Embassy: +372 667 4700

Ethiopia

- Population: 65.8 million ◆ Capital: Addis Ababa ◆ Currency: Birr
- Language: Amharic, English, plus more than 70 traditional languages
- Religion: Orthodox, Muslim, Animist ◆ British Embassy: +251 1 612354

The FCO advises against all travel to the following areas: within 20km of border with Eritrea in the Tigray & Afar regions, parts of Gambella & Awash, Metahara/Awash National Park and the immediately surrounding areas. The border with Somalia. The FCO advises against travel to the following areas except on essential business: East of the Harar to Gode line.

Fiji

- Population: 840,000 ◆ Capital: Suva
- Currency: Fiji Dollar
- Language: English, Fijian and Hindi
- Religion: Methodist, Hindu
- British High Commission: +679 311033

The Fijian prime minister and cabinet ministers held hostage for 56 days were released in July 2000, but Fiji's constitutional problems are unresolved. Travellers should not hitch-hike or travel alone after dark, and be careful swimming in the sea, because there are sometimes dangerous rips between gaps in the reef even at low tide. There have also been a number of minor incidents and one serious accident on domestic flights. ICAO standards are now mandatory on domestic flights in Fiji and flight operations are being improved, and anyway you don't have much choice other than air travel to some outer islands. The national maximum speed limit is 50mph and animals frequently wander on to roads, causing a serious hazard.

Finland

- Population: 5.1 million ◆ Capital: Helsinki
- Currency: Euro
- Language: Finnish, Swedish, English
- Religion: Evangelical Lutheran, Orthodox
- British Embassy: +358 09 2286 5100

France

- Population: 59 million ◆ Capital: Paris ◆ Currency: Euro
- Language: French, Breton, Basque ◆ Religion: Roman Catholic
- British Embassy in Paris: +331 44 51 31 00

Travellers should take the E111 form and take out complementary insurance to cover extra medical costs, repatriation, or in Savoie and Haute-Savoie departements, possible transfer to Switzerland for hospital treatment. For sports activities such as skiing, potholing and mountaineering travel insurance must include mountain rescue services and helicopter costs. In Corsica sporadic bomb attacks by the Corsican nationalist group (FLNC) on public buildings continue. Visitors to the island should take care, particularly in the town centres and near public buildings, and be wary of unattended packages.

Gabon

- Population: 1.2 million ◆ Capital: Libreville
- Currency: Franc CFA
- Language: French, Fang, Myene
- Religion: Catholic, Protestant
- British Consulate: +241 762200; +241 742041

Gambia

- Population: 1.4 million ◆ Capital: Banjul
- Currency: Dalasi
- Language: traditional languages, English
- Religion: Muslim, Christian, indigenous beliefs
- British Embassy: +220 495133/4; +220 497590 (Visa)

Appendix 2

Georgia

- Population: 5 million ♦ Capital: Tbilisi ♦ Currency: Lari
- Language: Georgian, Russian, Armenian
- Religion: Georgian Orthodox, Russian Orthodox, Armenian Orthodox, Muslim
- British Embassy: +995 32 955 497; +995 32 998 447

Germany

- Population: 83 million ♦ Capital: Berlin ♦ Currency: Euro
- Language: German ♦ Religion: Protestant, Roman Catholic, Muslim
- British Embassy: +49 30 20457 0

Ghana

- Population: 19.9 million ♦ Capital: Accra ♦ Currency: Cedi
- Language: English, native languages
- Religion: indigenous beliefs, Muslim, Christian
- British Embassy: +233 21 221 665; +233 7010721 (Visa)

Greece

- Population: 10.6 million ♦ Capital: Athens ♦ Currency: Euro
- Language: Greek ♦ Religion: Greek Orthodox, Muslim
- British Embassy: +30 210 727 2600

Personal attacks are rare but lone travellers are strongly advised not to accept lifts from strangers at night or in the early hours of the morning. Visitors are strongly advised against hiring motor-cycles, scooters and mopeds as accidents involving these forms of transport are common and can often result in fatal injury. Wearing of crash helmets is a legal requirement in Greece, and stiff fines can be imposed for non-compliance. Drink driving offences are also heavily penalised.

Grenada

- Population: 90,000 ♦ Capital: St George's
- Currency: East Caribbean Dollar ♦ Language: English
- Religion: Roman Catholic, Anglican
- British High Commission: +1 473 440 3222/3536

Guatemala

- Population: 12.9 million ♦ Capital: Guatemala City ♦ Currency: Quetzal
- Language: Spanish, Garifuna, Mayan languages
- Religion: Roman Catholic, Protestant, Mayan
- British Embassy: +502 367 5425/6/7/8/9

Guinea

- Population: 7.6 million ♦ Capital: Conakry
- Currency: Guinean Franc ♦ Language: French, native languages
- Religion: Muslim, indigenous beliefs, Christian
- British Consulate: +224 45 58 07; +224 45 60 20

The FCO advises against all travel to the following areas: border region with Liberia & Sierra Leone.

Guinea-Bissau

- Population: 1.3 million ◆ Capital: Bissau ◆ Currency: Guinea-Bissau Peso
- Language: Portuguese, Crioulo, French
- Religion: traditional religious beliefs, Muslim, Christian
- British Consulate: +245 20 12 24/16

Guyana

- Population: 700,000 ◆ Capital: Georgetown ◆ Currency: Guyana Dollar
- Language: English ◆ Religion: Hindu, Protestant, Roman Catholic
- British High Commission: +592 226 5881/2/3/4

Haiti

- Population: 7 million ◆ Capital: Port-au-Prince ◆ Currency: Gourde
- Language: Creole, French ◆ Religion: Roman Catholic, Voodoo, Protestant
- British Consulate: +509 257 3969

The FCO advises against travel to this country except on essential business.

Honduras

- Population: 6.4 million ◆ Capital: Tegucigalpa ◆ Currency: Lempira
- Language: Spanish, English ◆ Religion: Roman Catholic
- British Embassy: +504 232 0612/5144

Hungary

- Population: 10.1 million ◆ Capital: Budapest ◆ Currency: Forint
- Language: Hungarian ◆ Religion: Roman Catholic, Protestant
- British Embassy: +36 1 266 2888

Iceland

- Population: 278,000 ◆ Capital: Reykjavik ◆ Currency: Icelandic Krona
- Language: Icelandic ◆ Religion: Evangelical Lutheran
- British Embassy: +354 550 5100

Harsh winters can leave Iceland covered by snow and ice with routes in the interior closed and other roads impassable, so drivers should be aware that weather conditions can suddenly deteriorate, making driving extremely hazardous. Vehicles should be fitted with snow tyres. Visitors planning to travel off road are advised to contact the local authorities prior to departure. Visitors should check with Vegagerdin (office in charge of roads, Tel: +354 563 1400) before departing on any journey outside Reykjavik. Vegagerdin have a website at: **www.vegag.is/faerd/indexe.html** which gives up-to-date information.

India

- Population: Just over 1 billion ◆ Capital: New Delhi ◆ Currency: Rupee
- Language: Hindi, English, Bengali, Gujarati, Kashmiri, Malayalam, Marathi, Oriya, Punjabi, Tamil, Telugu, Urdu, Kannada, Assamese, Sanskrit, Sindhi and many dialects
- Religion: Hindu, Muslim, Christian, Sikh, Buddhist
- British High Commission in New Delhi
  (further offices elsewhere): +91 11 2687 2161

Appendix 2   **COUNTRY INFO**

In view of the heightened tension and increase in troop movements along the border with Pakistan the FCO is currently advising against all travel to the border regions. The FCO also strongly advise against travel to all parts of the state of Jammu and Kashmir, except Ladakh, where visitors should be cautious.

The FCO advises against all travel to the following areas: Jammu and Kashmir, areas of Gujarat, Rajasthan and Punjab close to the border, and areas of Ladakh close to the Line of Control.

Indonesia

- ◆ Population: 231.3 million ◆ Capital: Jakarta ◆ Currency: Rupiah
- ◆ Language: Bahasa Indonesia (official, modified form of Malay), English, Dutch, local dialects, the most widely spoken of which is Javanese
- ◆ Religion: Muslim, Protestant, Roman Catholic, Hindu, Buddhist
- ◆ British Embassy: +62 21 315 6264; 62 811 802435 (Out of hours emergency)

The FCO advises against travel to this country except on essential business.

Iran

- ◆ Population: 66.1 million ◆ Capital: Tehran ◆ Currency: Rial
- ◆ Language: Persian, Azari, Kurdish, Arabic
- ◆ Religion: Shi'ite Muslim, Sunni Muslim
- ◆ British Embassy: +98 21 6705011/19

Iraq

- ◆ Population: 23.3 million ◆ Capital: Baghdad ◆ Currency: Iraqi Dinar
- ◆ Language: Arabic, Kurdish ◆ Religion: Muslim
- ◆ There is no UK Mission, and the FCO warns that British nationals should not attempt to visit Iraq

The FCO advises against all travel to this country.

Israel

- ◆ Population: 5.9 million (including Israeli settlers in the West Bank, Golan Heights, the Gaza Strip and East Jerusalem)
- ◆ Capital: Jerusalem proclaimed capital in 1950, but most countries maintain embassies in Tel Aviv ◆ Currency: Shekel
- ◆ Language: Hebrew, Arabic, English ◆ Religion: Jewish, Muslim, Christian
- ◆ British Embassy: +972 3 725 1222

The FCO advises against all travel to the following areas: West Bank and Gaza and Israel/Lebanon and Israel/Gaza border areas.

Italy

- ◆ Population: 57.6 million ◆ Capital: Rome ◆ Currency: Euro
- ◆ Language: Italian ◆ Religion: Roman Catholic
- ◆ British Embassy: +39 06 4220 0001

Jamaica

- ◆ Population: 2.6 million ◆ Capital: Kingston ◆ Currency: Jamaican Dollar
- ◆ Language: English ◆ Religion: Protestant, Roman Catholic
- ◆ British Embassy: +1 876 510 0700; +1 876 926 1022/3 (Visa)

Most visits to Jamaica are trouble-free. However, violent crime can be a problem, particularly in Kingston. Visitors should be particularly alert for thieves. Do not offer resistance in the event of an attempted robbery. Visitors are advised against walking at night or using public transport (including taxis) unless authorised by the Jamaica Union of Travellers Association (JUTA) and ordered from hotels. Take care when walking in isolated areas even in daylight hours. Sporadic gang violence and shootings are usually concentrated in inner city and poor neighbourhoods of Kingston, including West Kingston, Grant's Pen, August Town and Harbour View, but can occur in other areas. These areas have occasionally been under curfew and should be avoided. The motive for most attacks is robbery and the Jamaican government has now instituted a new system of mobile police patrols, which have helped to ease the problem.

Japan

- Population: 126 million ◆ Capital: Tokyo
- Currency: Yen ◆ Language: Japanese
- Religion: Shintoist, Buddhist, Christian
- British Embassy: +81 3 5211 1100

Kazakhstan

- Population: 16.7 million ◆ Capital: Astana
- Currency: Tenge ◆ Language: Kazak, Russian
- Religion: Muslim, Russian Orthodox, Protestant
- British Embassy: +73272 506191/2; +73272 508280 (Visa/Consular)

Kenya

- Population: 30.8 million ◆ Capital: Nairobi
- Currency: Kenyan Shilling ◆ Language: English, Swahili
- Religion: Protestant, Roman Catholic, Muslim, traditional beliefs
- British High Commission: +254 2 2714699

Kiribati

- Population: 94,200 ◆ Capital: Tarawa ◆ Currency: Australian Dollar
- Language: English ◆ Religion: Roman Catholic, Protestant
- British High Commission: +686 22501

Korea (North)

- Population: 22 million ◆ Capital: Pyongyang ◆ Currency: Won
- Language: Korean ◆ Religion: Buddhist, Confucianist
- British Embassy: +850 2 381 7980/4 (International); 02 382 7980/2 (Local dialling); +850 02 381 7993 (Out of hours emergency)

Korea (South)

- Population: 48 million ◆ Capital: Seoul ◆ Currency: Won
- Language: Korean ◆ Religion: Christian, Buddhist, Confucianist
- British Embassy: +82 2 3210 5500

Kuwait

- Population: 2 million ◆ Capital: Kuwait ◆ Currency: Kuwaiti Dinar
- Language: Arabic, English ◆ Religion: Muslim
- British Embassy: +965 240 3334/5/6

Kyrgyzstan

- Population: 4.7 million ◆ Capital: Bishkek
- Currency: Som
- Language: Kyrgyz, Russian ◆ Religion: Muslim, Russian Orthodox
- British DFID Country Office: +996 312 220 354; +996 312 666 637

The FCO advises against all travel to the following areas: South & west of Osh and the Ferghana Valley Region only.

Laos

- Population: 5.6 million ◆ Capital: Vientiane
- Currency: Kip
- Language: Lao, French, English ◆ Religion: Buddhist, Animist
- British Embassy: +856 21 413606

Latvia

- Population: 2.4 million ◆ Capital: Riga
- Currency: Lat ◆ Language: Latvian
- Religion: Lutheran, Roman Catholic, Russian Orthodox
- British Embassy: +371 777 4700

Lebanon

- Population: 3.6 million ◆ Capital: Beirut
- Currency: Lebanese Pound
- Language: Arabic ◆ Religion: Muslim, Christian
- British Embassy: +961 1990 400

Lesotho

- Population: 2.2 million ◆ Capital: Maseru ◆ Currency: Loti
- Language: English, Sesotho ◆ Religion: Christian, indigenous beliefs
- British High Commission: +266 22313961

Liberia

- Population: 3.2 million ◆ Capital: Monrovia ◆ Currency: Liberian Dollar
- Language: English, tribal dialects
- Religion: traditional religions, Muslim, Christian
- British Honorary Consulate: +231 226 056; +231 6516 973 (mobile)

The FCO advises against all travel to this country.

Libya

- Population: 5.2 million ◆ Capital: Tripoli ◆ Currency: Libyan Dinar
- Language: Arabic, English ◆ Religion: Muslim
- British Embassy: +218 21 355 1084

Liechtenstein

- Population: 32,500 ◆ Capital: Vaduz ◆ Currency: Swiss Franc
- Language: German, Alemmanic dialect
- Religion: Roman Catholic, Protestant

Lithuania

- Population: 3.6 million ◆ Capital: Vilnius
- Currency: Lit ◆ Language: Lithuanian
- Religion: Roman Catholic, Protestant, Russian Orthodox
- British Embassy: +370 5 212 70 71; +370 5 212 20 70

Madagascar

- Population: 16 million ◆ Capital: Antananarivo
- Currency: Malagasy Franc ◆ Language: Malagasy, French
- Religion: traditional religious beliefs, Christian, Muslim
- British Embassy: +261 20 2249 380

Malawi

- Population: 10.5 million ◆ Capital: Lilongwe ◆ Currency: Kwacha
- Language: English, Chichewa ◆ Religion: Christian, Muslim
- British High Commission: +265 1 772 400 / 683 / 701

Malaysia

- Population: 22 million ◆ Capital: Kuala Lumpur
- Currency: Ringgit
- Language: Bahasa Malaysia, English, Chinese, Tamil
- Religion: Sunni Muslim, Daoist, Christian
- British High Commission in Kuala Lumpur: +60 3 2170 2200

There are severe penalties for all drug offences including, in some cases, the death penalty, or, in the case of possession, whipping in addition to any custodial sentence imposed. This also includes the possession of or trafficking in Amphetamine-type stimulants. Travellers should be aware that there is a possibility that they could be asked to take a urine test on arrival in Malaysia if they are suspected of having used drugs prior to their visit. Should the test prove positive, the person concerned could be referred for rehabilitation treatment or deported. The importation of unlicensed firearms and ammunition into Malaysia is prohibited. Possession can carry the death penalty. It is believed that Malaysia is one of a number of countries where there is an increased threat to British interests from global terrorism. Entry to Malaysia is normally refused to visitors holding passports with less than six months validity.

Maldives

- Population: 310,000 ◆ Capital: Male
- Currency: Maldivian Rufiyaa
- Language: Dhivehi, Arabic, Hindi, English ◆ Religion: Muslim
- British High Commission staff resident in British High Commission, Colombo, Sri Lanka

Mali

- Population: 11 million ◆ Capital: Bamako ◆ Currency: Franc CFA
- Language: French, African languages
- Religion: Muslim, Christian
- British Consulate: +223 223 34 12

Malta

- Population: 394,000 ◆ Capital: Valletta
- Currency: Maltese Lira
- Language: Maltese, English ◆ Religion: Roman Catholic
- British High Commission Floriana: +356 2323 0000

British nationals receive free medical treatment, under a reciprocal agreement, during the first 30 days of their stay. Caution should be exercised while driving as some roads are not in a good state of repair.

Mauritania

- Population: 2.7 million ◆ Capital: Nouakchott ◆ Currency: Ouguyia
- Language: Arabic, French ◆ Religion: Muslim
- British Honorary Consul: +22 25 29 20 53

Mauritius

- Population: 1.2 million ◆ Capital: Port Louis
- Currency: Mauritian Rupee
- Language: English, French, Creole, Hindi, Urdu
- Religion: Hindu, Christian, Muslim
- British High Commission: +230 202 9400

Mexico

- Population: 102 million ◆ Capital: Mexico City
- Currency: Peso ◆ Language: Spanish, Indian languages
- Religion: Roman Catholic, Protestant
- British Embassy: +52 55 5242 8500

Moldova

- Population: 4.5 million ◆ Capital: Chisinau ◆ Currency: Moldovan Lem
- Language: Moldovan, Russian ◆ Religion: Eastern Orthodox
- British Ambassador resides at Bucharest, Romania: +3732 238 991

Monaco

- Population: 32,000 ◆ Capital: Monaco
- Language: French, English, Italian, Monegasque
- Religion: Roman Catholic ◆ British Consulate: +377 93 50 99 66

Mongolia

- Population: 2.65 million ◆ Capital: Ulaanbaatar ◆ Currency: Tugrik
- Language: Mongolian, Kazak, Chinese, Russian
- Religion: Tibetan Buddhist, Muslim ◆ British Embassy: +976 11 458 133

Morocco

- Population: 30.6 million ◆ Capital: Rabat ◆ Currency: Dirham
- Language: Arabic, French ◆ Religion: Muslim, Christian
- British Embassy: +212 0 37 23 86 00

Mozambique

- Population: 19.4 million ◆ Capital: Maputo
- Currency: Metical ◆ Language: Portuguese, Bantu
- Religion: traditional religious beliefs, Christian, Muslim
- British High Commission: +2581 320 111/2/5/6/7

Myanmar (Burma)

- Population: 42 million ◆ Capital: Rangoon ◆ Currency: Kyat
- Language: Burmese, other minority languages
- Religion: Buddhist, Christian
- British Embassy: +95 1 295300; +95 1 370 863/864/865/867

Nauru

- Population: 12,000 ◆ Capital: Yaren
- Currency: Australian Dollar ◆ Language: Nauruan, English
- Religion: Protestant, Roman Catholic, Confucianism, Taoism
- British High Commission staff resident in Suva, Fiji

Nepal

- Population: 25.3 million ◆ Capital: Kathmandu
- Currency: Nepalese Rupee ◆ Language: Nepali, Newari, Bhutia, Maithali
- Religion: Hindu, Buddhist, Muslim
- British Embassy: +977 1 410583; +977 1 411281

New Zealand

- Population: 3.8 million ◆ Capital: Wellington
- Currency: New Zealand Dollar ◆ Language: English, Maori
- Religion: Christian
- British High Commission in Wellington: +64 4 924 2888

Reports of thefts from unattended vehicles, especially hire cars/camper vans in major tourist areas (*eg* the Coromandel peninsula and Rotorua) are on the increase. Visitors to the remote areas of New Zealand should check with local tourist authorities for advice before setting out and ensure that the local authorities are aware of their journey details. Visitors intending to participate in adventure activities, such as bungee jumping, white water rafting, *etc* should ensure that their travel insurance covers these types of activities.

Nicaragua

- Population: 5 million ◆ Capital: Managua
- Currency: Cordoba
- Language: Spanish ◆ Religion: Roman Catholic, Protestant
- British Embassy: +505 2 780 014/887; +505 2 674 050

Niger

- Population: 10.3 million ◆ Capital: Niamey ◆ Currency: Franc CFA
- Language: French, Hausa, Songhai, Arabic
- Religion: Muslim, Animist, Christian
- British Vice Consulate: +227 722 722

Appendix 2 **COUNTRY INFO**

Nigeria

- Population: 127 million ◆ Capital: Abuja ◆ Currency: Naira
- Language: English, Hausa, other traditional languages
- Religion: Muslim, Christian, indigenous beliefs
- British High Commission: +234 9 413 2010/2011

The FCO advises against travel to the following area except on essential business: Kaduna.

Norway

- Population: 4.5 million ◆ Capital: Oslo ◆ Currency: Krone
- Language: Norwegian ◆ Religion: Evangelical Lutheran
- British Embassy: +47 23 13 27 00

Oman

- Population: 2.6 million ◆ Capital: Muscat ◆ Currency: Omani Rial
- Language: Arabic, English ◆ Religion: Muslim
- British Embassy: +968 693 077; +968 9200865 (Out of hours emergencies)

Pakistan

- Population: 144.6 million ◆ Capital: Islamabad ◆ Currency: Rupee
- Language: Punjabi, Sindhi, Siraiki, Pashtu, Urdu and others
- Religion: Muslim
- British High Commission: +92 51 220 6071/5; +92 51 2822 131/5

Following the attacks in the USA on September 11 2001, FCO advice for visitors to the region is to exercise caution, remain vigilant and keep up to date with events. Visitors are advised by the FCO to avoid travel to the Northern Areas and Northern Baluchistan, and to inaccessible areas of the North West Frontier Province. It is important for visitors to be aware of the heightened tension along the border with India. The FCO also advises against areas adjacent to the Line of Control.

The FCO advises against travel to this country except on essential business

Panama

- Population: 2.8 million ◆ Capital: Panama City ◆ Currency: Balboa
- Language: Spanish, English ◆ Religion: Roman Catholic, Protestant
- British Embassy: +507 269 0866

Papua New Guinea

- Population: 5 million ◆ Capital: Port Moresby ◆ Currency: Kina
- Language: English, Tok Pisin, Hiri Motu and over 700 native languages
- Religion: Christian, indigenous
- British High Commission: +675 325 1643/45

The FCO advises against travel to the following areas except on essential business: Southern Highland Province and Enga Province.

Paraguay

- Population: 5.7 million ◆ Capital: Asuncion
- Currency: Guarani
- Language: Spanish, Guarani ◆ Religion: Roman Catholic
- British Embassy: +595 21 612 611

Peru

- Population: 27.5 million ◆ Capital: Lima
- Currency: Nuevo Sol
- Language: Spanish, Quechua ◆ Religion: Roman Catholic
- British Embassy: +51 1 617 3000

Philippines

- Population: 82.8 million ◆ Capital: Manila
- Currency: Peso
- Language: Filipino, English, regional languages
- Religion: Roman Catholic, Protestant, Muslim, Buddhist
- British Embassy: +63 2 816 7116

The FCO advises against all travel to the following areas: Central Mindanao, parts of Mindanao south and west of, and including, Davao City, and the Sulu archipelago.

Poland

- Population: 38 million ◆ Capital: Warsaw
- Currency: Zloty
- Language: Polish ◆ Religion: Roman Catholic
- British Embassy in Warsaw: +48 22 628 1001 5; +48 22 625 6262

There is a serious risk of robbery at main rail stations and on train services. Driving on Polish roads can be hazardous. Poland is a major east-west transit route for heavy vehicles. Even major roads can be narrow, crowded and the surfaces crinkled and rutted. British driving licence holders must hold a valid international driver's licence to drive legally in Poland. Theft of and from vehicles is common. Cases of vehicles with foreign number plates being stopped by gangs posing as policemen are rising, particularly in rural areas. If in doubt when flagged down, do not stop but continue to the nearest police station to report the matter. More details are available to motorists at Polish road borders. Non-Polish citizens (including dual nationals) should check Polish exchange control regulations before bringing in or taking out funds of more than €5000, (or the sterling equivalent of approx £3200). Those visiting forested areas are advised to seek medical advice about inoculations for tick borne encephalitis.

Portugal

- Population: 10.1 million ◆ Capital: Lisbon ◆ Currency: Euro
- Language: Portuguese ◆ Religion: Roman Catholic
- British Embassy: +351 21 392 4000

Qatar

- Population: 770,000 ◆ Capital: Doha ◆ Currency: Qatari Riyal
- Language: Arabic, English ◆ Religion: Muslim
- British Embassy: +974 442 1991

Republic of Ireland

- Population: 3.8 million ◆ Capital: Dublin ◆ Currency: Euro
- Language: English, Gaelic
- Religion: Roman Catholic, Anglican
- British Embassy: +353 1 205 3700

Romania

- ◆ Population: 22.3 million ◆ Capital: Bucharest ◆ Currency: Leu
- ◆ Language: Romanian, Hungarian, German
- ◆ Religion: Orthodox, Roman Catholic
- ◆ British Embassy Bucharest: +40 21 201 7200

Visitors should beware of petty theft in large towns and cities. Visitors should also beware of pickpockets and bag snatchers in crowded areas, particularly near exchange shops, on buses (especially to the airport), main railway stations and inside airport areas. Do not change money on the streets. It's illegal – only change it in recognised exchange shops, banks and hotels. British visitors have reported thefts of valuables including passports from hotel rooms. Deposit items of value, including passports and credit cards, in hotel safes. There have been reports of policemen stopping foreign cars and demanding payment of fines in hard currency for spurious offences. Some policemen may be bogus.

Russia

- ◆ Population: 145.4 million ◆ Capital: Moscow ◆ Currency: Ruble
- ◆ Language: Russian ◆ Religion: Russian Orthodox, Muslim
- ◆ British Embassy: +7 095 956 7200

The FCO advises against all travel to the following areas: Chechen Republic & north Caucasus region.

Rwanda

- ◆ Population: 7.3 million ◆ Capital: Kigali ◆ Currency: Rwanda Franc
- ◆ Language: Kinyarwanda, French, English
- ◆ Religion: Roman Catholic, Protestant, Animist, Muslim
- ◆ British Embassy: +250 84098; +250 85771

The FCO advises that most visits to the country are trouble-free, but visitors to the border areas with DRC, the north west and the south west should be particularly vigilant.

The FCO advises against travel to the following areas except on essential business: rural areas in Cyangugu Province bordering Burundi (Gishoma, Dugarama, Kibangiro, Bugumya, Gasumo & Bweyeye).

Saint Lucia

- ◆ Population: 158,000 ◆ Capital: Castries ◆ Currency: East Caribbean Dollar
- ◆ Language: English, dialects ◆ Religion: Roman Catholic, Protestant, Anglican
- ◆ British High Commission: +1 758 45 22484/5

Saint Vincent and the Grenadines

- ◆ Population: 116,000 ◆ Capital: Kingstown
- ◆ Currency: East Caribbean Dollar ◆ Language: English, French patois
- ◆ Religion: Anglican, Methodist, Roman Catholic
- ◆ British High Commission: +784 457 1701

Samoa

- ◆ Population: 180,000 ◆ Capital: Apia ◆ Currency: Tala
- ◆ Language: Samoan, English ◆ Religion: Christian
- ◆ British High Commission: +64 4 472 6049

San Marino

- Population: 27,000 ◆ Capital: San Marino
- Language: Italian ◆ Religion: Roman Catholic
- British Ambassador resides in Rome, Italy: +39 055 284133

Saudi Arabia

- Population: 22.8 million ◆ Capital: Riyadh
- Currency: Riyal
- Language: Arabic, English ◆ Religion: Muslim
- British Embassy: +966 1 488 0077

Senegal

- Population: 10.2 million ◆ Capital: Dakar
- Currency: Franc CFA
- Language: French, Wolof, Serer
- Religion: Muslim, Indigenous, Christian
- British Embassy: +221 823 7392/2766

Seychelles

- Population: 80,000 ◆ Capital: Victoria
- Currency: Seychelles Rupee
- Language: English, French ◆ Religion: Roman Catholic
- British High Commission: +248 283666

Sierra Leone

- Population: 5.4 million ◆ Capital: Freetown
- Currency: Leone
- Language: English, Mende, Temne
- Religion: Muslim, Christian, indigenous beliefs
- British High Commission: +232 22 232 961 / 362

The FCO is currently advising against all holiday and non-essential travel to Sierra Leone and British nationals should seek advice from the British High Commission before travelling outside the Freetown Peninsula.

Singapore

- Population: 4.3 million ◆ Capital: Singapore
- Currency: Singapore Dollar
- Language: Malay, Mandarin, Tamil, English
- Religion: Muslim, Christian, Buddhist, Hindu, Taoism
- British High Commission: +65 4244200

Slovakia

- Population: 5.4 million ◆ Capital: Bratislava
- Currency: Koruna
- Language: Slovak, Hungarian
- Religion: Roman Catholic, Protestant, Orthodox
- British Embassy: +421 2 5998 2000 (General); +421 905 601 741 (Out of hours)

Solomon Islands

- Population: 480,000 ◆ Capital: Honiara
- Currency: Solomon Islands Dollar
- Language: English, pidgin English, indigenous Melanesian languages
- Religion: Anglican, Roman Catholic, South Seas Evangelical, Seventh-Day Adventist
- British High Commission: +677 21705/6

The FCO advises against travel to the following areas except on essential business: Guadalcanal and Malaita.

Somalia

- Population: 7.5 million ◆ Capital: Mogadishu ◆ Currency: Somali Shilling
- Language: Somali, Arabic, English ◆ Religion: Sunni Muslim
- There is currently no British representation in Somalia. Refer to the British Embassy in Ethiopia: +252 1 20288/9; 252 1 21472/3

The FCO believes that Somalia is one of a number of countries where there is now an increased threat to British interests from global terrorism, and is advising against all travel.

The FCO advises against all travel to the following areas: Southern Somalia, the north-eastern area (Puntland and the Sool and Sanaag regions of Somaliland).

South Africa

- Population: 43.5 million ◆ Capital: Pretoria (Administrative)
- Currency: Rand ◆ Language: Xhosa, Zulu, English, Afrikaans and others
- Religion: Christian, Hindu, Muslim
- British High Commission: +27 12 483 1200

Though most visits are trouble-free, visitors should be aware that crime throughout the country remains high. The FCO recommends taking all usual precautions and staying alert to the threat of crime at all times.

Spain

- Population: 40 million ◆ Capital: Madrid ◆ Currency: Euro
- Language: Spanish, Catalan, Galician, Basque
- Religion: Roman Catholic
- British Embassy: +34 91 308 5201

Sri Lanka

- Population: 19.4 million ◆ Capital: Colombo ◆ Currency: Sri Lankan rupee
- Language: Sinhala, Tamil, English
- Religion: Buddhist, Hindu, Muslim, Christian
- British High Commission: +94 1 437336-43; +94 1 451924-6

There is a relatively high level of terrorist activity in Sri Lanka at the moment, with the International Airport having been targetted in July 2001. The FCO strongly advises against visiting the east and north east of the island, though also warns of the possibility of visitors to Colombo being caught up in terrorist attacks. The risk is low, but FCO advice is to take particular care and remain vigilant because of the indiscriminate nature of the attacks.

The FCO advises against all travel to the following areas: north & east only unless as with an international agency or NGO.

St Kitts and Nevis

- Population: 39,000 ◆ Capital: Basseterre
- Currency: East Caribbean Dollar ◆ Language: English
- Religion: Anglican, Methodist, Roman Catholic, Baptist
- British High Commission: +268 462 0008/9; +268 463 0010

Sudan

- Population: 36 million ◆ Capital: Khartoum ◆ Currency: Sudanese Pound
- Language: Arabic, English, tribal languages
- Religion: Muslim, indigenous beliefs, Christian
- British Embassy: +249 11 777105

The FCO advises against all travel to the following areas: Eritrean border/ Kassala area.

The FCO advises against travel to the following areas except on essential business: southern Sudan, except for those engaged in relief work.

Suriname

- Population: 434,000 ◆ Capital: Paramaribo ◆ Currency: Suriname Guilder
- Language: Dutch, Surinamese, English
- Religion: Hindu, Protestant, Roman Catholic, Muslim, indigenous beliefs
- British Embassy: +597 402 558/870

Swaziland

- Population: 1.1 million ◆ Capital: Mbabane ◆ Currency: Lilangeni
- Language: English, Swazi ◆ Religion: Christian, indigenous
- British High Commission: +268 404 2581/2/3/4

Sweden

- Population: 8.8 million ◆ Capital: Stockholm
- Currency: Krona ◆ Language: Swedish
- Religion: Evangelical Lutheran, Roman Catholic, Pentecostal
- British Embassy: +46 8 671 3000

Switzerland

- Population: 7.2 million ◆ Capital: Bern ◆ Currency: Swiss Franc
- Language: Swiss German, French, Italian
- Religion: Roman Catholic, Protestant
- British Embassy: +41 31 359 7700

Syria

- Population: 16.7 million ◆ Capital: Damascus ◆ Currency: Syrian Pound
- Language: Arabic, English, French ◆ Religion: Muslim, Christian
- British Embassy: +963 11 373 9241/2/3/7

Taiwan

- Population: 22.3 million ◆ Capital: Taipei ◆ Currency: New Taiwan Dollar
- Language: Mandarin ◆ Religion: Buddhist, Taoism, Protestant, Catholic
- British Embassy: see China

Appendix 2 **COUNTRY INFO**

Tajikistan

- ♦ Population: 6.5 million ♦ Capital: Dunshanbe ♦ Currency: Tajik Ruble
- ♦ Language: Tajik (similar to Persian) ♦ Religion: Sunni Muslim
- ♦ Dunshanbe British Ambassador resides in Tashkent, Uzbekistan: +992-91-901 5079 (International); 24-22-21 (Local)

The FCO advises against travel to the following areas except on essential business: specifically the Karategin (Rasht) valley, Kofarnihon and Tavildara areas (all in Central Tajikistan), mountainous areas bordering Kyrgyzstan & Uzbekistan & districts bordering Afghanistan.

Tanzania

- ♦ Population: 36.2 million ♦ Capital: Dar es Salaam
- ♦ Currency: Tanzanian Shilling ♦ Language: Swahili, English, local languages
- ♦ Religion: Christian, Muslim, traditional beliefs
- ♦ British High Commission: +255 22 211 0101; 255 744 242242 (Emergency)

Thailand

- ♦ Population: 61.8 million ♦ Capital: Bangkok ♦ Currency: Baht
- ♦ Language: Thai, Chinese, English ♦ Religion: Buddhist, Muslim, Hindu
- ♦ British Embassy: +66 2 305 8333

The Netherlands

- ♦ Population: 16 million ♦ Capital: The Hague ♦ Currency: Euro
- ♦ Language: Dutch ♦ Religion: Roman Catholic, Protestant, Muslim
- ♦ British Embassy: +31 0 70 427 0427; British Consulate-General helpline:(020) 676 4343.

Amsterdam is a busy city and visitors should exercise caution particularly in the centre (especially Central Station). As in many large cities, pick-pocketing is commonplace. Pick-pockets often operate in gangs (usually on the trams): while one distracts you, another picks your pocket. Where possible, travellers should avoid carrying passports, valuables and large sums of money on their person, but it is important to carry copies of identification details. In the event of theft, contact the nearest police station and obtain a police report. If your passport is stolen a police report is accepted by some carriers in lieu of a passport. A police report is required as part of the application for a replacement passport.

Tibet

- ♦ Capital: Lhasa ♦ Currency: Yuan ♦ Language: Putonghua
- ♦ Religion: Buddhist ♦ (A Chinese autonomous region)

Togo

- ♦ Population: 5.1 million ♦ Capital: Lome ♦ Currency: Franc CFA
- ♦ Language: French, Ewe, Mina, many dialects
- ♦ Religion: indigenous beliefs, Christian, Muslim
- ♦ British Consulate: +228 264606 or contact Embassy staff in Accra, Ghana

Tonga

- ♦ Population: 104,000 ♦ Capital: Nuku'alofa ♦ Currency: Pa'anga
- ♦ Language: Tongan, English ♦ Religion: Christian
- ♦ British High Commission: +676 24285/24395

visit: www.gap-year.com

Trinidad and Tobago

- Population: 1.2 million ◆ Capital: Port-of-Spain
- Currency: Trinidad and Tobago Dollar
- Language: English, Hindi, French, Spanish
- Religion: Roman Catholic, Hindu, Anglican, Muslim
- British High Commission: +1 868 622 2748; +1 868 622 8960/1/2

Tunisia

- Population: 9.7 million ◆ Capital: Tunis ◆ Currency: Tunisian Dinar
- Language: Arabic (plus Berber) ◆ Religion: Sunni Muslim
- British Embassy: +216 71 846 184 (Consular); +216 71 793 322 (Visa)

Some 250,000 British tourists visit Tunisia every year. Visits to Tunisia are generally trouble-free, but care should be taken in areas close to the Algerian border. Specific advice should also be sought from tour operators or the British Embassy when travelling independently to the desert areas in the south. Travel insurance which includes the cost of local hospitalisation and possible medical evacuation is strongly recommended. Visitors should bring sufficient funds for their visit and declare any large amounts of cash on arrival. The export of Tunisian dinars is prohibited.

Turkey

- Population: 66.5 million ◆ Capital: Ankara ◆ Currency: Lira
- Language: Turkish, Kurdish ◆ Religion: Sunni Muslim
- British Embassy: +90 312 455 3344

Although there have not been terrorist incidents in resort areas recently, and the security situation in Eastern Turkey has improved considerably, there continue to be sporadic incidents involving the PKK and Turkish security forces, particularly in the Emergency Rule Region (Van, Hakkari, Sirnak, Diyarbakir, Tunceli provinces); and neighbouring provinces in the south-east. Travel to these areas should be avoided. Those who must travel in south-east Turkey should keep to main roads and towns; and avoid travel at dusk or after dark. Visitors should ensure that inoculations are up to date as contagious diseases are on the increase. They should also advise the Consular Section at the British Embassy in Ankara, or the British Consulate General in Istanbul (tel: +90 212 293 7540) of their travel plans.

Visitors should stay only at hotels and guest houses that have been approved by the Ministry of Tourism – these cost from $US20 per night. Street robbery is a regular occurrence in the major Istanbul tourist areas. Stay alert and be wary of approaches by strangers. There have been instances of tourists being offered drink and food which is drugged. Take particular care when travelling by road throughout Turkey. Serious traffic accidents occur frequently.

Turkmenistan

- Population: 4.6 million ◆ Capital: Ashgabat ◆ Currency: Manat
- Language: Turkmen, Russian, Uzbek
- Religion: Muslim, Eastern Orthodox
- British Embassy: +993 12 363 462/63/64

Tuvalu

- Population: 11,000 ◆ Capital: Funafuti
- Currency: Tuvaluan Dollar, Australian Dollar
- Language: Tuvaluan, English
- Religion: Congregationalist ◆ British Embassy staff resident at Suva, Fiji

Uganda

- Population: 24 million ◆ Capital: Kampala ◆ Currency: Ugandan Shilling
- Language: English, Swahili, Luganda, Ateso, Luo
- Religion: Christian, Muslim ◆ British High Commission: +256 78 312000

The FCO advises against all travel to the following areas: Gulu (inc. Murchison Falls Nat. Pk.), Kitgum, Adjumani, Apac & Lira Districts, the Karamoja region of Eastern Uganda (Kotido, Moroto & Nakapiripiri Districts), Katakwi District & Bundibugyo District inc. Semliki Nat. Pk. (not the Game Reserve).

Ukraine

- Population: 48.7 million ◆ Capital: Kiev ◆ Currency: Hryvna
- Language: Ukranian, Russian ◆ Religion: Orthodox, Catholic, Jewish
- British Embassy: +380 44 462 0011 4

Ukraine has relatively low levels of street and car crime. However, foreigners offer lucrative targets and visitors should be vigilant, keeping expensive possessions out of sight. Particular care should be taken on public transport and in crowded areas where pickpockets and bag snatchers operate. If travelling by overnight train, secure the compartment door from the inside by tying it closed with wire or cord. Visitors to Ukraine should seek medical advice before travelling. Diphtheria is endemic in some parts of Ukraine, namely Kmelnitsky, Ivano-Frankisvsky and Lvivsky regions (all in Western Ukraine), and tick-borne encephalitis is prevalent in forested areas. Do not drink tap water without first boiling it. British nationals visiting Ukraine require entry visas, which should be obtained before departure. All visitors to Ukraine who intend to stay more than three days are required to register with the Ministry of Internal Affairs. If staying at a hotel visitors should confirm on check-in that this will be done automatically by the hotel. Registration must be done within three days of arrival. Carry your passport at all times. There are strict customs regulations governing the export from Ukraine of antiques and items of historical interest. If in doubt seek prior permission from customs authorities. British nationals intending to drive in Ukraine should be in possession of an International Driving Licence. British nationals are advised to register with the British Embassy in Kiev.

United Arab Emirates

- Population: 2.4 million ◆ Capital: Abu Dhabi ◆ Currency: UAE Dirham
- Language: Arabic, English ◆ Religion: Muslim
- British Embassy: +971 2 6326600/1364

United Kingdom

- Population: 59 million ◆ Capital: London ◆ Currency: Pound Sterling
- Language: English, Welsh, Gaelic
- Religion: Protestant, Roman Catholic, Methodist, Congregational, Baptist, Jewish, Muslim

United States of America

- Population: 281 million ◆ Capital: Washington DC ◆ Currency: US Dollar
- Language: English, Spanish ◆ Religion: Protestant, Roman Catholic, Jewish
- British Embassy in Washington DC: +1 202 588 6500

Comprehensive travel and medical insurance is essential. Medical treatment can be very expensive; there are no special arrangements for medical treatment for British visitors. The British Embassy and Consulates-General cannot assist with medical expenses. If staying in a hotel, do not leave your door open at any time. Do not wear ostentatious jewellery and avoid walking in obviously run-down areas. If arriving at night, take a taxi to your hotel and collect your hire car the next day. If departing on an evening flight avoid leaving luggage and souvenirs on view in your hire car during the day. Gangs of thieves are targeting these vehicles and stealing the contents. Drive on main highways and use well-lit car parks. Do not stop if your car is bumped from behind. Instead, indicate to the other driver to follow you to the nearest public area and call for police assistance. Do not sleep in your car on the roadside or in rest areas.

Uruguay

- Population: 3.3 million ♦ Capital: Montevideo ♦ Currency: Peso
- Language: Spanish ♦ Religion: Roman Catholic, Protestant, Jewish
- British Embassy: +598 2 622 3630/50

Uzbekistan

- Population: 25.2 million ♦ Capital: Tashkent ♦ Currency: Uzbekistani Som
- Language: Uzbek, Russian, Tajik ♦ Religion: Muslim, Eastern Orthodox
- British Embassy: +99871 120 6822/6451

Vanuatu

- Population: 193,000 ♦ Capital: Port Vila ♦ Currency: Vatu
- Language: Bislama (pidgin English), English, French
- Religion: Presbyterian, Roman Catholic, Anglican, indigenous beliefs
- British High Commission: +678 23100

Vatican City State

- Population: 880 ♦ Language: Italian ♦ Religion: Roman Catholic

Venezuela

- Population: 24 million ♦ Capital: Caracas ♦ Currency: Bolivar
- Language: Spanish, indigenous languages
- Religion: Roman Catholic, Protestant
- British Embassy: +58 212 263 8411

The FCO advises against all travel to this country.

Vietnam

- Population: 80 million ♦ Capital: Hanoi ♦ Currency: Dong
- Language: Vietnamese, French, English, Khmer, Chinese
- Religion: Buddhist, Roman Catholic, Muslim, Taoist, Confucianism, Animist
- British Embassy: +84 4 936 0500

Yemen

- Population: 18.1 million ♦ Capital: Sanaa ♦ Currency: Rial
- Language: Arabic ♦ Religion: Muslim
- British Embassy: +967 1 264081/82/83/84

The FCO advises against all travel to this country.

Appendix 2 **COUNTRY INFO**

Yugoslavia, the Federal Republic of

- Population: 10.7 million ◆ Capital: Belgrade
- Currency: Yugoslav New Dinar
- Language: Serbian, Albanian
- Religion: Orthodox, Muslim, Roman Catholic
- British Embassy: +381 11 645 055; +381 11 3615 660

The FCO advises that the situation in both Serbia and Montenegro is generally calm, though it recommends keeping abreast of developments. Specific areas to avoid include the Preservo Valley in southern Serbia, and border regions. The situation in Kosovo is regarded as being dangerous, and FCO advice is to avoid all holiday and other non-essential travel. British nationals should avoid drawing attention to themselves or becoming involved in political discussions. Local ethnic Albanians may react violently to use of the Serbian language. ID should be carried at all times.

Diplomatic relations between the UK and the Federal Republic of Yugoslavia were restored on 17 November 2000. The British Embassy is located at Generala Zdanova (Resavska) 46, 11000, Belgrade with visitors advised to register their presence. Emergency Consular services are also available from the Honorary Consulate in Podgorica, Montenegro (tel +381 81 625 816), where visitors to Montenegro are also advised to register thier presence.

The FCO states that FRY law requires British nationals to obtain a valid visa in advance of travel, and to have had it stamped at an authorised border point recognised by the Federal government. Visas are not available at the border, so must be obtained from the FRY Embassy, 5 Lexham Gardens, London W8 5JJ (Tel 020 7370 6105) before setting off.

Although Montenegro has waived all visa requirements, it has done so without consent from the Federal government. The FCO therefore advises that travellers entering Montenegro without a visa should not attempt to travel into Serbia. If travelling to this part of the world it is advisable to contact the FRY Embassy in order to find out the latest information.

The FCO advises against travel to the following areas except on essential business: Kosovo.

Zambia

- Population: 10 million ◆ Capital: Lusaka
- Currency: Kwacha
- Language: English, local dialects
- Religion: Christian, Muslim, Hindu, indigenous beliefs
- British High Commission: +260 1 251133

Zimbabwe

- Population: 11.4 million ◆ Capital: Harare
- Currency: Zimbabwean Dollar
- Language: Shona, English, Ndebele
- Religion: Syncretic, Christian, Animist
- British High Commission: +263 4 772990; +263 4 774700

The FCO is warning that political tension and lawlessness in both rural and urban areas is high. Disturbances in Bulawayo have led to advice to avoid the city centre and high density suburbs. The FCO also recommends avoiding Kadoma, in Midlands province. To date tourists have been unaffected by the campaign of extortion and intimidation being waged by liberation war veterans,

Appendix 2

though in rural areas many farms and hunting reserves are still illegally occupied by these groups.

Another worrying statistic is the high rate of opportunistic theft. Care should always be taken with baggage, and the FCO warns visitors to be particularly careful when leaving banks and ATMs. Victoria Falls and other tourist centres are highlighted by the FCO as being places where tourists, particularly backpackers, are at an increased risk from casual thieves.

TRAVEL WITH CARE
Information provided by Homeway

When you go on your gap-year travels you want to know for sure that you're going to be healthy, comfortable and safe - that's where Homeway comes in. Homeway has been providing quality products and advice that you can trust to gappers since 1989. They have all the latest gadgets as well as the essentials. Homeway is a family company, they're always happy to talk to you and answer your questions. What's more - they operate a fast, efficient mail order service and guaranteed next working day delivery for telephone orders.

Take a look over the next few pages to get an idea of what Homeway can offer you. All of the products you see here are available from the Gap-Year Shop by mail order - phone 0870 748 9565 or you can order direct from www.gap-yearshop.com which has the complete up-to-date range.

Potable Aqua

WATER AND WATER PURIFICATION

One of the main ways gap travellers get ill is by drinking contaminated water - it can ruin your gap experience and the health problems can last long after you've come home.

It's usually best not to drink the local water in Africa, India, the Far East, Central and South America. Don't use it to brush your teeth or to wash food either. If you don't have the facilities to wash food with safe water, the best rule is: don't eat it unless you can peel it!

There are different ways to get 'safe water':

- ❒ Bottled, as long as checked for secure cap and no discolouration (fizzy water is safest)
- ◉ Boiled water – minimum boiling time 5 minutes. Not always 100% effective
- ❒ Iodine – short term use, not recommended for more than 28 days. Not effective on some cysts
- ◉ Chlorine (Puritabs) + filter – satisfactory and can be used long term
- ❒ Combined filter and purifier – ideal: easy to use and TOTALLY SAFE.

SUN PROTECTION

Just because you're not lying around on a beach sunbathing doesn't mean you can't get sunburned. Remember to protect all exposed skin at all times in sunny climates and at high altitudes. If you allow your skin to burn it increases your chances of getting skin cancer later. You need to use products that protect you from UVA and UVB rays - the lotions that bind to your skin are the easiest because they don't wash off so you only have to apply it once a day. After a while, say 3 to 4 weeks, your skin will acclimatise so you won't need to use so much.

Ultrasun range

Tel: 0870 748 9565   www.gap-yearshop.com

— GAP-YEAR SHOP IN ASSOCIATION WITH HOMEWAY —

PROTECTION AGAINST INSECTS

DEET Repellents
Repel Range

Insect bites are not only irritating but can be life threatening as they can transmit diseases including Malaria. They can be a problem wherever you go in the world, but if you travel to Africa, India, the Far East and Central & South America you will almost certainly need insect protection: skin repellents, a room vapouriser/coil and a net. Make sure you take the right level of insect protection for where you are travelling. You must also talk to your doctor before you go to any malarial areas, as prophylaxis will also be needed.

Insect repellents for the skin

DEET (Diethyltoluamide) repellents, which have been around for nearly 50 years, are regarded by most experts to be the most effective repellents available. Independent safety tests have shown there are no dangerous side effects on people or the environment if DEET is used correctly. DEET is designed for use on your skin. It can also be applied to natural fabrics but will destroy synthetic fabrics and plastics. Remember to take your watch off before using DEET-based repellents.

100% DEET: 5-6 hours protection. Use when re-application is impractical. Short-term use. Not suitable for sensitive or sunburnt skin.

55% DEET: 4-5 hours protection. Considered safe for everyday use.

25% DEET: 2-3 hours protection. Ideal for sensitive skins and faces.

Non-DEET repellents come in many formulations, mostly made using natural ingredients. Generally regarded as a good alternative, but DEET is the No1 choice for malarial areas.

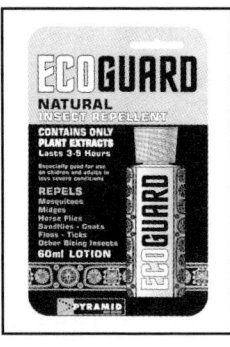

Non-DEET Repellents
EcoGuard

Insect repellents for fabrics and clothing:
DEET-free sprays, formulated for fabrics. Use on collars, cuffs, hat brims *etc*. Used with skin repellents, they provide a real armour against insect bites.

Insect repellents for the room:
Room Spray: to kill flying and crawling insects.

Room Vapouriser: ideal if you know you will have electricity. Vapourisers plug into electric sockets and can be switched on and off.

Coils: useful for the outdoors.

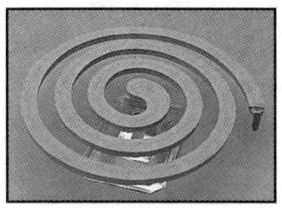

Mosquito Coil

Tel: 0870 748 9565   www.gap-yearshop.com

— GAP-YEAR SHOP IN ASSOCIATION WITH HOMEWAY —

Nets

Bed Nets: Insects are most active at night. Using a bed net impregnated with the insecticide permethrin will ensure protection from bites and in many countries is essential to protect you against Malaria. If you are using your net for more than 6 months then it will need re-impregnating. Nets come in various styles and you need to choose what will suit your trip best. Gap-Year Shop has a wide range of nets and are always happy to advise you on your choice, but these are the general guidelines for choosing your net:

- Hostels and outdoor use: *wedge net* or *pop up net*
- Long term static use with periods of travel: *wedge* and *bell nets*
- Long term use where there is a frame facility: *box net*.

Wedge Net

Head Nets: Useful for keeping biting insects away from the face and neck.

Mattress covers: mattresses can harbour all sorts of creepy crawlies. A lightweight impregnated mattress cover will make sure you sleep undisturbed.

HEALTH

First Aid kit

You won't be able to just walk into a chemist so it is sensible to carry the basics with you.

A good First Aid Kit should definitely have:

Plasters ▫ Scissors ◉ Bandages ▫ Non-stick dressings ◉ Skin closure strips (steristrips) ▫ Micropore tape ◉ Safety pins ▫ Antiseptic wipes and cleanser ◉ Painkiller tablets such as paracetamol ▫ Anti diarrhoea tablets.

For international travel you should also consider:

Re-hydration sachets (in case you get diarrhoea) ◉ sting relief ▫ anti-biotics (*see your doctor*) ◉ sterile medical/needle kit ▫ DVT anti-embolism socks ◉ insect repellents ▫ net ◉ water purification kit.

Homeway International First Aid Kit

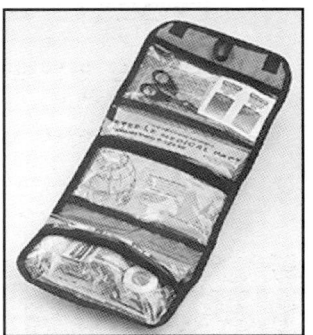

Dental check-up

Go to see your dentist before you travel - toothache will ruin your trip and you might find it difficult to get treatment abroad. If you have crowns or fillings then it is sensible to carry a *Dental First Aid Kit* – see the Gap-Year Shop at www.gap-year.com

Tel: 0870 748 9565   www.gap-yearshop.com

— GAP-YEAR SHOP IN ASSOCIATION WITH HOMEWAY —

DVT - Deep Vein Thrombosis

DVT is a clot of blood formed in the deep vein of your lower leg. To start with you might feel intense pain in the calf of your leg. Chest pain and breathlessness may follow. You are particularly at risk during long flights and journeys if you :

- Are taking the contraceptive pill
- Are over 6 foot or under 5 foot
- Are overweight
- Have a history of heart problems, varicose veins or family history of blood clots
- Have had recent surgery

If you are at all worried, then go to see your doctor. Avoid alcohol, tea and coffee and drink lots of water and soft drinks on flights. Take regular exercise. Wear medically approved flight socks, fitted by calf and leg measurement and not by shoe size. See www.gap-yearshop.com for fitting advice.

HIV/AIDS

AIDS (Acquired Immune Deficiency Syndrome) is caused by the HIV (Human Immuno-Deficiency) virus . HIV infection is incurable and there is no vaccine. HIV/AIDS can be caught through:

- an infected needle or syringe during medical and dental treatment, skin piercing, tattooing or drug use.
- blood transfusions of HIV-infected blood.
- unprotected sex with an infected person.

Homeway Sterile Medical Pack

To protect yourself when travelling (you are particularly at risk in Asia, Africa, India, Central and South America) we suggest you:

- Carry a *Sterile Medical Pack*. For use by medical personnel, this is a heat sealed pack containing sterile needles, syringes *etc*. Remember, simple procedures such as a blood test require a needle.
- Don't have tattoos, body piercing or acupuncture unless you are sure that sterilised needles are being used.
- Ensure that blood is screened if you need a blood transfusion. The British Consulate can assist.
- Use condoms every time.

SAFETY

Remember that every country has people who are happy to steal or hurt you. You are especially vulnerable as a traveller because you won't know the surrounding area and can easily be spotted.

Photocopy all important documents and details like your passport numbers, traveller's cheques, card details, insurance documents, tickets, itinerary *etc*

Tel: 0870 748 9565   www.gap-yearshop.com

GAP-YEAR SHOP IN ASSOCIATION WITH HOMEWAY

and leave one set at home with someone you can contact easily in case they are stolen. It is also a good idea to keep a set of copies somewhere in your luggage when travelling.

Here are a few tips for your safety:

- Don't carry large sums of money around.
- Don't wear expensive jewellery.
- Try not to draw attention to yourself.
- Treat locals respectfully.
- Keep valuables/money/tickets/passports safely hidden in a money belt or waist wallet etc
- Carry a personal attack alarm

Pacsafe Waist Wallet

Locks

Pacsafe combination lock

It is worth investing in some locks and padlocks to keep you and your gear safe and deter thieves. Gap-Year Shop has a wide range of locks and padlocks including:

- *Combination padlocks* which are great as there's no key to lose - as long as you can remember the number!
- *Rucksack locks:* these fit on the rucksack straps which can be a deterrent to opportunist thieves.
- *Cable locks:* secure your luggage to an immovable object.
- *Door Locks:* easily fitted to inward opening doors (at hostels for example) to stop intruders coming into your room.
- *Pacsafe:* a mesh cage which fits over your rucksack and can be secured to an immovable object. Prevents anyone slashing your rucksack. Good for overland truck expeditions.

Torches

A good torch is essential. The bright LED torches are good because they are small but very bright – the key ring torch can clip to your rucksack. A head torch is good for night reading and hands free carrying.

TRAVEL ACCESSORIES

Rucksacks, suitcases and backpacks

A 65 litre bag is a good general size, especially for women. Higher capacity may seem a good idea when you're trying to pack every thing in - but remember you're going to have to carry it. *Rucksacks:* Look for padded adjustable back system, internal support bars, padded shoulder straps and hip belt. Side pockets and a double accessed main compartment are

Aztec Tacuba
65 +10 litre

Tel: 0870 748 9565   www.gap-yearshop.com

— GAP-YEAR SHOP IN ASSOCIATION WITH HOMEWAY —

useful too. *Convertible bags:* give great versatility. You might also want to consider a rucksack travel bag – a large lockable bag for protecting a rucksack when travelling by air or coach. Also doubles as an extra storage bag.

Sleeping bags

Sold as 2, 3 or 4 season bags (light, medium and warm). A mid-range priced bag (£55-£75) will give years of wear and unless you're going somewhere very cold, a 2/3 season bag should be fine. Look out for lightweight bags with full and half-length zips and a good compression stuff bag.

Sleeping bag liners: Cotton or silk sheets sewn up to fit in a sleeping bag. Highly recommended as they save washing the sleeping bag, add another layer and are needed in certain hostels where sleeping bags aren't allowed.

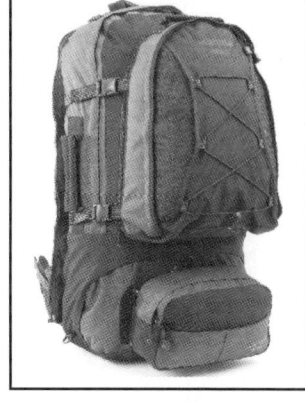

Aztec Hobo Convertible Travel Sack

Elite Micro 2 - 3 Season before 50% compression

Practical stuff

Washing: it's a good idea to take ◉ liquid bio-degradable soap for washing in all types of water and temperatures ❑ travel bath & sink plug (it's impossible to improvise if one is missing!) ◉ travel wash for clothing ❑ pegless washing line.

Penknife or multi-purpose tool: Lots of types depending on your budget. Remember: you are not allowed to carry these in your hand luggage on a plane.

Keeping dry: A *rain cape* can double up as a ground sheet and fits over you and your rucksack. *Waterproof pouches* are available in a range of shapes and sizes to fit pretty much anything you own. The *AquaPac Range* is suitable for watersports, diving and underwater photography.

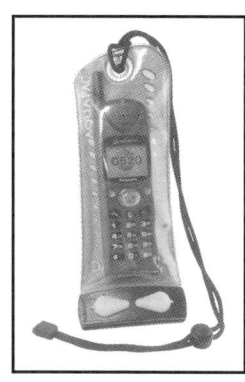

AquaPac Phone case

Useful extras:

◉ Sewing Kit ❑ Cutlery set with Can/Bottle Opener ◉ Waterproof matches ❑ Whistle/compass ◉ 10 Band World Radio ❑ Alarm clock ◉ Duck/Gaffer tape ❑ Travel Towel ◉ Pillow

'Cyclone' Windproof and waterproof matches

Homeway Tel: 0870 748 9565 www.gap-yearshop.com